McGraw-Hill/Contemporary's

The Math Problem Solver

A Breakthrough Approach to Learning Math

2nd edition

Myrna Manly

 Contemporary

Acknowledgments

Chart on page 286 "Body Mass Index" adapted from "Understanding Adult Obesity" on *Weight-control Information*. Network website ww.niddk.nih.gov.

Chart on page 289 "Exchange Rates" from www.exchangerate.com. Reprinted by permission.

Chart and graphs on page 290 from "Why Do Gas Prices Differ Across the USA?" by James R. Healey, *USA Today,* December 11, 2001. Copyright ©2001, USA TODAY. Reprinted with permission.

Chart on page 292 "U.S. Highpoints Guide" as appeared on www.americasroof.com. Reprinted by permission.

Chart on page 293 "The Price of Power," *Los Angeles Times,* January 19, 2001. Copyright ©2001, Los Angeles Times. Reprinted by permission.

Graphs on page 294 "Decade of change for USA" by Sam Ward and Dave Merrill, *USA Today,* June 5, 2002. Copyright © 2002, USA TODAY. Reprinted with permission.

Executive Editor: Linda Kwil
Production Manager: Genevieve Kelley
Marketing Manager: Sean Klunder
Cover Design: Michael E. Kelly

Send all inquiries to:
McGraw-Hill/Contemporary
130 East Randolph Street, Suite 400
Chicago, Illinois 60601

ISBN 0-07-294300-9

Printed in the United States of America.

1 2 3 4 5 6 7 8 9 10 QPD 09 08 07 06 05 04 03

Table of Contents

Fractions and Decimals

To the Teacher

The Math Problem Solver cultivates the learning of valuable mathematics while it prepares students with the mathematics they need for proficiency tests. The text is structured to aid you in promoting number and operation sense, mental flexibility, and problem-solving skills.

To accomplish these goals, *The Math Problem Solver* has been designed to help students

- build genuine understanding of mathematical procedures

- investigate mathematical relationships and apply them in realistic settings

- use a range of math tools—including paper and pencil, mental math, and calculators

In keeping with the demands of many stardardized mathematics tests, this text

- focuses on problem solving and reasoning as it reviews procedures

- encourages estimation

- integrates the topics of algebra, geometry, and data analysis from the outset

- provides practice with both multiple-choice and gridded-response formats

The Math Problem Solver is organized into 25 lessons that can be adapted to a variety of class structures.

- The problems within the lessons examine the concepts in an incremental way that encourages student participation in ongoing informal class discussion, practice, and assessment.

- Each lesson ends with problems that check individual understanding and proficiency. Half are formatted similar to standardized mathematics test items.

- Skill-maintenance and checkup sections provide review of previous topics.

- Using Data activities throughout the book refer to data files in the Appendix.

- Calculator Exploration activities use a scientific calculator to explore concepts being studied.

- A detailed answer key at the end of the book is a valuable resource.

This student text is only one part of *The Math Problem Solver* program. An ancillary text, *The Math Problem Solver Teacher's Guide*, contains lesson-by-lesson information and suggestions as well as dozens of classroom activities. This teacher's guide supports the types of group interactions and critical-thinking activities needed to develop genuine mathematical understanding.

To the Student

The knowledge and skills that are emphasized in this book were chosen to help you weave a strong web of ideas, principles, and procedures that will enable you to pass many mathematics proficiency tests. It is no accident, however, that they are also the knowledge, understanding, and skills that you will use outside of school to cope with the mathematical aspects of your life.

The mathematical content that often serves as the basis for mathematics tests represents four strands of mathematics that are taught in high school:

Number, Number Sense, & Operations   Measurement & Geometry

Data, Statistics, & Probability   Algebra, Functions, & Patterns

Modern standardized mathematics tests are written to assess more than just computational skill. The questions are designed to find out if you know more about math than how to add, subtract, multiply, and divide. Thus, in this book, you will learn (or relearn) the procedures, but you will spend most of your time thinking about how the numbers, ideas, and rules fit together to form a connected approach to solving mathematical problems. By emphasizing the strategies of estimating, reasoning, and problem solving to find answers, this book prepares you not only for a test but also for the numeracy demands that confront people daily.

Recommendations for using this book:

Practice reading the problems carefully.

- Learn the significance of the mathematics vocabulary.

- Learn to recognize the underlying mathematics of the situations that are described.

Be curious. Look beyond the answers.

- Ask "What if?" questions. Make up a question that is similar.

- Connect the procedures of one problem to those of another.

- Don't be satisfied with knowing "how;" try to reason "why."

Be flexible.

- Learn more about the concepts and principles by seeing how other strategies work in the situation.

- Look for more than one way to find the answer to test items. Use them to check whether your answer is reasonable.

Relax and enjoy learning math.

- Become an estimator. Notice how mathematically powerful it makes you.

- Find situations in your own life where your improved knowledge of mathematics will make a difference.

- Use your common sense and reasoning power rather than trying to remember rules. This will work for many problems on tests as well as in your daily experience.

"Seeing" Addition and Subtraction

1 Picture the Situation

Think about these problems. Don't try to find the answers—yet.

EXAMPLE A

Roberta has 5 children, and her sister Ronnie has 3. When their families get together, how many children are there in all?

EXAMPLE B

George traveled 187 miles one day before lunch, then continued for another 290 miles in the afternoon. How many miles did he travel that day?

├———187———┼————290————┤
                    ?

When the action in a situation is **combining** or **joining**, you can **add** to find the **sum**.

PROBLEM 1

Ⓐ Make a sketch of this situation: Magdelena bought two packages of Halloween candy. One contains 14 miniature candy bars and the other contains 12. How many individual treats did she buy?

Ⓑ Think of a situation in your life that requires addition (joining or combining). Make a sketch of the problem.

Look at the following problems. Don't try to find the answers—yet.

When the action in a situation is **separating** or **comparing** to find the **difference**, you should **subtract**.

EXAMPLE C

Maria had $18.00 in her purse. After she spends $7.00 in the grocery store, how much does she have left?

X̶ X̶ X̶ X̶ X̶ X̶
X̶ $ $ $ $
$ $ $ $ $

EXAMPLE D

George traveled 180 miles one day before lunch, then continued for another 290 miles in the afternoon. How many more miles did he travel in the afternoon than he did in the morning?

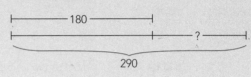

PROBLEM 2

Ⓐ Draw a sketch of this situation: A bag contained 14 oranges. How many are left after 5 are eaten?

Ⓑ Think of a personal situation that involves the difference between two quantities or distances. Make a sketch of the problem.

Ⓒ Use your experience (or imagination) to make up problems that could be shown by each of the following pictures. Look for ways to combine, separate, or compare in your story problems.

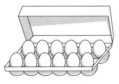

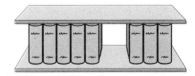

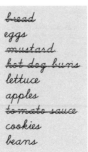

bread
eggs
mustard
hot dog buns
lettuce
apples
tomato sauce
cookies
beans

2 Write the Problem

The order of the **addends** (numbers being added) does not matter. Because of this, the operation of addition is said to be **commutative**.

After you "picture a problem," the next step is to write it mathematically.

EXAMPLE

Roberta has 5 children, and her sister Ronnie has 3. When their families get together, how many children are there in all?

This problem can be written mathematically in two ways:

$$5 + 3 \quad \text{or} \quad 3 + 5$$

PROBLEM 3   Write two addition problems for each picture.

Ⓐ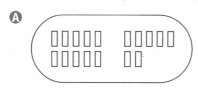

Ⓑ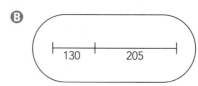

When you subtract, the order in which the problem is written *is* important. You *cannot* change the order of numbers in a subtraction problem.

Since the order *does* make a difference when you are subtracting, subtraction is *not* **commutative**.

EXAMPLE

A bag contained 14 oranges. How many are left after 5 are eaten?

This can *only* be written as $14 - 5$.

The original number, the 14, *must* come first in the problem. The number being taken away, the 5, comes second, after the subtraction sign.

PROBLEM 4   Write a subtraction problem for each picture.

Ⓐ

Ⓑ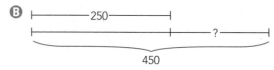

PROBLEM 5   Write either an addition or a subtraction problem based on these diagrams.

Ⓐ 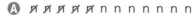   Ⓓ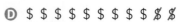

Ⓑ    Ⓔ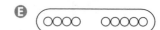

Ⓒ    Ⓕ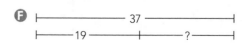

Using Letters to Represent Unknowns

EXAMPLE

A letter that is used to represent a number in an expression is called a **variable**. Its value is unknown and may change from problem to problem.

Juan deposited $150 into his checking account. He was not sure how much money he originally had in the account, so at this point, he knew only that he had $150 more than his previous balance.	$150 + balance or balance + $150 $150 + ? ? + $150 $150 + x x + $150

Notice that the x is the variable in this problem—it represents the original amount in Juan's account.

EXAMPLE

When you write an expression, you can use any letter to represent the unknown quantity.

How many nails are left in a bag after 7 are used?

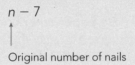

$n - 7$

↑

Original number of nails

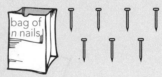

We don't know the number of nails in the bag.

Study these examples of writing a problem:

four more than 5	4 + 5 or 5 + 4
? + 5	x + 5 or 5 + x
ten more than Jane has (x)	10 + x or x + 10
the difference between 13 and 5	13 − 5
the difference between 13 and x	13 − x
nine less than 21	21 − 9
nine less than the maximum (m)	m − 9

PROBLEM 6 | Write an expression for each of the following.

Ⓐ

Ⓑ (n   • • • •)

Ⓒ nine increased by 2

Ⓓ the books on the table (*b*) increased by 2

Ⓔ twelve decreased by 4

Ⓕ twelve decreased by x

Ⓖ

Ⓗ four taken away from 12 (be careful)

Ⓘ four taken away from the total (*t*)

Ⓙ seven less than 15

Ⓚ seven less than the full bag (*b*)

3 Find the Answer

The two earlier steps in problem solving, picturing the situation and writing the problem, require you to do a great deal of mathematical thinking before you even think about what you will do to find the answer. When you take the time to write the problem first, it will be easier to decide *how* you will find the answer. Usually you have three choices:

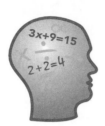

① **Figure it out by using mental math or estimation strategies.** This is the quickest and often the easiest method, especially if you are confident of the basic math facts. You will often be able to choose the correct answer on a multiple-choice test by merely estimating. This book will help you to develop some strategies and will give you a lot of practice, but you may also need to spend some time individually reviewing the addition and multiplication tables.

② **Use paper and pencil calculations to figure out the answers.** You may think that there is only one "right" way to calculate. However, there are many methods that can be used. For example, on page 296 of the Appendix, there are some interesting ways to add without carrying and to subtract without borrowing. These may inspire you to invent some methods of your own. Choose the method that is easiest for you to remember or the one that fits the kind of problem you are facing.

③ **Use a calculator.** Often when we use a calculator, we can find the answer more quickly and accurately than with paper and pencil methods. Many people use a calculator regularly in their everyday lives, and you will be allowed to use one on sections of many tests. This book requires that you use a scientific calculator for some explorations and allows you to use it for most problems, but it also prohibits its use on some problems that are intended to give you practice estimating and calculating. If you see the symbol, you should not use the calculator for that problem.

Class Activity

Discuss the following questions with your classmates:

Ⓐ Which of the three choices, estimation, paper and pencil, or calculator, do you use most often?

Ⓑ Describe the situations in your life when you are most likely to estimate. When do you use paper and pencil? When do you use the calculator?

Ⓒ Which method is the one that you need the most help with?

Adding and Subtracting Mentally

The answer to an addition problem is called the **sum**.

The answer to a subtraction problem is called the **difference**.

Using Zeros

Adding zero to a number gives the same number.

$34 + 0 = 34$ $0 + 49 = 49$

Subtracting zero from a number gives the same number.

$34 - 0 = 34$ $49 - 0 = 49$

Building on Basic Facts

Use the basic facts of addition and subtraction along with what you know about zeros to solve more problems in your head.

$200 + 700 = 900$

- Ignore the common zeros while you add or subtract the digits on the front.
- Then replace the zeros to get the answer.

PROBLEM 7

Add or subtract the digits that have the same place value—that is, add tens to tens, hundreds to hundreds, thousands to thousands, and so on.

Ⓐ $2 + 3 = 5$
$20 + 30 = 50$
$200 + 300 = 500$
$2,000 + 3,000 =$

Ⓑ $7 + 8 = 15$
$70 + 80 =$
$700 + 800 =$
$7,000 + 8,000 =$

Ⓒ $7 - 3 = 4$
$70 - 30 =$
$700 - 300 =$
$7,000 - 3,000 =$

Take the next step with more difficult numbers. Often, reading or saying the numbers will help you keep track of the place values when you find answers mentally.

$\underline{8}00 + \underline{1}80 =$ "$\underline{8}$ hundred plus $\underline{1}$ hundred 80 equals $\underline{9}$ hundred 80" (980)

PROBLEM 8

Find the answers to the following problems mentally.

Ⓐ $740 - 200 =$
Ⓑ $100 + 920 =$

Ⓒ $420 - 300 =$
Ⓓ $300 + 710 =$

Ⓔ $2,100 + 400 =$
Ⓕ $8,400 - 300 =$

Other problems require you to focus on the endings of numbers. Use simple addition or subtraction facts as the basis for solving more difficult problems.

PROBLEM 9

Notice the pattern and complete the following.

Ⓐ $6 + 8 = 14$
$36 + 8 = 44$
$56 + 8 = 64$
$86 + 8 = 94$
$126 + 8 =$

Ⓑ $11 - 7 = 4$
$31 - 7 = 24$
$61 - 7 =$
$91 - 7 =$
$101 - 7 =$

Ⓒ $4 + 9 = 13$
$24 + 9 =$
$74 + 9 =$
$94 + 9 =$
$234 + 9 =$

Ⓓ $12 - 3 = 9$
$52 - 3 = 49$
$72 - 3 =$
$102 - 3 =$
$552 - 3 =$

4 Check for Reasonableness

Whether you have found the answer mentally, with paper and pencil, or with a calculator, the final step in mathematical problem solving is to check your answer to see if it is reasonable.

Sometimes the situation itself can be a check. For example, if you were given $6.25 in change after you gave the clerk only a $5 bill to pay for an item, you would know immediately that there was a mistake.

When the mistake is less obvious, you should know how to estimate to check whether your answer makes sense. Estimation is also a timesaving tool when answering multiple-choice items on a test. Often it is all you need to choose the correct answer.

Place Value, Rounding, and Estimating

CALCULATOR EXPLORATION

Erase the Eights

Take note of the position of the 8 in each number given. Write the number you could subtract that would erase the eight, changing it to zero while leaving the other digits alone. Carry out the subtraction on the calculator to check if you are correct.

EXAMPLE Erase the 8 in 584.32.
Enter: 584.32 − 80 = [504.32]

Ⓐ 7,894.2 − _____ = [   ]

Ⓑ 184.35 − _____ = [   ]

Ⓒ 38.50 − _____ = [   ]

Ⓓ 78,433 − _____ = [   ]

Ⓔ 900,184 − _____ = [   ]

Ⓕ 10,450.85 − _____ = [   ]

Ⓖ 5,832,023 − _____ = [   ]

Ⓗ 182.08 − _____ = (Try to erase both at once.) [   ]

When you need to add or subtract numbers that are not as "nice" (easy to work with) as the ones in the previous section, round them to the closest "nice" number first, then add.

REMINDER: ROUNDING GUIDELINES

① Circle the digit in the place you are rounding to.

② Look at the digit immediately to the right of the circled digit.

   If the digit is less than 5, leave the circled digit alone.

   If the digit is greater than or equal to 5, add 1 to the circled digit.

③ Replace all the digits to the right of the circled digit with zeros.

EXAMPLE

367 + 717

Where would you place the 367 on the number line below? Is it more or less than halfway between 300 and 400? How about the 717? Ask yourself, which *hundred* is the number closest to?

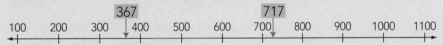

Round each number to the nearest hundred. Use the number line to picture what the rounding guidelines are telling you to do.

Use the rounded numbers and mentally estimate an answer.

$$400 + 700 = 1,100$$
$$\text{so}$$
$$367 + 717 \approx 1,100$$

(The symbol $\approx$ means "is approximately equal to.")

PROBLEM 10

CLASS ACTIVITY Discuss the connection between the "5" in the rounding guidelines and the 'halfway' marks on the number line.

Use both the guidelines and the number line of 100s above to round the numbers and estimate the answers.

Ⓐ 488 + 577 ≈ 500 + 600 = 1,100   Ⓓ 822 + 1,088 ≈

Ⓑ 562 − 318 ≈   Ⓔ 1,075 − 888 ≈

Ⓒ 98 + 612 ≈   Ⓕ 733 − 688 ≈

PROBLEM 11

Use both the guidelines and the number line of 10s to round and estimate the following.

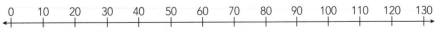

Ⓐ 56 + 32 ≈ 60 + 30 =   Ⓓ 119 − 42 ≈

Ⓑ 71 + 24 ≈   Ⓔ 98 − 59 ≈

Ⓒ 83 + 37 ≈   Ⓕ 64 − 31 ≈

USING DATA

The bar graph shows the number of calories in an average amount of each popular topping for baked potatoes. Answer the questions below by estimating the length of the bars. Explain your reasoning.

CALORIES IN BAKED POTATO TOPPINGS

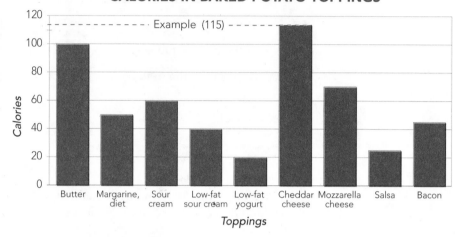

EXAMPLE About how many calories would be added to the baked potato if you topped it with cheddar cheese?

Estimate: 115

Reasoning: Draw a line straight across from the top of the cheddar cheese bar back to the axis. Make a mark that is about halfway between the lines for 100 and 120. This would be 110. You can see that the bar is close to halfway between 110 and 120, or 115.

Ⓐ Which topping adds the most calories? Which topping adds the least?

Ⓑ How many calories would butter add?

Ⓒ Approximately how many calories would diet margarine add?

Ⓓ Regular sour cream adds how many more calories than low-fat sour cream?

Ⓔ About how many calories would salsa add?

Ⓕ About how many calories less than cheddar cheese is mozzarella cheese?

Ⓖ About how many calories would you add if you topped your potato with both sour cream and bacon?

✔ CHECK YOUR UNDERSTANDING

You may use your calculator on any problem except where noted by this symbol:

Write the problem as a mathematical expression.

1. ⬭ ▯▯▯▯▯   ▯▯▯▯▯ ⬭

2. ⬭ ▦ ▦ ▦ ▦ | b | ⬭

3. ▯ ▯ ▯ ▯ ☒ ☒ ☒

4. ├──────── 14 ────────┤
      ├──── 8 ────┼── ? ──┤

5. six added to three

6. six added to those in the box (*x*)

7. eighteen reduced by 9

8. eighteen reduced by *x*

9. 10 less than 54

10. 10 less than *x*

11. 0.3 meter farther than the record (*r*)

12. 15° higher than the day's low (*l*)

13. 8° less than the record high (*h*)

14. the amount in the bank (*b*) plus a deposit of $75

15. the amount in the bank (*b*) minus a withdrawal of $25

16. 7 more points than his average (*a*)

17. 7 fewer points than his average (*a*)

 Find the answers to the following problems **mentally.**

18. $500 + 800 =$

19. $1,300 - 700 =$

20. $3,000 + 4,500 =$

21. $7,800 - 2,000 =$

22. $510 + 30 =$

23. $3,440 - 10 =$

24. $775 + 20 =$

25. $775 + 30 =$

26. $56 + 5 =$

27. $86 + 5 =$

28. $96 + 5 =$

29. $236 + 5 =$

30. $72 - 7 =$

31. $92 - 7 =$

32. $102 - 7 =$

33. $452 - 7 =$

Round the numbers to the closest 10, 100, 1,000, or 10,000. Then estimate the answers **mentally.**

34. $23 + 59 \approx$

35. $37 + 78 \approx$

36. $17 + 52 \approx$

37. $188 + 521 \approx$

38. $375 + 283 \approx$

39. $1,212 + 2,111 \approx$

40. $79 - 43 \approx$

41. $98 - 33 \approx$

42. $437 - 109 \approx$

43. $3,988 - 1,756 \approx$

44. $4,102 - 1,444 \approx$

45. $976 - 622 \approx$

46. $5,987 + 3,421 \approx$

47. $49,822 - 24,788 \approx$

TEST-TAKING PRACTICE

Is estimation a valuable skill when taking tests? Absolutely. Look over the answer choices to see which one is closest to your estimated answer. Many times you will find that estimation is all you need to do to choose the correct answer. It will save you time on the test.

You may use your calculator on any problem except where noted by this symbol:
Refer to the number grid directions on page 281 whenever needed.

1. Sam traveled 671 miles last month on business and 913 miles this month. What is his total mileage for the 2 months?

   (1) 121
   (2) 242
   (3) 1,584
   (4) 2,255
   (5) 3,168

2. The Lincoln Adult School raised $815 at its fund-raiser. However, the students had $295 in expenses. How much money did the school make after paying the expenses?

   (1) $ 430
   (2) $ 520
   (3) $ 720
   (4) $1,050
   (5) $1,110

Problems 3–5 refer to the following table.

The heat index chart below indicates how warm it feels under various air temperatures and percentages of relative humidity. For example, when it is 90° and the relative humidity is 60%, it will feel more like 100°.

HEAT INDEX
Air Temperature (°F)

Relative Humidity (%)	80	85	90	95	100
30	78	84	90	96	104
40	79	86	93	101	110
50	81	88	96	107	120
60	82	90	100	114	132
70	85	93	106	124	144
80	86	97	113	136	
90	88	102	122		

3. What is the heat index temperature, in °F, when the air temperature is 85° and the relative humidity is 90%?

   Write your answer in the boxes at the top of the grid, using one box per digit. Then mark your answer by filling in the circles below.

4. When the air temperature is 85° but it feels more like 90°, what is the percentage of relative humidity?

   (1) 15
   (2) 60
   (3) 70
   (4) 80
   (5) 90

5. One day the air temperature was 100° with a relative humidity of 30% in Reno, and the air temperature was 100° with a relative humidity of 60% in Minneapolis. What is the difference, in degrees, between the heat-index temperatures in the two cities?

   (1) 132
   (2) 104
   (3) 40
   (4) 32
   (5) 28

Grouping to Add More Than Two Numbers

MENTAL MATH

1. 32 + 8

2. 56 + 4

3. 73 + 7

4. 85 + 5

5. 67 + 3

6. 31 + 9

Did you notice that each of the numbers above has ending digits that add to 10? This makes the numbers compatible pairs for addition. **Compatible pairs** can be grouped for easy mental addition. Remember that compatible pairs can make adding and subtracting easier.

Perimeters

A common use of adding more than two numbers is finding the **perimeter** of a figure.

The **perimeter** of a figure is the distance around it.

Add the lengths of the sides of a figure to find its perimeter.

EXAMPLE

How many feet of edging does Geraldo need to put around the garden?

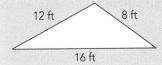

You can combine the three quantities in any order.

16 + 8 + 12
or 12 + 16 + 8
or 8 + 12 + 16

The order of the numbers (called **addends**) in an addition problem does not affect the answer. To add more than two numbers, start by adding any two of them, then add that answer to the next number, one step at a time.

16 + 8 + 12	or	12 + 16 + 8	or	8 + 12 + 16
24 + 12		28 + 8		20 + 16
36 ft		36 ft		36 ft

All three problems end up with the same answer, but the last one is easiest because you add compatible numbers first.

Addition is associative. This means that the way you group the addends does not affect the answer. You can use the associative property of addition to make problems easier to solve.

PROBLEM 1

In the following problems, parentheses group the compatible pairs that add up to 10. Complete the steps in parentheses first and find the answers.

Ⓐ $37 + (27 + 3)$ Ⓑ $(11 + 19) + 24$ Ⓒ $(6 + 14) + (13 + 7) + 56$

$37 + 30$

PROBLEM 2

First place the parentheses in the following problems to show the easiest order in which to complete the addition. Then find the answers by working one step at a time.

Ⓐ $56 + 99 + 1$ Ⓒ $17 + 3 + 24$ Ⓔ $15 + 5 + 26 + 4 + 32$

Ⓑ $56 + 4 + 37$ Ⓓ $15 + 9 + 21$ Ⓕ $22 + 8 + 3 + 37 + 24$

PROBLEM 3

Look for compatible pairs whose last digits add to 10. Rearrange the addends so that you can answer the problem easily, and then solve it.

Ⓐ $23 + 9 + 7 + 11 + 42$ Ⓒ $53 + 12 + 4 + 18 + 26$

Ⓑ $46 + 21 + 9 + 17 + 4$ Ⓓ $35 + 17 + 16 + 3 + 5$

Grouping with Variables

As you saw in Lesson 1, a letter is often used in a problem to indicate an unknown number. When a letter (**variable**) is one of the numbers being added, you cannot actually carry out that addition. You can only write an expression to indicate that the number and letter are to be added.

■ **: : : :**   eight more than what's in the box   can be written as $x + 8$ or $8 + x$

When there are more than two numbers and/or letters to be added, group the numbers together and add them. Then indicate the remaining addition in a single expression.

$8 + x + 13$
$21 + x$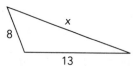
    $x + 11 + y + 8$
$19 + x + y$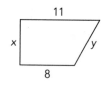

PROBLEM 4

First write the problem. Then find the perimeter of each figure.

Ⓐ   Ⓑ   Ⓒ 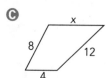   Ⓓ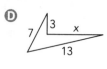

Evaluating Expressions

EXAMPLE

What would the perimeter be if the value of *x* were 16?

Write the problem.	$14 + 6 + x$
Add the numbers, and indicate the remaining addition.	$20 + x$
Substitute 16 for *x* in the expression.	$20 + 16$
Add.	36

PROBLEM 5 Find the perimeter of the triangle above.

Ⓐ Assume that *x* is 13.   Ⓑ Assume that *x* is 18.

PROBLEM 6 Write an expression and find the perimeter for Figures A and B below, if the value of *x* is Ⓐ 6, Ⓑ 8, Ⓒ 11.

FIGURE A   12
x   *x*
13

FIGURE B   *x*
x   *x*
x   *x*

PROBLEM 7 Ⓐ Express the perimeter of this triangle using the letters and numbers.

What is the perimeter if

Ⓑ *x* = 4 and *y* = 6?

Ⓒ *x* = 5 and *y* = 7?

y
x
8

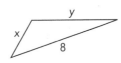

USING DATA

Study the Women's Shoe Size Conversion Chart on page 294 in the Appendix.

Ⓐ Compare the sizes in the U.S. and United Kingdom. Let *x* represent any U.S. size and write an expression to represent the equivalent size in the United Kingdom. Evaluate your expression to find the UK size that is equivalent to a size 12 in the U.S.

Ⓑ Compare the Japanese sizes with the U.S. sizes. Letting *n* represent any Japanese size, write an expression to represent the equivalent size in the U.S. Evaluate your expression to find the U.S. size that is equivalent to a size 31 in Japan.

How Much Is the Total Cost?

Estimating and Calculating with Money

EXAMPLE

Doris had only $10 in her purse and stopped at a convenience store for a can of coffee ($5.99), a box of cereal ($2.79), and a loaf of bread ($1.49). Before she went to the cashier, she wondered if she had enough money for the items she had chosen.

> If a front-end estimate leaves you uncertain, take a second look and round the numbers before you add.

Doris needed to **estimate** the total cost in order to avoid embarrassment at the checkout counter. To guess at the total, she focused on the first numbers, because these front-end digits gave her a general idea about how much each item costs. Since that front-end estimate came fairly close to her limit of $10, she needed a more accurate estimate. Doris took a second look, rounding the numbers to the nearest dollar, then adding.

FRONT-END ESTIMATION	SECOND LOOK (ROUNDING)
$5.99 + $2.79 + $1.49	$5.99 is nearly $6.00
5 + 2 + 1 = 8	$2.79 is closer to $3.00
	These add to $9.00
	$9.00 plus $1.49 is about $10.50

Doris can be pretty sure that she does not have enough money. Use the calculator to find the exact amount Doris will need.

5	.	9	9	+	2	.	7	9	+	1	.	4	9	=	. 10.27
decimal point				plus sign	decimal point				plus sign	decimal point				equals sign	

The total ($10.27) shows that Doris's second look was important—$10 was not enough money.

PROBLEM 8 | Do a front-end estimate of these totals, and then take a second look by rounding to get closer. Finally, use your calculator to find the precise answer.

		FRONT END	SECOND LOOK ROUNDING	CALCULATOR ANSWER
Ⓐ	$2.27 + $4.07 + $1.49 ≈	☐	_____	_____
Ⓑ	$7.16 + $11.99 + $.99 ≈	☐	_____	_____
Ⓒ	$6.49 + $1.79 + $1.99 ≈	☐	_____	_____

Grouping in Estimating

A third method of estimating is grouping to find easy numbers to work with. This is most useful when the original numbers are not very close to whole numbers.

EXAMPLE

$7.29 + $1.68 + $2.50 = ?

First add the dollars.	($7 + $1 + $2)	$10.00
Then group the cents	($.29 + $.68 is nearly $1, plus $.50)	+ 1.50
into dollar groups.		$11.50
Finally, add the two sums.		

You may want to group amounts that combine to form nice numbers that you can add mentally.

EXAMPLE

$16.35 + $3.69 + $5.25 + $4.99 = ?

    about $20   +   about $10 = about $30

PROBLEM 9 | From the prices shown below, find pairs that group to about $5, about $10, and about $15. You may use prices more than once.

Ⓐ about $5   **Ⓑ** about $10   **Ⓒ** about $15

Ⓐ about $5	Ⓑ about $10	Ⓒ about $15
_____ + _____	_____ + _____	_____ + _____
_____ + _____	_____ + _____	_____ + _____
	_____ + _____	_____ + _____
	_____ + _____	_____ + _____

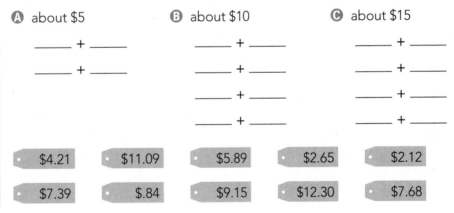

$4.21	$11.09	$5.89	$2.65	$2.12
$7.39	$.84	$9.15	$12.30	$7.68

Money and Decimals

Use your familiarity with money as a stepping-stone to understanding the value of decimal fractions.

money form		pure decimal form (Enter this in calculator.)
$.01 (one-hundredth of a dollar)	penny	0.01
$.10 (ten-hundredths or one-tenth of a dollar)	dime	0.10 or 0.1
$.25 (twenty five-hundredths or one-fourth of a dollar)	quarter	0.25
$.05 (five-hundredths of a dollar)	nickel	0.05

CALCULATOR EXPLORATION

How Much Money Is Here?

Money	Find total mentally	Calculator — Enter the value of each coin and add. Compare.
Ⓐ 4 pennies and 2 dimes	_____	___ + ___ + ___ + ___ + ___ + ___ = ___
Ⓑ 3 dimes and 2 pennies	_____	___ + ___ + ___ + ___ + ___ = ___
Ⓒ 1 half dollar and 5 pennies	_____	___ + ___ + ___ + ___ + ___ + ___ = ___
Ⓓ 3 nickels and 3 pennies	_____	___ + ___ + ___ + ___ + ___ + ___ = ___
Ⓔ 1 half dollar, 2 nickels, and 3 pennies	_____	___ + ___ + ___ + ___ + ___ + ___ = ___
Ⓕ 2 quarters and 4 pennies	_____	___ + ___ + ___ + ___ + ___ + ___ = ___
Ⓖ 4 dimes and 2 nickels	_____	___ + ___ + ___ + ___ + ___ + ___ = ___

Decimals on a Number Line

Which is greater, 0.05 or 0.5?   0.01 or 0.1?

Apply what you know about money and these questions are not as confusing as they look.

YOU KNOW THAT:	SO YOU ALSO KNOW THAT:
fifty cents is more than five cents	0.5 is greater than 0.05
ten cents is more than one cent	0.1 is greater than 0.01

Locate the values of these coins on a decimal **number line** to make their relative size more obvious. (Numbers on a number line increase as you move from left to right.)

EXAMPLE

Find the location of $.19, $.20, $.38, and $.40 on the number line.

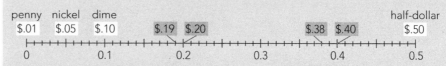

Their locations on the number line show that 0.2 ($.20) is greater than 0.19 ($.19) and that 0.4 ($.40) is greater than 0.38 ($.38).

PROBLEM 10

On the number line below, mark the approximate location of the following numbers. (The first one is done for you.) **Think:** 0.09 is the same as $.09. $.09 is less than 0.1, which is equivalent to $.10.

A 0.09	**C** 0.25	**E** 0.59	**G** 0.8	**I** 0.11
B 0.1	**D** 0.3	**F** 0.6	**H** 0.75	**J** 1.1

Use data from the table on page 288 in the Appendix to complete the bar graph. Insert bars to represent (approximately) the amount of tax per gallon of gasoline in each of these states.

STATE TAX ON GASOLINE

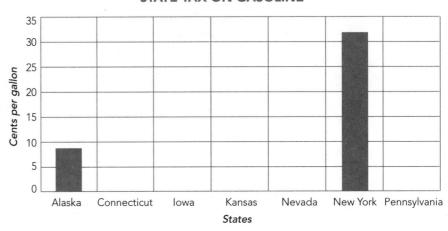

Comparing Decimal Numbers

Adding or removing trailing zeros to a decimal number does not change its value.

EXAMPLE

Which is greater 0.45 or 0.4?

- Add zeros to the end so that the numbers have the same number of digits after the decimal point.

  0.45   0.40

- Disregard the decimal point and choose the greater number.

  45   40

45 is greater, so 0.45 is greater than 0.4.

PROBLEM 11 | Which number in each pair is greater?

Ⓐ 0.6 or .07

Ⓑ 0.677 or 0.7

Ⓒ 0.04 or 0.2

Ⓓ 3.9 or 3.09

Ⓔ 1.3 or 0.13

Ⓕ 1.005 or 1

Ⓖ 2 or 0.5

Ⓗ 70.8 or 7.08

Both the > and < signs open to the greater number.

These are three of the signs used in mathematics to tell the relationship between numbers:

$<$ means "is less than"

$=$ means "is equal to"

$>$ means "is greater than"

PROBLEM 12

The following statements are true. Write them using the words above to understand their meaning.

EXAMPLES $6 > 3$ "6 is greater than 3" $2 < 4$ "2 is less than 4"

Ⓐ $8 > 6$ Ⓓ $10 < 40$

Ⓑ $6 < 8$ Ⓔ $1.6 > 0.67$

Ⓒ $40 > 10$ Ⓕ $7.2 < 10$

PROBLEM 13

Write one of the signs $<$, $=$, or, $>$ between each pair of numbers to make true statements.

Ⓐ 0.45 _____ 0.7 Ⓔ 0.7 _____ 0.70

Ⓑ 3 _____ 3.00 Ⓕ 0.69 _____ 0.7

Ⓒ 0.08 _____ 0.8 Ⓖ 0.12 _____ 1.2

Ⓓ 90 _____ 0.09 Ⓗ 1 _____ 0.89

PROBLEM 14

How Much Greater? Once you have added zeros so that the numbers have the same number of digits after the decimal point and have determined which one is greater, subtract them to find the difference between them. Arrange the numbers from problem 13 into a subtraction problem (writing the greater number first) and then do the subtraction.

Ⓐ **EXAMPLE** $0.70 - 0.45 = 0.25$ Ⓔ _____

Ⓑ _____   Ⓕ _____

Ⓒ _____   Ⓖ _____

Ⓓ _____   Ⓗ _____

Explain how knowing the compatible pairs helped you subtract these numbers.

Subtracting Decimals

Enter the following subtraction problems into the
calculator and write the answer that appears on the display.

Ⓐ 5.6 − 0.56 = _____   0.56 − 5.6 = _____

Ⓑ 0.9 − 0.75 = _____   0.75 − 0.9 = _____

Ⓒ 15 − 12.8 = _____   12.8 − 15 = _____

Ⓓ 1 − 0.83 = _____   0.83 − 1 = _____

Write a few sentences to tell how you could use a calculator to decide
which of two numbers is greater.

_____

_____

Reading Word Problems

To solve word problems, you must first be able to understand the situation
that the words describe. There is no one approach that will work for all word
problems, but there are some questions to ask and techniques to use that may
help you to understand what a situation is about.

PROBLEM 15

A word problem contains this sentence: "Marcus drove 10 miles farther than Ben."

Ⓐ **Ask a broad "big picture" question.**
Who drove the longer distance?

Ⓑ **Insert some easy number in place of one of the unknowns.**
If Ben drove 15 miles, how far did Marcus drive?

Ⓒ **Make a table of specific values
to help in recognizing a relationship.**
Complete the table at the right.

Ⓓ **Sketch a picture of the situation.**

Ⓔ **Write a mathematical expression that
represents the situation.**
*If b represents the number of miles that
Ben drove, which expression tells how
many miles Marcus drove?*

Ben	Marcus
2	
8	
	19
	23
20	

(1) $10b$ **(2)** $\frac{b}{10}$ **(3)** $b + 10$ **(4)** $10 - b$ **(5)** $b - 10$

Check your answer choice by substituting some of the values from the
table above.

CHECK YOUR UNDERSTANDING

You may use your calculator on any problem except where noted by this symbol:

 *When adding, you can change both the order and grouping of the numbers without changing the answer. Rearrange the following expressions and place parentheses so that you can do all the adding, step by step, in your head. Then add.*

1. 45 + 8 + 5 + 12

2. 21 + 3 + 9 + 16 + 17

3. 36 + 15 + 15 + 4 + 29

4. 19 + 8 + 32 + 56 + 11

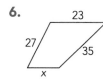 *Find the perimeters of the following figures. Try to find the sums mentally by grouping first.*

5.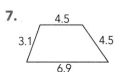

7.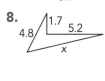

6.

8.

Problems 9 and 10 are based on this figure.

9. Write the perimeter as an expression.

10. What would the perimeter be if the value of x were

Ⓐ 16?
Ⓑ 13?
Ⓒ 17.7?

11. When manufactured material is put in a shipping box, 3 extra inches are allowed for packing. If an article were x inches high, write an expression for the height of the packing box.

12. Allowing 3 inches for packing, how high would a box be for an article that is

Ⓐ 24 inches high?
Ⓑ 32 inches high?
Ⓒ 18 inches high?

13. Estimate each total cost, using the method that seems best for you. Then find the exact answer.

Ⓐ $3.89 + $2.12 + $6.49 =
Ⓑ $15.35 + $22.98 + $4.66 =
Ⓒ $11.98 + $5.04 + $6.22 + $1.75 =
Ⓓ $2.75 + $12.88 + $7.30 + $1.21 =

14. Joe Swift jogged the following distances during one week:

Monday	7.8 km
Tuesday	10.0 km
Wednesday	4.1 km
Friday	12.05 km
Saturday	5.9 km

Ⓐ Estimate the total number of kilometers he jogged.
Ⓑ Then find the exact answer.

15. Write <, =, or, > to make these statements true.

Ⓐ 6 ___ 0.6
Ⓑ 0.3 ___ 2.3
Ⓒ 2.3 ___ 2.25
Ⓓ 10 ___ 10.00
Ⓔ 0.9 ___ 0.09
Ⓕ 50 ___ 0.05
Ⓖ 1.04 ___ 1.4
Ⓗ 0.33 ___ 0.3

16. Find the difference between each pair of numbers. First write the mathematical expression and then find the answer.

Ⓐ 0.68 and 2
Ⓑ 11 and 9.56
Ⓒ 0.4 and 0.04
Ⓓ 0.77 and 0.7
Ⓔ 1.5 and 15
Ⓕ 0.3 and 0.33

TEST-TAKING PRACTICE

You may use your calculator on any problem except where noted by this symbol:
Refer to the number grid directions on page 281 whenever needed.

1. On Monday, Sam's Service Station charged $1.47 for a gallon of Supreme Unleaded. On Thursday, Sam raised the price by $.03, and on Friday, he raised it $.04 more. What was the price of gas on Saturday?

(1) $1.40
(2) $1.45
(3) $1.50
(4) $1.53
(5) $1.54

2. How much change, in dollars, should Juan receive if he gives the clerk a $20 bill when he purchases a can of shaving cream for $4.79, a greeting card for $2.95, and a bottle of aspirin for $7.35? (Disregard any tax.)

Mark your answer in the circles in the grid.

3. Packages weighing 0.26 lb, 0.2 lb, 0.06 lb, and 0.6 lb were taken to the post office. Which of the following arranges these weights in order from least to greatest?

(1) 0.2, 0.26, 0.6, 0.06
(2) 0.2, 0.26, 0.06, 0.6
(3) 0.06, 0.26, 0.2, 0.6
(4) 0.06, 0.2, 0.26, 0.6
(5) 0.2, 0.06, 0.6, 0.26

Problems 4 and 5 refer to the following graph.

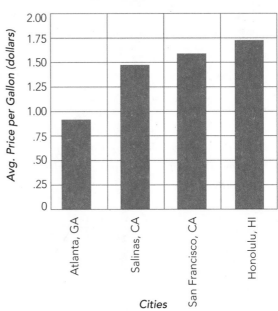

**GASOLINE PRICES IN SELECTED CITIES
DECEMBER 2001**

Source: *USA Today,* "Why do gas prices differ across the USA?"

4. Which of the following was the approximate price of gasoline in San Francisco?

(1) $ .90
(2) $1.05
(3) $1.30
(4) $1.60
(5) $1.75

5. From the graph, estimate the difference, in cents, between the highest and the lowest price per gallon for gas. Which of the following is closest to your estimate?

(1) 30
(2) 40
(3) 50
(4) 70
(5) 80

Equivalent Equations: Addition and Subtraction

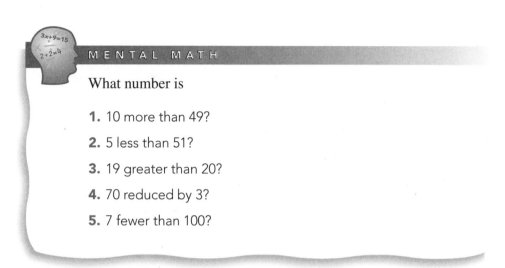

MENTAL MATH

What number is

1. 10 more than 49?

2. 5 less than 51?

3. 19 greater than 20?

4. 70 reduced by 3?

5. 7 fewer than 100?

In this lesson, you will expand on the expressions above and learn to make equations—full mathematical sentences—to solve problems such as this:

EXAMPLE

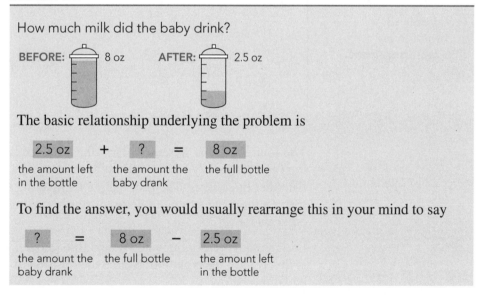

How much milk did the baby drink?

BEFORE: 8 oz   AFTER: 2.5 oz

The basic relationship underlying the problem is

2.5 oz	+	?	=	8 oz
the amount left in the bottle		the amount the baby drank		the full bottle

To find the answer, you would usually rearrange this in your mind to say

?	=	8 oz	–	2.5 oz
the amount the baby drank		the full bottle		the amount left in the bottle

This lesson will show you how you can write an equation for a problem so it is easy to solve.

Writing Equivalent Equations Using "Fact Families"

An **equation** is a mathematical sentence that contains an equals sign. It says that the expression on one side of the equals sign *has the same value* as the expression on the other side.

expression = expression

The three numbers 6, 9, and 15 are related by addition and subtraction. The relationship is pictured by the triangle and written mathematically by the equations below.

	ADDITION		SUBTRACTION	
	6 + 9 = 15	9 + 6 = 15	15 − 9 = 6	15 − 6 = 9

Equations can be reversed without changing their meaning. The equation 6 + 9 = 15 says the same thing as 15 = 6 + 9. For our purposes, we won't consider them as being "different."

PROBLEM 1

Write four equivalent equations that follow from each of the following:

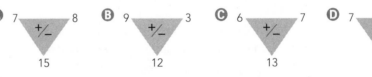

Ⓐ 7, 8, 15   **Ⓑ** 9, 3, 12   **Ⓒ** 6, 7, 13   **Ⓓ** 7, 9, 16

What addition does, subtraction undoes.

Addition and subtraction are **inverse operations.**

EXAMPLE

7 + 8 = 15

8 + 7 = 15

15 − 8 = 7

15 − 7 = 8

The four equations are **equivalent**; the sentences are different, yet they say the same thing. If you know the addition fact 7 + 8 = 15, then you also know the other three facts. The four equations (making up a "fact family") show that addition and subtraction are inverse operations—what one does, the other undoes.

Use the same reasoning when a **variable** (a letter used in place of a number) is involved in the equation. Notice the position of the boxed number in the equations below.

	ADDITION		SUBTRACTION	
	$x + 6 = \boxed{14}$	$6 + x = \boxed{14}$	$\boxed{14} - x = 6$	$\boxed{14} - 6 = x$

The number in the box is the sum of the addition problems and must come first in the subtraction problems.

PROBLEM 2 | Write four equivalent equations for each of the following. Later in the lesson, you will solve these equations by finding the numbers that will make them true.

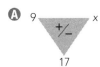 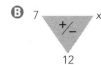 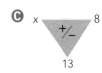 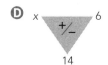

PROBLEM 3 | Write two equivalent equations using subtraction for each. If the triangle helps you to organize your thoughts, draw and label it first.

EXAMPLE For $14 + x = 30$, write $30 - x = 14$ and $30 - 14 = x$.

Ⓐ $8 + x = 12$ Ⓓ $x + 45 = 100$

Ⓑ $17 = x + 9$ Ⓔ $30 = x + 29.9$

Ⓒ $15 = x + 12$ Ⓕ $81 + x = 100$

PROBLEM 4 | Write two equivalent equations, one with subtraction and one with addition.

EXAMPLE For $x - 18 = 10$, write $x - 10 = 18$ and $10 + 18 = x$.

Ⓐ $17 - x = 9$ Ⓓ $x - 8 = 6$

Ⓑ $15 = 20 - x$ Ⓔ $32 = x - 8$

Ⓒ $x - 15 = 20$ Ⓕ $40 = 75 - x$

> You can reverse the order of equations. For example, $6 + x = 7$ is the same as $7 = 6 + x$.

Writing Equations to Solve Problems

You have learned to rearrange equations into equivalent ones. To use this in real life, you must first be able to write an equation that describes the situation. Follow the sequence of the pictures and see how they lead to the equations that follow them.

 + **=** $20 $25

money in   money Jack found   Jack's new total $20 + x = $25
Jack's pocket   in the dresser

 **−** **=**

24 sodas − x = 18 sodas

case of   sodas that   case with 18
24 sodas   were finished   sodas left

In solving word problems, the most critical step is writing the equation. The following two techniques are helpful.

1 Describe the Action of the Problem

One way to describe the action in the problem is to simply *translate* from the English words into mathematical symbols.

To write an equation for a word problem, you do not need to know in advance how to solve it, but you must understand what is going on in the problem.

EXAMPLE

When they were married, Roberto weighed 58 pounds more than his wife, Maria. If Roberto weighed 188 pounds, how much did Maria weigh?

└─58 lb

① Represent the unknown quantity with a letter.
Let m = Maria's weight.

② **Translate** the action sentence.
Roberto weighed **58 lb more than Maria** is the same as
$188 = 58 + m$

The equation is a mathematical **translation** of the problem situation. Writing it did not require you to think ahead as to what you will do to find the answer. You merely translated. Later in this lesson, you will solve this equation for m (Maria's weight).

EXAMPLE

Joan, whose present weight is 166 pounds, wants to lose some weight so that she will weigh only 140 pounds. How much should she lose?

The question asks how much weight she should lose, so this is the **unknown**.

Let x = how much weight Joan should lose.

The action of the problem is losing weight—a subtraction action. Think of this in **time order** (the order something happens) and then translate.

$166 - x = 140$

Joan starts at 166, loses some weight (x), then weighs 140.

PROBLEM 5

Write an equation that follows the action or time order in each of these problems.

Ⓐ Andy has already saved $500 to buy a used motorcycle. How much more does he have to save if the bike costs $1,125?

Ⓑ LaTonya starts on a shopping trip with $100. When she is finished shopping, she has $12 left. How much did she spend?

2 Use a Known Relationship as a Guideline

Your experience and prior knowledge are important when writing equations.

For example, consider a store owner who sells items at a higher price (**selling price**) than what he paid for them (**cost**) so that he can make a **profit**.

cost + profit = selling price

This equation is a simplified formula for the relationship.

EXAMPLES

A furniture store buys a sofa for $525 and sells it for $750. The profit the store makes on the sofa is $225.	cost + profit = selling price $525 + $225 = $750	

Lucille buys bracelets from a supplier for $.85 each. She personalizes them by putting people's names on them, then sells them for $2.50 each. What is her profit per item?	The questions asks for the **profit**. Use the formula and **substitute** the values.	Let p = profit. cost + profit = selling price $.85 + p = $2.50

PROBLEM 6

Write an equation for each of the following problems by either (1) following the action or time order of the problem (translating) or (2) using a known relationship as shown in the examples above. Use any letter for the unknown. **Do not solve.**

Ⓐ Wade, who trades baseball cards, purchased a 1986 José Canseco rookie card for $8. He later sold it for $49. What was his profit on this card alone?

Ⓑ At the start of a trip, the odometer on Juan's car read 11,031.8 miles. At the end of the trip, it read 11,988.2 miles. How many miles did he drive on this trip? (**Note:** Write the equation in time order.)

Ⓒ After losing 32 pounds, Jim is back to his "fighting weight" of 185 pounds. How much did he weigh before he lost the weight?

Ⓓ A used-car dealer paid $8,500 for a car, shined it up, and then put it on his lot with a price of $9,999 on the windshield. If he sells it for that price, how much profit will he make?

PROBLEM 7

Write an equation to represent the types of problems that you saw in Lessons 1 and 2. **Do not solve.**

Ⓐ One side of a triangular lot measures 100 feet, another measures 80 feet. If the perimeter of the triangle is 230 feet, how long must the third side be?

Ⓑ The economy-size box of cereal weighs 121 grams more than the regular-size box. If the economy size weighs 567 grams, how much does the regular size weigh?

Solving Equations

Use Guessing

Some equations are easy to solve. Just look at them and come up with the answer mentally.

When you replace x with the number that is the solution, the equation is true.

> To solve an equation, find the number that makes it true.

	ask yourself	solution
$x + 5 = 12$	What added to five results in 12?	$x = 7$
$3 + x = 13$	Three plus what number equals 13?	$x = 10$
$15 - x = 7$	Subtracting what number from 15 leaves 7?	$x = 8$
$20 - x = 12$	20 minus what number leaves 12?	$x = 8$

PROBLEM 8

Solve these equations by the guessing method described above. The solution is the number that makes the equation true.

Ⓐ $7 + x = 13$ Ⓒ $x + 15 = 20$ Ⓔ $17 - x = 9$ Ⓖ $20 - x = 9$

$x =$ _____ $x =$ _____ $x =$ _____ $x =$ _____

Ⓑ $35 + x = 95$ Ⓓ $x + 125 = 200$ Ⓕ $50 - n = 30$ Ⓗ $870 - p = 800$

$x =$ _____ $x =$ _____ $n =$ _____ $p =$ _____

Write an Equivalent Equation

Sometimes it is difficult to guess at a solution. When it is difficult to guess at a solution, you can rearrange an equation so that it is easier to solve.

Compare these two equivalent equations by trying to solve each of them. Which seems easier to solve? Why?

$$45 + x = 96 \qquad 96 - 45 = x$$

It is usually easier to solve an equation when the variable (the letter) is alone on one side of the equals sign. Compare these equations. Which is easier to solve? Why?

$$99 - x = 35 \qquad 99 - 35 = x$$

Because the second equation tells you specifically what to do, it is easier for most people to solve.

PROBLEM 9

Rearrange these equations to make them easier to solve. Then solve them.

Ⓐ $100 + x = 125$ Ⓓ $x - 100 = 225$

Ⓑ $100 - x = 70$ Ⓔ $p + 30 = 56$

Ⓒ $x + 100 = 225$ Ⓕ $56 - p = 30$

Revisit a few examples from pages 28 and 29. In each case, to solve the equations you will follow these steps:

STEP 1 Picture the situation.

STEP 2 Write an equation that follows the action.

STEP 3 Write an equivalent equation that is easy to solve.
Use mental math, paper and pencil, or a calculator to find the answer.

STEP 4 Check your answer for reasonableness.

EXAMPLE A

When they were married, Roberto weighed 58 pounds more than his wife, Maria. If Roberto weighed 188 pounds, how much did Maria weigh?

STEP 1 Roberto weighed 58 pounds more than Maria.

STEP 2 Write the equation. $188 = 58 + m$

STEP 3 Rearrange the equation. $188 - 58 = m$
$$130 = m$$

STEP 4 Maria weighed 130 pounds, which is reasonable.
Do a formal check by replacing m with 130 in the original equation.
Original equation $188 = 58 + m$
Replace m with 130. $188 = 58 + (130)$
Since the statement is true, $188 = 188$
130 is the solution.

EXAMPLE B

Lucille buys bracelets from a supplier for $.85 each. She personalizes them by putting people's names on them, then sells them for $2.50 each. What is her profit per item?

STEP 1 cost + profit = selling price

STEP 2 $\$.85 + p = \$2.50$

STEP 3 $\$2.50 - \$.85 = p$
$$\$1.65 = p$$

STEP 4 Lucille's profit is $1.65, a number between $1 and $2, which makes sense here.
A formal check: $\$.85 + p = \$2.50$
$$\$.85 + (\$1.65) = \$2.50$$
$$\$2.50 = \$2.50$$

PROBLEM 10 | Go back to problems 6 and 7 on page 29. Solve the equations that you wrote earlier. Be sure to check your answers.

Rewriting Equations Using Algebraic Rules

Another way to find equivalent equations is to use the properties of equality from elementary algebra.

ADDITION PROPERTY OF EQUALITY	If $a = b$, then $a + c = b + c$ If $a = b$, then $a - c = b - c$

Equals added to equals remain equal.

Picture an equation as a balanced scale. If the same weight were added to (or subtracted from) both sides, the scale would still be balanced.

For equations, the addition property says that the same number can be added to (or subtracted from) both sides and they will remain equal.

In algebra, we use these rules to get the variable alone on one side of the equation.

EXAMPLE

$x + 27 = 56$	Notice that 27 is being added to x on its side of the equation. Remember that we want x to be alone.
$x + 27 - 27 = 56 - 27$	To undo "adding 27," following the Addition Property of Equality, we have to subtract 27 from both sides of the equation.
$x + 0 = 56 - 27$ $x = 29$	Because $27 - 27 = 0$, we have succeeded in getting x alone on its side of the equation. Subtracting 27 from 56 leaves 29 as the solution.
CHECK: $(29) + 27 = 56$ $56 = 56$	Replace x with 29 in the original equation.

EXAMPLE

$n - 15 = 42$	Notice that 15 is being subtracted from n on its side of the equation.
$n - 15 + 15 = 42 + 15$	Add 15 to both sides of the equation.
$n + 0 = 42 + 15$	Because $-15 + 15 = 0$, we have succeeded in getting n alone on it side of the equation.
$n = 57$	Adding 15 to 42 leaves 57 as the solution.
CHECK: $(57) - 15 = 42$ $42 = 42$	Replace n with 57 in the original equation.

PROBLEM 11 | Solve the following equations using the Addition Property of Equality. Check your answers.

A $x + 25 = 76$ **F** $100 = x - 45$

B $y + 34 = 80$ **G** $32 = 17 + x$

C $51 + m = 99$ **H** $y - 88 = 102$

D $x - 75 = 24$ **I** $49 = n - 14$

E $m - 21 = 49$ **J** $72 = b + 24$

Equations and Test-Taking

In this lesson you have learned to

- write equations to solve problems

- simplify problems by changing to equivalent equations using either the fact families or the Addition Property of Equality

- check answers

You will use these skills when taking a test, especially for an item that asks you to choose the equation that could be used to correctly solve a problem. You should be aware that the correct answer may not be exactly the equation that you come up with; it could be an **equivalent equation**. You must be able to recognize when an equation is merely a rearrangement of yours.

PROBLEM 12 | A repairman bought a part for $78. He charged his customer $109 for the same part. Letting p represent profit, which of the following equations represents the situation?

(1) $\$78 - p = \$109$
(2) $\$78 + \$109 = p$
(3) $\$109 + p = \$78$
(4) $\$109 - \$78 = p$
(5) $p - \$78 = \$109$

PROBLEM 13 | On the highway between Capitol City and Bridgeport, you pass through the village of Walker. It is 103 miles between Capitol City and Bridgeport and 37 miles from Walker to Bridgeport. Which equation shows how many miles (m) it is between Capitol City and Walker?

(1) $m = 103 + 37$
(2) $103 = m - 37$
(3) $37 = m - 103$
(4) $37 = 103 - m$
(5) $m = 37 - 103$

CHECK YOUR UNDERSTANDING

You may use your calculator on any problem except where noted by this symbol:

1.

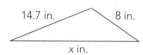

14.7 in. 8 in.

x in.

- **A** Write an expression for the perimeter of the figure above.
- **B** Write an equation if the perimeter were 30 inches.
- **C** Write an equivalent equation using subtraction so that x is alone on one side of the equals sign.
- **D** Solve the equation.
- **E** Check your answer.

2. A football player lost 41 pounds getting in shape for the season. After losing this weight, he weighed 299 pounds. How much did he weigh previously?

- **A** Choose a letter for the unknown, and write the equation suggested by the time order in the problem. (**Hint:** It is a subtraction action.)
- **B** Rewrite the equation so it is easier to solve. Use addition.
- **C** Solve the equation.
- **D** Check your answer.

3. After paying $98 dollars (cash) for a jacket, Dolores saw that she had a total of $64 left in her wallet. How much did she have before she bought the jacket?

- **A** Choose a letter for the unknown, and write the equation suggested by the time order in the problem. (**Hint:** It is a subtraction action.)
- **B** Rewrite the equation so it is easier to solve.
- **C** Solve the equation.
- **D** Check your answer.

4. After 7 years of owning a house in which they invested $46,500, the Johnsons sold it for $90,000. What was their profit?

- **A** Fit the information into the known formula, letting a letter stand for the unknown.
- **B** Rewrite the equation.
- **C** Solve the equation.
- **D** Check your answer.

5. Write a subtraction sentence that is equivalent to each addition equation. Write one where the variable is alone on one side of the equation. (Remember that the sum of an addition problem becomes the first number of a subtraction problem.)

- **A** $4 + x = 15$
- **B** $y + 9 = 20$
- **C** $45 = x + 15$
- **D** $35 = 30.5 + n$

6. Show the steps in finding the solution to the following equations. Use the "fact family" idea for these problems.

EXAMPLE
$$74 - n = 19$$
$$74 - 19 = n$$
$$55 = n$$

- **A** $23 - a = 15$
- **B** $54 + x = 75$
- **C** $s + 39 = 68$
- **D** $t - 49 = 61$
- **E** $104 = p + 85$
- **F** $138 = n - 32$

7. Show the steps that indicate that you are using the Addition Property of Equality in solving the following equations.

EXAMPLE
$$14 = z - 68$$
$$14 + 68 = z - 68 + 68$$
$$82 = z$$

- **A** $62 + x = 81$
- **B** $y + 47 = 55$
- **C** $p - 66 = 15$
- **D** $79 = m - 31$

TEST-TAKING PRACTICE

You may use your calculator on any problem except where noted by this symbol:

1. Nancy is a sales representative. On her last road trip, she covered 855 miles in 3 days. She drove 327 miles the first day and 288 miles the third day. If x represents the number of miles that she covered the second day, which of the following equations describes the situation?

(1) $x = 327 + 288$
(2) $x = 855 - 288$
(3) $x = 855 - 327 + 288$
(4) $855 = 327 + x + 288$
(5) $855 = 327 + 288 - x$

2. Rachel rides her bike 15 miles each evening for exercise. She follows the same triangular route each time so she knows how far she's gone. Part of her route is 5 miles and another is 7 miles. Which equation could be used to find m, the length of the third part of her route?

(1) $m = 15 + 5 + 7$
(2) $15 = 5 + 7 + m$
(3) $15 + m = 5 + 7$
(4) $m - 5 = 15 - 7$
(5) $m = 15 - 5 + 7$

3. At her annual physical, Mrs. Slimbody weighed in at 106 pounds. Her physician mentioned that for her height and frame, the ideal weight would be 125 pounds. How many pounds would she need to gain to achieve the ideal weight?

Mark your answer in the circles in the grid.

Problems 4 and 5 refer to the following table.

HEAT INDEX
Air Temperature (°F)

Relative Humidity (%)	80	85	90	95	100
30	78	84	90	96	104
40	79	86	93	101	110
50	81	88	96	107	120
60	82	90	100	114	132
70	85	93	106	124	144
80	86	97	113	136	
90	88	102	122		

4. Estimate the heat-index temperature, in degrees Fahrenheit, when the relative humidity is 75% and the air temperature is 85°.

(1) 85
(2) 95
(3) 103
(4) 106
(5) 110

5. Which equation could be used to determine d, the difference, on a 90° day, between the heat-index temperatures when the relative humidity is 80% and when the relative humidity is 50%?

(1) $d = 80 - 50$
(2) $80 = d - 50$
(3) $113 = 96 + d$
(4) $96 = d - 113$
(5) $d - 96 = 113$

Skill Maintenance
Lessons 1–3

Part One

In Lessons 1–3 you covered a lot of ground. Before going on, use the following exercises to maintain your skills. If you are having difficulty, this is a good time to go back and review. You may use your calculator on any problem except where noted by this symbol:

PROBLEM 1   Write an expression for each of the following problems.

Ⓐ $ $ $ 💲 💲 💲

Ⓑ $23 more than Hilary's salary (*s*)

Ⓒ $10 off the original price (*p*)

Ⓓ 1,250 more than the minimum (*m*)

Ⓔ 9 inches wider than the frame (*f*)

Ⓕ
```
 |‾‾‾‾‾‾‾⌒‾‾‾‾‾|
 |—————|————|
     17      n
```

PROBLEM 2   Write an expression for and find the perimeters of the figures shown below. Group the numbers to make adding easier.

Ⓐ parking lot

Ⓑ garden

Ⓒ coffee table

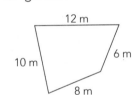

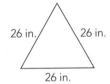

parking lot: 100 ft, 125 ft, 130 ft, 75 ft

garden: 12 m, 10 m, 6 m, 8 m

coffee table: 26 in., 26 in., 26 in.

PROBLEM 3   Write a subtraction equation that is equivalent to each addition equation. Make sure the variable is alone on one side of the equation.

Ⓐ $650 + x = 1,000$ Ⓑ $y + 99 = 470$ Ⓒ $300 + x = 430$

PROBLEM 4   Write equations and solve the problems below.

Ⓐ After she drove 300 miles, Linda had only 675 miles left to go to her grandmother's house. How long was her entire trip?

Ⓑ Samantha sold a painting for $200 more than she had paid for it. If she sold it for $925, how much had she paid for it?

Ⓒ Todd's grocery bill came to $78 after he was credited $7 for coupons. What would his bill have been without coupons?

Ⓓ Alaska's highest peak, Mt. McKinley, is 20,320 feet high. This is 5,910 feet higher in elevation than Washington state's highest peak, Mt. Rainier. What is the elevation of Mt. Rainier?

Part Two

1. There are five boxes on Kim's shelf. They weigh 0.2 lb, 0.15 lb, 0.17 lb, 1.1 lb, and 1.2 lb. Which box is the lightest?

(1) 0.2 lb
(2) 0.15 lb
(3) 0.17 lb
(4) 1.1 lb
(5) 1.2 lb

2. Estimate the total of this bill to the nearest dollar.

(1) $ 3
(2) $10
(3) $14
(4) $18
(5) $22

Date: 11/18	Server: Joan
Pizza	13.75
Pitcher Coke	3.45
Tax	1.04
Total	_____

Problems 3 and 4 refer to the chart below.

	Ryan	Kelley
Precinct 1	1,215	930
Precinct 2	672	1,177
Precinct 3	829	990

3. In total, how many people voted for Ryan?

Mark your answer in the circles in the grid.

4. How many more votes did Kelley receive than Ryan in Precinct 2?

(1) 161
(2) 285
(3) 405
(4) 505
(5) 1,849

5. The states on the graph below rank the lowest in a list of the highest peaks in each of the 50 states. From the graph, estimate the elevation, in feet, of the highest peak in Florida (FL).

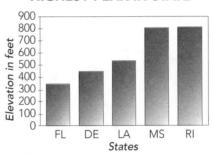

HIGHEST PEAK IN STATE

(1) 810
(2) 530
(3) 450
(4) 390
(5) 350

6. At the beginning of June, Alfred's checking account balance was $233.12. During the month, he wrote checks for a total of $980.12 and made deposits of $1,180.00. Disregarding any interest or check charges, what is his balance at the end of the month?

(1) $ 233.12
(2) $ 433.00
(3) $ 980.12
(4) $1,180.00
(5) $2,393.24

7. How many centimeters of weatherstripping does a maintenance engineer need to put around the window shown below?

(1) 57
(2) 400
(3) 557
(4) 657
(5) 15,000

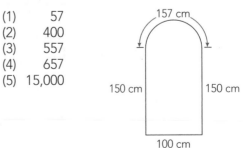

MENTAL MATH

1. $40 + n = 180$
2. $35 + x = 180$
3. $85 + p = 180$
4. $44 + n = 100$
5. $78 + c = 100$

In this lesson involving geometry topics, you will first learn the vocabulary and some special geometry relationships. Then you will be able to write equations like the ones above and solve them.

Angles

You see angles around you every day.

A This is an angle.

This is an angle.

An **angle** is formed between two sides when they extend from one point. The point is called the **vertex**.

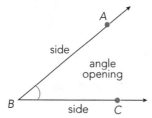

Angles can be named in three ways. For example, this angle can be named

① $\angle ABC$ (**Note:** *B*, the vertex, is in the middle.)

② $\angle CBA$

③ $\angle B$

The **measure** of an angle depends on the size of the opening between its sides. The unit of measure for angle openings is the **degree** (°).

There are 360° in a full circle.

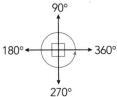

You should know the measures of these common angles.

A **right angle** has a measure of 90°.

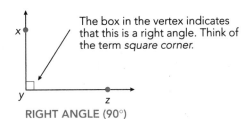

The box in the vertex indicates that this is a right angle. Think of the term *square corner*.

RIGHT ANGLE (90°)

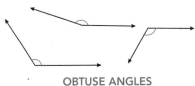

STRAIGHT ANGLE (180°)

Since this angle results in a straight line, the name is easy to remember.
90° + 90° = 180°

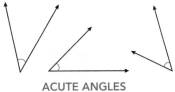

ACUTE ANGLES

Acute angles have smaller openings than right angles. Their measure is between 0° and 90°.

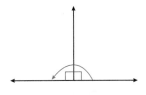

OBTUSE ANGLES

An **obtuse angle** is one whose measure is greater that 90° but less than 180°. These angles have larger openings than right angles, but smaller openings than straight angles.

PROBLEM 1 | Identify the following angles as acute, right, obtuse, or straight.

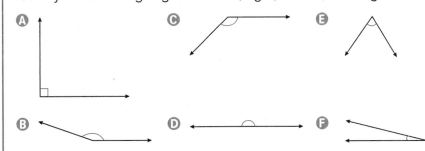

Complementary and Supplementary Angles

The following pairs of angles are complementary. Their total measure is 90°.

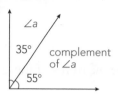
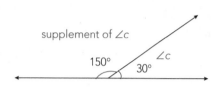

$$35° + 55° = 90°$$
$$30° + 60° = 90°$$

The following pairs of angles are supplementary. Their total measure is 180°.

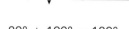

$$30° + 150° = 180°$$
$$80° + 100° = 180°$$

Two angles are **complementary** if the sum of their measures is 90°.

Two angles are **supplementary** if the sum of their measures is 180°.

PROBLEM 2 | If a pair of angles is complementary, each angle must be

_____. (acute, right, obtuse, or straight)

PROBLEM 3 | Two angles are both supplementary and equal to each other. They must

both be _____ angles. (acute, right, obtuse, or straight)

Equations and Geometry

You can use the steps of writing, rearranging, and solving the equations that you learned in Lesson 3 to find the answers to these geometry problems.

EXAMPLE 1

Find the complement of an angle whose measure is 35°.

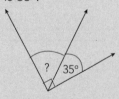

Let x = unknown angle
$$35° + x = 90°$$
$$x = 90° - 35°$$
$$x = 55°$$

EXAMPLE 2

Find the supplement of an angle whose measure is 65°.

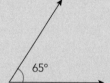

Let n = unknown angle
$$65° + n = 180°$$
$$n = 180 - 65$$
$$n = 115°$$

Write an equation to describe the relationship.

Rearrange the equation to get the variable alone.

Solve to find the value of the variable.

"Seeing" How to Solve a Problem

EXAMPLE

A brace makes an angle of 40° with the post it supports. What is the measure of the second angle formed?

SOLUTION 1

$40° + x = 180°$
$x = 180° - 40°$
$x = 140°$

SOLUTION 2

$x = 180° - 40°$
$x = 140°$

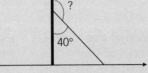

Both solutions are correct, even though solution 2 skipped the first step. You can often begin with an equation that does not need to be arranged if you can "see" what to do to solve it.

PROBLEM 4 | Write an equation to find the complement of the angle shown. Then do the same to find the supplement of the angle. (**Note:** Some angles may only have a supplement.) Solve.

EXAMPLE For an angle of 30°.

COMPLEMENT
$x = 90° - 30°$
$x = 60°$

SUPPLEMENT
$x = 180° - 30°$
$x = 150°$

Ⓐ

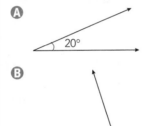

Ⓒ

Ⓑ

Ⓓ

PROBLEM 5 | Josh had to replace a piece of tile that was part of a design on his bathroom floor. Find the size of the angle the tile must have in order to fit in the design.

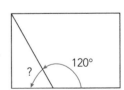

PROBLEM 6 | Ⓐ What is the measure of ∠m?
Ⓑ What is the measure of ∠n?

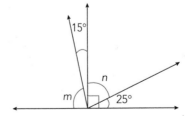

PROBLEM 7 | The complement of an angle whose measure is $b°$ can be expressed as $90° - b°$. Write an expression for the measure of the supplement of an angle that measures $m°$.

Triangles

Triangles are closed figures made up of three angles.

EXAMPLE

Find the measure of angle *b* in this triangle.

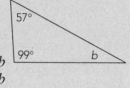

SOLUTION 1	SOLUTION 2
$57° + 99° + b = 180$	$180° - (57° + 99°) = b$
$156° + b = 180°$	$180° - 156° = b$
$b = 180° - 156°$	$24° = b$
$b = 24°$	

CALCULATOR EXPLORATION

Which Expressions Are Equal?

Most scientific calculators have parentheses keys (**(** and **)**) to use when evaluating expressions. Find the answers to each of the following expressions using your calculator and entering the symbols in exactly the order that they are written. (**Note:** You need to press the **=** key to complete the problem.)

Ⓐ $180 - (57 + 99) =$ Ⓑ $180 - (11 + 47) =$ Ⓒ $180 - 52 + 107 =$

  $180 - 57 + 99 =$ $180 - 11 - 47 =$ $180 - 52 - 107 =$

  $180 - 57 - 99 =$ $180 - 11 + 47 =$ $180 - (52 + 107) =$

Compare your results and complete this statement: $a - (b + c) =$

PROBLEM 8

A tile setter cut a square tile on the line shown. If one of the new angles formed is 30°, what is the measure of the other new angle?

PROBLEM 9 | Find the measure of angle *m* in each of the following triangles.

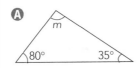
Ⓐ *m*, 80°, 35°

Ⓑ *m*, 110°, 22°

Ⓒ *m*, 37°

PROBLEM 10 | Which expression could be used to find the third angle of this triangle?

(1) 180° − x°
(2) 180° − (90° − x°)
(3) 180° − (90° + x°)
(4) 180° − 90°
(5) 90° + x°

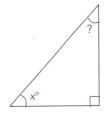

REASONING ACTIVITY

Exterior Angles of Triangles

Exterior angles are formed when a side of a triangle is extended beyond the vertex. For example, in the diagram of triangle *LUV* at the right, the *interior* angles are numbered 1, 2, and 3, and one *exterior* angle is ∠ALU.

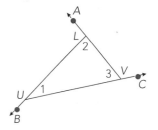

Ⓐ Name the other exterior angles that are pictured.

Ⓑ If you know that the measure of ∠2 is 75°, what is the measure of ∠ALU? How do you know?

Ⓒ If you know that the measure of ∠2 is 75°, what is the sum of the remaining interior angles? That is, ∠1 + ∠3 = _____. How do you know that? Compare your answer to your answer for part Ⓑ.

Ⓓ Knowing that ∠1 = 55°, what two statements can you make? (**Hint:** Repeat parts Ⓑ and Ⓒ for this angle.)

Ⓔ Knowing that ∠3 = 50°, make two similar statements.

Your statements are examples of a theorem in geometry that says:

THEOREM | The measure of an exterior angle is equal to the sum of the opposite interior angles.

Special Types of Angles

Parallel and Perpendicular Lines

Two lines are **parallel** (//) if they
lie on the same plane and do
not meet.

When two lines form right angles, the
two lines are said to be **perpendicular** (⊥)
to each other.

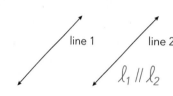

Line 1 and line 2 are parallel.

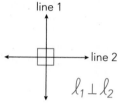

Line 1 and line 2 are perpendicular.

PROBLEM 11 | Name one place in the room you are in where you can see parallel lines.

PROBLEM 12 | Name one place in the room you are in where you can see perpendicular lines.

Angles Formed by Intersecting Lines

> When two angles
> have the same
> measure, we say that
> they are **congruent**
> and use this symbol: ≅
> If ∠A and ∠B both
> measure 45°, then
> ∠A ≅ ∠B.

In the diagram at the right, two lines have
been drawn to form four angles. These angles
have special relationships.

Opposite angles have the same measure.

For example: ∠1 ≅ ∠4; ∠2 ≅ ∠3

These are called **vertical angles**.

Pairs of angles on a straight line equal 180°.

∠1 + ∠2 = 180°   ∠3 + ∠4 = 180°

You know these angles as supplementary angles.

PROBLEM 13 | For the lines shown at the right:

Ⓐ List the two pairs of angles that are congruent
to each other.

Ⓑ List the four pairs of angles that equal 180°.

Ⓒ If the measure of ∠2 = 145°, what is the
measure of ∠3?

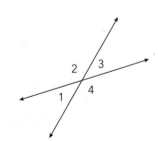

Corresponding Angles Are Equal

In the diagram below, a third line has been drawn across two parallel lines. The eight angles are numbered.

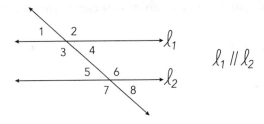

> Angles that occupy similar positions on parallel lines have the same measure.

Look at a pair of angles, $\angle 2$ and $\angle 6$.

Both $\angle 2$ and $\angle 6$ lie above a parallel and to the right of the intersecting line. They form a pair of **corresponding angles** that are congruent to each other.

Problems 14–16 are based on the sketch below.

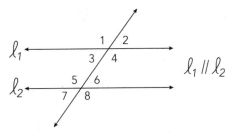

PROBLEM 14 | Name the pairs of corresponding angles on the drawing above.

EXAMPLE $\angle 1$ and $\angle 5$

Ⓐ $\angle 2$ and _____.

Ⓑ $\angle 3$ and _____.

Ⓒ $\angle 4$ and _____.

16 | If $\angle 5 = 140°$, what is the measure of

Ⓐ $\angle 1$?

Ⓑ $\angle 6$?

Ⓒ $\angle 7$?

Ⓓ $\angle 8$?

PROBLEM 15 | If $\angle 5 = 140°$, which expression shows how to find the measure of $\angle 6$?

(1) $180° + 140°$
(2) $180° - 140°$
(3) $140° - 90°$
(4) $140° + 90°$
(5) $180° + 90°$

17 | Find the measure of the following angles and discuss your reasoning.

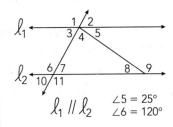

$\angle 5 = 25°$
$\angle 6 = 120°$

Ⓐ $\angle 3$

Ⓑ $\angle 4$

Ⓒ $\angle 8$

✓ CHECK YOUR UNDERSTANDING

You may use your calculator on any problem except where noted by this symbol:

1. Write three ways to name this angle.

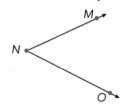

2. Which pairs of angles are supplementary?

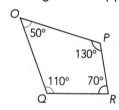

Problem 3 refers to the triangle below.

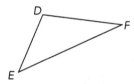

3. Ⓐ ∠D = 95° and ∠E = 51°
Write an expression to find ∠F.

Ⓑ What is the measure of ∠F?

Ⓒ ∠D = 95° and ∠E = x°
Write an expression to find ∠F.

Ⓓ If ∠D is a right angle and ∠F = 27°,
what is the measure of ∠E?

Ⓔ If ∠D is a right angle, what do you know
about the pair of remaining angles?

4. Main Street crosses Walnut Avenue and forms
the intersection shown in the sketch below.

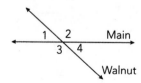

If corner 4 measures 45°, how many degrees
does corner 2 measure?

Problem 5 refers to the angle below.

5. Ⓐ What is the measure of the complement
of ∠NOP?

Ⓑ What is the measure of the supplement
of ∠NOP?

6. 🖩 What is the measure of ∠2?

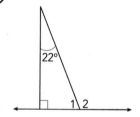

Problem 7 refers to the diagram below.

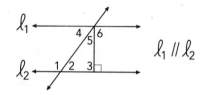

$\ell_1 \parallel \ell_2$

7. 🖩 Ⓐ What is the measure of ∠3?

Ⓑ Assuming that ∠1 = 130°, find the
measure of ∠2.

Ⓒ Assuming that ∠1 = 130°, find the
measure of ∠5.

Ⓓ What is the reason that you know
that ∠2 + ∠3 + ∠5 = 180°?

Ⓔ How do you know that
∠4 + ∠5 + ∠6 = 180°?

TEST-TAKING PRACTICE

You may use your calculator on any problem except where noted by this symbol:

1.

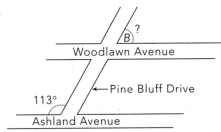

Pine Bluff Drive connects Woodlawn and Ashland Avenues as shown in the illustration above. If Woodlawn is parallel to Ashland, what is the value of ∠B, the acute angle that Pine Bluff makes with Woodlawn?

(1) 23°
(2) 67°
(3) 87°
(4) 90°
(5) 113°

2.

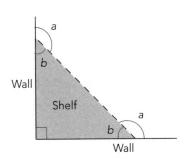

To cut a piece of shelving to fit in the corner sketched above, Dennis must rotate the blade of his table saw through the measure of ∠b. How large is ∠b?

(1) 90°
(2) 60°
(3) 50°
(4) 45°
(5) Not enough information is given.

3. Ally's monthly salary is $4,215. However, after deductions are made for taxes and insurance, her monthly take-home pay is $3,572.75. How much is deducted from her salary each month?

(1) $ 615.00
(2) $ 642.25
(3) $ 643.75
(4) $ 778.78
(5) $7,787.75

Problems 4 and 5 refer to the following diagram.

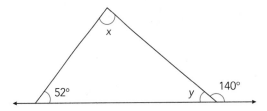

4. What is the measure, in degrees, of ∠x?

Mark your answer in the circles in the grid.

5. Which expression gives the measure, in degrees, of ∠y?

(1) 140 + 52
(2) 140 − 52
(3) 180 − 52
(4) 180 − (52 + x)
(5) 180 − 52 + x

MENTAL MATH

If:	You know that:
1. 20 + 13 = 33	18 + 13 is (less or greater) than 33
2. 60 + 40 = 100	58 + 36 is (less or greater) than 100
3. 75 + 25 = 100	77 + 29 is (less or greater) than 100
4. 100 − 40 = 60	100 − 38 is (less or greater) than 60
5. 30 − 15 = 15	32 − 15 is (less or greater) than 15

The Number Line

You already know about **positive** and **negative numbers** on a thermometer.

A **number line** looks something like a thermometer on its side. On a number line, such as the one below, the negative numbers are to the left of zero.

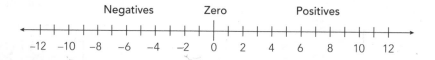

Numbers on a number line increase as you move to the right. Notice that

- The values of all negative numbers are less than 0.

- Since −2 is to the right of −10, −2 > −10 (−2 is greater than −10).

PROBLEM 1 In each pair of numbers, decide which is greater. For help, think of either the thermometer or the number line.

Ⓐ 8 or −10　　Ⓑ 0 or −25　　Ⓒ −50 or −25　　Ⓓ −6 or −5.6

PROBLEM 2 Insert the symbol >, <, or = to make each statement true. Remember, > means "is greater than," and < means "is less than."

Ⓐ −9 _____ −8　Ⓒ 5 _____ −6　Ⓔ 2 _____ −2　Ⓖ −5.4 _____ −5.5

Ⓑ 5 _____ 6　　Ⓓ −5 _____ −6　Ⓕ 5.4 _____ 5.5　Ⓗ −2 _____ −1.2

PROBLEM 3 Place the following numbers in order, from least to greatest.

Ⓐ 9, −10, 5, −15, 3　　　　　　Ⓑ 8, −10, 0, −2, −9

Adding and Subtracting on the Number Line

We can show addition and subtraction as movements on a number line.

EXAMPLE A	**EXAMPLE B**
To *add* a number to another, start at the first number and move the second number of spaces *to the right*.	To *subtract* a number, move that many spaces *to the left*.

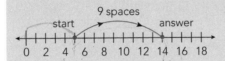

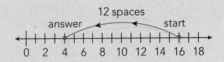

$$5 + 9 = x$$

$$16 - 12 = x$$

Start at 5. Move 9 spaces to the right. $x = 14$	Start at 16. Move 12 spaces to the left. $x = 4$

If you think of the number line as extending to the left of the zero, you can picture subtracting a greater number from a smaller one.

$$7 - 18 = x$$

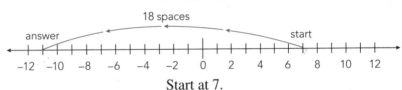

Start at 7.
Move 18 spaces to the left.
$x = -11$

Attaching a real situation to the problem often makes it easier to understand.

EXAMPLE A

Imagine the zero as the original line of scrimmage in a football game. On the first play, your team gains 7 yards, and on the second play it loses 18 yards. Where is your team now with respect to the original line of scrimmage?

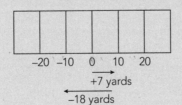

This can be expressed as
$7 - 18 = -11$

EXAMPLE B

You may prefer to think in terms of money. Imagine earning $7 in the same hour that you spend $18.

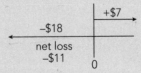

The hour ends with a net loss of $11.
This can be expressed as
$\$7 - \$18 = -\$11$

You can also picture problems that start with negative numbers.

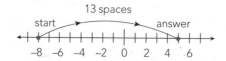

| $(-8) + 13 = x$ | $(-2) - 5 = x$ |

Start at −8.
Move 13 spaces *to the right*.
$x = 5$

Start at −2.
Move 5 spaces *to the left*.
$x = -7$

THINK: a loss of 8 followed by a gain of 13

THINK: a loss of 2 followed by a loss of 5

PROBLEM 4 | Write the problem illustrated by each of the following diagrams.

EXAMPLE

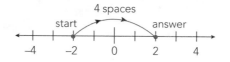

$$-2 + 4 = 2$$

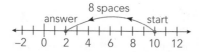

Ⓐ

Ⓒ

Ⓑ

Ⓓ

The equation $10 + (-8) = x$ can be written as $10 - 8 = x$ and solved in the same way as before.

$$10 - 8 = x$$

Start at 10.
Move 8 spaces *to the left*.
$x = 2$

Think of two money losses, first a loss of $7 and then a loss of $11. They can be written in an equation as $(-7) + (-11) = x$, which is the same as:

$$(-7) - 11 = x$$

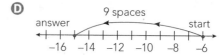

Start at −7.
Move 11 spaces *to the left*.
$x = -18$

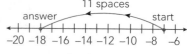

SUMMARY | Adding a negative number has the same result as subtracting a positive number. $5 + (-3) = 5 - 3 = 2$

CALCULATOR EXPLORATION

How Can You Do This on Your Calculator?

On some calculators, you use the **+/−** key to enter a negative number.

EXAMPLE $(-7) - 11$ Watch the display as you press these keys.
7 **+/−** **−** **1** **1** **=** The **+/−** key changes the sign of whatever is in the display.

Find the answers to the following. If you use the **+/−** key, you do not have to enter the parentheses that enclose a negative number. Note which answers in each column are the same.

$56 - (-43) =$	$(-16) - (-28) =$	$113 - (-176) =$
$56 - 43 =$	$(-16) - 28 =$	$113 + 176 =$
$56 + 43 =$	$(-16) + 28 =$	$113 - 176 =$

Compare your results and complete this statement without using a calculator: $45 - (-80) = 45$ _____ $80 =$ _____

SUMMARY | Subtracting a negative number has the same result as adding a positive. $7 - (-2) = 7 + 2 = 9$

Using the Number Line

Problems involving negatives are easier to solve because you can use your life experience to make sense of the problem.

The windchill temperature depends on both the actual recorded temperature and the wind speed. The following table is a record of some winter temperatures. Use it for problem 5 below.

	S	M	T	W	Th	F	S
recorded temps (°F)	20	12	−3	−1			5
windchill temps (°F)	3	−10		−24	−22	−20	−8

100 —
90 —
80 —
70 —
60 —
50 —
40 —
30 —
20 —
10 —
0 —
−10 —
−20 —
−30 —

°F

If you lay a thermometer on its side, you can see a number line.

PROBLEM 5 | Use the thermometer at the left to help you "picture the problem." What was the difference between the recorded temperature and the windchill temperature

Ⓐ on Sunday?

Ⓑ on Monday? (Picture the numbers on the thermometer and determine the number of spaces between them.)

Ⓒ on Wednesday?

Ⓓ If the windchill temperature was 13° lower than the recorded temperature on Tuesday, what was the windchill temperature? (Write the mathematical sentence first.)

PROBLEM 6 | Solve the following equations. Remember that it is more important to understand the problem than to be speedy in solving it. (To help yourself, "picture the problem" on a thermometer or number line.)

A $15 - 27 = x$ **C** $47 + (-67) = x$ **E** $(-32) + 16 = b$

B $(-34) + (-44) = n$ **D** $(-22) - 33 = k$ **F** $(-18) - 4 = s$

Use the calculator to solve the following equations.

G $106 - 277 = x$ **I** $890 + (-536) = y$ **K** $(-744) + 406 = m$

H $(-309) - (-447) = n$ **J** $186 - (-244) = b$ **L** $214 + (-316) = r$

The Coordinate Grid

Placing two number lines perpendicular to each other so that they intersect at the zeros creates a **coordinate plane**.

This is a pair of **axes**.

The horizontal axis is called the **x-axis**, and the vertical axis is the **y-axis**.

The point at which they meet is called the **origin** and represents 0 for both axes.

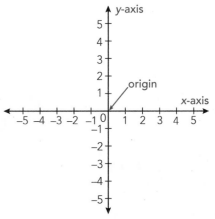

COORDINATE PLANE

Note that on the x-axis, the positive numbers are to the right of the origin and the negatives are to the left of the origin.

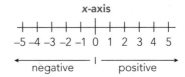

Likewise, on the y-axis, the positive numbers are above the origin and the negatives are below.

The axes are used to pinpoint the position of any point on a plane.

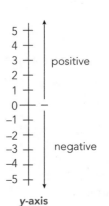

EXAMPLE A

Find the distance from point A to each of the axes.

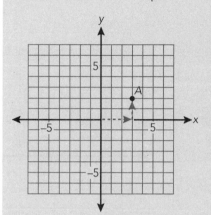

To find or plot the point (x, y) on a graph, start at the origin, move x units to the left or right, then move y units up or down.

Starting at the origin, move to the right (or left) until you are directly under (or over) the point. How far to the right (or left) did you move? Count the lines.

You moved 3 spaces to the right. That is +3 (or just 3) on the x-axis.

Then move up (or down) until you reach the point, counting the units as you go. How far up (or down) did you go?

You moved 2 spaces up. That is +2 (or just 2) on the y-axis.

We use the **ordered pair** notation (3, 2) to tell the position of this point. The two numbers are called the **coordinates** of point A. The first number of the pair tells how far to the left or right the point is; it is called the **x-coordinate**. After the comma, the second number—the **y-coordinate**—tells how far up or down the point is. Think of this as the point (x, y).

EXAMPLE B

Compare the positions of points A (3, 6) and B (–3, 6).

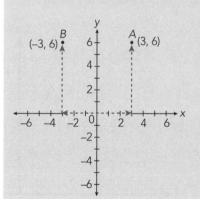

Look at the first number of each ordered pair.

The first number tells you how far *to the left or right* of the origin to move.

If the first number is negative, move to the left. If it is positive, move to the right.

Both of these points have a positive y-value. They both lie above the x-axis.

EXAMPLE C

Compare the positions of points C (−5, 2) and D (−5, −2).

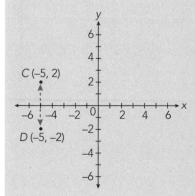

Look at the second number of these ordered pairs.

The second number tells you how far *up or down* to move.

If the second number is positive (as in point C), *move up* from the x-axis. If it is negative (as in point D), *move down*.

Both of these points have a negative x-value; they are located to the left of the y-axis.

PROBLEM 7 | Plot the following points on the coordinate grid below. That is, locate the position, mark it with a dot, and label it with the letter.

Ⓐ (4, 3)

Ⓑ (−4, −3)

Ⓒ (3, −4)

Ⓓ (−5, 2)

Ⓔ (−2, 5)

Ⓕ (5, −2)

Ⓖ (2, 0)

Ⓗ (0, −6)

Ⓘ (−3, 0)

Ⓙ (−2, −4)

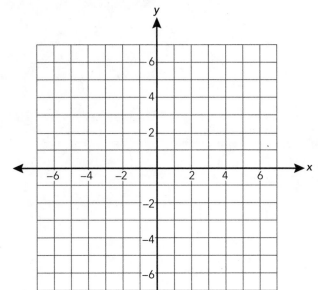

PROBLEM 8 | Write the coordinates of the following points. Use ordered pair notation.

EXAMPLE The coordinates of Ⓐ are (3, 6).

Ⓑ _____

Ⓒ _____

Ⓓ _____

Ⓔ _____

Ⓕ _____

Ⓖ _____

Ⓗ _____

Ⓘ _____

Ⓙ _____

Ⓚ _____

Ⓛ _____

Ⓜ _____

Ⓝ _____

Ⓟ _____

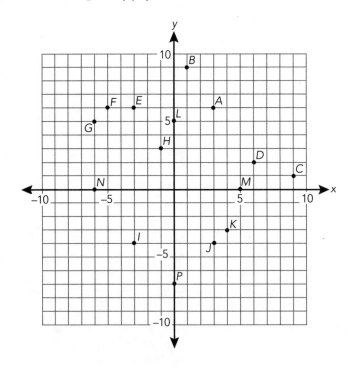

PROBLEM 9 | Use ordered pair notation to answer the following.

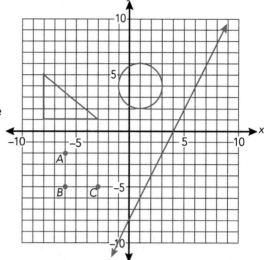

Ⓐ What are the coordinates of the point where the line crosses the *x*-axis?

Ⓑ What are the coordinates of the center of the circle?

Ⓒ Points *A*, *B*, and *C* are three corners of a square. What are the coordinates of the fourth corner?

Ⓓ What are the coordinates of the highest point of the triangle?

PROBLEM 10 | When a figure is "**reflected** over the *y*-axis" it is "flipped" over the axis so that its mirror image is on the other side of the axis. What are the coordinates of the highest point of the mirror image of triangle *ABC*?

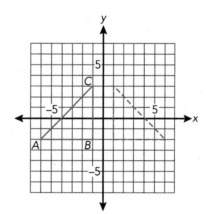

CHECK YOUR UNDERSTANDING

You may use your calculator on any problem except where noted by this symbol:

1. Insert one of the symbols <, =, or > to make each statement true.

   Ⓐ 7_____2   Ⓔ −7_____−2

   Ⓑ −3_____−4   Ⓕ 0_____9

   Ⓒ 0_____−9   Ⓖ 7_____6.5

   Ⓓ −7_____−6.5   Ⓗ −7_____6.5

2. Some high and low temperatures of cities around the United States on a winter day are recorded in the following table. All temperatures are given in degrees Fahrenheit.

	high	low
Fargo, ND	−7	−18
Chicago, IL	8	−8
Washington, D.C.	15	
Denver, CO		−4
Buffalo, NY	−2	

   Ⓐ In Washington, the temperature fell 18° from the high to the low. What was the low temperature that day? (Write the equation first.)

   Ⓑ What was the difference between Chicago's high and low temperatures?

   Ⓒ What is the difference between Fargo's high and low temperatures? (Picture the numbers on a thermometer and determine the number of spaces between them.)

   Ⓓ Denver's low temperature occurred at 4:00 A.M. By 2:00 P.M., the temperature had risen 31° to the high for the day. What was the high temperature? (Write the equation first.)

   Ⓔ If Buffalo's low temperature was n° lower than the high, how would you represent the low temperature?

3. Solve the following equations. You may use a calculator if you wish, but always check the answers for reasonableness.

   Ⓐ $25 - 34 = k$

   Ⓑ $57 + (-45) = m$

   Ⓒ $-75 + 21 = n$

   Ⓓ $-39 + 103 = x$

   Ⓔ $48 - (-48) = n$

   Ⓕ $(-72) - 128 = p$

4. Write the coordinates of each lettered point.

   Ⓐ _____
   Ⓑ _____
   Ⓒ _____
   Ⓓ _____
   Ⓔ _____
   Ⓕ _____
   Ⓖ _____
   Ⓗ _____
   Ⓘ _____

   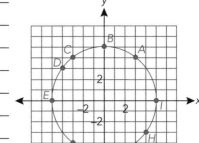

5. Plot the following points on the graph below.

   Ⓐ (−4, −1)
   Ⓑ (1, 5)
   Ⓒ (−2, 0)
   Ⓓ (0, 2)

   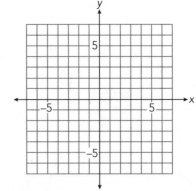

TEST-TAKING PRACTICE

You may use your calculator on any problem except where noted by this symbol:

1. Which one of the following statements is true?

(1) $-13 > -4$
(2) $-4 > -0.03$
(3) $-4 > 0$
(4) $-4 > -2$
(5) $-4 > -14$

2. The graph of a line segment is shown on the grid below. If the line were extended, at what point would it cross the *y*-axis?

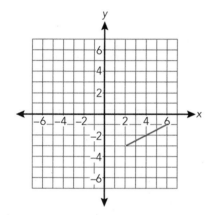

(1) $(7, 0)$
(2) $(0, 7)$
(3) $(0, -4)$
(4) $(-4, 0)$
(5) $(-3, 0)$

3. Today's temperature rose to 10°F. This was 13° higher than yesterday's high temperature. What was the high temperature yesterday?

(1) $-13°$
(2) $-10°$
(3) $-3°$
(4) $3°$
(5) $23°$

4. If triangle *CAT* shown on the grid below were reflected over the *x*-axis, which point would be the image of point *A*?

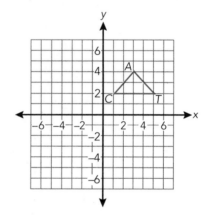

(1) $(-3, 4)$
(2) $(-3, -4)$
(3) $(4, -3)$
(4) $(3, -4)$
(5) $(-4, 3)$

Test-Taking Tips

MENTAL MATH

1.	600 + 700	**6.**	600 − 700
2.	87 − 9	**7.**	87 + 9
3.	100 − 16	**8.**	100 − 135
4.	340 − 200	**9.**	340 + 200
5.	246 + 50	**10.**	50 − 70

Were you able to do all of the problems mentally? If so, you have already made a lot of progress. This lesson gives a quick review of what you learned in this section and some tips on applying it when taking a test.

REVIEW EXAMPLE

Chris intended to complete the 488-mile trip from Boise, Idaho, to Seattle, Washington, in one day. By noon, she had driven 203 miles. How much farther did she have to go?

1 Understand the problem.

Remember what the operations do. *Addition* combines or joins. *Subtraction* compares or separates.

You can help yourself understand the problem by sketching the situation.

2 Write the problem.

The relationship in the problem can be represented as the equation

$203 + x = 488$.

Write an equivalent equation where x is alone on one side of the equation:

$488 − 203 = x$.

If you can see the path to the answer immediately, write the problem as

$x = 488 − 203$.

3 Find the answer.

Estimate first:

203 is close to 200;
488 is nearly 500.

500 − 200 is approximately
300 miles.

Do you need a precise answer?

Find it mentally, with paper and
pencil, or with a calculator.

You can subtract these precisely:

488 − 203 = **285 miles**.

4 Check that your answer is reasonable.

What if you had mistakenly added 488 + 203 = 691? The answer doesn't
make sense that the remainder of a trip would be longer than the entire trip!
You can avoid costly mistakes by taking a moment to ask yourself, "Does this
answer make sense?"

Two Problem-Solving Tips

Estimation and Multiple-Choice Tests

For a number of the multiple-choice problems that appear on tests, good
estimation skills are all you need to choose a correct answer. Besides being
easier than actually computing an answer, estimating is faster. Time is
valuable when you are taking a test.

The diagram below shows a good approach to use for test problems.

PROBLEM-SOLVING MODEL

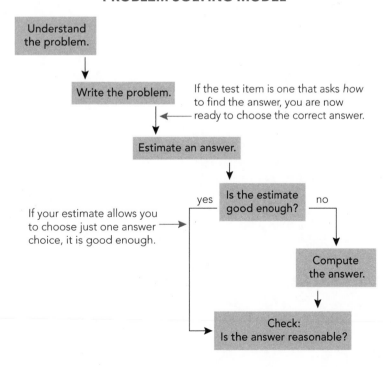

Study the examples to see how you might be able to use your estimation skills for two different problems.

EXAMPLE A

Estimate first.

It may be all you need to do to choose the correct option.

A woman read 68 pages of her biology book, 123 pages of literature, and 80 pages of psychology. How many pages did she read in all? (1) 28 (2) 43 (3) 148 (4) 191 (5) 271	**ESTIMATE** 68 is about 70. 123 is about 120. 70 + 120 + 80 = 270 **COMPARE** 270 is very close to choice **(5)** and not close at all to the other choices. **CHOOSE** **(5) 271**

EXAMPLE B

Angel spent $35.85 on a new hairdryer. If her purchase came to $37.80 including tax, how much tax did Angel pay? (1) $ .65 (2) $ 1.55 (3) $ 1.95 (4) $ 2.05 (5) $73.65	**ESTIMATE** $35.85 is about $36. $37.80 is about $38. $38 − $36 = $2 **COMPARE** $2 is very close to both choices **(3)** and **(4)**, so you will have to calculate an answer. **CALCULATE** $37.80 − $35.85 = $1.95 **CHOOSE** **(3) $1.95**

Deciding When There Is Not Enough Information

On some tests, one possible answer choice may be "not enough information is given."

- It can be the correct answer choice for one or more problems on the test.

- Use caution and think twice before choosing this answer. Can you identify what information is missing? Be sure that there is no way for you to find an answer.

EXAMPLE A

Alicia drove 245 miles from Houston to Dallas. If she drove straight through and arrived at 6:00 P.M., how long did it take her to drive to Dallas?

(1) 4 hr
(2) 4 hr 30 min
(3) 5 hr
(4) 5 hr 30 min
(5) Not enough information is given.

The correct answer would be **(5) Not enough information is given.**

Since you don't know how fast Alicia drove or what time she left Houston, you can't find the solution.

EXAMPLE B

Roberto pays $400 per month in rent. How much rent does he pay in a year?

(1) $ 400
(2) $ 800
(3) $4,000
(4) $4,800
(5) Not enough information is given.

The correct answer choice is **(4) $4,800.**

400×12 months = $4,800

At first glance, you see that there is only one number in the problem—$400 per month. You may jump to the conclusion that choice **(5) Not enough information is given** is correct.

However, you do know that there are 12 months in a year, and you can use this information to solve the problem.

On most tests, you will be expected to know everyday math relationships and use them to solve real-life problems.

On the test below, try to solve as many problems as possible with mental math and estimating. You may use a calculator on any problem that does not have this symbol: **You may use the formulas page (page 280) and the number grid directions (page 281) whenever you wish.**

1. The following amounts are weights, in pounds, of packages of cheddar cheese in the supermarket.

   1.01   0.9   1.2   0.95   1.11

   Which of the following sequences is arranged in order from *least* to *greatest*.

   (1) 0.9, 0.95, 1.01, 1.2, 1.11
   (2) 1.2, 1.01, 1.11, 0.9, 0.95
   (3) 1.01, 1.2, 1.11, 0.9, 0.95
   (4) 0.9, 0.95, 1.01, 1.11, 1.2
   (5) 0.9, 0.95, 1.2, 1.01, 1.11

2. On Tuesday, April 18, Robin was given one week to finish a project. What is the due date?

   (1) April 21
   (2) April 25
   (3) April 28
   (4) May 1
   (5) Not enough information is given.

3. Elizabeth's present weight is *x* pounds. She is trying to lose 35 pounds. Which of the following expressions represents her target weight?

   (1) $35x$
   (2) $35 + x$
   (3) $x + 35$
   (4) $x - 35$
   (5) $35 - x$

4. From the tip of an antenna on top of a building to the ground is a drop of 331 feet. The floor of the sub-basement of the same building is 37 feet *below* the ground. How far, in feet, is it from the top of the antenna to the bottom of the sub-basement?

   (1) 257
   (2) 294
   (3) 368
   (4) 405
   (5) Not enough information is given.

Problem 5 refers to the following diagram.

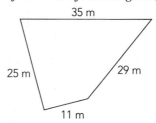

5. How many meters of fencing would be necessary to fence in the irregularly shaped lot pictured above?

   Mark your answer in the circles in the grid.

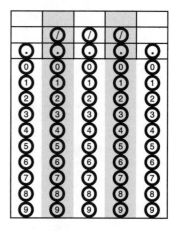

6. Locate the point $(-1, -3)$ on the coordinate plane grid.

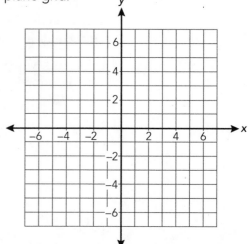

Problems 7 and 8 refer to the following diagram.

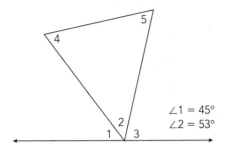

∠1 = 45°
∠2 = 53°

7. What is the measure of ∠3?

(1) 45°
(2) 53°
(3) 82°
(4) 98°
(5) Not enough information is given.

8. If ∠2 ≅ ∠4, what is the measure of ∠5?

(1) 45°
(2) 53°
(3) 74°
(4) 106°
(5) Not enough information is given.

9. Use the graph to estimate how many more electoral votes were allocated to California than to Florida in the 2000 presidential election.

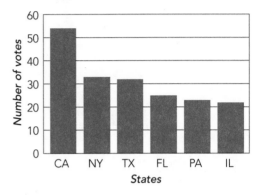

ELECTORAL VOTES IN 2000 PRESIDENTIAL ELECTION

Source: National Archives and Records

(1) 54
(2) 41
(3) 29
(4) 21
(5) 9

SELF-EVALUATION CHART

After you have checked your answers, evaluate your progress and mistakes.

1. On how many problems did you estimate?

2. Did you use the calculator on all the items where it was allowed?

3. Can you identify areas that you need to review?

problems	skill	lessons
1	Decimal comparisons	2
3	Recognizing expressions	all
4	Positive and negative numbers	5
5	Perimeter	2
7, 8	Angles	4
9	Bar graphs	1, 2
6	Coordinate plane	5
1, 2, 5, 7, 8, 9	Solving problems without a calculator	all

"Seeing" Multiplication and Division

MENTAL MATH

1. 2 + 2 + 2 + 2 = ?
2. 5 + 5 + 5 = ?
3. 4 + 4 + 4 + 4 + 4 = ?
4. 7 + 7 + 7 + 7 = ?
5. 10 + 10 + 10 + 10 + 10 = ?

Adding the same number over and over can get to be tedious. This lesson introduces a much shorter way. You know it as multiplication.

1 Picture the Situation

Consider these problems. Do not try to find the answers.

EXAMPLE A

A teacher bought 4 packages of pencils. Each package contained 3 pencils. How many pencils did the teacher buy?

EXAMPLE B

When the men's choir performs, the men line up in 4 rows. There are 9 men in each row. How many men are in the choir?

Both of these problems ask you to **combine** groups that are the same size.

> Multiply when you want to combine or join groups of the same size.

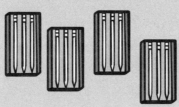

3 + 3 + 3 + 3
or 4 × 3 = 12

You multiplied 4 and 3 to get 12. 4 and 3 are called **factors** of 12. 12 is called a **multiple** of both 4 and 3.

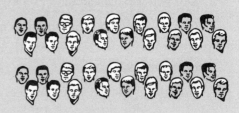

9 + 9 + 9 + 9
or 4 × 9 = 36

You multiplied 4 and 9 to get 36. _____ and _____ are factors of 36. 36 is a _____ of both 4 and 9.

Now think about the following situations. Do not try to find the answers.

EXAMPLE C

How many 8-passenger vans are necessary to transport 24 people to the ball game?

This problem asks, "How many groups of 8 are there in 24?"

You know the size of the group but need to find the number of groups.

EXAMPLE D

Sal needs to cut a 54-inch-long piece of wood into 6 stakes. How long should each piece be?

This problem asks, "How long is each of the 6 stakes?"

| ? | ? | ? | ? | ? | ? |

54

You know the number of groups but need to find the size of each one.

Divide when you want to separate a large group into smaller, equal-sized groups.

In Example C, you could have subtracted 8 over and over. However, **division** is a shorter way to do repeated subtractions.

24 ÷ 8 asks the same question as "How many times can you subtract 8 from 24?"

$$24 \div 8 = 3 \qquad\qquad 24 - 8 = 16 \text{ (once)}$$
$$16 - 8 = 8 \text{ (twice)}$$
$$8 - 8 = 0 \text{ (three times)}$$

We say that 24 **is divisible by** 8 because there was nothing left over after we subtracted 8 three times.

In Example D, 54 is _____ by 6 because we can cut 6 equal-sized stakes and have no wood left over.

2 Write the Problem

Does Order Make a Difference?

With multiplication and addition, the order **does not** affect the result. They are said to be **commutative**.

Subtraction and division are not commutative. The order **is important** when you subtract or divide.

Look at these sketches. Changing the order of the numbers in a multiplication problem does not affect the result.

$3 \times 5 = 15$ is the same total number as $5 \times 3 = 15$

But the order *is* very important when you divide.

EXAMPLE

Enter these two problems into your calculator and compare the answers. Are they different?

The answers are different—the order does affect the result when you divide.

The problem $54 \div 6$ is read as 54 *divided by* 6 (or 6 *divided into* 54). It asks, how many 6s there are in 54. Or, if 54 is separated into 6 equal groups, how many will be in each group?

The problem $6 \div 54$, 6 *divided by* 54, asks how many 54s there are in 6! Or, if 6 is separated into 54 groups, how many will be in each group? The answer is a decimal number that is less than 1 (as you would expect).

PROBLEM 1 | Think of a situation in your life that would require the use of multiplication. Draw a picture or tell how it fits the description of multiplying as combining equal groups.

PROBLEM 2 | Draw a picture or describe a situation that requires division. How does it fit into the description of division as separating into equal groups?

PROBLEM 3 | Write a mathematical expression describing each of the following situations.

Ⓐ There are 8 chairs at each of 6 tables.

Ⓑ There are 40 cookies to be shared equally among 20 students.

Ⓒ A 36-inch ribbon is to be cut into 4 equal pieces.

Ⓓ There are 3 packages of paper, each containing 500 sheets.

PROBLEM 4 | Solve the following pairs of problems **with your calculator**, and compare the answers. Which pairs of answers indicate that the order is important?

Ⓐ $695 + 42$ $42 + 695$ Ⓒ $56 - 34$ $34 - 56$

Ⓑ 45×62 62×45 Ⓓ $625 \div 25$ $25 \div 625$

Notation

You are already familiar with two ways to show *multiplication*:

$$65 \qquad\qquad 65 \times 11 =$$
$$\underline{\times\ 11}$$

This same problem can also be written as: $65 \bullet 11$ or $(65)(11)$ or $65(11)$

When there is no sign next to the parentheses, multiply.

There are many ways to write *division* problems. 56 *divided by* 8 can be written as:

$$56 \div 8 \qquad \text{or} \qquad 8\overline{)56} \qquad \text{or} \qquad \frac{56}{8} \qquad \text{or} \qquad 56/8$$

(**Note:** The form $\frac{56}{8}$ is used most often in this book. Begin at the top and read it as 56 *divided by* 8.)

Using Variables

EXAMPLE

| There are 6 desks in each row in a classroom. If there are *n* rows, how many desks are in the room? | This example describes a situation where there are *n* groups of equal size. The expression is written as: $6 \times n$ or $6(n)$ or, more simply, just $6n$. |

EXAMPLE

| There are *x* pieces of candy in a package. If Fran shares the bag with 3 other friends, how many pieces will each get? | The large group is made up of *x* objects to be divided into 4 equal groups (Fran and her friends). $x \div 4$ or $\frac{x}{4}$ |

PROBLEM 5 Write each problem in an equivalent form, then in numbers and words.

EXAMPLES $4(5)$ $4 \bullet 5$ 4 times 5

$\quad\qquad\qquad \frac{6}{m} \quad\ 6 \div m$ 6 divided by *m*

A $21 \div 7$ _____ _____

B $(21) - (7)$ _____ _____

C $20x$ _____ _____

D $\frac{m}{3}$ _____ _____

E $4 + (15)$ _____ _____

F $6\overline{)36}$ _____ _____

Translating Words to Problems

You know that writing a mathematical expression is key to solving problems.

EXAMPLES

4 more than 7 . . . . 4 + 7	6 less than 15 . . . . 15 − 6
4 more than y . . . . 4 + y	x less than 15 . . . . 15 − x
4 times as great as 5 . . . . 4 × 5	the number of 6s in 42 . . . . $\frac{42}{6}$
4 times as great as n 4n	the number of 6s in p . . . . $\frac{p}{6}$
the number of doughnuts in 3 dozen . . . . 12(3)	the number of 5-member teams formed from 40 people . . . . $\frac{40}{5}$
the number of doughnuts in d dozen 12d	the number of x-member teams formed from 40 people . . . . $\frac{40}{x}$
98 divided by 7 . . . . $\frac{98}{7}$	
98 divided into 7 . . . . $\frac{7}{98}$	

PROBLEM 6 | Write a mathematical expression for each problem. Think about why some problems seem harder than others.

EXAMPLE   63 divided by 9 $\frac{63}{9}$ 63 ÷ 9 $9\overline{)63}$

Ⓐ 32 divided by 8   Ⓔ 6 times 3

Ⓑ 32 divided into 8   Ⓕ 6 more than 3

Ⓒ 32 divided by b   Ⓖ the number of 3s in 6

Ⓓ x divided into 8   Ⓗ 3 less than 6

PROBLEM 7 | Translate the following situations into mathematical expressions. It will help if you ask yourself, "Am I *combining* equal amounts or *separating* into equal amounts?" Write your reason after the expression.

EXAMPLES	EXPRESSION	REASON
the number of cents in 4 nickels (5¢)	5 × 4	combining 4 equal groups
the number of nickels (5¢) in 75¢	$\frac{75}{5}$	separating into equal groups
Ⓐ the number of cents in 10 nickels	_____	_____
Ⓑ the number of nickels in 20 cents	_____	_____
Ⓒ the number of 12s in 36	_____	_____
Ⓓ the number of feet in y yards (**Note:** 3 feet = 1 yard)	_____	_____
Ⓔ the number of months in 2 years (**Note:** 12 months = 1 year)	_____	_____
Ⓕ the number of months in x years	_____	_____
Ⓖ the number of 25s in 100	_____	_____
Ⓗ the number of quarters (25¢) in 125¢	_____	_____

3 Find the Answer—Mentally

Multiplying and Dividing by 1

The answer to a multiplication problem is called the **product**. When you multiply any number by 1, the product is that same number back again. This is also true when you multiply variables by 1.

$$7 \times 1 = 7 \qquad 1 \bullet 578 = 578 \qquad 1(149) = 149 \qquad 1 \bullet a = 1a = a$$

In some situations, you may have to think of a variable alone as being 1 times that variable.

For example, $x = 1x$, $b = 1b$, $y = 1y$.

> When you multiply or divide any number by 1, the answer is the same as the original number.

The answer to a division problem is called the **quotient**. When you *divide by 1*, the quotient is the same as the number you were dividing into.

$$7 \div 1 = 7 \qquad \frac{67}{1} = 67 \qquad \frac{625}{1} = 625 \qquad \text{BUT} \qquad \frac{1}{625} = 0.0016$$

(You are dividing by 625, not by 1.)

Multiplying and Dividing with 0

Whenever you multiply by 0, the product is 0. Try the examples below on your calculator.

$$9(0) = 0 \qquad 0 \times 58 = 0 \qquad 489 \times 0 = 0 \qquad 0(1,025) = 0$$

Division is a bit more complicated. There are two separate cases to learn:

> When you multiply or divide 0 by any number, the answer is 0. However, do not *divide* by 0.

① When you *divide into 0* (that is, when 0 is the top number), the quotient (answer) is always 0, as long as the divisor is not zero.

$$\frac{0}{9} = 0 \qquad \frac{0}{39} = 0 \qquad \frac{0}{529} = 0 \qquad \frac{0}{2,376} = 0$$

② However, when you *divide by 0*, you run into trouble. Division of a non-zero number by 0 is **undefined**. In other words, it is not allowed in our system of arithmetic. 0 cannot be the divisor, the bottom number in a problem.

$$\frac{67}{0} \qquad\qquad 49 \div 0 \qquad\qquad 0\overline{)38} \qquad\qquad 23 \div 0$$

PROBLEM 8 | Find the answers mentally. When a problem can't be done, write "undefined."

Ⓐ $10,000 \times 1 = $ _____

Ⓑ $10,000 \times 0 = $ _____

Ⓒ $10,000 + 0 = $ _____

Ⓓ $10,000 - 1 = $ _____

Ⓔ $10,000 \div 0 = $ _____

Ⓕ $10,000 + 1 = $ _____

Ⓖ $10,000 \div 1 = $ _____

Ⓗ $10,000 - 0 = $ _____

Ⓘ $1 \div 10,000 = $ _____

Ⓙ $0 \div 10,000 = $ _____

Ⓚ $0 \times 10,000 = $ _____

Ⓛ $0 + 10,000 = $ _____

Ⓜ $n \times 1 = $ _____

Ⓝ $n \div 1 = $ _____

Ⓞ $n \times 0 = $ _____

Ⓟ $0 \div n = $ _____

Building on Basic Facts

Multiplication

Multiples of 10 (10; 100; 1,000; and so on) are easy to multiply mentally.

$4 \times 1\underline{0} = 4$ tens $= 4\underline{0}$
$4 \times 1\underline{00} = 4$ hundreds $= 4\underline{00}$
$4 \times 1\underline{,000} = 4$ thousands $= 4\underline{,000}$

① Think of the problem in this way: Ignore the **trailing zeros** while you multiply the digits at the front. Then replace the trailing zeros in the answer. Now you can do even more problems mentally.

$6 \times 200 = 1,200$	$3 \times 90 = 270$	$500 \times 7 = 3,500$	$700 \times 6 = 4,200$
$6 \times 2 = 12$	$3 \times 9 = 27$	$5 \times 7 = 35$	$7 \times 6 = 42$

② When both multipliers have trailing zeros, forget about all of them while you multiply the digits at the front ends. Then replace all the zeros in the answer.

	90×60	80×600	900×700	$50 \times 4,000$
Think:	$9 \times 6 = 54$	$8 \times 6 = 48$	$9 \times 7 = 63$	$5 \times 4 = 20$
Replace 0s:	5,400	48,000	630,000	200,000
	two 0s	three 0s	four 0s	four 0s

Division

① The process is similar when you divide. Ignore the trailing zeros that are not involved with the division, then replace them in the answer.

$\frac{800}{4} = 200$	$\frac{3,600}{4} = 900$	$\frac{640}{8} = 80$	$\frac{4,000}{8} = 500$
$8 \div 4 = 2$	$36 \div 4 = 9$	$64 \div 8 = 8$	$40 \div 8 = 5$

② When both numbers in a division problem have trailing zeros, cancel the ones they have in common. Then proceed as before.

Cancel:	$\frac{6,000}{30} = \frac{6,00\cancel{0}}{3\cancel{0}}$	$\frac{180,000}{200} = \frac{180,0\cancel{00}}{2\cancel{00}}$	$\frac{3,000,000}{60} = \frac{3,000,00\cancel{0}}{6\cancel{0}}$
Think:	$6 \div 3 = 2$	$18 \div 2 = 9$	$30 \div 6 = 5$
Replace 0s:	200	900	50,000

PROBLEM 9

Find the answers to the problems below using the techniques you have learned.

Ⓐ $4 \times 300 =$ _____ Ⓔ $1,500 \div 5 =$ _____ Ⓘ $9,000 \div 30 =$ _____

Ⓑ $600 \times 9 =$ _____ Ⓕ $600 \times 50 =$ _____ Ⓙ $4,900 \div 700 =$ _____

Ⓒ $80 \times 40 =$ _____ Ⓖ $900 \times 800 =$ _____ Ⓚ $800 \times 500 =$ _____

Ⓓ $640 \div 8 =$ _____ Ⓗ $900 + 800 =$ _____ Ⓛ $40,000 \div 80 =$ _____

Divisibility and Multiples

Divide using a calculator: $\dfrac{900}{36}$ $\qquad$ $\dfrac{1{,}000}{36}$ $\qquad$ $\dfrac{1{,}200}{36}$ $\qquad$ $\dfrac{1{,}800}{36}$

If there are *no* digits to the right of the decimal point in the answer, we know that the first number **is divisible by** 36. Above, you saw that both 900 and 1,800 are divisible by 36. It is also correct to say that these numbers are **multiples** of 36.

A Use a calculator and circle the numbers below that are divisible by 36.

432 $\qquad$ 933 $\qquad$ 540 $\qquad$ 345

B Use a calculator and circle the numbers below that are divisible by 10.

910 $\qquad$ 345 $\qquad$ 990 $\qquad$ 999 $\qquad$ 322 $\qquad$ 300 $\qquad$ 144

Notice the last digit of each circled number. In a complete sentence, describe numbers that are divisible by 10.

_____

C Use a calculator and circle the numbers below that are multiples of 5.

910 $\qquad$ 345 $\qquad$ 990 $\qquad$ 999 $\qquad$ 322 $\qquad$ 305 $\qquad$ 144

In a complete sentence, describe numbers that are divisible by 5.

_____

D Use a calculator and circle the numbers below that are divisible by 2.

910 $\qquad$ 345 $\qquad$ 996 $\qquad$ 999 $\qquad$ 322 $\qquad$ 308 $\qquad$ 144 $\qquad$ 147

In a complete sentence, describe numbers that are multiples of 2.

_____

You can tell when a number is divisible by 3 if the sum of its digits is divisible by 3. For example, you know that 48 is divisible by 3 because 12 (the sum of 4 and 8) is divisible by 3.

78 is divisible by 3 because $7 + 8 = 15$, and 15 is divisible by 3.

E Without using the calculator, circle the numbers below that are divisible by 3.

910 $\qquad$ 345 $\qquad$ 996 $\qquad$ 322 $\qquad$ 144 $\qquad$ 441 $\qquad$ 803 $\qquad$ 12,543

Check your selections by dividing on a calculator.

Perhaps you learned the divisibility rule for 9s when you learned the multiplication facts. Like the rule of 3s, a number is divisible by 9 if the sum of its digits is divisible by 9.

F Without using the calculator, circle the numbers below that are divisible by 9.

117 $\qquad$ 435 $\qquad$ 144 $\qquad$ 441 $\qquad$ 585 $\qquad$ 9,468 $\qquad$ 47,520 $\qquad$ 12,543

Check your selections by dividing on a calculator.

▟ Check for Reasonableness

Comparing your answer to an estimate is a quick way to check your calculations.

Rounding and Estimating

Estimating an answer can also save you time when answering the multiple-choice questions on a test.

Multiplication

EXAMPLE

Pam is collecting trading stamps from her grocery store for a new set of dishes. Each book of stamps has 38 pages that can hold 30 stamps per page. How many stamps does each book hold?

(1) 68
(2) 114
(3) 680
(4) 980
(5) 1,140

By estimating the problem to be 30×40, you can see the answer is near 1,200.

Only choice **(5) 1,140** is close.

Round the numbers that are being multiplied (factors) to estimate the answer.

ROUNDING ONE FACTOR

Estimate 7×582.

```
500           550      582   600
|--------------+--------|-----|
```

$7 \times 600 = 4,200$

So, $7 \times 582 \approx 4,200$

ROUNDING BOTH FACTORS

Estimate $58(321)$.

```
300    321        350          400
|------|----------+------------|
```

$60(300) = 18,000$

So, $58(321) \approx 18,000$

PROBLEM 10

Use rounding to estimate answers to the following problems. Then find the exact answer using a calculator—the two answers should be close!

Ⓐ $3 \times 49 \approx$

Ⓑ $8 \times 411 \approx$

Ⓒ $769 \times 7 \approx$

Ⓓ $53 \times 78 \approx$

Ⓔ $92 \times 39 \approx$

Ⓕ $27 \times 63 \approx$

Ⓖ $\$6.18 \times 43 \approx$

Ⓗ $\$24.75 \times 105 \approx$

Now use estimating to solve the sample problem below.

PROBLEM 11 | To complete a construction project, 18 workers each worked 120 hours. How many man-hours did the project take?

(1)   108
(2)   138
(3)   216
(4) 2,160
(5) 6,666

Division

You can also round numbers to make division easier. Look at the two problems below.

EXAMPLES

Which is easier to divide mentally?

$\frac{628}{3}$ or $\frac{600}{3}$

$\frac{600}{3}$ is easier because you can think:

$6 \div 3 = 2$ so $\frac{600}{3} = 200$.

Which is easier to divide mentally?

$\frac{318}{5}$ or $\frac{300}{5}$

$\frac{300}{5}$ is easier because you can think:

$30 \div 5 = 6$, so $\frac{300}{5} = 60$

When you estimate with division, you often have to think ahead about the multiples of the divisor before you round the number. Use the multiplication facts that you know to create an easy problem that you can divide mentally.

PROBLEM 12 | First, circle the rounded number that will make these problems easier to divide. Then find an estimated solution.

		ROUND TO NEAREST 10	ROUND TO NEAREST 100	SOLVE
EXAMPLE	$\frac{152}{3}$	$\frac{150}{3}$ ⃝	$\frac{200}{3}$	$\frac{150}{3} = 50$
Ⓐ	$\frac{213}{4}$	$\frac{210}{4}$	$\frac{200}{4}$	
Ⓑ	$\frac{877}{8}$	$\frac{880}{8}$	$\frac{900}{8}$	
Ⓒ	$\frac{1,157}{60}$	$\frac{1,160}{60}$	$\frac{1,200}{60}$	
Ⓓ	$\frac{1,574}{40}$	$\frac{1,570}{40}$	$\frac{1,600}{40}$	

PROBLEM 13 | Estimate answers to the following problems.

Ⓐ $\frac{418}{7}$ Ⓓ $\frac{779}{4}$ Ⓖ $\frac{1,221}{40}$

Ⓑ $\frac{1,823}{3}$ Ⓔ $\frac{1,486}{50}$ Ⓗ $\frac{1,221}{400}$

Ⓒ $\frac{537}{9}$ Ⓕ $\frac{1,486}{500}$ Ⓘ $\frac{12,211}{4,000}$

Compatible Numbers for Division

Sometimes, rounding to the nearest 10, 100, or 1,000 will not give you easy numbers to work with. In that case, round to a close number that is a multiple of the divisor and is easy to divide mentally. A number and one of its multiples make up a **compatible pair** for division.

> To find compatible pairs for division, you must know your multiplication and division facts very well.

If rounding to the nearest 10:

$\frac{349}{9}$ would round to $\frac{350}{9}$.

If rounding to the nearest 100:

$\frac{349}{9}$ would round to $\frac{300}{9}$.

Neither of these is easy to do in your head. Instead, round 349 to a multiple of 9 that is easy to divide mentally:

$\frac{349}{9} \approx \frac{360}{9} = 40$ Why choose 360?

Because 36 is divisible by 9 and 36 is close to 34.

PROBLEM 14

Estimate answers to the following problems. Write the math fact you used to get each estimate.

	PROBLEM	FACT
EXAMPLE	$\frac{418}{7} \approx \frac{420}{7} = 60$	$42 \div 7 = 6$

Ⓐ $\frac{230}{3} \approx \frac{240}{3} = ?$

Ⓑ $\frac{621}{8} \approx$

Ⓒ $\frac{1,853}{3} \approx$

Ⓓ $\frac{2,234}{3} \approx$

Ⓔ $\frac{3,816}{6} \approx$

Ⓕ $\frac{443}{5} \approx$

Ⓖ $\frac{745}{9} \approx$

Use the estimating techniques you learned in this lesson to solve the problem below.

PROBLEM 15

A rummage sale raised $6,270 for 5 neighborhood projects. If the money was divided equally, how much went to each project?

(1) $ 125
(2) $ 655
(3) $1,254
(4) $1,395
(5) $1,500

CHECK YOUR UNDERSTANDING

You may use your calculator on any problem except where noted by this symbol:

1. Write a multiplication or division expression for each. Do not solve.

   A the number of eggs in 2 dozen
   B the number of 3s in 42
   C the number of days in 21 weeks
   D the number of years in 104 weeks (there are 52 weeks in a year)
   E the number of chairs in each row when 72 chairs are arranged into 6 rows
   F the number of centimeters (cm) in y meters (there are 100 cm in one meter)
   G the number of shoes in p pair

2. A group of 10 workers won a lottery prize of $2,600,000. If the workers divide the winnings equally, how much will each worker get (before taxes)?

   A Write the problem as a mathematical expression.
   B Find the answer.

3. A ream of paper contains 500 sheets. What is the total number of sheets in 8 reams?

   A Write the problem as a mathematical expression.
   B Find the answer.

4. Bart ate a breakfast of 450 calories and a lunch of 350 calories. What is the total number of calories he consumed in those two meals?

   A Write the mathematical expression.
   B Find the answer.

5. How many $200 payments will be necessary to pay off a debt of $1,000?

   A Write the mathematical expression.
   B Find the answer.

6. What is the seating capacity of a restaurant that has 30 tables, each of which seats n persons? Write the mathematical expression.

7. Find the following answers mentally.

   A 6×70 **H** $240 \div 8$
   B $60(70)$ **I** $\frac{2,400}{80}$
   C 60×700 **J** $24,000 \div 800$
   D $600(700)$ **K** $\frac{24,000}{8}$
   E $600 + 700$ **L** $2,400 - 800$
   F $300 \div 5$ **M** $5 \bullet 600$
   G $\frac{3,000}{5}$ **N** $5(6,000)$

8. Which of the following numbers
   140 765 258 602 405 1,200
is divisible by

   A 10?
   B 5?
   C 2?
   D 3?

9. Estimate the answers to the following problems.

   A $7 \bullet 683 \approx$ **G** $4,188 \div 6 \approx$
   B $3(926) \approx$ **H** $733 + 319 \approx$
   C $43 \times 68 \approx$ **I** $1,010 - 397 \approx$
   D $92(79) \approx$ **J** $\frac{532}{9} \approx$
   E $98 \times 438 \approx$ **K** $\frac{532}{8} \approx$
   F $\frac{566}{3} \approx$ **L** $\frac{532}{5} \approx$

10. A number for monthly expenses was rounded to $2,000.   *2,499*

   A If the actual number had been rounded to the nearest 1,000, what is the largest it could have been? the smallest?
   B If the actual number had been rounded to the nearest 100, what is the largest it could have been? the smallest?

TEST-TAKING PRACTICE

You may use your calculator on any problem except where noted by this symbol:

1. Laura's new car gets 27 miles to the gallon. How many miles does she travel on 48 gallons of gas?

   (1)   96
   (2)   960
   (3) 1,296
   (4) 2,096
   (5) Not enough information is given.

2. Pedro loads cartons onto a truck for shipping. Each carton weighs 40 pounds. One truck to be loaded has a load limit of 2,000 pounds. Which expression below tells how many cartons can be loaded on this truck?

   (1) $\frac{40}{2,000}$

   (2) 2,000(40)

   (3) 40(2,000)

   (4) $\frac{2,000}{40}$

   (5) 2,000 + 40

3. The following data concerning electrical energy usage is provided by Southern California Edison.

usage	cost
ceiling fan, 3 hr per day	3¢ per day
central air conditioner, 3 hr per day	$1.29 per day

   How much cheaper, in dollars per week, is it to run 5 ceiling fans 3 hours per day than to run the central air conditioner 3 hours per day?

   (1) $1.05
   (2) $1.26
   (3) $3.78
   (4) $7.98
   (5) $9.03

Problems 4 and 5 refer to the graph below.

SPORTS UTILITY VEHICLES REGISTERED IN CANO COUNTY

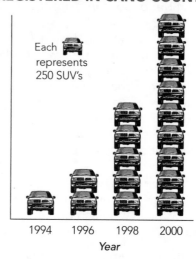

4. How many sports utility vehicles were registered in Cano County in 1998?

   Mark your answer in the circles in the grid.

5. If 2,750 sports utility vehicles (SUVs) were registered in 2002, how many of the SUV symbols would need to be drawn on the graph?

   (1)   6
   (2)   9
   (3) 11
   (4) 13
   (5) 15

Measurement: Multiplying More Than Two Numbers

Units of Measure

Two systems of measurement are used in the United States today. One is the **customary** or **standard system**, whose common units of length are shown in the table below.

12 inches (in.) = 1 foot (ft)
3 feet = 1 yard (yd)
5,280 feet = 1 mile (mi)

Since there is no fixed pattern to the relationships between the units in the customary system, you need to learn the equivalents to be able to change from one unit to another. Tables of equivalent measurements can be found in the Appendix (page 295).

Most of the rest of the world uses the **metric system**, in which the standard unit of length is the meter. The commonly used units are millimeter, centimeter, meter, and kilometer.

1,000 millimeters (mm) = 1 meter (m)
100 centimeters (cm) = 1 meter
1,000 meters = 1 kilometer (km)

To change from one unit to another in this system, you only need to multiply or divide by multiples of 10.

PROBLEM 1 | Develop your own personal "body ruler." Find the part of *your* hand that you could use to approximate the length of 1 inch. (Try the length of the last joint of a finger.) Find some part of your hand that measures about 1 centimeter. (Try the width of a fingernail.)

The units of length are the basis for other measurements, area and volume.

one dimension	two dimensions	three dimensions
Length is measured in inches, feet, meters, and kilometers.	Area is measured in **square** units.	Volume is measured in **cubic** units.
length	area — To indicate square units, write sq in. sq ft, cm², mm², and so on	volume — To indicate cubic units, write cu ft cu yd, m³, cm³, and so on

PROBLEM 2 | Use the chart above to tell which unit in the customary system would most likely be used to make each of the following measurements.

   Ⓐ How far is it from Minneapolis to Des Moines?

   Ⓑ How far is it from your car in the parking lot to the building?

   Ⓒ How much carpet should you buy for the living room?

   Ⓓ How much storage room is in a public warehouse?

Area

Area is a 2-dimensional measure of how much surface is inside a region. When you find the area of a figure, you find out how many *square units* are inside.

Rectangles

Remember to indicate area in square units, for example, sq ft, sq in., m² (square meters).

This rectangle has been divided into square units. There are 6 rows and there are 8 squares in each row.

The two dimensions of the rectangle, length and width, are 8 units and 6 units.

Find the area of the rectangle.

To find the answer, you could count the squares one by one, or you could add 8 six times. Or you could multiply 6×8 to find the number of squares. By any of these methods, the area is 48 squares.

PROBLEM 3 | Multiply to find the area of each of the following rectangles. Write your answer in square units.

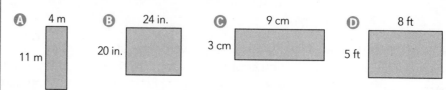

Reasoning About Rectangles on a Grid and Divisibility

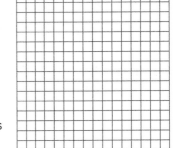

Ⓐ On the grid, draw three differently shaped rectangles whose area is 24 squares. (For this exercise, the sides of the rectangles should be on the grid lines.) Write the dimensions, length and width, by each one.

Ⓑ Write a sentence that tells the relationship between 24 and each of the dimensions you have found.

Ⓒ Why can't you draw a rectangle on the grid that has 5 rows of squares and an area of 24 squares?

Ⓓ **A real situation:** Glass blocks for windows come in two sizes: 8-inch squares and 12-inch squares. Only whole blocks, all the same size, can be used in a window. What are two possible sets of dimensions for a rectangular window that can use either size block?

Ⓔ **A puzzle:** Juanita has a number of square tiles that is less than 100. When she tries to use them to make a rectangle that is 5 squares wide, she has three tiles left over. When she tries to make a rectangle that is 4 squares wide, she also has three left over. However, when she makes a rectangle that is 9 squares wide, she uses all the tiles. How many tiles does she have? Explain how you found the answer.

PROBLEM 4 | On the formulas page of this book (page 280), there is a formula for the area of a rectangle.

> **FORMULA** Area = length × width

Explain how this formula describes what you have been doing to find the area.

PROBLEM 5 | A hallway measures 2.9 feet by 19.5 feet.

Ⓐ Estimate how many square feet of tile are needed to resurface the floor.

Ⓑ Use your calculator to find the precise number of square feet in the hallway.

Ⓒ Which answer would you use when you went to purchase the tile? Why?

PROBLEM 6 | Sarah bought some plastic sheeting to cover her garden. Which expression represents the size, in square feet, of the plastic?

(1) $A = (5 + 2) + (5 + 2)$
(2) $A = 2(5 - 2)$
(3) $A = 2(5) + 2(2)$
(4) $A = 2(5)$
(5) $A = 5 - 2$

2 ft

5 ft

Parallelograms

Any four-sided figure whose opposite sides are both equal and parallel is called a **parallelogram**.

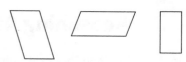

How do you find the area of a parallelogram? Notice in Figure 1 below that the slanted lines make it hard to see exactly how many square units are inside.

When you cut off one slanted end (shaded part) and slide it over to the opposite side of the parallelogram, you make a rectangle. (Figure 2)

FIGURE 1 **PARALLELOGRAM**

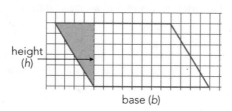

FIGURE 2 **RECTANGLE**

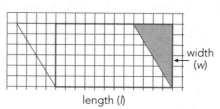

The area of the parallelogram is the same as that of the rectangle.

Notice

- The base (*b*) of the parallelogram is the same as the length (*l*) of the rectangle.
- The height (*h*) of the parallelogram is the same as the width (*w*) of the rectangle.

The height (*h*) of the parallelogram is not the slanted side. It is the perpendicular (⊥) distance between two opposite sides.

Height can be indicated with a straight, dotted line drawn either inside or outside the parallelogram.

PROBLEM 7

Use what you have learned about parallelograms to find the area of these figures. Look carefully for the heights.

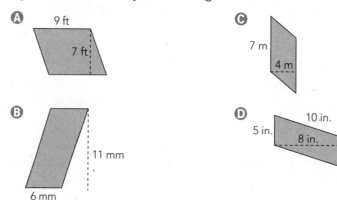

PROBLEM 8 | The formula for the area of a parallelogram is on the formulas page (page 280) of this book.

> **FORMULA** Area = base × height

Explain how this formula describes the same process that you have been using.

PROBLEM 9 | Which of the following shows the difference, in square units, between the areas of the two figures below?

(1) $(10 \times 7) - (10 \times 5)$
(2) $(10 \times 7) - (4 \times 5)$
(3) $(10 + 7) - (10 + 4)$
(4) $(10 + 7) - (10 + 5)$
(5) $(10 \times 7) - (10 \times 4)$

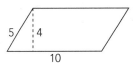

A page of formulas is often included as a reference to use during tests.

Triangles

How many square units are in a triangle?

It is hard to tell by looking at the figure on the grid.

However, from the sketches below, notice that these triangles, when doubled, become parallelograms.

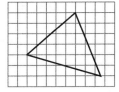

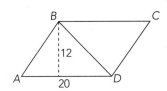

You can see that the area of a triangle would be half a parallelogram's area. On the formulas page, the formula for the area of a triangle appears as

> **FORMULA** Area = $\frac{1}{2}$ × base × height

To find the area of a triangle, you find $\frac{1}{2}$ of the area of a parallelogram with the same base and height.

Area of parallelogram *ABCD*: $A = bh$
$$A = 20 \times 12 = 240 \text{ square units}$$

Area of triangle *ABD*: $A = \frac{1}{2}bh$
$$A = \frac{1}{2}(20 \times 12) = 120 \text{ square units}$$

Regrouping to Multiply

EXAMPLE

To find the answer when you multiply, you can **regroup** the numbers—as you did in addition.

To determine the amount of fertilizer to buy, Robert Lin must know the area of this triangular garden plot.

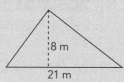

$A = \frac{1}{2}bh$

$A = \frac{1}{2} \times 21 \times 8$

Which of these problems would be the easiest for Robert to multiply?

(**Note**: Multiplying by $\frac{1}{2}$ is the same as dividing by 2.)

$$(\frac{1}{2} \times 21) \times 8 \qquad \frac{1}{2} \times (21 \times 8) \qquad (\frac{1}{2} \times 8) \times 21$$

The third solution would be the easiest. You can even do this in your head.

$(\frac{1}{2} \times 8) \times 21 \qquad 4 \times 21 = 84$ m² or 84 square meters

PROBLEM 10

Find the area of each of the following triangles. Regroup when possible.

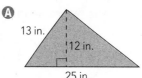

Ⓐ 13 in.   12 in.   25 in.

Ⓑ 33 m   37 m   20 m

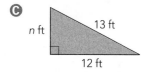

Ⓒ n ft   13 ft   12 ft

PROBLEM 11

Ⓐ What is the area, in square feet, of triangle *ABD* below?

(1) 10
(2) 12
(3) 16
(4) 24
(5) 30

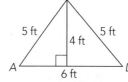

Ⓑ What is the perimeter, in feet, of triangle *ABD*?

(1) 10
(2) 12
(3) 16
(4) 24
(5) 30

Irregular Figures

Shapes in your everyday experience may be combinations of the ones you have studied. You can find the area of these irregular figures by separating them into shapes you know.

EXAMPLE

One side of Gloria's house is sketched in the figure. How many square feet of surface are on this side of the house?

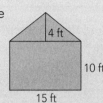

This shape consists of a rectangle *plus* a triangle.

$A = lw + \frac{1}{2}bh$

$A = (10 \times 15) + \frac{1}{2}(15 \times 4)$

$A = 150 + 30$

$A = 180$ sq ft

EXAMPLE

The area that is shaded in the sketch represents a lawn that will be covered with sod. How many square meters of sod are needed?

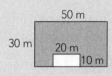

The shaded area is a larger rectangle *minus* a smaller rectangle.

$A = lw - lw$

$A = (50 \cdot 30) - (20 \cdot 10)$

$A = 1,500 - 200$

$A = 1,300 \ m^2$

PROBLEM 12 | Find the area of the *shaded* parts of the figures below. (Decide whether you need to add or subtract the two areas.)

Ⓐ
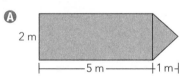

Ⓒ
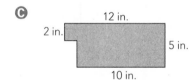

Ⓑ
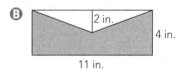

Ⓓ
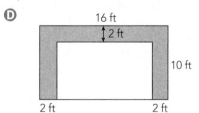

Volume

Perimeter can be thought of as fencing around a figure, and area can be visualized as the covering on a surface. **Volume**, then, can be thought of as packing inside a box or carton.

EXAMPLE

To find the volume of the figure at the right, you to want know how many cubes could be packed into the carton.

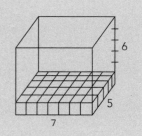

How many cubes are in the bottom layer? (5×7)
How many of these layers will fit into the box? (6)

How many cubes can be packed in the box?
$6 \times 5 \times 7 = 210$ cubes

Again, the formula for finding the volume of a rectangular solid on the formulas page (page 280) confirms the common sense method.

FORMULA | Volume = length × width × height

PROBLEM 13

Find the volume of the following rectangular containers. If you cannot find a number answer, write an expression using numbers and letters.

EXAMPLE $V = (3\ \text{in.})(6\ \text{in.})(x\ \text{in.}) = 18x$ cu in.

Remember to write volume as cubic units: cu ft, m^3, and so on.

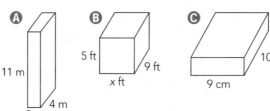
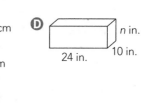

PROBLEM 14

How many cubic inches of sand can be carried in this wagon if it is packed level with the top?

(1)   66
(2)   432
(3)   648
(4) 7,776
(5) Not enough information
     is given.

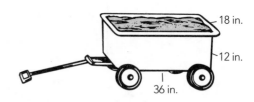

Finding the Answer Mentally

Compatible Numbers for Multiplication

Finding areas of triangles and volumes of rectangular solids requires you to multiply three numbers, called **multipliers** or **factors**. By grouping **compatible factors** (those that make computing easier), you can make these problems easy to solve mentally.

$4 \times 13 \times 25$ $8 \times 9 \times 5$ $4 \times 11 \times 50$

$(4 \times 25) \times 13$ 4 and 25 are $(8 \times 5) \times 9$ 8 and 5 are $(4 \times 50) \times 11$ 4 and 50 are
compatible   compatible   compatible

100×13 40×9 200×11

1,300   360   2,200

PROBLEM 15

Find a pair of compatible factors for each problem and multiply.

Ⓐ $2 \times 57 \times 5$ **Ⓒ** $4 \times 89 \times 25$ **Ⓔ** $4 \times 5 \times 41$

Ⓑ $5 \times 13 \times 6$ **Ⓓ** $2 \times 44 \times 50$ **Ⓕ** $2 \times 15 \times 22$

Doubling and Halving

Some of the most common math in your everyday life requires you to double or to find half of a number. These exercises will help you to solve more of these problems mentally.

Double 36.
Break 36 up into its parts ($36 = 30 + 6$),
and double each of them.
Then add.

double 30:	60
double 6:	12
add:	72

In a similar way, you can mentally find half of an even number by breaking up the number into parts.

Halve 428, or find $\frac{428}{2}$.

Break up 428 ($428 = 400 + 20 + 8$),
and find half of each part.

half of 400:	200
half of 20:	10
half of 8:	4
add:	214

Halve 94, or find $94 \div 2$.
Break up 94 into parts that can be
halved easily ($94 = 80 + 14$).

half of 80:	40
half of 14:	7
add:	47

PROBLEM 16

Find the answers by using the methods shown above.

Ⓐ 58×2 **Ⓒ** 127×2 **Ⓔ** 177×2

Ⓑ $\frac{58}{2}$ **Ⓓ** $\frac{284}{2}$ **Ⓕ** $\frac{76}{2}$

✓ CHECK YOUR UNDERSTANDING

You may use your calculator on any problem except where noted by this symbol:

1. Fill in the blanks, using the equivalencies given on page 77.

  Ⓐ 1 yd = _____ in.
  Ⓑ 1 mi = _____ yd

First draw a sketch of each of these on a grid.

  Ⓒ 1 sq ft = _____ sq in.
  Ⓓ 1 sq yd = _____ sq ft

2. Write an equation to find the area of each of the following figures. Solve if possible, or write an expression using letters and numbers.

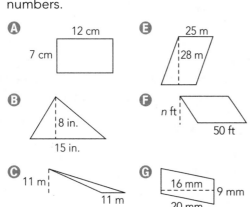

3. The sketch below shows the dimensions of a pennant that Trudy has agreed to sew for her son's soccer team.

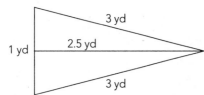

  Ⓐ How much trim will she need in order to bind around the edges of the pennant?
  Ⓑ What is the area of the pennant?

4. The shaded area below represents a deck. The unshaded area represents a hot tub.

  Ⓐ What is the area of the deck?
  Ⓑ If the hot tub is $1\frac{1}{2}$ yards deep, what is its volume?

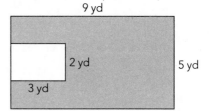

5. The sketch below shows a carton made to hold sugar.

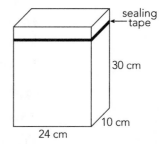

  Ⓐ How much sealing tape will be needed to encircle the carton as shown?
  Ⓑ How much shelf space will each carton take up if the cartons stand as shown in the sketch?
  Ⓒ What volume of sugar can this carton hold?

T E S T - T A K I N G   P R A C T I C E

You may use your calculator on any problem except where noted by this symbol:

1. The rectangular box of ornaments pictured below holds 84 ornaments. Into how many layers are they arranged?

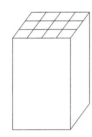

Mark your answer in the circles in the grid.

Problems 3 and 4 refer to the following diagram.

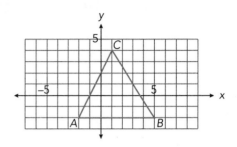

3. What are the coordinates (*x, y*) of the highest point of the triangle?

(1) (4, 1)
(2) (1, 4)
(3) (−2, −2)
(4) (2, −5)
(5) (5, −2)

4. What is the area, in square units, of the triangle?

(1) 42
(2) 36
(3) 24
(4) 21
(5) 18

2. Which equation represents the volume of the container below?

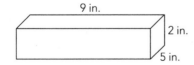

(1) $V = 5 \times 2$

(2) $V = 2 \times 9$

(3) $V = 9 \times 5 \times 2$

(4) $V = 5 \times \frac{9}{2}$

(5) $V = \frac{1}{2}(5 \times 2)$

5. What is the area of the sidewalk around the garden, shown by the shaded portion in the sketch below?

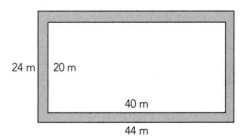

(1)   256
(2)   272
(3)   800
(4)   1,056
(5)   Not enough information is given.

9 LESSON
Equivalent Equations: Multiplication and Division

In this lesson, you will use two everyday relationships to see how division and multiplication are fundamentally related.

Finding Total Cost

PROBLEM 1

EXAMPLE A CD costs $14. Follow the pattern in the table below. Two CDs would cost ($2 \times 14), or $28.

Ⓐ What is the cost of 5 CDs?

Ⓑ What is the cost of 10 CDs?

Ⓒ Paul has a collection of 70 CDs. How much has he spent on his collection?

Ⓓ How did you find the total cost? Fill in the blank: To find the total cost, multiply 14 by _____.

number	cost
1	$14
2	*$28*
3	$42
4	$56
5	

(EXAMPLE marks the row: 2 | $28)

Look at this formula from the formulas page (page 280).

FORMULA Total cost = (number of units) × (price per unit), or $c = nr$

Notice that your experience and common sense have again led you to a mathematical rule. The formula above describes exactly what you did to find the answers for problem 1.

The graph at the right is a picture of the same information that was in the table. The points (1, 14), (2, 28), and so on, lie on a straight line, so we say that the relation between the number of CDs and the total cost is a **linear function**.

EXAMPLE

How much do 3 CDs cost?

Find 3 on the **horizontal** (bottom) axis, and move straight up until you reach the line. From that point move across to the **vertical** (side) axis and estimate ($42).

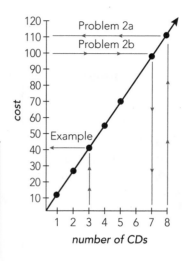

PROBLEM 2

Ⓐ *Estimate* the total cost of 8 CDs by reading the graph.

Ⓑ Use the graph to *estimate* how many CDs can be purchased for $100.

Ⓒ How would you find the answer to problem Ⓑ without the graph?

Ⓓ Make a rule: To find the number of CDs you can buy, divide _____ by 14.

Finding Distance

EXAMPLE

The table below summarizes the flight of a small airplane that cruises at 250 miles per hour (mph). Follow the pattern shown in the table. If the airplane were flying for 2 hours at this rate, it would travel (2 × 250) or 500 miles.

PROBLEM 3

Ⓐ How far would the airplane travel in 5 hours?

Ⓑ How far would it travel in 10 hours?

Ⓒ Think about what you did in problems Ⓐ and Ⓑ. Make a rule: To find the distance flown, multiply 250 by _____.

Ⓓ Write the mathematical expression for the distance it would travel if the airplane continued at this rate for *n* hours.

time	distance
1	250
2	500
3	750
4	1,000
5	

Look at this formula from the formulas page (page 280). Does it look familiar?

FORMULA Distance = rate × time, or $d = rt$

The graph below pictures the information from the table on page 89. Notice that it is another linear function.

PROBLEM 4

Ⓐ Use the graph to estimate the number of miles this airplane would travel in 8 hours.

Ⓑ From the graph, estimate the number of hours it would take to travel 1,500 miles.

Ⓒ How would you have determined the answer to problem Ⓑ without the graph?

Ⓓ Make a rule: To find the number of hours it would take this airplane to travel a certain distance, divide _____ by 250.

> Multiplication and division are inverse operations. You can use one to undo the other.

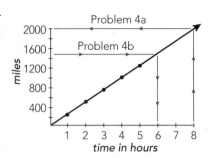

• Notice that the graphs of these two functions ($c = nr$ and $d = rt$) were constructed to show what happens when you **multiply**.

• However, you also used the graphs to **divide**—to find the number of CDs in problem 2Ⓑ and the number of hours in problem 4Ⓑ.

Writing Equivalent Equations Using "Fact Families"

The three numbers 8, 7, and 56 are related by multiplication and division. We can picture the relationship using a triangle and write it mathematically by the equations below.

$$7 \times 8 = \boxed{56} \qquad 8 \times 7 = \boxed{56} \qquad \frac{56}{7} = 8 \qquad \frac{56}{8} = 7$$

Each of these equations is different, yet the underlying fact is the same. Notice that the boxed number is the answer to the multiplication problems and is the top number in the division problems.

PROBLEM 5

Write four equivalent equations that can be written about the relationship shown in each triangle.

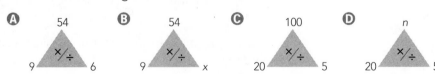

PROBLEM 6 | Write two equivalent equations, one with multiplication and one with division. If the triangle helps you to organize your thoughts, draw and label it first.

EXAMPLE $\frac{32}{x} = 4$ is equivalent to $4 \times x = 32$ or $4x = 32$ and $\frac{32}{4} = x$

Ⓐ $\frac{72}{n} = 6$ Ⓑ $\frac{128}{2} = t$ Ⓒ $\frac{p}{5} = 600$ Ⓓ $\frac{1,200}{24} = m$

PROBLEM 7 | Rearrange these equations into equivalent equations where the variable (the letter) is alone on one side of the equation. Do not solve.

EXAMPLE Rewrite $10 = 4r$ as $r = \frac{10}{4}$ and rewrite $11 = \frac{132}{n}$ as $n = \frac{132}{11}$.

Ⓐ $45 = 9w$ Ⓓ $5x = 95$ Ⓖ $125 = \frac{m}{10}$

Ⓑ $8 = 96k$ Ⓔ $11 = \frac{99}{t}$ Ⓗ $21b = 105$

Ⓒ $39 = 13p$ Ⓕ $75 = 15n$ Ⓘ $\frac{w}{9} = 6$

> Remember that you can reverse the order of equations. For example, $35 = 7x$ is the same as $7x = 35$.

The two basic relationships from pages 88 and 89 can also be pictured with triangles.

COST RELATIONSHIP

PROBLEM 8 | Ⓐ Write two division equations that are equivalent to $c = nr$.

Ⓑ Consider the situation where CDs cost \$14 apiece and the total cost is \$280. Write a division equation to find n, where n is alone on its side of the equation.

Ⓒ Use the equation from Ⓑ to find the number of CDs you could buy for \$350.

DISTANCE RELATIONSHIP

PROBLEM 9 | Ⓐ Write two division equations that are equivalent to $d = rt$.

Ⓑ Consider the situation where an airplane cruises at 250 mph and has traveled 750 miles. Write a division equation to find t, where t is alone on its side of the equation.

Ⓒ Use the equation from Ⓑ to find the time it would take this airplane to fly 1,500 miles.

Solving Multiplication and Division Equations

When you solve problems involving the cost relationship ($c = nr$) or the distance relationship ($d = rt$), you can either

① start with the basic formula, or

② start with an equivalent equation.

EXAMPLE

Rick wants to be at his destination, which is 385 miles away, in 7 hours. What would his average speed need to be? Let r stand for rate (the speed).

The basic equation:	$d = rt$	Or, an equivalent equation: $r = \dfrac{d}{t}$

Substitute known values: $385 = r \times 7$

Substitute values: $r = \dfrac{385}{7}$

Rearrange: $r = \dfrac{385}{7}$

Solve:	$r = 55$ mph	Solve:	$r = 55$ mph
Check:	$385 = 55 \times 7$	Check:	$55 = \dfrac{385}{7}$

Some people like the first way because they find it easier to write equivalent equations *after* the numbers have replaced some of the variables. Others like the second way because it has fewer steps.

> Remember: To solve an equation, find the number that makes it true.

PROBLEM 10

For each part below, write an equation, solve, and check. These real-life problems may contain more information than you need or not enough information to solve them. If not enough information is given, just write "Not enough information is given" as your answer.

Ⓐ A bicyclist can maintain a speed of 20 mph for long periods. At this rate, how long must he ride to travel 90 miles?

Ⓑ In 2002, Ward Burton won the Daytona 500 (an auto race that is 500 miles long) with a speed close to 143 mph. At what time did he finish?

Ⓒ A package of 25 nails costs $.69. Find the price per nail to the nearest tenth of a cent.

Ⓓ A jogger stays in shape by running an average of 8 hours a week. How far does he run if he maintains a pace of 8.5 km/hr for 1.4 hours?

Ⓔ Ears of corn are on sale, 7 for a dollar. What is the price per ear to the nearest cent?

Ⓕ How many light bulbs can you buy with $10 if a package of 2 bulbs costs $1.25?

Rewriting Equations Using Algebraic Rules

Another way to find equivalent equations is to rewrite them by following the **Multiplication Property of Equality** from elementary algebra. You can only use this property if your starting point is an *equation*.

MULTIPLICATION PROPERTY OF EQUALITY	Let a, b, and c represent numbers and c does not equal 0. If $a = b$, then $ac = bc$ If $a = b$, then $\frac{a}{c} = \frac{b}{c}$

The multiplication property says that if you multiply or divide both sides of an equation by the same non-zero number, the sides of the equation will remain equal.

These examples use the algebraic rules to rewrite equations so the variable is alone on its side of the equation.

EXAMPLE

$13x = 234$	Notice that x is being *multiplied* by 13 on its side of the equation. Remember that you want to get x alone.
$\frac{13x}{13} = \frac{234}{13}$	To *undo* "multiplying by 13," divide by 13. To follow the multiplication property, you also have to divide the other side of the equation by 13.
$x = 18$	$\frac{13}{13} = 1$ and 1 times x is x. You have succeeded in getting x alone. Dividing 234 by 13 gives 18 as the solution to the equation.
Check: $13(18) = 234$	Replace x with 18 in the original equation.

EXAMPLE

$\frac{n}{25} = 25$	Notice that n is being *divided* by 25 on its side of the equation.
$25\left(\frac{n}{25}\right) = 25\,(25)$	Multiply both sides of the equation by 25.
$n = 625$	Multiplying by 25 undoes dividing by 25, so n is alone on its side of the equation. Multiplying 25 by 25 gives 625.
Check: $\frac{625}{25} = 25$	Replace n with the solution, 625, in the original equation.

PROBLEM 11

Solve the following equations using the Multiplication Property of Equality. Show that you understand what you are doing by showing the step in your work where you do the same thing to both sides of the equation. Check your answers.

Ⓐ $5z = 60$

Ⓑ $78 = 6y$

Ⓒ $\frac{p}{7} = 14$

Ⓓ $15 = \frac{x}{30}$

Ⓔ $364 = 14t$

Ⓕ $88x = 2{,}024$

Analyzing Answers

What Happens When You Multiply?

Use the formula $c = nr$ to make some discoveries.

Consider this situation: The gas tank of a small automobile holds 12 gallons of gasoline. How much does it cost to fill the tank?

Let $n = 12$, and watch what happens to c (the total cost) as r (the price per gallon) changes: $c = 12r$.

PROBLEM 12 Complete the table to show the changing cost of 12 gallons of gas. Use your calculator when necessary.

Use the table in problem 12 to solve problem 13.

price per gallon (r)	total cost (c)
.50	$6.00
.75	
.85	
.99	
1.00	$12.00
1.50	
2.00	
3.00	

PROBLEM 13

Ⓐ As the price per gallon increases, what happens to the total cost? Does it increase or decrease?

Ⓑ When the price was less than a dollar per gallon, the total cost was (less than or greater than) $12.

Ⓒ When the price was greater than a dollar per gallon, the total cost was greater than _____ .

Ⓓ Complete these statements so they will be true for positive numbers:

When a number is multiplied by a value less than 1, the result is _____ than the original number.

When a number is multiplied by a value greater than 1, the result is _____ than the original number.

Estimating Answers

PROBLEM 14 Use the principle you discovered in problem 13Ⓓ to estimate whether the answer would be greater than or less than the value given. Choose *greater than* or *less than*.

Ⓐ 36×1.38 is (greater than or less than) 36?

Ⓑ 158×0.87 is (greater than or less than) 158?

Ⓒ 212×0.45 is (greater than or less than) 106?

Ⓓ 54×2.09 is (greater than or less than) 108?

Ⓔ 785×1.223 is (greater than or less than) 785?

What Happens When You Divide?

Consider this situation: You have $12 to spend on cheese. Various kinds of cheese have different prices per pound. The equation $n = \frac{c}{r}$ can be used to find the number of pounds of cheese you can buy. Let $c = \$12$, and watch what happens to n (the number of pounds) as the value of r (the price per pound) is changed: $n = \frac{12}{r}$.

PROBLEM 15
Complete the table to show the changing number of pounds of cheese.

Use the table in problem 15 to solve problem 16.

price per lb (r)	number of lb (n)
.50	24
.75	
1.00	
4.00	
6.00	
12.00	
24.00	

PROBLEM 16

Ⓐ As the price per pound increases, the number of pounds you can buy with $12 _____.

Ⓑ When the price per pound was less than a dollar, the number of pounds you could buy was _____ than 12.

Ⓒ When the price per pound was more than a dollar, the number of pounds you could buy was _____ than 12.

Ⓓ When the price per pound was greater than $12, the number of pounds you could buy was less than _____.

Ⓔ Complete these statements so they will be true for positive numbers:

When a number is divided by a value less than 1, the result is _____ than the original number.

When a number is divided by a value greater than 1, the result is _____ than the original number.

When a number is divided by a value greater than itself, the result is less than _____.

Estimating Answers

PROBLEM 17
Decide whether the answer will be greater than or less than the value given. Choose *greater than* or *less than*. It may help to interpret each division problem as asking, "How many _____s are there in _____?"

Ⓐ $\frac{59}{0.92}$ is (greater than or less than) 59?

Ⓑ $\frac{43}{1.19}$ is (greater than or less than) 43?

Ⓒ $\frac{79}{80}$ is (greater than or less than) 1?

Ⓓ $\frac{356}{311}$ is (greater than or less than) 1?

Multiplying and Dividing with Negative Numbers

On a winter day in Minnesota when the high temperature for the day was 0°, a weather forecast predicted that the temperature would fall in a regular pattern, 2° every hour for 6 hours.

We can picture this drop on a number line.

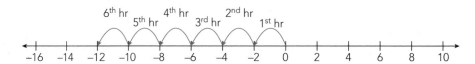

The temperature after 6 hours is −12°. Mathematically, we could write the equation

$$(-2) + (-2) + (-2) + (-2) + (-2) + (-2) = -12$$

or $6(-2) = -12$

The temperature example suggests this algebraic rule.

> **ALGEBRAIC RULE** The product of a negative number and a positive number is negative.

Another algebraic rule says:

> **ALGEBRAIC RULE** The product of a negative number and another negative number is positive.

Remember that the answer to a multiplication problem is called the **product**.

Study the pattern in the following tables:

The first factor *decreases* by 1 each row.
The second factor is negative.

3(−4)	−12
2(−4)	−8
1(−4)	−4
0(−4)	0

The product *increases* by 4 each row.

When the table is continued, the pattern also continues in the same fashion.

The first factor continues to *decrease* by 1 each row.

(−1)(−4)	4
(−2)(−4)	8
(−3)(−4)	12

The product continues to *increase* by 4 each row.

Notice that, in a mathematical sense, it is necessary for a negative times a negative to equal a positive.

PROBLEM 18

Find the products.

   Ⓐ (−9)(8)   Ⓒ (−15)(−6)   Ⓔ (−16)(2)(−5)

   Ⓑ (7)(−12)   Ⓓ (−11)(−11)   Ⓕ (4)(17)(−25)

Division

Because multiplication and division are inverse operations, you can use the rules for multiplying to create rules for dividing.

Because $4(-7) = -28$, it is true that $\frac{-28}{4} = -7$ and $\frac{-28}{-7} = 4$.

And since $(-3)(-9) = 27$, it is true that $\frac{27}{-3} = -9$ and $\frac{27}{-9} = -3$.

The examples suggest the following:

> **Remember that the answer to a division problem is called the quotient.**

ALGEBRAIC RULE	The quotient of a negative and a positive number is negative. The quotient of two negative numbers is positive.

PROBLEM 19 Find the quotients.

Ⓐ $\frac{100}{-4}$ Ⓒ $\frac{-120}{-5}$ Ⓔ $\frac{625}{-25}$

Ⓑ $\frac{-96}{12}$ Ⓓ $\frac{-450}{9}$ Ⓕ $\frac{-630}{-30}$

Equations and Problem Solving

Use your understanding of formulas, equivalent equations, and estimation to solve these problems.

Problem 20 refers to the table and the graph.

The cost of apples at a fruit stand is described in the following table and graph.

number of pounds	total cost
3	$2.00
6	$4.00
12	$8.00

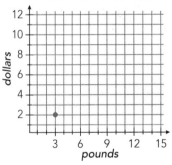

PRICE OF APPLES

PROBLEM 20

Ⓐ What is the total cost of 9 pounds of apples?

(1) $18.00
(2) $12.00
(3) $ 6.00
(4) $ 4.50
(5) $ 3.00

Ⓑ The point that corresponds to 3 pounds of apples costing $2 has been placed on the graph. Plot the other two points from the table and draw a line connecting them.

Ⓒ Approximately how many pounds of apples could you buy with $5? Explain your answer.

Ⓓ What is the price per pound of the apples? Using *n* to stand for the number of pounds, write an equation that could be used to find *c*, the cost in dollars of any number of pounds.

CHECK YOUR UNDERSTANDING

You may use your calculator on any problem except where noted by this symbol:

1. Write two equivalent division equations for $40 = 8 \times 5$.

2. **Ⓐ** Write an equation to find the cost (c) of 6 shirts at $24.99 each.

   Ⓑ Find the cost of the shirts (without tax).

3. **Ⓐ** Write an equation to find the price (r) of 1 shirt if 6 cost $186.

   Ⓑ Find the cost of each shirt.

4. A rectangle contains 84 square feet. If its length is 7 feet, what is its width?

   Ⓐ Write the formula for the area of a rectangle and substitute the known values.

   Ⓑ Write an equivalent equation so that the unknown is alone on one side of the equation.

   Ⓒ Find the width.

5. Manny saves $50 a week from his paycheck. How many weeks does he have to save before he has savings of $1,000?

   Ⓐ Substitute values into the total savings formula.

FORMULA	Total savings = number of weeks × weekly savings

   Ⓑ Write an equivalent equation and solve.

6. A package of hamburger meat contains 1.2 pounds of meat. The price per pound is $2.45.

   Ⓐ Substitute the values into the equation $c = nr$.

   Ⓑ Will the cost be greater than or less than $2.45?

7. **Ⓐ** A trucker finds that he can average 50 mph on interstate highways. Write an equation to find how far he can travel (d) in t hours.

   Ⓑ Write an equation for the number of bottles (n) that can be purchased with $12.00 if each bottle costs $b.

   Ⓒ The cost of 12 ears of corn was n. Write an expression for the price (c) of one ear (r).

8. A rental car company charges the rates shown in the table below. Continuing the pattern shown, determine the total cost for renting a car for 5 days.

number of days	total cost
1	$19.95
2	$39.90
3	$59.85
4	$79.80
5	

9. Perform each operation.

   Ⓐ $(-15)(-8)$

   Ⓑ $\frac{-720}{9}$

   Ⓒ $(-7) + 11$

   Ⓓ $(-7) - 11$

   Ⓔ $(-7)(11)$

   Ⓕ $\frac{-930}{-30}$

   Ⓖ $(-930) + 30$

   Ⓗ $(-930) - 30$

10. Solve the following algebraic equations. Show the step in your solution where you used the Addition or Multiplication Properties of Equality. Check your answers.

   Ⓐ $t - 27 = 51$

   Ⓑ $14x = 210$

   Ⓒ $m + 25 = 25$

   Ⓓ $t + 30 = 25$

   Ⓔ $\frac{n}{17} = 17$

   Ⓕ $\frac{y}{17} = -1$

   Ⓖ $12x = -108$

   Ⓗ $36d = -1,800$

TEST-TAKING PRACTICE

You may use your calculator on any problem except where noted by this symbol:

1. How long would it take an airliner traveling at 520 miles per hour to fly 3,640 miles from New York to Paris?

Mark your answer in the circles in the grid.

2. If x books, all the same price, cost $49.95, which expression tells you the price of one book?

(1) $49.95 + x

(2) $49.95 − x

(3) ($49.95)(x)

(4) $\frac{\$49.95}{x}$

(5) ($49.95)($49.95)x

3. Tracy walks 0.8 of a mile to school. Which expression shows how far she walks to and from school in a 5-day week?

(1) (0.8)(5)

(2) (0.8)(2)(5)

(3) (0.8) + (2)(5)

(4) (0.8)(2)

(5) (0.8)(5) − (2)

4. The shipping boxes each hold 36 light bulbs. How many boxes are needed for a shipment of 1,000 bulbs?

(1) 52

(2) 48

(3) 36

(4) 28

(5) 27

Problems 5 and 6 refer to the following road sign.

Ramon saw this sign beside the highway. He knows that Gary and Chicago are on the same road.

| Gary | 70 miles |
| Chicago | 100 miles |

5. Which of the following expressions tells how far it is from Gary to Chicago?

(1) 70 + 100

(2) 100 − 70

(3) 100 × 70

(4) $\frac{100}{70}$

(5) Not enough information is given.

6. If Ramon drives 65 miles per hour, about how long will it take him to get to Chicago?

(1) $\frac{1}{2}$ hour

(2) 1 hour

(3) $1\frac{1}{2}$ hours

(4) $2\frac{1}{2}$ hours

(5) Not enough information is given.

Multistep Problems

MENTAL MATH

If it is true that:	Can it be true that:
1. $50 \times 75 = 3{,}750$	$45 \times 75 = 3{,}825$?
2. $5{,}700 \div 100 = 57$	$5{,}700 \div 95 = 60$?
3. $36 \times 10 = 360$	$36 \times 10.5 = 378$?
4. $100 \div 5 = 20$	$100 \div 5.5 = 22.5$?
5. $4.6 \times 2.5 = 11.5$	$4.42 \times 2.5 = 11.05$?

Until now, you have been working mostly with problems that take one step to solve. Many problems will take more than one step to solve. Before you can solve multistep problems, you need to learn how to write them.

Order of Operations

What is the answer to this problem: $4 + 5 \times 6 = ?$

Is it 54? ($4 + 5 = 9$; $9 \times 6 = 54$)   or   Is it 34? ($5 \times 6 = 30$; $30 + 4 = 34$)

To avoid this kind of uncertainty when problems involve more than one step, mathematicians have agreed on an **order of operations**. The order of operations has been programmed into scientific calculators, so you can rely on one to do the problem above in the correct order. Here are two parts of the order of operations:

① **Multiply and divide before you add and subtract.**

EXAMPLES $9 + 30 \div 3$ $100 - 25 \times 3$ $4 + 5 \times 6$

$9 + 10 = 19$ $100 - 75 = 25$ $4 + 30 = 34$

② **Do each *level* of operations in order from left to right.**

Notice in the following examples that multiplication and division are carried out, from left to right, before addition and subtraction.

$20 - 8 \div 2$	Divide first.	$40 \div 2 \times 5$	Only multiplication and division. Work from left to right.
$20 - 4 = 16$	Then subtract.	$20 \times 5 = 100$	
$12 - 8 - 3$	Only subtraction.	$30 \div 6 + 24 \div 6$	Complete the divisions first. Then add.
$4 - 3 = 1$	Work from left to right.	$5 + 4 = 9$	

PROBLEM 1 | Use the rules for order of operations to solve these problems.

A $12 \div 4 + 2$ $\qquad$ $5 + 2 \times 3$ $\qquad$ $24 - 6 \div 2$ $\qquad$ $32 \div 8 \div 2$

B $12 + 3 \div 3$ $\qquad$ $33 \div 3 + 8 \div 4$ $\qquad$ $5 + 8 \div 4 - 3$ $\qquad$ $6 \times 3 + 6 \times 2$

C $5 \times 13 \times 4$ $\qquad$ $17 + 16 + 3$ $\qquad$ $15 - 3 + 3$ $\qquad$ $49 \div 7 \times 7$

Parentheses and Division Bars

How do **parentheses**, ( ) or [ ], fit into these rules about the order of operations? You have already used them to indicate which operations are to be done first.

Parentheses have the highest priority. First do the operations within parentheses, then multiply or divide, and then add or subtract.

For example, $34 + (7 + 43)$ $\qquad$ The parentheses make the addition
$\qquad$ $34 + 50 = 84$ $\qquad$ easier by grouping compatible pairs.

In most cases, however, parentheses are placed in a problem for the purpose of changing the standard order of operations.

Without the parentheses, multiply first. $\qquad$ With the parentheses, add first.
$7 \times 4 + 5$ $\qquad\qquad\qquad\qquad\qquad$ $7 \times (4 + 5)$
$28 + 5 = 33$ $\qquad\qquad\qquad\qquad\qquad$ $7 \times 9 = 63$

The **fraction line** (or **division bar**) is also a **grouping symbol**. The line in a division problem means "divided by," but it can enclose another operation as well.

> Operations within parentheses or on top and bottom of the division bar (fraction line) should be done first.

$\dfrac{24 - 6}{3}$ means the same as $\dfrac{(24 - 6)}{3}$. $\qquad$ $\dfrac{5 + 7}{4 - 2}$ is the same as $\dfrac{(5 + 7)}{(4 - 2)}$.

$\dfrac{18}{3}$ Do the operation on top first. $\qquad$ $\dfrac{12}{2}$ Do the operations above and below the line first.

6 $\quad$ Then divide. $\qquad\qquad\qquad\qquad$ 6 $\quad$ Then divide.

PROBLEM 2 | Do the indicated operations. Compare the answers of pairs grouped by the word *and*.

A $12 - 6 \div 2$ and $(12 - 6) \div 2$ $\qquad$ **D** $\dfrac{12 - 7}{-5}$

B $3 + 12 \times 2$ and $(3 + 12) \times 2$ $\qquad$ **E** $\dfrac{21 - 7}{7 - 5}$

C $6 \times 3 + 2$ and $6 \times (3 + 2)$ $\qquad$ **F** $15 \div (6 - 4 + 1)$

The Distributive Property

In Lesson 8, you learned to find the areas of rectangles. Find these areas.

The **distributive property of multiplication** states:

$a(b + c)$ is the same as $ab + ac$, and $a(b - c)$ is the same as $ab - ac$.

$6 \times (3 + 2)$
6×5
30

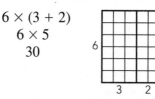

Area = $6(3 + 2)$
= 30 square units

$(6 \times 3) + (6 \times 2)$
$18 \quad + \quad 12$
30

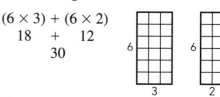

Area = $6 \cdot 3 + 6 \cdot 2$
= 30 square units

The answers to both problems are the same, just as both areas are the same.

$$6(3 + 2) = 6 \cdot 3 + 6 \cdot 2$$

This is an example of the **distributive property** of multiplication over addition.

The distributive property allows you to work problems two ways. Sometimes one is easier than the other.

Remember that $15 \times (20 + 3)$ can also be written without the times sign $15(20 + 3)$.

EXAMPLE A		EXAMPLE B	
$15 \times (20 + 3)$		$13(15 + 5)$	
FACTORED FORM	**EXPANDED FORM (EASIER)**	**FACTORED FORM (EASIER)**	**EXPANDED FORM**
$15 \times (20 + 3)$ Add first:	$(15 \times 20) + (15 \times 3)$ Multiply first:	$13(15 + 5)$	$13(15) + 13(5)$
15×23	$300 + 45$	$13(20)$	$195 + 65$
345	345	260	260

Multiply to Write the Expanded Form: $ab + ac$

The distributive property states that a factor in front of the parentheses is distributed to each of the numbers inside. This results in the **expanded form**.

We show this as:
$a(b + c) = ab + ac$
$a(b - c) = ab - ac$

$7(15 - 9) = 7(15) - 7(9)$ Use the minus sign.

$m(10 + 4) = 10(m) + 4(m)$ Multiply numbers and variables.

$9(4n + 7) = 36n + 63$ Multiply numbers and variables.

PROBLEM 3 | Use the distributive property to write these expressions in expanded form.

EXAMPLE $12(40 + 6) = 12(40) + 12(6)$

Ⓐ $8(2 + 5)$

Ⓑ $34(21 + 19)$

Ⓒ $12(10 - 5)$

Ⓓ $5(4 + 3 + 8)$

Ⓔ $13(x + 3)$

Ⓕ $k(8 - 3)$

Ⓖ $3(11m + 5)$

Ⓗ $10(8y - 8)$

Ⓘ $\frac{1}{2}(60 - 6x)$

Factor to Write the Factored Form: $a(b + c)$

If you look at it from the other direction, the distributive property also says that if the same number (a) is a **factor** of both terms, you can divide it out and write it outside of the parentheses.

> We show this as:
> $ab + ac = a(b + c)$
> $ab - ac = a(b - c)$

Algebraic terms that have the same variable are called **like terms**.

$5x$ and $8x$ are like terms.

$5a$ and $5b$ are not.

$3(9) - 3(2) = 3(9 - 2)$ 3 is a factor of both terms. Use the minus sign.

$7x + 35 = 7(x) + 7(5) = 7(x + 5)$ The common factor is 7. Use the plus sign.

$5n + 6n = n(5 + 6)$ A variable can be a common factor.

The last example could be written as: $5n + 6n = 11n$.

It shows how "like terms" are added and subtracted. Because the variable is the same in both terms, you can just add or subtract the numbers in front, and carry the variable along.

EXAMPLES

Combining like terms simplifies an expression.

$4x + 13x = 17x$ $12b - 7b = 5b$ $4a + a = 5a$ (Remember, a means 1a.)

$4 + 13 = 17$ $12 - 7 = 5$ $4 + 1 = 5$

PROBLEM 4

Use the distributive property to write these expressions in factored form. Simplify.

A $6 \cdot 8 + 6 \cdot 5$ **D** $6b - 30$ **G** $25m + 22p$

B $12(7) - 12(3)$ **E** $7x + 6x$ **H** $15x + x$

C $10d + 20$ **F** $13n - 9n$ **I** $y + 8y - 3y$

For multiple-choice questions, you must recognize that the factored form and the expanded form are equal to each other. For example, this type of item could appear on a test.

PROBLEM 5

Sam worked for 7 hours on Saturday for $6 per hour and also worked for 3 hours on Sunday for $6 per hour. Which expression shows how much, in dollars, Sam was paid for his work?

(1) $7 + 6 + 3 + 6$
(2) $7 \times 6 \times 3 \times 6$
(3) $6(7 + 3)$
(4) $7(6 + 3)$
(5) $3(7 + 6)$

Order of Operations

You need to learn what to expect from your scientific calculator when you press a sequence of keys that represents a multistep problem.

Which operation does your calculator do first?

Watch the calculator display as you key in each step of the next two problems.

Notice that it waits to carry out the addition once it knows the next operation is multiplication.

KEY IN: **3** **+** **2** **×** **4** **=**

DISPLAY: 3. 3. 2. 2. 4. 11.

But it carries out the multiplication as soon as it knows the next operation is addition.

KEY IN: **3** **×** **2** **+** **4** **=**

DISPLAY: 3. 3. 2. 6. 4. 10.

The order of operations rules have been programmed into scientific calculators.

When do you need to use the parentheses keys?

Since the calculator will automatically follow the standard order of operations, you need the parentheses keys only when the problem demands an order of operations that is not standard—the same times that you *need* grouping symbols when you write a problem. Compare answers when you insert parentheses and when you do not.

EXAMPLE A $108(45 + 79)$

Enter **1** **0** **8** **×** **(** **4** **5** **+** **7** **9** **)** **=**

Press the equals sign to get the final answer.

13392.

OR

Enter **1** **0** **8** **×** **4** **5** **+** **7** **9** **=**

4939.

The answers are different—you need the parentheses to do the addition before the multiplication.

EXAMPLE B $\dfrac{9}{72 - 27}$

Enter **9** **÷** **(** **7** **2** **−** **2** **7** **)** **=**

Press the equals sign to get the final answer.

0.2

OR

Enter **9** **÷** **7** **2** **−** **2** **7** **=**

−26.875

The parentheses keys are needed to carry out the subtraction before the division.

Find the answers to these problems with your calculator. Decide in advance when you need to use the parentheses keys.

Ⓐ $(256 \div 32) \times 4$

Ⓑ $(437 + 78) \times 31$

Ⓒ $2{,}604 - (45 \times 32)$

Ⓓ $\dfrac{650 + 376}{3}$

Ⓔ $(30 \times 72) + (25 \times 43)$

Ⓕ $\dfrac{1{,}364}{45 + 79}$

Use Formulas to Solve Real Problems

Perimeters of Rectangles

The distributive property applies when finding the perimeter (sum of the lengths of the sides) of a rectangle.

The **perimeter** of any closed figure is the entire distance around it.

Notice:
2 sides are 8 units long.
2 sides are 3 units long.
You can write
$P = (2 \times 8) + (2 \times 3)$ expanded form

However, notice:
The sum of $8 + 3$ is *halfway* around the entire rectangle.
You can write
$P = 2(8 + 3)$ factored form

In both cases, the perimeter is 22.

On the formulas page (page 280), the formula for the perimeter of a rectangle follows the expanded form above: $P = 2l + 2w$.

The perimeter formula written in factored form would be $P = 2(l + w)$.

You may use either form when solving problems.

EXAMPLE A

Find the perimeter of a rectangle whose length = 8.5 cm and whose width = 3.5 cm.

$P = 2l + 2w$ or $P = 2(l + w)$

$P = 2(8.5) + 2(3.5)$ $P = 2(8.5 + 3.5)$

$P = 17 + 7 = 24$ cm $P = 2(12) = 24$ cm

EXAMPLE B

How much fencing is required to enclose a rectangular garden that is *b* ft long and 5 ft wide?

$P = 2l + 2w$ or $P = 2(l + w)$

$P = 2 \cdot b + 2 \cdot 5$ $P = 2(b + 5)$

$P = 2b + 10$ $P = 2b + 10$

PROBLEM 6

For the perimeter of the rectangle at the right

Ⓐ Write an equation in expanded form: $P = 2l + 2w$

Ⓑ Write an equation in factored form: $P = 2(l + w)$

Ⓒ Find the perimeter of the rectangle, using the form that makes the computation easier.

3.9 m

5.1 m

Find the Mean (Average)

The **average** of a group of numbers is one number that is typical of the group, a measure of central tendency.

EXAMPLE

In four games of a tournament, a basketball player scored 25, 28, 19, and 35 points, respectively. What is her mean (average) points per game in the tournament?

STEP 1 Add the scores. $25 + 28 + 19 + 35 = 107$

STEP 2 Divide by 4, the number of scores. $\frac{107}{4} = 26.75$

The two steps in the problem above can be written as one equation:

$$\text{Mean} = \frac{25 + 28 + 19 + 35}{4} \longleftarrow \text{This means "divided by."}$$

Discuss: Compare this example with the formula for the mean found on the formulas page (page 280). What is the value of n in the example above? What is the purpose of the subscripts, 1, 2, … n?

Find the Median

Another measure of central tendency is the **median**, the middle number of a group.

EXAMPLE A When the number of numbers is **odd**

Find the median of the following prices: $200,000, $30,000, $60,000, $30,000, and $250,000.

Arrange the values in order.   median

$30,000 $30,000 $60,000 $200,000 $250,000

Choose the number in the middle. The median is $60,000.

EXAMPLE B When the number of numbers is **even**

Find the median of the following prices: $90,000, $65,000, $30,000, $90,000, $60,000, and $80,000.

Arrange the values in order.   median

$30,000 $60,000 $65,000 $80,000 $90,000 $90,000

Here the median is the number that is *halfway* between 65,000 and 80,000.

$$\frac{65,000 + 80,000}{2} = \frac{145,000}{2} = \$72,500$$

PROBLEM 7

The high temperatures for five summer days were recorded as shown below.

Ⓐ Write a single equation and find the mean temperature.

Ⓑ What is the median temperature?

M	T	W	Th	F
85°	90°	70°	80°	85°

PROBLEM 8 | At one real estate office, the prices of the houses that were sold one week were $90,000; $250,000; $125,000; $1,600,000; $95,000; and $300,000.

Ⓐ Write a single equation and find the mean (average) price.

Ⓑ Find the median price.

Ⓒ Which of the two averages do you consider to be more typical of the group?

PROBLEM 9 | The following listing shows the salaries of all the employees in a small company.

President	$250,000
Manager	$ 70,000
Secretary	$ 25,000
Shipping Clerk	$ 23,000
Machinist (2)	$ 24,000 each
Assembler (2)	$ 24,000 each

Ⓐ Find the mean and median for this group of 8 numbers.

Ⓑ Which of the measures of central tendency (mean or median) would you suggest that the president use if he were trying to convince stockholders that he was running a cost-conscious ("lean and mean") business?

Ⓒ Which of these measures of central tendency would the president use on a report if he wanted the company to look as if it paid a high average salary?

Ⓓ Change the original listing by adding $20,000 to each of the salaries. Find the mean and median now. How are they different from the ones you found in Ⓐ?

Ⓔ Make a different change to the original. Add $100,000 to the president's salary only. Find the new mean and median and compare it to the ones you found in Ⓐ.

Translate a Situation into Mathematics— "Mathematize"

Before you try to translate a real situation into an equation, practice translating some simple expressions from English to mathematics.

six times five increased by 8	$6 \times 5 + 8$	
eight less than 4 times 12	$4 \times 12 - 8$	Order is important in subtraction.
three times the sum of 8 and x	$3(8 + x)$	Needs parentheses to show that you add first.
three more than the product of 8 and 7	$3 + 8 \times 7$	No parentheses necessary.
44.99 divided by the sum of 5 and 6	$\dfrac{44.99}{5 + 6}$	

Remember that the **sum** is the answer when you add and the **product** is the answer when you multiply.

PROBLEM 10 | Choose the correct mathematical expression for each statement. **Do not solve.**

Ⓐ 3 more than 4 dozen $\qquad$ $(3 + 4) \times 12$ $\quad$ or $\quad$ $3 + 4 \times 12$

Ⓑ 3 quarters less than 5 dollars $\qquad$ $\$5 - (3 \times \$.25)$ $\quad$ or $\quad$ $(3 \times \$.25) - \$5$

Ⓒ the number of legs on 5 birds and 3 dogs $\qquad$ $5 + 2 + 3 + 4$ $\quad$ or $\quad$ $5(2) + 3(4)$

Ⓓ the number of shoes in 5 men's pairs and 8 women's pairs $\qquad$ $5(2) + 8(2)$ $\quad$ or $\quad$ $5(2 + 8)$

PROBLEM 11 | Write these expressions mathematically. **Do not solve.**

Ⓐ six more than three times seven

Ⓑ 10 times the difference between 15 and 7

Ⓒ 6 times the sum of 5 and 8

Ⓓ half of the difference between 35 and 25

Ⓔ 98.99 divided by the sum of 4 and 3

Ⓕ the price of five $.37 stamps and seven $.21 stamps

Ⓖ the amount earned in 8 hours at $8 per hour and 3 hours at $12 per hour

More Multistep Problems

When situations are described in word problems, take time to do the following:

① Read carefully, extracting the mathematical essence of the situation.

② Think of a plan, taking notes if it helps.

③ Write the steps of your plan as an equation.

EXAMPLE A

A small office purchased 20 boxes of computer paper in January and 9 boxes in September. If the cost of each box was $6.25, what was the total amount the office spent on computer paper that year?

HOW TO PLAN IT:

You could choose to add the 20 boxes and 9 boxes, then to multiply that sum by $6.25.

You could find the same answer by multiplying 20 boxes by $6.25 and 9 boxes by $6.25, then adding those products.

HOW TO WRITE IT:

$t = 6.25(20 + 9)$
$t = 6.25(29)$
$t = \$181.25$

$t = 6.25 \cdot 20 + 6.25 \cdot 9$
$t = 125 + 56.25$
$t = \$181.25$

The next example shows the fraction bar serving two purposes: it means "divided by," and it also is a grouping symbol indicating which operation to do first.

EXAMPLE B

A case of 12 cans of motor oil costs $11.50. For a limited time, a discount of $2.50 per case was given. What was the price per can at this special price?

HOW TO PLAN IT:

First find the discounted price by subtracting $2.50 from $11.50.

Divide the difference by 12, the number of cans.

HOW TO WRITE IT:

$$p = \frac{11.50 - 2.50}{12}$$

$$p = \frac{9.00}{12}$$

$$p = \$.75$$

PROBLEM 12

Write a single equation for each problem and solve. Compare your equation with those written by others in the class, and determine whether or not the equations are equivalent.

Ⓐ The package on a coil of rope indicates that it is 50 feet long. George cuts off 12 pieces, each of which is 3 feet long. How long is the rope remaining in the coil?

Ⓑ The expenses of a trip were shared by four people. They spent $283 on gas and $165 on lodging. What was each person's share of the expenses?

Ⓒ What is the total cost of 3 cheeseburgers at $2.05 each, 3 orders of fries at $.70 each, and 3 medium soft drinks at $.85 each?

Example C shows how a multistep problem can be written as one equation.

EXAMPLE C

A used car is priced at $4,500. Under a time payment plan, Carlos would make a down payment of $500 and 36 monthly payments of $150 each. How much extra would Carlos pay if he used the time payment plan?

HOW TO PLAN IT:
Multiply 36 payments by $150, and add the sum to $500. Then subtract $4,500.

HOW TO WRITE IT:
$d = 36 \cdot 150 + 500 - 4,500$
$d = 5,400 + 500 - 4,500$
$d = 5,900 - 4,500$
$d = \$1,400$

PROBLEM 13

Write a single equation for each problem. Estimate the answer. Then solve. Use your calculator if necessary.

Ⓐ The Blackwells found some carpeting they liked for a price of $17.95 per square yard installed. They need 50 square yards. If they purchase this carpet, how much of their redecorating budget of $2,000 will be left?

Ⓑ Ray earns a salary of $23,245 per year, and his wife, Rowena, earns $10,755 per year. To the nearest cent, what is their combined *monthly* income?

Ⓒ Vance earns $6.25 an hour for the first 8 hours he works each day. He is paid $10 an hour for each additional hour that he works. One day he worked 11.5 hours. How much did he earn that day?

✓ CHECK YOUR UNDERSTANDING

You may use your calculator on any problem except where noted by this symbol:

1. Which pairs of expressions are equal to each other?

   Ⓐ $20 - 4 + 5$ $20 - (4 + 5)$
   Ⓑ $7 + k + 1$ $7 + (k + 1)$
   Ⓒ $8 \times 6 \div 6$ $8 \times (6 \div 6)$
   Ⓓ $(4)(m) + 2$ $4m + 2$
   Ⓔ $50 - (5 \bullet 3)$ $50 - 5 \times 3$
   Ⓕ $7 \times 6 + 8$ $7 \times (6 + 8)$
   Ⓖ $6 \bullet 3 + 4 \bullet 5$ $(6 \bullet 3) + (4 \bullet 5)$
   Ⓗ $10(8 + 7)$ $10 \bullet 8 + 10 \bullet 7$
   Ⓘ $6x + 3x$ $9x^2$
   Ⓙ $12(3x - 5)$ $36x - 60$
   Ⓚ $(4 + 13)y$ $17y$

2. 📵 Use the rules for the order of operations to find the value of each expression.

   Ⓐ $19 - 7 \div 7$ Ⓔ $48 \div 6 \times 2$
   Ⓑ $19 - 7 + 7$ Ⓕ $48 - 6 \times 2$
   Ⓒ $3 + 4(6 - 5)$ Ⓖ $8 \bullet 9 + 8 \bullet 10$
   Ⓓ $\dfrac{10 + 14}{8}$ Ⓗ $\dfrac{22 - 6}{13 - 9}$

3. Use your calculator to find the answer to each of these problems.

   Ⓐ $13 + 11 \times 12$ Ⓓ $30 \bullet 15 + 31 \bullet 16$
   Ⓑ $(13 + 11) \times 12$ Ⓔ $176 - 148 \div 4$
   Ⓒ $\dfrac{33 + 127}{5}$ Ⓕ $\dfrac{840}{27 + 8}$

4. Write a single mathematics expression that means the same as

   Ⓐ 5 times 9 decreased by 3
   Ⓑ 10 times the sum of 30 and 8
   Ⓒ 6 more than the product of 4 and b
   Ⓓ the sum of 12 and m divided by 15
   Ⓔ 78 divided by the difference of 18 and 5
   Ⓕ half the sum of 62 and 68

5. Find the perimeter and the area of this rectangle.

   7 in. ⎜ [rectangle] ⎜ 13 in.

For problems 6–10, do the following:

   Ⓐ Write the problem in a single equation.
   Ⓑ Estimate the answer.
   Ⓒ Then solve. Use your calculator if necessary.

6. How much change should Paul get from $10.00 if he bought 5 candy bars that cost $.65 each?

7. Barbara is paid $7.20 an hour for the first 40 hours she works during a week. If she works more than 40 hours, she is paid 1.5 times her normal rate for each hour over 40 hours. How much should she be paid for a week in which she works 45 hours?

8. A car rental agency advertises a rate of $24 per day plus $.15 a mile for every mile driven. How much would the agency charge for a 2-day rental in which the car was driven 200 miles?

9. Four luxury cars were tested for fuel efficiency. The number of miles they got per gallon of gasoline were 23, 20, 27, and 21, respectively. What is the mean (average) fuel efficiency for these cars?

10. According to one source, an egg contains 26 mg of calcium and a piece of toast contains 43 mg of calcium. How many mg of calcium are in a breakfast of 2 eggs and 3 pieces of toast?

TEST-TAKING PRACTICE

You may use your calculator on any problem except where noted by this symbol:

1. Which expression indicates the total cost (without tax) of an order of 5 lunch specials at $3.95 each and 5 coffees at $.50?

   (1) 5 + $3.95 + 5 + $.50
   (2) 5($3.95 + $.50)
   (3) 10($3.95 + $.50)
   (4) 5 × $3.95 × $.50
   (5) 25($3.95 + $.50)

2. What is the area, in square inches, of the trapezoid shown below? (Use the formula on page 280.)

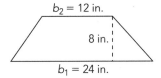

   (1)   48
   (2)   96
   (3)   144
   (4)   192
   (5)   2,304

3. Sue watches about 1.5 hours of television on Monday and Wednesday nights. On Tuesdays and Thursdays, she watches 2.5 hours of television. Choose the expression that shows how many hours of television she watches for these 4 days of the week.

   (1) 1.5 + 2.5 + 4
   (2) 4(1.5 + 2.5)
   (3) 1.5 × 2.5
   (4) 2(1.5 + 2.5)
   (5) 2(1.5 + 2.5 + 4)

4. Two tall skyscrapers are being built in Asia. The Shanghai World Financial Center will be 1,509 feet tall and Union Square in Hong Kong will be 1,575 feet tall. What is the average height, in feet, of these two buildings?

   Mark your answer in the circles in the grid.

5. Pictures in a yearbook are arranged so that there are 7 rows on a page and 5 pictures in each row. How many pages are needed to include all 225 students in the senior class?

   (1)   6
   (2)   7
   (3)   12
   (4)   35
   (5)   45

6. The regular price of bananas is $.55 per pound. This week they are on sale for 3 pounds for a dollar. Which equation shows how to find s, the amount in dollars, one would save by buying 3 pounds at the sale price rather than at the regular price?

   (1) $s = 3(.55)$
   (2) $s = 3(1 - .55)$
   (3) $s = 3(.55) - 3$
   (4) $s = 1 - 3(.55)$
   (5) $s = 3(.55) - 1$

Part One

Before going on further in this book, use the following exercise to maintain your skills. If you are having difficulty, this is a good time to go back and review.

PROBLEM 1 | Write an expression for each of the following. **Do not solve.**

A area: _____   **B** perimeter: _____   **C** volume: _____

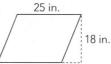
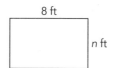
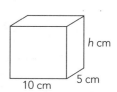

PROBLEM 2 | Write an expression for each of the following. Simplify if possible.

A the amount of money earned by each of 4 waitresses if $344 in tips is shared equally among them

B the cost of 2 dozen cupcakes if one cupcake costs $.43

C the seating capacity of an auditorium with 50 rows of *y* seats

D the number of balloons each child gets if a package of 30 balloons is shared evenly among 4 girls and 6 boys

PROBLEM 3 | Estimate an answer to the following.

A $2{,}073 \div 500$ **B** 8×189 **C** $99(12)$ **D** $187 \div 90$ **E** $403 \div 7$

PROBLEM 4 | What is the area of the floor shaded in the diagram at the right?

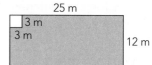

PROBLEM 5 | Continuing the pattern shown on the chart at the right, how much does Gallagher Landscaping charge for 6 cubic feet of bark mulch?

GALLAGHER MULCH PRICES

1 cu ft	$22.50
2 cu ft	$45.00
3 cu ft	$67.50
4 cu ft	$90.00

PROBLEM 6 | Use the rules of order of operations to simplify each expression.

A $20 - 14 \div 2$ **D** $(12 + 20) \div 4 + 102$

B $\dfrac{122 - 50}{-8}$ **E** $\dfrac{(-10) + 2 + 7 + (-2) + 3}{5}$

C $9(20 - 9)$ **F** $(5)(-4) + (5)(5)$

Part Two

1. A Jumboburger contains 1,119 grams of sodium. Large french fries contain 689 grams of sodium. Which of the following expressions gives the grams of sodium in 4 Jumboburgers and 4 large fries?

(1) $1,119 + 689 + 4 + 4$

(2) $\dfrac{1,119 + 689}{4}$

(3) $4(1,119 + 689)$

(4) $\dfrac{4}{1,119 + 689}$

(5) $\dfrac{1,119 - 689}{4}$

Problems 2 and 3 refer to the following graph and information.

For copies made by the attendants, Quikprint charges a $3.00 set-up fee and $.10 per page.

FULL SERVICE COPY PRICES

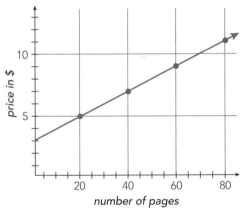

2. How many pages could be copied for $10?

(1) 60
(2) 65
(3) 70
(4) 75
(5) 100

3. How much, in dollars, would Mary Lou pay to have an 85-page document copied? (Disregard any tax.)

(1) $ 8.50
(2) $10.00
(3) $11.50
(4) $12.00
(5) $12.50

4. How many level cubic feet of sand can be poured into the sandbox shown below?

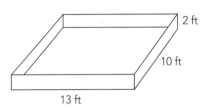

Mark your answer in the circles in the grid below.

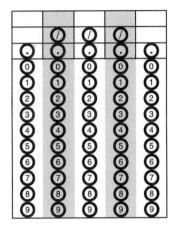

Problems 5 and 6 refer to the following sketch of a patio.

5. What is the least number of feet of edging needed to go around the shaded area?

(1) 25
(2) 50
(3) 75
(4) 150
(5) Not enough information is given.

6. How many square feet of area are shaded in the sketch?

(1) 25
(2) 50
(3) 75
(4) 150
(5) Not enough information is given.

Powers and Roots

1. 8 times itself = ?

2. 36 = ? times itself

3. 4 times itself = ?

4. 100 = ? times itself

5. ? = 12 times itself

The numbers that result from multiplying a number by itself are called **perfect squares**. In this lesson, you will learn how to write these numbers and use them to solve problems.

Exponents

Remember that multiplication is a short way to do repeated addition.

Instead of $7 + 7 + 7 + 7 + 7$ ⟶ write 7×5.

five addends that are the same

There is also a shorthand way to write repeated multiplications.

Instead of $2 \cdot 2 \cdot 2 \cdot 2$ ⟶ write 2^4. 2 is the **base**, and 4 is the **exponent**. Read "2 to the fourth power."

four factors that are the same

2^4 does *not* mean 2 times 4. It means $2 \times 2 \times 2 \times 2$.

EXAMPLE

4^3

4 is the base. It is the factor that is going to be multiplied.

3 is the exponent. It tells how many 4s to multiply.

4^3 means to use 4 three times as a factor.

You can enter $4 \times 4 \times 4 =$ into your calculator to find its value or you can use the $\boxed{x^y}$ (or $\boxed{y^x}$) key.

ENTER: $\boxed{4}$ $\boxed{x^y}$ $\boxed{3}$ $\boxed{=}$ [64.] The answer, 64, is displayed.

PROBLEM 1 | Complete this table.

Ⓐ 6×6 6^2 "6 to the second power" or "6 squared"   36

Ⓑ $5 \times 5 \times 5$ 5^3 "5 to the third power" or "5 cubed"   125

Ⓒ $7 \times 7 \times 7 \times 7$ 7^4 "7 to the fourth power"   2,401

Ⓓ _____ 8^2 _____   _____

Ⓔ _____   ____   "2 to the fifth power"   _____

Ⓕ 5×5 ____   _____   _____

Ⓖ _____   ____   "6 cubed"   _____

Ⓗ _____ 8^4 _____   _____

Ⓘ _____   ____   "4 to the eighth power"   _____

Ⓙ $m \times m$ ____   _____

Note: You can write numbers to the second and third powers in two different ways.

Squares

Only two of the powers have special ways to be named—the **squares** and the **cubes**. These powers have special names because they can be represented by real things in our lives.

Remember that you found the area of a rectangle by multiplying its length by its width.

Area = lw

When all sides of a rectangle are equal, it is a **square**. To find the area of a square, you multiply a side by itself.

Area = s^2

EXAMPLE A

Find the area of a square whose side is 11 meters long.

Area = s^2
$A = 11^2 = 11 \times 11$
$A = 121 \text{ m}^2$

> Remember that area is measured in square units.

EXAMPLE B

How many square inches are in a square foot?

A **square foot** is a square whose sides are each 1 foot (12 inches) long.

Area = s^2
$A = 12^2 = 12 \times 12$
$A = 144 \text{ sq in. (in a square foot)}$

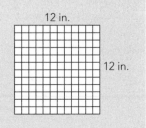

12 in.

12 in.

PROBLEM 2

Ⓐ Find the area of a square whose sides are each 15 millimeters long.

Ⓑ How many square *inches* are there in one square yard?
(**Hint:** 1 yd = 3 × 12 in. = ? in.)

Ⓒ The side of a square mirror measures 24 inches. What is its area?

Ⓓ There are 10 millimeters in 1 centimeter. How many square *millimeters* are there in one square centimeter?

Ⓔ A square section of grip tape for a skateboard measures 22 centimeters on each side. How many square centimeters are covered by its surface?

REASONING ACTIVITY

Finding Area

How many square yards of carpet are necessary to cover a floor that measures 15 feet by 12 feet?

Ⓐ Use grid paper to draw a rectangle that is 15 units long and 12 units wide. Think of each unit (the length of the side of a square in the grid) as being 1 foot long. How many square feet are in the area of the rectangle?

Ⓑ Using the fact that there are 3 feet in 1 yard, draw lines across the rectangle that divide its area into square yards. How many square yards are in the rectangle?

Ⓒ How many square feet are in 1 square yard?

Ⓓ Find the area, in square yards, of a floor that measures 9 feet by 18 feet.

Ⓔ Find the area, in square yards, of a piece of carpet that is 8 feet by 10 feet. Round to the nearest tenth.

Square Roots

In the last section, you performed the operation of squaring—multiplying a number by itself. In this section, you will find **square roots**—the opposite, or inverse, operation of squaring.

The inverse operation of squaring would have to *undo* what squaring *does*.

$\sqrt{}$ is a **radical sign**. The radical sign asks you to find the positive square root of the number under it.

EXAMPLE A

Because you know that: You also know that:
4 squared is 16 ⟶ the square root of 16 is 4
$4^2 = 16$ ⟶ $\sqrt{16} = 4$

The equations, $4^2 = 16$ and $\sqrt{16} = 4$, are **equivalent**.

EXAMPLE B

Evaluate $\sqrt{49}$ and $\sqrt{81}$.

$\sqrt{49}$ Think: "What number times itself equals 49?" $\sqrt{49} = 7$

$\sqrt{81}$ Think: "What number times itself equals 81?" $\sqrt{81} = 9$

A helpful way to think of finding the square root of a number is to think of "unsquaring" it.

EXAMPLE C

What is the length of the side of a square whose area is 64 square inches?

$$\text{Area} = s^2$$
$$64 = s^2$$
$$\sqrt{64} = s \quad \text{Write the equivalent equation.}$$
$$8 \text{ in.} = s$$

? 64 sq in.

PROBLEM 3

Evaluate without a calculator.

A $\sqrt{16}$ **B** $\sqrt{25}$ **C** $\sqrt{100}$ **D** $\sqrt{144}$

PROBLEM 4

Write equivalent equations.

A $20^2 = 400$ **B** $\sqrt{625} = 25$ **C** $15^2 = 225$ **D** $\sqrt{121} = 11$

PROBLEM 5

Find the length of the side of a square whose area is 81 square feet.

Order of Operations

Order When Evaluating Expressions

Where do these new operations fit into the order of operations? They are at a higher level than multiplication, so they must be completed before you multiply or divide. The entire set of rules for order of operations is as follows:

A memorizing trick:

Please
Excuse
My **D**ear
Aunt **S**ally

ORDER OF OPERATIONS	1. Complete the operations within the **p**arentheses.
	2. Do the operations with **e**xponents and radicals.
	3. Complete the **m**ultiplications and **d**ivisions from left to right. Complete the **a**dditions and **s**ubtractions from left to right.

EXAMPLE A

$4(8) - 5^2$	No operations within parentheses, so square the five first, then multiply, and finally subtract.
$4(8) - 25$	
$32 - 25$	
7	

EXAMPLE B

$200 - 10(4)^2$	The exponent applies only to the 4. Square the 4 first, then multiply that product by 10, and finally subtract.
$200 - 10(16)$	
$200 - 160$	
40	

When there is an operation within parentheses, it must be done first.

$$(3 + 4)^2 = 7^2 = 49 \qquad\qquad (3 \times 4)^2 = (12)^2 = 144$$

PROBLEM 6

Evaluate without a calculator.

(A)	$5 + 3^2$	$(5 + 3)^2$	$5 + 3(2)$
(B)	$2(3)^2$	$(2 \times 3)^2$	$2 \times 3(2)$
(C)	$5(6) + 4^2$	$5^2 - \sqrt{4}$	$\sqrt{16} + \sqrt{4}$
(D)	$4(3) + 9^2$	$4(3 + 9)^2$	$4(3) + \sqrt{9}$

PROBLEM 7

Complete the table below.

x	5	2	0	–2	–5
$3x^2$	$3(5)(5) = 75$				

Order When Solving Equations

Think of the order in which you do an everyday two-step task. First you put on your socks and then you put on your shoes. When it is time to *undo* those steps, you do them in the opposite order—first you remove the shoes and then the socks.

The same thing is true in algebra. While the order of operations states that you should do multiplication and division before addition and subtraction when evaluating an expression, you should do them in the *reverse* order when you are solving an equation and *undoing* the operations that are shown. First, undo the addition and subtraction and then the multiplication and division.

EXAMPLE

Solve for *x*.

$6x + 7 = 91$	You can see that both multiplication and addition will need to be *undone* before *x* is alone on its side of the equation.
$6x + 7 - 7 = 91 - 7$	Undo the addition first by subtracting 7 from both sides.
$\dfrac{6x}{6} = \dfrac{84}{6}$ $x = 14$	Then undo the multiplication that is shown by dividing both sides by 6.
$6(14) + 7 = 91$	Check your solution by substituting it back into the original equation.

PROBLEM 8 | Solve the following equations, showing that you are using the Addition and Multiplication Properties of Equality.

Ⓐ $9x + 10 = 145$ Ⓓ $87 = 5n - 3$

Ⓑ $14y - 6 = 50$ Ⓔ $10b - 35 = -65$

Ⓒ $112 = 11n + 13$ Ⓕ $10b + 35 = -65$

Pythagorean Theorem

A right triangle has one right angle (90°). The lengths of the sides of any right triangle have a relationship that was first proven to be true by the Greek mathematician Pythagoras.

PYTHAGOREAN THEOREM	The square of the hypotenuse (longest side—opposite the right angle) of a right triangle is equal to the sum of the squares of the other two sides.

FORMULA | $a^2 + b^2 = c^2$

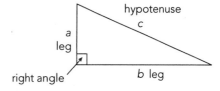

The Pythagorean theorem works both ways. If you have a right triangle, then you know that $a^2 + b^2 = c^2$. Conversely, if $a^2 + b^2 = c^2$ for the sides of some triangle, then you know that you have a right triangle.

Certain groups of whole numbers fit into this relationship nicely.

For example, $3^2 + 4^2 = 5^2$
$$9 + 16 = 25$$

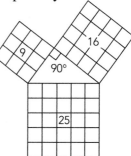

Because they make the formula true, 3, 4, and 5 are called a **Pythagorean triple**.

To decide whether three whole numbers can be sides of a right triangle, substitute them in the Pythagorean theorem: $a^2 + b^2 = c^2$.

EXAMPLE A   **EXAMPLE B**

Can the sets of three numbers below be the lengths of sides of a right triangle?

2 in., 3 in., and 4 in.

$2^2 + 3^2 \stackrel{?}{=} 4^2$
$4 + 9 \stackrel{?}{=} 16$

No, 13 *does not* equal 16, so 2, 3, and 4 are not sides of a right triangle.

30 m, 40 m, and 50 m

$30^2 + 40^2 \stackrel{?}{=} 50^2$
$900 + 1,600 \stackrel{?}{=} 2,500$

Yes, 2,500 = 2,500, so 30, 40, and 50 are sides of a right triangle.

PROBLEM 9 | Decide whether or not these sets of whole numbers can be sides of a right triangle. You may use your calculator.

Ⓐ 4, 5, and 6   Ⓓ 18, 24, and 30   Ⓖ 5, 12, and 13

Ⓑ 8, 15, and 17   Ⓔ 6, 11, and 12   Ⓗ 7, 24, and 25

Ⓒ 9, 12, and 15   Ⓕ 12, 16, and 20   Ⓘ 15, 20, and 25

The Pythagorean theorem allows you to find the length of the third side of a right triangle when you know the lengths of the other two sides. You can find the third side without actually measuring it.

EXAMPLE

Find the length of side a.

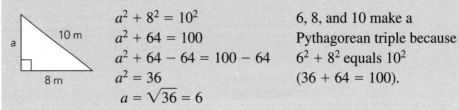

$$a^2 + 8^2 = 10^2$$
$$a^2 + 64 = 100$$
$$a^2 + 64 - 64 = 100 - 64$$
$$a^2 = 36$$
$$a = \sqrt{36} = 6$$

6, 8, and 10 make a Pythagorean triple because $6^2 + 8^2$ equals 10^2 ($36 + 64 = 100$).

On the GED Test, you may have to find the missing side of a right triangle.

EXAMPLES

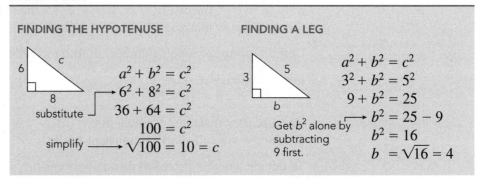

FINDING THE HYPOTENUSE

$$a^2 + b^2 = c^2$$
substitute → $6^2 + 8^2 = c^2$
$$36 + 64 = c^2$$
$$100 = c^2$$
simplify → $\sqrt{100} = 10 = c$

FINDING A LEG

$$a^2 + b^2 = c^2$$
$$3^2 + b^2 = 5^2$$
$$9 + b^2 = 25$$
Get b^2 alone by subtracting 9 first. → $b^2 = 25 - 9$
$$b^2 = 16$$
$$b = \sqrt{16} = 4$$

Use the Pythagorean theorem to solve problems 10 and 11.
Remember: This theorem applies only to right triangles.

PROBLEM 10 | Sondra drives her 5-year-old son to school, following the route shown at the right. How many miles is it from the school to her work?

(1)   5 mi
(2)   9 mi
(3) 144 mi
(4) 169 mi
(5) 313 mi

PROBLEM 11 | Which of the following expressions can be used to find the length of side *b*?

(1) $10^2 + 30^2 = b^2$
(2) $30^2 - 10^2 = b^2$
(3) $10^2 - b^2 = 30^2$
(4) $30^2 + b^2 = 10^2$
(5) $\sqrt{10} + \sqrt{30} = b$

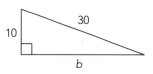

Estimating and Calculating Square Roots

To find the square root of a number that is not a perfect square, you can estimate the answer, or you can use your calculator to give you a more accurate answer.

To be a good estimator, you must know the squares of some key numbers.

Use the table below to estimate square roots. Notice one important feature on this table: as the numbers increase, so do their squares.

TABLE OF SQUARES

number	square
1	1
2	4
3	9
4	16
5	25
6	36
7	49
8	64
9	81
10	100
11	121
12	144
13	169
14	196
15	225
20	400
25	625
30	900
40	1,600
50	2,500
100	10,000

Example B: $\sqrt{55}$

Example A: $\sqrt{196}$

EXAMPLE A

Find the square root of 196.

• Move down the "square" column until you find 196.

• Look across to the left to find the 14.

EXAMPLE B

Estimate the square root of 55.

• Move down the "square" column until you come to the two numbers that 55 is between (49 and 64).

$\sqrt{55}$ is between $\sqrt{49}$ and $\sqrt{64}$ (7 and 8).

• Estimated square root: between 7 and 8

• Closer estimated square root: 7.5

Use the table for as long as you need it, but soon you will find that you can do this whole process mentally.

PROBLEM 12 | Use the table to estimate the answers.

Ⓐ The value of $\sqrt{50}$ is approximately _____.

Ⓑ The value of $\sqrt{75}$ is between _____ and _____.

Ⓒ The value of $\sqrt{500}$ is between _____ and _____.

Ⓓ The value of $\sqrt{1,000}$ is between _____ and _____.
It is closer to _____.

Ⓔ The value of $\sqrt{2,000}$ is between _____ and _____.
A good estimate is _____.

Ⓕ The value of $\sqrt{30}$ is between _____ and _____.
A good estimate is _____.

Ⓖ The value of $\sqrt{125}$ is between _____ and _____.
It is closer to _____.

Ⓗ The value of $\sqrt{70}$ is between _____ and _____.
A good estimate is _____.

Using the x^2 and $\sqrt{}$ Key

Use the x^2 key on your calculator to find the square of a number.

EXAMPLE

Find 23^2.

Press: **2** **3** x^2 The answer appears immediately: $\boxed{529.}$.

If the $\sqrt{}$ sign is written directly on your calculator instead of on a working key, press the **2nd** or [SHIFT] key first and then press the working key just under the $\sqrt{}$ sign.

EXAMPLE

Use the [$\sqrt{}$] function to find $\sqrt{55}$.

Press: **5** **5**, then [SHIFT] or **2nd**, then [$\sqrt{}$]

The display reads: $\boxed{7.416198487}$.

Note: Do not hold down the [SHIFT] or **2nd** key while you press the next key.

EXAMPLE

Estimate and then use the [$\sqrt{}$] key to find $\sqrt{80}$.

Estimate: 80 is between 64 and 81, so $\sqrt{80}$ is between 8 and 9.
$\sqrt{80}$ is very close to 9.

Press: **8** **0** [SHIFT], or **2nd**, [$\sqrt{}$] The display reads: $\boxed{8.94427191}$.

PROBLEM 13 | Watch the display on your scientific calculator while you enter the expression $3(2)^2 =$. (Use the times key instead of the parentheses and be sure to enter the equals sign to get the final answer.) Explain the order of operations that the calculator is using. Compare it to what you learned on p. 118.

EXAMPLE

The area of a square piece of carpet is 90 square feet. What is the approximate length of each side?	$90 = s^2$ $s = \sqrt{90}$ $s \approx$ halfway between 9 and 10 (estimate) $s = 9.49$ (calculator answer rounded to the nearest hundredth)

EXAMPLE

A side of a square lawn area in the municipal park measures 12 yards. How many *square feet* of lawn are there in the park?	Area $= s^2$ $A = (3 \cdot 12)^2 = 36^2$ $A = 1{,}296$ sq ft

PROBLEM 14 | Approximately how long is the side (s) of the square painting whose area is 500 square centimeters?

s

Area = 500 cm^2

PROBLEM 15 | A wire is attached to the top of a 15-foot pole and anchored at a spot 5 feet away from the base of the pole. Approximately how long must the wire be if the pole is perpendicular to the ground?

15 ft   ?

5 ft

PROBLEM 16 | The city created 5 "pocket parks" in the central area. If each of the small parks is a square with sides of 55 yards, how many *square feet* of parkland was added to the city?

CHECK YOUR UNDERSTANDING

You may use your calculator on any problem except where noted by this symbol:

1. 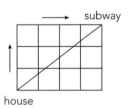 Evaluate.

   A 15^2
   B 4^3
   C $\sqrt{36}$
   D $\sqrt{121}$
   E $3 + \sqrt{64}$
   F $\frac{1,700}{10^2}$
   G $(4 \cdot 3)^2$
   H $8(5) + 6^2$
   I $20^2 - 10^2$
   J $(20 - 10)^2$
   K $11(10 - 8)^2$
   L $\frac{(8 + 24)}{4^2}$

2. Write an equivalent equation using exponents.

   EXAMPLE $\sqrt{100} = 10$; $10^2 = 100$
   A $\sqrt{81} = 9$
   B $\sqrt{361} = 19$
   C $\sqrt{2,025} = 45$

3. Which of the following groups of numbers can be the lengths of sides of a right triangle? (Are they Pythagorean triples?)

   A 3, 5, and 8
   B 600, 800, and 1,000
   C 16, 30, and 34
   D 10, 24, and 26

4. Estimate the value of each expression. Use your calculator to check your estimates. (You may use the table on page 121 if necessary.)

   A $\sqrt{10}$
   B $\sqrt{40}$
   C $\sqrt{150}$

5. Evaluate the expression $5x^2$ when

   A $x = 10$
   B $x = 3$
   C $x = 0$
   D $x = -3$
   E $x = -10$

6. The carton containing a tent says that the area of the tent's square floor is 196 square feet. How long is each side of the tent floor?

7. Solve the following equations using the Multiplication and Addition Properties of Equality.

   A $3n - 7 = 59$
   B $15x - 10 = -100$

8. To get from her house to the subway station, Martha walks 3 blocks north and 4 blocks east. If she were able to "cut across" the blocks, how far would she have to walk?

Problems 9 and 10 refer to the following information.

The Body Mass Index (BMI) is a number that reflects the relationship between one's height and weight. The formula for finding an adult's BMI is

$\text{BMI} = \frac{703w}{h^2}$, where w is weight in pounds and h is height in inches.

The following weight zones have been described for adults.

BMI	weight zone
below 18.5	underweight
18.5 – 24.9	healthy weight
25 – 29.9	moderately overweight
over 30	obese

9. Use the BMI formula and the weight zone chart to determine the weight zone of a person who weighs 220 pounds and is 70 inches tall.

10. What is the BMI, to the nearest tenth, of a 65-inch tall woman who weighs 135 pounds?

TEST-TAKING PRACTICE

You may use your calculator on any problem except where noted by this symbol:

1. A ramp leads to a loading dock that is 4 feet above the ground. The ramp begins at 8 feet away from the end of the dock. Approximately how long is the ramp?

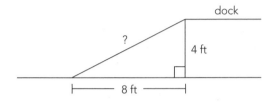

(1) between 3 ft and 4 ft
(2) between 4 ft and 5 ft
(3) between 5 ft and 7 ft
(4) between 7 ft and 8 ft
(5) between 8 ft and 9 ft

2. 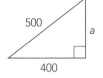 If $4x - 2 = 30$, what is the value of x?

(1) 8.0
(2) 7.5
(3) 7.0
(4) 6.5
(5) 6.0

3. Roy and Elena found the carpet they liked priced at about $20 per *square yard*. This price includes padding and installation. Without adding a waste allowance, which of the following is a good estimate of the cost of carpeting their room, which measures 15 feet by 18 feet?

(1) $ 270
(2) $ 600
(3) $1,200
(4) $1,800
(5) $5,400

4. Which of the following equations shows how to find the length of a?

(1) $500 - 400 = a$
(2) $500^2 - 400^2 = a^2$
(3) $500 + 400 = a$
(4) $500^2 + 400^2 = a^2$
(5) $a^2 + 500^2 = 400^2$

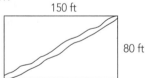

5. When auto accidents are investigated, authorities can use the formula

$$r = 2\sqrt{5L}$$

to estimate the speed, r, in miles per hour, of a car that has left a skid mark L feet long. What was the approximate speed, in miles per hour, of a car that left skid marks measuring 210 feet?

(1) 45
(2) 50
(3) 55
(4) 60
(5) 65

6. The diagram below shows where pedestrians have worn away the grass on a path that cuts through the park. How long, in feet, is the actual path?

150 ft

80 ft

Mark your answer in the circles in the grid.

1. $\sqrt{100} = ?$

2. $10^2 = \sqrt{?}$

3. $\sqrt{36} = ?$

4. $\sqrt{49} = ?$

5. $\sqrt{42} \approx ?$

Radius and Diameter

You can find the shape of a circle in many things you see each day.

Circles involve a vocabulary all their own. You will need to be able to use these terms for the GED Test:

radius   diameter   circumference   pi (π)

The size of a circle is determined by its **radius** (*r*)—the distance from the center to the edge of the circle.

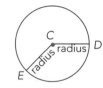

Every radius of a circle has the same length. $CD = CE$

The length of a circle's **diameter** (*d*) is double the length of its radius. The diameter is a line that extends from one side of a circle to the other and passes through the center.

Note: $r = \frac{1}{2}d$ and $d = 2r$

The length of a diameter is the greatest distance you can measure across a circle.

PROBLEM 1 | What is the length of the diameter of each circle below?

Ⓐ   Ⓑ   Ⓒ   Ⓓ

PROBLEM 2 | What is the length of the radius of each circle below?

Ⓐ   Ⓑ   Ⓒ   Ⓓ

Circumference and Pi (π)

Circumference can be thought of as the perimeter of a circle. It answers the question, "How long would the circle be if it were broken and laid straight out?" Circumference measures length, so it is a one-dimensional measure.

There is a special relationship between the diameter and the circumference of a circle.

The distance around the circle is a little more than 3 times the diameter, no matter what the size of the circle is.

"A little more than 3" is an estimate of π (pronounced "pie") which represents the ratio of $\frac{C}{d}$ in every perfect circle. The exact value of π cannot be written with decimals or fractions.

From the fact that $\frac{C}{d} = \pi$, we can derive the formula for the circumference of a circle.

> The Greek letter π represents a **constant** number. Unlike a variable, the value of a constant does not change.

FORMULA | $C = \pi d$

In most computations, the value of π is estimated as 3.14. It is a good idea to estimate the circumference first, simply by using "a little more than 3." Then find a more precise answer (if needed) using 3.14.

EXAMPLE

Find the circumference of this circle.

An estimate would be "a little more than 12."

$C = \pi d$ (substitute 3.14 for π and 4 for d)
$C \approx 3.14(4)$
$C \approx 12.56$ cm

PROBLEM 3

Pi Day is celebrated every year on March 14 (3.14).

First *estimate* the length of the circumference of each of these circles. Then find a more precise answer using π = 3.14. (You may use your calculator.)

Ⓐ 12 m

Ⓑ 5 in.

Ⓒ 4.5 ft

Ⓓ 10 in.

PROBLEM 4

Most scientific calculators have a special key for π which provides an estimate of its value that is even more accurate than 3.14. Repeat the exercises in problem 3 using the π key.

EXAMPLE In problem 3Ⓐ, 1 2 × π = 37.69911184

PROBLEM 5

The diameter of a bicycle tire is 2.25 feet. How far will the bicycle travel when the wheel goes around one time?

Ⓐ Find the answer three ways: First, estimate by using 3 for π, then use 3.14 for π, and finally use the π key on your calculator.

Ⓑ If you needed the answer to be correct to the nearest foot, which of the above three ways would be the easiest to find, yet be accurate enough?

CALCULATOR EXPLORATION

Approximating π

Measure the diameter and circumference of some common circular objects as accurately as you can. It will be easier if you use a tape measure marked in metric units (centimeters and millimeters).

Suggestion: To measure the circumference, mark a starting and ending point on the edge, and roll the object along the tape carefully, avoiding any slipping.

Complete the table with your results.

object	circumference (C)	diameter (d)	$\frac{C}{d}$
coin (quarter)			
jar lid			
soup can			
dinner plate			
trash can lid			

Ⓐ Each entry in the $\frac{C}{d}$ column should approximate what number?

Ⓑ Which one is the most accurate approximation of π?

Ⓒ Why are the others not as accurate?

Using Equivalent Equations

In some situations, you can measure the circumference, but it is difficult to measure the diameter. Using the idea of equivalent equations, you can rearrange the circumference formula so that you can find the diameter if you know the circumference.

FORMULA $\quad C = \pi d$ can be written as $d = \frac{C}{\pi}$

EXAMPLE

Since the diameter is twice as long as the radius, $(d = 2r)$, the formula for the circumference of a circle, $(C = \pi d)$, can also be written as $C = 2\pi r$.

A giant redwood tree is measured as 12 meters around the base of the trunk. Approximately how thick is the tree at this point? (**OR:** What is the length of the diameter?)

First, estimate. Since you are dividing by a little more than 3, the answer will be a little less than 4.

$$d \approx \frac{12}{3} \approx 4$$

Then calculate. Use either 3.14 or the $\boxed{\pi}$ key on your calculator.

$$d \approx \frac{12}{3.14}$$
$$d \approx 3.82$$

PROBLEM 6 | **Ⓐ** If the circumference of a circle is 10 meters, what is the diameter? (Use all three of the estimations for π and compare. Round to the nearest tenth of a meter.)

Ⓑ What is the radius?

PROBLEM 7 | The circular bottom of a lampshade has a diameter of 9.5 inches. To the nearest inch, how much trim is needed to go around the bottom of the lampshade?

Ⓐ Estimate the answer mentally.

Ⓑ Calculate the answer and round to the nearest inch.

Ⓒ What length of trim would you probably purchase?

PROBLEM 8 | A measurement around a football player's neck is 20 inches. Assuming his neck is circular, what is its approximate diameter?

PROBLEM 9 | The drawing at the right was included in a jewelry catalog.

Ⓐ Using a ruler, measure the length, in centimeters, of the circumference of a finger with ring size 8.

Ⓑ Approximately what would be the diameter of a size 8 finger in centimeters?

HOW TO MEASURE YOUR RING SIZE
Cut out measuring strip along the dotted line. Wrap it around the desired ring finger. The number on which the arrow rests is your proper ring size.

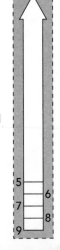

Area

In the last lesson, you learned to square numbers. To find the area of a circle, you need to square the radius. The formula for the area of a circle is found on the formulas page (page 280).

FORMULA | Area = π × radius²

Area is measured in square units. Square units are found by multiplying one *dimension* by another. These facts give you an idea why the radius must be multiplied by itself to find the area. But it is more difficult to "see" the sense of this formula than it was to "see" the area of a rectangle or square.

Follow the sequence of sketches to find out how the area formula makes sense.

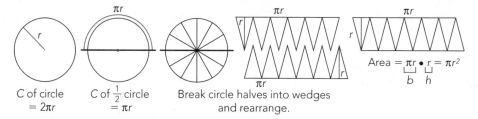

C of circle = 2πr   C of ½ circle = πr   Break circle halves into wedges and rearrange.   Area = πr • r = πr²

When using the area formula, remember that the order of operations says to square the radius before you multiply by π.

EXAMPLE

Find the area of a circle whose radius is 20 meters long.

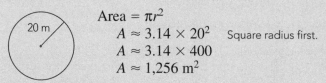

$$\text{Area} = \pi r^2$$
$$A \approx 3.14 \times 20^2 \quad \text{Square radius first.}$$
$$A \approx 3.14 \times 400$$
$$A \approx 1{,}256 \text{ m}^2$$

PROBLEM 10 | Find the areas of the circles below. Use the your calculator if necessary.

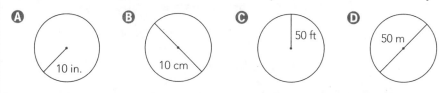

Ⓐ 10 in.   Ⓑ 10 cm   Ⓒ 50 ft   Ⓓ 50 m

PROBLEM 11 | Use the Multiplication Property of Equality to find approximately how long the radius would be of a circle that covers 50 square inches.

PROBLEM 12 | The circle in the diagram is enclosed by a square whose sides measure 16 inches. Find the approximate circumference and the area of the circle.

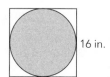

16 in.

Some irregular figures are made from joining parts of a circle to other figures.

EXAMPLE

A window has a half-circle of glass above the usual rectangular window. What is the total area of the window at the left?

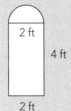

Total = rectangle + half-circle

Total area $= lw + \frac{1}{2}\pi r^2$

Area $\approx 2 \times 4 + \frac{1}{2} \times 3.14 \times 1^2$

Area $\approx 8 + 1.57 = 9.57$ sq ft

The diameter of the half-circle is 2 ft, so its radius is 1 ft.

PROBLEM 13 A reflecting pool has the shape shown at the right. How many feet of sealing tape are necessary to seal the edge of this pool?

PROBLEM 14 The gardener has divided a circular flowerbed into three equal plots as shown. Which expression below indicates how many square meters are to be planted with petunias?

(1) $3 \times \pi \times 4 \times 4$

(2) $3 \times \pi \times 4 \times 2$

(3) $3 \times \pi \times 4$

(4) $\dfrac{\pi \times 4 \times 4}{3}$

(5) $\dfrac{\pi \times 4 \times 2}{3}$

REASONING ACTIVITY

Which Shape Encloses the Greatest Area?

Using 100 feet of flexible edging material to surround a flower garden, which shape—a rectangle, square, or circle—will give you the most area?

shape	perimeter	dimensions	area formula	area
rectangle	100 ft	May vary.		
square	100 ft			
circle	100 ft			

Discuss situations where this principle, using the least amount of material to enclose the greatest area, may have been the reason for choosing the shape for familiar objects.

CHECK YOUR UNDERSTANDING

You may use your calculator on any problem except where noted by this symbol:

1. Estimate mentally. Then use the π key on your calculator to find the circumference (to the nearest hundredth) of a circle whose

   Ⓐ diameter is 9.8 cm
   Ⓑ diameter is 47 ft
   Ⓒ radius is 3.1 m
   Ⓓ radius is 47 ft

2. Consider the equator of the earth to be a large circle. It is approximately 25,000 miles around the earth at the equator. Use this information to estimate the diameter of the earth at the equator.

3. What is the area of the circular region irrigated by a sprinkler that covers a radius of 3 meters?

4. A college radio station upgraded its transmitter from one that reached listeners in a 10-mile radius to one that reaches those in a radius of 20 miles. While they doubled the radius of transmission, did they also double the number of square miles in the listening area? Explain your answer.

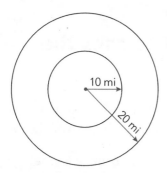

5. Sara baked a small cake for a celebration of Pi Day in an 8-inch square-baking pan. To honor the occasion, she decided that the cake should be in the shape of a circle. Sara has two options: (1) cut the cake as shown in Figure 1, later cutting it into pieces for the 16 guests, or (2) cut the cake into 16 small circles as shown in Figure 2.

FIGURE 1   **FIGURE 2**

Which option would leave the least amount of wasted cake? Use your calculations to explain your answer.

6. A circle of grass must have an area of at least 75 square feet. What is the approximate radius of such a circle?

7. The circular garden at the right is divided into equal plots by 6 spokes, each of which is 8 feet long.

   Ⓐ To the nearest tenth, what is the size of each small plot?
   Ⓑ Find the approximate distance around this garden.

8. A large pizza has a diameter of 16 inches, while a medium pizza has a diameter of 12 inches. About how many more square inches of pizza do you get with the large pizza?

TEST-TAKING PRACTICE

You may use your calculator on any problem except where noted by this symbol:

Problems 1 and 2 refer to the diagram below.

Point C is at the center of the circle.

1. Which of the following lines is a diameter of the circle?

   (1) *AC*
   (2) *AD*
   (3) *BC*
   (4) *BD*
   (5) *CD*

2. If the length of *AC* is 20 centimeters, which expression, in square centimeters, shows the area of the circle?

   (1) $20\pi^2$
   (2) $40\pi^2$
   (3) 40π
   (4) $(20)(20)\pi$
   (5) $(40)(40)\pi$

3. The minute hand on the clock below is 5 inches long. Through how many inches does its tip pass in one hour?

   (1) 15.7
   (2) 31.4
   (3) 78.5
   (4) 157.0
   (5) 314.0

4. The circle below is inscribed in the square whose side is 18 inches. Approximately how much larger, in square inches, is the square than the circle?

   (1) 27
   (2) 70
   (3) 140
   (4) 254
   (5) 324

   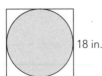
   18 in.

Problems 5 and 6 refer to the following diagram.

5. A pond, circular in shape, is ringed closely by a concrete pathway. When Javier walked the pathway, he counted it to be 310 paces long. If each pace is about 2.5 feet long, what is the approximate circumference of the pond?

   Mark your answer in the circles in the grid.

6. About how many of Javier's paces would equal the distance across the pond through its center?

   (1) 50
   (2) 100
   (3) 200
   (4) 900
   (5) Not enough information is given.

7. Which expression shows the approximate number of square feet in a circular pool cover that measures 15 feet in diameter?

   (1) (3.14)(15)(15)
   (2) (3.14)(15)(2)
   (3) (3.14)(15)
   (4) (3.14)(7.5)(7.5)
   (5) (3.14)(7.5)(2)

LESSON 13 — More Powers – Powers of Ten

MENTAL MATH

1. 35 × 10

2. 6 × 100

3. 925 × 10

4. 42 × 1,000

5. 691 × 1,000

Powers of 10 and Place Value

Multiplying by 10, 100, and 1,000 in the problems above involved simply tacking on zeros. It is so easy because 10, 100, and 1,000 are powers of 10 and because our number system is based on 10. First study the powers of 10.

exponent	expanded	long way	word name
10^0	—	1	one
10^1	—	10	ten
10^2	10×10	100	one hundred
10^3	$10 \times 10 \times 10$	1,000	one thousand
10^4	$10 \times 10 \times 10 \times 10$	10,000	ten thousand
10^5	$10 \times 10 \times 10 \times 10 \times 10$	100,000	one hundred thousand
10^6	$10 \times 10 \times 10 \times 10 \times 10 \times 10$	1,000,000	one million
10^9	—	1,000,000,000	one billion
10^{12}	—	1,000,000,000,000	one trillion
10^{15}	—	1,000,000,000,000,000	one quadrillion

Notice that the place before the decimal point, the ones place, is labeled 10^0: $10^0 = 1$.

PROBLEM 1

Compare the exponential notation of a power of 10 and the long way of writing it. Use the table to complete the following:

EXPONENTIAL NOTATION (10^n)

Ⓐ 10^3

Ⓑ _____

Ⓒ 10^6

Ⓓ _____

Ⓔ What pattern do you see?

LONG WAY (HOW MANY ZEROS?)

1,000 (3)

10 (1)

_____ ( )

1,000,000,000 (9)

134

Raising 10 to powers is easy to do because our number system is based on 10—it is a **decimal system**. The chart below shows the place-value names, the same word names as the powers of 10 seen in the previous chart. Use this chart as a guide for the next section.

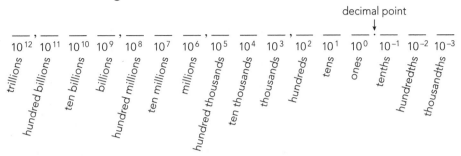

The places to the right of the decimal point are **decimal fractions**. The **negative exponents** tell you to divide by that number.

EXAMPLES $10^{-1} = \dfrac{1}{10} = 0.1$ $10^{-2} = \dfrac{1}{10^2} = \dfrac{1}{100} = 0.01$

$10^{-3} = \dfrac{1}{10^3} = \dfrac{1}{1,000} = 0.001$

On the place value chart, the place value names do *not* center around the decimal point. They center around the *ones place*. The names to the left of the ones place match up with the names to the right.

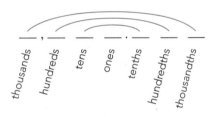

Writing a number in expanded notation, digit by digit, often helps when estimating or doing mental math. Expanded notation shows the place value of each digit, either in long form or using exponents.

EXAMPLES

number	long form	exponential form
329	3(100) + 2(10) + 9(1)	$3(10)^2 + 2(10)^1 + 9(10)^0$
30.285	3(10) + 2(0.1) + 8(0.01) + 5(0.001)	$3(10)^1 + 2(10)^{-1} +$ $8(10)^{-2} + 5(10)^{-3}$
30,504,000	3(10,000,000) + 5(100,000) + 4(1,000)	$3(10)^7 + 5(10)^5 + 4(10)^3$

The pattern you saw between the exponent and the number of zeros in the powers of 10 is the basis for the next observation.

PROBLEM 2 | Complete each number with exponents.

NUMBER	OBSERVATION	PLACE VALUE OF THE 5
Ⓐ 5,040.2	3 places between the 5 and the decimal point	10—
Ⓑ 57,300,000.9	7 places between the 5 and the decimal point	10—
Ⓒ 58,333.002	____ places between the 5 and the decimal point	10—

PROBLEM 3 | Expand each of the following numbers by place value. Use exponential notation.

A 380   **B** 5,000.02   **C** 60,400   **D** 29,000,000   **E** 100.004

PROBLEM 4 | Write each of the following numbers as a digit times a power of 10.

EXAMPLES $4{,}000{,}000 = 4(10)^6$ $600{,}000{,}000 = 6(10)^8$ $0.06 = 6(10)^{-2}$

A 50   **C** 80,000   **E** 0.09   **G** 30,000   **I** 600,000,000

B 0.5   **D** 800   **F** 9,000   **H** 0.006   **J** 30,000,000

Multiplying and Dividing a Number by a Power of 10

You have already seen how to carry trailing zeros along when you multiply by powers of 10.

Adding on trailing zeros can also be thought of as moving the decimal point to the right.

EXAMPLES

$49 \times 100 = 4{,}900$

$49.00 \times 100 = 4{,}900.$

You can multiply by 100 (10^2) by moving the decimal point 2 places *to the right*. (Add 0s when necessary.)

$32.5 \times 1{,}000 = 32{,}500$

$32.500 \times 1{,}000 = 32{,}500.$

You can multiply by 1,000 (10^3) by moving the decimal point 3 places *to the right*. (Add 0s when necessary.)

When you divide by powers of 10, you know to cancel the common zeros.

Instead of canceling common zeros, think of moving the decimal point—this time to the left.

EXAMPLES

$\dfrac{6{,}000}{100} = 60$

$6{,}000 \div 100 = 60.00$

To divide by 100 (10^2), move the decimal point 2 places *to the left*.

$\dfrac{40{,}000}{10{,}000} = 4$

$40{,}000 \div 10{,}000 = 4.0000$

To divide by 10,000 (10^4), move the decimal point 4 places *to the left*.

How can you remember which direction to move the decimal point? Rather than trying to remember rules about right and left, try to make sense of what you are doing.

- Remember that **multiplying** a positive number by a number greater than 1 *increases* the original number. So does moving the decimal point to the **right**.

- **Dividing** a positive number by a number greater than 1 *decreases* the original number. So does moving the decimal point to the **left**.

PROBLEM 5 | Complete the table using the technique of moving the decimal point to multiply and divide.

	NUMBER	× 10	÷ 1,000	× 1,000
EXAMPLES	308.5	3,085	0.3085	308,500
	5.004	50.04	0.005004	5,004
Ⓐ	730.2	_____	_____	_____
Ⓑ	2.105	_____	_____	_____
Ⓒ	45	_____	_____	_____
Ⓓ	0.08	_____	_____	_____

Scientific Notation

Scientific notation is a method used to write large numbers as well as small numbers in a shorthand way.

For example, 29,600,000 is written as 2.96×10^7 and 0.00025 is written as 2.5×10^{-4}.

Focus on two parts of the notation: $a \times 10^{b}$

① The value of the number in front is at least 1, but less than 10. These numbers will have just one digit to the left of the decimal point.

② The exponent of 10 can be either a positive number (for large values) or a negative number (for small values between 0 and 1).

EXAMPLE

Write 8,200 in scientific notation.

STEP 1	Move the decimal point so that there is just one digit to the left.	8200
	How many places did you move it?	3
STEP 2	Place the 3 as the exponent of the 10. 8,200 is a large number; 3 is a positive number.	8.2×10^3

EXAMPLE

Write 0.00029 in scientific notation.

STEP 1	Move the decimal point so that there is just one non-zero digit to the left.	0.00029
	How many places did you move it?	4
STEP 2	Place the –4 as the exponent of the 10. 0.00029 is a small number; the exponent, –4, is a negative number.	2.9×10^{-4}

EXAMPLE

Write 4.39×10^7 in standard notation.

The positive exponent indicates that this will be a large number. The single digit 4 is before the decimal point. Add enough zeroes so that the 4 is in the 10^7 place. (The *10^7 place* means that there are 7 digits between the 4 and the decimal point.)

4 3, 9 0 0, 0 0 0

PROBLEM 6 Write the following numbers in scientific notation.

Ⓐ 75,000   Ⓒ 870,000,000   Ⓔ 0.008   Ⓖ 0.0000095

Ⓑ 309,000   Ⓓ 9,140,000,000   Ⓕ 0.00003   Ⓗ 0.00000028

PROBLEM 7 In 2002, Michael R. Bloomberg spent more than $76 million of his own money to become mayor of New York City. Write the number of dollars in scientific notation.

PROBLEM 8 It is estimated that 1.89×10^{11} individual Lego tiles have been sold in the 50 years since their introduction. Write this amount in standard notation.

PROBLEM 9 A pollen grain measures 0.0004 meter in diameter. Write this measurement in scientific notation.

PROBLEM 10 The wavelength of visible/infrared radiation is measured in microns. One micron is equal to 1×10^{-6} meter. Write this in standard notation.

Estimating with Multiplication and Division

Scientific notation is important in another method to determine the magnitude of the answer when estimating with either multiplication or division. You will be able to use this method to choose an answer on the GED Test, but, more importantly, you can use it to estimate large and small numbers that are common in your life.

ALGEBRAIC PROPERTIES Multiplication: $a^m \bullet a^n = a^{m+n}$ Division: $\dfrac{a^m}{a^n} = a^{m-n}$ $(a \neq 0)$

The algebraic properties say that when the base of the powers is the same, you can multiply two powers by adding the exponents and divide two powers by subtracting the exponents.

We will use these properties with numbers that are written in scientific notation.

EXAMPLES

$300 \times 43{,}000$		$450{,}000{,}000 \div 3{,}000$	
$3 \times 10^2 \times 4.3 \times 10^4$	Write in scientific notation.	$\dfrac{4.5 \times 10^8}{3 \times 10^3}$	
$3 \times 4.3 \times 10^2 \times 10^4$	Rearrange. Multiply or divide numbers in front.		
12.9×10^6	Add or subtract exponents.	1.5×10^5	
$12{,}900{,}000$	Write in standard notation.	$150{,}000$	

CLASS ACTIVITY

Try a few problems to satisfy yourself that the properties of exponents work. Find each answer in the following two ways and compare the results:

① Carry the trailing zeros if multiplying, or cancel common zeros if dividing.

② Use the properties of exponents.

Ⓐ $8{,}400{,}000 \times 200$ Ⓑ $8{,}400{,}000 \div 200$ Ⓒ $10{,}000 \times 0.05$

TEST-TAKING EXAMPLE

What is the cost, in dollars, of a fleet of 40 new compact cars, each of which cost $18,450?

(1)   224,500
(2)   738,000
(3) 1,845,000
(4) 2,245,000
(5) 7,380,000

A possible strategy:

By rounding, the problem becomes $40 \times 20{,}000$. You can tell that the first digit of the answer is close to 8.

Both **(2)** and **(5)** satisfy that requirement.

What is the magnitude of the answer?

$4 \times 10^1 \times 2 \times 10^4 = 8 \times 10^5 = 800{,}000$

The correct answer is **(2)** 738,000.

Stories in the newspapers and on TV seem to be using large numbers more often than ever before. To fully understand the impact of the story, you need to be able to analyze the numbers being used.

PROBLEM 11

As a result of a new tax law, each household in a school district will be required to pay about $200 in extra taxes per year. If there are 9,256 households in the district, about how much extra revenue is generated by this new law every year?

PROBLEM 12

It was reported in the news that investors lost a total of $358 billion in the second quarter of 2002, when the value of stocks declined sharply. The population of the U.S. was about 285 million people at that time. If the loss were divided equally among the entire population, approximately what would each person's loss be?

PROBLEM 13

The annual salary of Alex Rodriguez, who plays shortstop for the Texas Rangers, was $22 million in 2001. During this same year, the median salary for full-time workers in the U.S. was about $30,000. About how many of the median salaries could have been paid with Alex's salary?

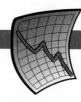

USING DATA

In their 2001 World Population Data Sheet, the Population Reference Bureau released data about the world's population and land area. Use the chart on page 287 in the Appendix to answer the problems below.

Ⓐ A bar graph of the population numbers would tell the story more dramatically than the column of figures. Decide how the vertical axis of this graph should be scaled so that all the population numbers can be shown. Insert the numbers and the title for the axis. Finally, insert bars of the correct length so that the population data is shown as accurately as possible.

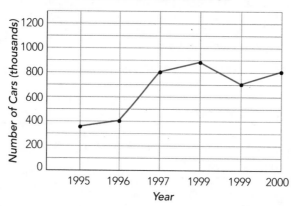

**STAR-LITE DRIVE-IN THEATRE
ANNUAL ATTENDANCE**

Ⓑ Rank the regions from least (1) to greatest (6) in terms of both population and area.

POPULATION

1. _____
2. _____
3. _____
4. _____
5. _____
6. _____

AREA

1. _____
2. _____
3. _____
4. _____
5. _____
6. _____

Ⓒ Round each of the population figures to two significant digits and write them in scientific notation.

EXAMPLE Africa: $818,000,000 \approx 8.2 \times 10^8$ Asia _____

North America _____   Europe _____

Latin America & Carribean _____   Oceania _____

Ⓓ Round each of the area figures to two significant digits and write them in scientific notation.

Ⓔ Which region has the highest population density? That is, which one has the most people per square mile? Use your answers to **Ⓒ** and **Ⓓ** to estimate the answer without actually dividing the numbers in the table.

Problem Solving with Multiplication and Division

At the end of this chapter on multiplication and division, take time to clarify which kind of situations require you to multiply and which require you to divide. It is important to understand the situation and the relationships that are described rather than to rely on clue words that can mislead you.

Multiply when

- you are combining a number of equal amounts. For example, if you know the price or size of one and want to know the price or size of many.

Divide when

- you are separating a large amount into smaller, equal-sized pieces. For example, if you want to know how many individual portions are in a large container.

- you are looking for the price or size of only 1 in a group when you know the price or size of many.

- you are comparing two quantities and want to know how many times as large one quantity is compared to the other.

PROBLEM 14 | A carton of fruit punch contains 8 eight-ounce servings. Each serving has 120 calories. Which of the following expressions shows how many calories are in a full carton?

(1) 8×8
(2) 8×120
(3) $8 \times 8 \times 120$
(4) $(8 + 8)120$
(5) $120 \div 8$

PROBLEM 15 | A new car model can travel 522 miles on 1 tank of gasoline. The gasoline tank holds 9 gallons. Which expression shows how many miles per gallon the car gets?

(1) 522×9

(2) $522 \times 9 \times 1$

(3) 522×10

(4) $\frac{522}{9}$

(5) $\frac{522}{10}$

PROBLEM 16 | What is the cost for 5 pages of $.37 stamps if each page costs $5.55?

(1) $ 1.85
(2) $ 2.05
(3) $15.00
(4) $10.27
(5) $27.75

CHECK YOUR UNDERSTANDING

You may use your calculator on any problem except where noted by this symbol:

1. What is the place value of the six in each number?

    Ⓐ 561
    Ⓑ 78.6
    Ⓒ 6,329
    Ⓓ 560,489
    Ⓔ 44,744.26

2. Write each power of 10 in exponential notation.

    Ⓐ 100,000

    Ⓑ $\frac{1}{100}$ or 0.01

    Ⓒ $\frac{1}{10}$ or 0.1

    Ⓓ 1,000,000

3. Expand each of the following numbers by place value. Use exponential notation.

    EXAMPLE $1,300 = 1(10)^3 + 3(10)^2$

    Ⓐ 78
    Ⓑ 62,000
    Ⓒ 5,030.9
    Ⓓ 93,000,000
    Ⓔ 40.73

4. Write the following numbers in scientific notation.

    Ⓐ 90,000
    Ⓑ 0.007
    Ⓒ 4,500,000
    Ⓓ 0.000029
    Ⓔ 88,000,000

5. By July 4, 2002, wildfires had destroyed 2.5 million acres in the West, much greater than the usual toll for that early in the season. Write this figure in scientific notation.

6. Approximately 30 million Lego bricks were used in the construction of Legoland in Carlsbad, California, a 125-acre park. About how many bricks per acre is that?

7. Ⓐ To measure long distances in space, astronomers use a unit of measurement called a light-year. A light-year is approximately 5.88 trillion miles. Write this in scientific notation.

    Ⓑ Barnard's star is 5.94 light years from our sun. In scientific notation, approximately how many miles is that?

8. The headline of a conservation pamphlet reads, "Insects Outnumber Humans 200,000 to 1." If the world population is 6 billion, what is the insect population?

Do problems 9–14 using the following steps:

    Ⓐ Write the equation.
    Ⓑ Study the equation you have written, and decide on an appropriate **estimated answer** for the problem.
    Ⓒ Find the **exact answer**.

9. A recreational vehicle averages 8 miles for each gallon of gasoline. How many gallons would be used on a trip of 550 miles?

10. Each six-pack of soda costs $2.49. How much would 4 six-packs cost?

11. A roll of 24-exposure film costs $4.95. To the nearest cent, what is the film's cost per exposure?

12. A package of 6 drinking glasses costs $4.39. To the nearest cent, what is the price of each glass?

13. Each gallon of milk contains 16 cups. How many gallons are needed to provide 100 cups of milk?

14. A computer printer can print 12 pages per minute. How long would it take to print a document that contains 58 pages? Round your answer to the nearest tenth.

TEST-TAKING PRACTICE

You may use your calculator on any problem except where noted by this symbol:

Problems 1–3 refer to the graph below.

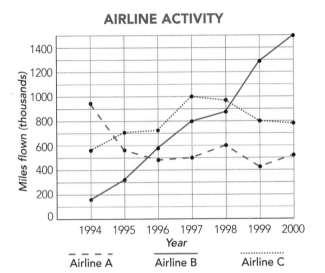

AIRLINE ACTIVITY

Miles flown (thousands)

1994 1995 1996 1997 1998 1999 2000
Year

- - - - Airline A   —— Airline B   ········ Airline C

1. Approximately how many miles did Airline C fly in 1997, their best year?

(1)   1,000
(2)   10,000
(3)   100,000
(4)   1,000,000
(5) 1,000,000,000

2. Which year was the first year that Airline B flew more miles than Airline A?

(1) 1996
(2) 1997
(3) 1998
(4) 1999
(5) 2000

3. Early in 1999, Airline B was awarded some new routes. Estimate the increase in the number of miles in 1999 over the number of miles in 1998.

(1)   200,000
(2)   400,000
(3)   130,000,000
(4)   200,000,000
(5)   400,000,000

4. Sonja earns $2,200 a month on her job. How much does she earn each year?

(1) $ 2,200
(2) $ 4,400
(3) $22,000
(4) $26,400
(5) Not enough information is given.

5. Sonya pays $18.50 every 2 weeks in insurance premiums for her dental plan. How much does she pay for dental insurance each year? (52 weeks = 1 year)

(1) $ 185
(2) $ 444
(3) $ 481
(4) $ 962
(5) $1,924

6. A local charity set a goal of raising $350,000 during their annual fund drive. From previous campaigns, they expect to get contributions from approximately 25,000 donors. What is the average donation, in dollars, that each donor needs to give in order to meet the goal?

Mark your answer in the circles in the grid.

Test-Taking Tips

In this lesson, you will apply the math skills that you have been learning to a sample of the types of questions that typically appear on tests. When you take a standardized test, you must be confident of your math skills, but you also need to go in with a positive problem-solving attitude. The problems on the test are not just *exercises* to see if you know how to carry out some procedure, they are *problems* to see if you know how to reason and to apply the procedures to new situations. Expect to see unfamiliar contexts, but be confident that you can analyze them and figure out what to do to answer the questions.

Read the problems and explanations on the next page. Then refer to them again as you read the tips below.

1 General Relationships

Ask yourself, "What do I know about this?" For example, in previous lessons, you explored the relationship between cost, selling price, and profit. In **problem 1** on the next page, you must recognize that the cost of materials gets added to the labor and the overhead costs to reach a total cost.

You also are expected to remember some of the **measurement equivalents** (for example, 12 inches = 1 foot) and **geometric relationships** (for example, 180° is the sum of the angles in a triangle). Do not expect these relationships to be spelled out in each problem. Remember that many basic relationships are summarized on the formulas page of the test.

2 Extra Information or Not Enough Information

Ask yourself, "What do I need to find the answer?"
In **problem 2** on the next page, the number of hours the Quik Lube stayed open is not needed to find out how many quarts of oil the business uses each hour.
In **problem 3**, you need to know the number of hours worked before you can find the answer.

Both demand that you take the time to understand the problem situation rather than to make quick assumptions. Reread the problem. Pick out the relevant information and check for any information that you may have overlooked.

Problems 1–3 are based on the following information.

Some problems on the test are part of a set. More than one question is asked about a single situation.

Art's Quik Lube specializes in oil changes for automobiles. An oil change involves changing the oil (4 quarts) and replacing the filter. Art's has 3 stalls, each of which averages 3 oil changes an hour. The business stays open 10 hours a day.

Read the passage well enough to know the situation—more than once if necessary. Do not anticipate the kind of question that will be asked.

1. The charge for an oil change at Art's is $27.95. If it costs Art $4.00 for each filter and $1.75 for each quart of oil that he uses, how much of that money is left to cover labor costs and overhead?

   (1) $ 5.75
   (2) $ 7.00
   (3) $11.00
   (4) $16.95
   (5) $22.20

GENERAL RELATIONSHIPS

The fee must cover the cost of materials plus the labor and overhead costs (and hopefully leave some profit). Each oil change uses 1 filter and 4 quarts of oil. Subtract the total cost of materials from the $27.95. Let x stand for what's left.

$$\$27.95 - (\$4.00 + 4 \times \$1.75) = x$$

The materials total $11, leaving **(4)** $16.95.

2. If each oil change requires 4 quarts of oil, how much oil must Art have in stock for each hour of operation?

   (1) 12
   (2) 24
   (3) 36
   (4) 90
   (5) 360

EXTRA INFORMATION

There are 3 stalls, each stall averages 3 oil changes an hour, and each change requires 4 quarts. Each step involves combining equal amounts so each step requires multiplication.

Write the equation: $x = (3 \times 3) \times 4$

Look back at the problem and determine whether or not the 10 hours a day is relevant to this question, or if it is extra information that is not involved.

The question asks for how much he needs for each hour, so the 10 hours is not relevant to this question.

$x = (3 \times 3) \times 4 = $ **(3)** 36 quarts

3. Manuel is a mechanic who works at Art's. His weekly take-home pay is $475. How much is he being paid an hour?

   (1) $ 6.78
   (2) $ 9.50
   (3) $11.87
   (4) $15.83
   (5) Not enough information is given.

NOT ENOUGH INFORMATION

To find Manuel's hourly rate of pay, need to divide the total pay by the number of hours he works each week. The number of hours is not given.

Can you figure it out from something else that is given? You know that Art's stays open 10 hours a day. Does Manuel work all 10 hours? How many days a week does he work?

Don't assume anything. You don't know enough about Manuel's work situation to solve this problem. Choose **(5)** Not enough information is given.

CHECK YOUR SKILLS

On the test below, try to solve as many problems as possible with mental math and estimating. You may use a calculator on any problem that does not have this symbol: You may use the formulas page (page 280) and the number grid directions (page 281) whenever you wish.

1. The value of $\sqrt{150}$ is between which of the following pairs of numbers?

(1) 10 and 11
(2) 11 and 12
(3) 12 and 13
(4) 13 and 14
(5) 70 and 80

2. What is a train's rate of speed, in miles per hour, if it travels 375 miles in 2.5 hours?

(1) 55
(2) 65
(3) 90
(4) 150
(5) 937.5

3. A gallon of paint for patios can cover 400 square feet of cement surface. How many gallons would Sam need to buy to cover the patio (shaded area) below?

(1) 2
(2) 4
(3) 5
(4) 6
(5) 21.5

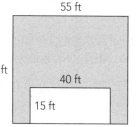

4. One auto-transport trailer holds 7 vehicles. Which expression can be used to find how many such trailers it would take to transport 48 vehicles from the port of entry to a dealership 1,050 miles away?

(1) $\dfrac{7}{48}$

(2) $\dfrac{48}{7}$

(3) $\dfrac{1,050 - 48}{7}$

(4) $\dfrac{1,050}{48 \times 7}$

(5) $\dfrac{1,050 \times 7}{48}$

5. A self-service storage company charges \$.50 per month for each cubic foot of space rented. Martin and Gloria rented a rectangular unit that measures 5 feet by 5 feet. All the units in the building are 8 feet high. How much, in dollars, was their monthly rent?

Mark your answer in the circles in the grid.

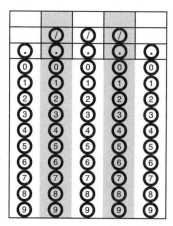

6. Which expression could be used to find the number of meters of fencing that would be required to surround the circular area shown below?

(1) 3.14×5
(2) 3.14×7
(3) 3.14×10
(4) $3.14 \times (5)^2$
(5) $3.14 \times (10)^2$

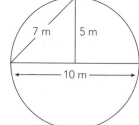

7. In the diagram below, angle *COD* is a right angle, and angle *BOD* measures 115°. What is the measure of angle *AOB*?

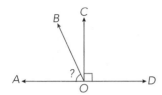

(1) 15°
(2) 25°
(3) 65°
(4) 90°
(5) Not enough information is given.

8. A breakfast order of 2 coffees and 3 Danish rolls costs a total of $5.95 before tax. Each of the rolls costs $1.25. What is the price of each coffee?

(1) $ .55
(2) $1.10
(3) $2.20
(4) $3.75
(5) Not enough information is given.

9. The high temperature for the 5 days of the Browns' vacation was 92°F. The low temperature that occurred was 64° F. What was the average daily temperature during the family's 5-day vacation?

(1) 31.2°
(2) 64°
(3) 78°
(4) 92°
(5) Not enough information is given.

Problems 10 and 11 refer to the following graph.

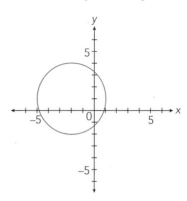

10. Approximately how many square units are in the area of the circle in the graph?

(1) 28
(2) 19
(3) 9.42
(4) 9
(5) 6

11. What are the coordinates of the center of the circle in the graph?

(1) (1, −2)
(2) (−2, 1)
(3) (2, −2)
(4) (−2, 2)
(5) (0, 0)

12. Renting a Rototiller costs $25 plus $4 for each hour that it is rented. Which expression below tells how many dollars it would cost to rent the Rototiller for *n* hours?

(1) $25 + 4 + n$

(2) $(25)(4)(n)$

(3) $\frac{25}{4n}$

(4) $25 + 4n$

(5) $\frac{25 + 4}{n}$

13. The total amount Richard earns each month is $2,790. His employer then deducts $420 each month for taxes and social security. How much is Richard's take-home pay for the year?

(1) $ 1,950
(2) $ 2,370
(3) $19,500
(4) $28,440
(5) $38,520

14. To travel by road from Centerville to Gotham, one must go 9 miles north and 12 miles east. How many miles would it be if one could go directly ("as the crow flies") from Centerville to Gotham?

(1) 3
(2) 15
(3) 18
(4) 24
(5) Not enough information is given.

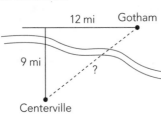

15. Find the value of *h* in the following equation if $t = 8$.

$$h = t^2 + t$$

(1) 4
(2) 16
(3) 24
(4) 32
(5) 72

16. For each mile that Bernie walks, he estimates that he burns 100 calories. He walked 6 miles on Tuesday, 3 on Wednesday, and 7 on Friday. Which expression below shows the number of calories he burned walking those 3 days?

(1) $100(6 + 3 + 7)$

(2) $100(6 \times 3 \times 7)$

(3) $6(100) \times 3(100) \times 7(100)$

(4) $(6 + 100) \times (3 + 100) \times (7 + 100)$

(5) $\frac{6 + 3 + 7}{100}$

17. What is the height of this triangle, in centimeters, if its area is 30 square centimeters?

(1) 6
(2) 10
(3) 12
(4) 20
(5) 60

Problem 18 refers to the graph below.

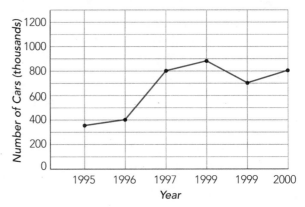

18. Which year showed the greatest increase in attendance?

(1) 1996
(2) 1997
(3) 1998
(4) 1999
(5) 2000

19. What is the measure, in degrees, of ∠ADB?

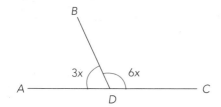

(1) 30
(2) 45
(3) 54
(4) 60
(5) 80

20. In a survey, 20 people were asked how many trips to the grocery store they made in a typical month. The responses are summarized in the table below.

number of trips per month	number of people
15	2
12	1
10	3
8	3
4	8
2	3

What is the median number of trips per month?

(1) 4
(2) 6
(3) 8
(4) 9
(5) 10

SELF-EVALUATION CHART

Check your answers and compare your solutions to those given in the answer key. When you compare solutions, you can learn another way to do the problem and adopt the new way if you like it better than yours.

Review the questions again, trying to gain some insight into the kinds of problems to expect on large-scale assessments.

1. How many of the problems required you to use paper-and-pencil computations to find the answer? Could you have answered any of these by estimating instead?

2. For which questions would you have used your calculator if it had been allowed?

3. For how many questions did you refer to the formulas page?

4. Can you identify any skill that you need to study?

Use the following chart to identify skills that you may need to review further before you go on to the next section of the book.

problems	skill	lessons
1, 10, 14, 15	Squares and square roots	11
5, 8, 9, 12, 13, 16, 20	Multistep problems	10
4, 12, 16	Recognizing expressions	7, 10
6, 10	Circles	12
3, 5, 6, 17	Perimeter, area, and volume	8, 10, 12
2, 4	"Seeing" multiplication and division	7, 9
7, 19	Angles	4
11	Coordinate plane	5
18	Informational graphs	all

Size of Fractions

Divide. Watch for a pattern.

1. $\frac{12}{12}$　　　　3. $\frac{12}{4}$　　　　5. $\frac{12}{2}$

2. $\frac{12}{6}$　　　　4. $\frac{12}{3}$　　　　6. $\frac{12}{1}$

As the divisors (the numbers on the bottom that you were *dividing by*) got smaller, the answers increased in value. You also saw this mathematical principle in Lesson 9. It will be an important one to remember as you learn about fractions in this lesson.

Common fractions are not as important in people's lives as they once were. Although common fractions are used in some measurements in the United States, in many cases the decimal form has replaced fractions. For example, the prices of stocks on the Stock Exchanges are now listed using decimals instead of fractions.

EXAMPLE

When the Hensons saw this sign,　　the odometer in their car read

REST STOP
$1\frac{1}{4}$ mi

| | 7 | 5 | 4 | 8 | 1 | .6 |

What will the odometer read by the time the Hensons get to the rest stop?

To figure out what the odometer will read by the time the Hensons get to the rest stop, you need to know about the relationship between common and decimal fractions, the main topic of this lesson.

What Does a Fraction Mean?

$\frac{2}{5}$ ←—— The number on top is called the **numerator**.

←—— The number on the bottom is called the **denominator**.

A fraction can be thought of as part of a whole.

The denominator (bottom number) tells how many *equal* parts the whole is divided into.

The numerator (top number) tells how many of those parts are shaded.

These figures have 5 equal parts.

These represent the fraction $\frac{2}{5}$.

A fraction can also be thought of as a division problem.

The line in a fraction means "divided by," so the fraction $\frac{3}{4}$ can be read as "3 divided by 4" and the fraction $\frac{6}{2}$ can be read as "6 divided by 2."

By carrying out the division, you will find the decimal value of a common fraction. Think of the *value of a fraction* as a single number rather than thinking about its two parts separately.

The decimal value and the fraction are equivalent so they will both name the same point on a number line.

EXAMPLE

Compare the values of the fractions $\frac{4}{5}$ and $\frac{5}{4}$ by dividing to find their decimal equivalents. Show their position on a number line.

$\frac{4}{5} =$  $\qquad \frac{5}{4} =$

```
              4                5
              ─                ─
              5                4
  ◄──┼──┼──┼──┼──┼──┼──┼──┼──┼──►
     0       0.5     1       1.5
```

> If a fraction has a numerator that is equal to its denominator, the fraction is equal to 1.

Fractions with Values Close to 1

What is the value of $\frac{5}{5}$? of $\frac{4}{4}$? When a non-zero number is divided by itself, the answer is 1.

EXAMPLES $\frac{5}{5} = 5 \div 5 = 1$, $\qquad \frac{523}{523} = 523 \div 523 = 1$

PROBLEM 1 | Use your calculator to find the decimal value for the following fractions. Show where they fall on the number line. The first one is done for you.

(A) $\frac{1}{4} = 0.25$ (D) $\frac{4}{2}$ (G) $\frac{12}{5}$

(B) $\frac{1}{5}$ (E) $\frac{4}{16}$ (H) $\frac{12}{8}$

(C) $\frac{1}{8}$ (F) $\frac{4}{20}$ (I) $\frac{12}{15}$

PROBLEM 2 | Notice the fractions in problem 1 whose value is *greater than 1*. Their numerators (numbers on top) are *greater* than their denominators.

Finish this statement about positive fractions that are *less than 1*. A fraction whose value is less than 1 has a numerator (top number) that is _____ than its denominator.

PROBLEM 3 | Which of the fractions below are less than 1? Which fractions are greater than 1? What is the value of the remaining fractions?

(A) $\frac{2}{3}$ (D) $\frac{5}{2}$ (G) $\frac{4}{4}$

(B) $\frac{6}{5}$ (E) $\frac{3}{7}$ (H) $\frac{10}{11}$

(C) $\frac{7}{6}$ (F) $\frac{7}{8}$ (I) $\frac{11}{11}$

PROBLEM 4 | Insert numbers into the following fractions so that they are very close to, but less than, 1.

EXAMPLE $\frac{7}{8}$

(A) $\frac{}{12}$ (B) $\frac{}{6}$ (C) $\frac{}{20}$ (D) $\frac{6}{}$ (E) $\frac{13}{}$ (F) $\frac{9}{}$

A fraction whose value is greater than 1 can be written as a **mixed number**. A mixed number tells how many ones (wholes) the number contains (the **whole number part**) as well as what remains (the **fractional part**).

EXAMPLES

Rewrite $\frac{5}{3}$ and $\frac{24}{5}$ as mixed numbers.

$\frac{5}{3}$ can be written as $1\frac{2}{3}$.
(1 one $\left(\frac{3}{3}\right)$ with $\frac{2}{3}$ remaining)
$\frac{24}{5}$ can be written as $4\frac{4}{5}$.
(4 ones $\left(\frac{20}{5}\right)$ with $\frac{4}{5}$ remaining)

You can also change a fraction to a mixed number by simply carrying out the division mentally.

$\frac{5}{3} = 5 \div 3 = 1$ with 2 remaining $= 1\frac{2}{3}$

$\frac{24}{5} = 24 \div 5 = 4$ with 4 remaining $= 4\frac{4}{5}$

PROBLEM 5 | Write the following fractions as mixed numbers. Use either method.

EXAMPLE $\frac{7}{3} = \frac{6}{3} + \frac{1}{3} = 2\frac{1}{3}$ or $7 \div 3 = 2$ with 1 remaining $= 2\frac{1}{3}$

A $\frac{4}{3}$ **C** $\frac{7}{4}$ **E** $\frac{14}{3}$ **G** $\frac{17}{6}$

B $\frac{5}{2}$ **D** $\frac{10}{7}$ **F** $\frac{11}{5}$ **H** $\frac{20}{3}$

> If twice the numerator of a fraction is greater than the denominator, the value of the fraction is greater than $\frac{1}{2}$.

Fractions with Values Close to $\frac{1}{2}$

What is the value of $\frac{4}{8}$? of $\frac{3}{6}$? of $\frac{7}{14}$? If you enter these fractions into your calculator as division problems, the display will read 0.5 for each answer. They are all equal to $\frac{1}{2}$. The top number equals half of the bottom number.

PROBLEM 6 | Each of the following fractions is equal to or close to $\frac{1}{2}$ in value. Which fractions are exactly $\frac{1}{2}$ in value? Which fractions are greater than $\frac{1}{2}$?

A $\frac{3}{5}$ **C** $\frac{5}{10}$ **E** $\frac{7}{13}$ **G** $\frac{35}{70}$

B $\frac{2}{4}$ **D** $\frac{6}{11}$ **F** $\frac{5}{9}$ **H** $\frac{51}{100}$

PROBLEM 7 | For a sewing project, Sasha needs a length of fabric at least $\frac{1}{2}$ yard long. Which length should she choose?

(1) $\frac{1}{8}$ yd   (2) $\frac{3}{8}$ yd   (3) $\frac{9}{16}$ yd   (4) $\frac{1}{3}$ yd   (5) $\frac{1}{4}$ yd

Comparing Fractions

You can compare the values of two fractions by entering them into your calculator as division problems and comparing the resulting decimals.

EXAMPLE

Which is greater, $\frac{3}{7}$ or $\frac{5}{11}$?

3 **÷** **7** **=** 0.428571428, **5** **÷** **11** **=** 0.454545454

By comparing decimal equivalents, you can see that $\frac{5}{11}$ is greater.

You can also reason about the size of certain fractions by using your understanding of their characteristics.

Compare fractions with the same denominator.

> If two fractions have the same denominator, the one with the greater numerator is greater in value.

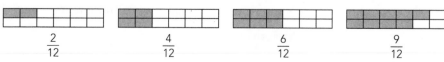

$\frac{2}{12}$ $\frac{4}{12}$ $\frac{6}{12}$ $\frac{9}{12}$

As the *numerators increase in value*, more of the pieces are shaded, and the size of the shaded region *increases*.

Compare fractions with the same numerator.

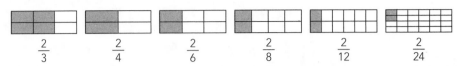

$$\frac{2}{3} \qquad \frac{2}{4} \qquad \frac{2}{6} \qquad \frac{2}{8} \qquad \frac{2}{12} \qquad \frac{2}{24}$$

As the *denominators increase in value,* the size of the pieces gets smaller, and the size of the shaded region *decreases.*

Sometimes you can reason in other ways to help you decide.

> If two fractions have the same numerator, the one with the smaller denominator is greater in value.

EXAMPLE

Which is greater, $\frac{8}{15}$ or $\frac{9}{19}$?

The values of both are *close to* $\frac{1}{2}$. $\frac{8}{15}$ is greater than $\frac{1}{2}$, and $\frac{9}{19}$ is less. So $\frac{8}{15}$ has the greater value.

PROBLEM 8

Decide which fraction in each pair is *greater.* Try to do all of these mentally. You can check your reasoning with your calculator.

A $\frac{4}{5}$ or $\frac{4}{7}$ **D** $\frac{9}{10}$ or $\frac{10}{9}$ **G** $\frac{5}{10}$ or $\frac{11}{20}$

B $\frac{8}{11}$ or $\frac{7}{11}$ **E** $\frac{13}{5}$ or $\frac{13}{10}$ **H** $\frac{5}{8}$ or $\frac{4}{9}$

C $\frac{5}{6}$ or $\frac{5}{8}$ **F** $\frac{3}{11}$ or $\frac{6}{11}$ **I** $\frac{5}{9}$ or $\frac{8}{17}$

Decimal and Fractional Equivalents

You will be a more confident and flexible estimator when you know the decimal equivalents of the common fractions that appear often in your life. Many are easy to learn because of what you already know about money.

you know:	because:
$\frac{1}{2}$ = 0.50 or 0.5	$\frac{1}{2}$ of a dollar is $.50
$\frac{1}{4}$ = 0.25	one quarter is $.25
$\frac{3}{4}$ = 0.75	three quarters are $.75
$\frac{1}{10}$ = 0.10 or 0.1	one dime is $.10
$\frac{1}{100}$ = 0.01	one penny is $.01

Not so obvious is that $\frac{1}{5}$ = 0.20 (there are five $.20 in a dollar).

Moreover, since $\frac{2}{10}$ (2 dimes) also equals $.20, you can reason that $\frac{1}{5} = \frac{2}{10}$.

PROBLEM 9 | Use what you know about money to find the decimal equivalents.

Ⓐ 3 dimes = $._____ $\frac{3}{10}$ = _____

Ⓑ 7 dimes = $._____ $\frac{7}{10}$ = _____

Ⓒ 9 dimes = $._____ $\frac{9}{10}$ = _____

Ⓓ 4 dimes = $._____ $\frac{4}{10} = \frac{2}{5}$ = _____

Ⓔ 6 dimes = $._____ $\frac{6}{10} = \frac{3}{5}$ = _____

Ⓕ 8 dimes = $._____ $\frac{8}{10} = \frac{4}{5}$ = _____

Ⓖ 2 quarters = $._____ $\frac{2}{4} = \frac{1}{2}$ = _____

Ⓗ 5 dimes = $._____ $\frac{5}{10} = \frac{1}{2}$ = _____

Although the thirds are not often used with money, you should also know them.

Enter $\frac{1}{3}$ into your calculator.   Enter $\frac{2}{3}$ into your calculator.

The display reads $\boxed{0.333333333}$. The display reads $\boxed{0.666666666}$.

These numbers are called **repeating decimals** because the same digit (or pattern of digits) keeps repeating itself and *never* comes out evenly. Rather than write out so many digits, you can show that a decimal is a repeating decimal by

① placing a line or a dot above the digits that repeat $\frac{1}{3} = 0.\dot{3} = 0.\overline{3}$, or

② placing three dots after the digits $\frac{2}{3} = 0.66\ldots$

You should learn all of these equivalents—halves, thirds, fourths, fifths, and tenths—just as you learned the addition and multiplication facts.

PROBLEM 10

Quiz yourself by writing *decimal equivalents* for the fractions or *fraction equivalents* for the decimals.

Ⓐ $\frac{4}{5}$ = _____   Ⓕ 0.2 = _____   Ⓚ 0.66 . . . = _____

Ⓑ $\frac{1}{3}$ = _____   Ⓖ 0.25 = _____   Ⓛ 0.6 = _____

Ⓒ $\frac{3}{10}$ = _____   Ⓗ 0.7 = _____   Ⓜ $\frac{9}{10}$ = _____

Ⓓ $\frac{3}{4}$ = _____   Ⓘ 0.1 = _____   Ⓝ $\frac{10}{10}$ = _____

Ⓔ $\frac{1}{2}$ = _____   Ⓙ 0.4 = _____   Ⓞ $\frac{11}{10}$ = _____

Equivalent Fractions

Equivalent fractions have the same value.

Reading a ruler can help you learn about equivalent fractions, and learning about equivalent fractions can help you read a ruler.

Think of a ruler as a number line that starts at zero. The inch marks are labeled as a number line.

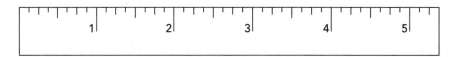

Find the half-inch marks. Finish labeling them on the ruler below.

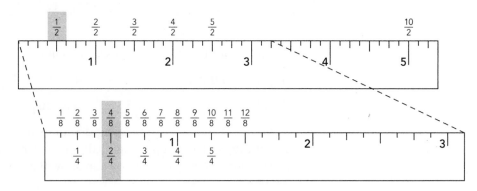

Fractions that name the same mark on the ruler are equal to each other.

Finish marking the fourth-inch marks and the eighth-inch marks on the blown-up version of the ruler above.

Notice that many ruler marks have more than one label. For example, the $\frac{1}{2}$ mark is also labeled $\frac{2}{4}$ and $\frac{4}{8}$.

By blowing up the ruler a little more, we can show the sixteenths.

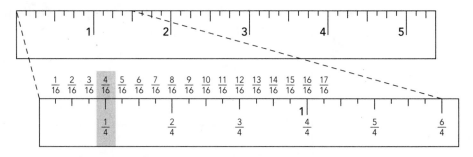

Since $\frac{4}{16}$ and $\frac{1}{4}$ are both labeling the same point, you can see that they are equal to each other. You can confirm that this is true by entering both fractions into your calculator as division problems: $\frac{4}{16} = 0.25$, and $\frac{1}{4} = 0.25$.

FUNDAMENTAL PRINCIPLE OF FRACTIONS	If both the numerator and the denominator of a fraction are multiplied or divided by the same non-zero number, the value of the fraction remains the same.

Notice that both the top and bottom numbers in these fractions are being multiplied (or divided) by the same number.

$\frac{12}{16}$ and $\frac{6}{8}$ are equal. $\frac{12}{8}$ and $\frac{3}{2}$ are equal.

$$\frac{6 \times 2}{8 \times 2} = \frac{12}{16} \qquad \frac{12 \div 2}{16 \div 2} = \frac{6}{8} \qquad\qquad \frac{12 \div 4}{8 \div 4} = \frac{3}{2} \qquad \frac{3 \times 4}{2 \times 4} = \frac{12}{8}$$

You can see from the problems above that this principle is based on another fundamental principle.

IDENTITY PROPERTY FOR MULTIPLICATION	Multiplying or dividing a number by 1 does not change its value. $n \times 1 = n$ $n \div 1 = n$

PROBLEM 11 | Complete the following equalities. For help, look back at the ruler markings on page 156.

A $\frac{4}{16} = \frac{}{8}$ **D** $\frac{6}{4} = \frac{}{8}$ **G** $\frac{5}{8} = \frac{}{16}$

B $\frac{3}{4} = \frac{}{8}$ **E** $\frac{1}{8} = \frac{}{16}$ **H** $\frac{5}{2} = \frac{}{4}$

C $\frac{10}{8} = \frac{}{4}$ **F** $\frac{6}{16} = \frac{}{8}$ **I** $\frac{5}{4} = \frac{}{16}$

PROBLEM 12 | If you remember which fractions are equal, you can determine which are greater than or less than another. Insert >, <, or = to make the following expressions true. Use the rulers again to help you.

EXAMPLE $\frac{5}{16} > \frac{1}{4}$. Remember that $\frac{1}{4} = \frac{4}{16}$, so $\frac{5}{16} >$ (is greater than) $\frac{1}{4}$.

A $\frac{5}{8}$ ____ $\frac{1}{2}$ **C** $\frac{3}{8}$ ____ $\frac{1}{4}$ **E** $\frac{5}{16}$ ____ $\frac{3}{8}$

B $\frac{7}{8}$ ____ $\frac{3}{4}$ **D** $\frac{3}{8}$ ____ $\frac{1}{2}$ **F** $\frac{1}{2}$ ____ $\frac{9}{16}$

A fraction whose numerator and denominator do not have any factors in common is in **simplest form**. You can recognize a fraction in simplest form when no number (other than 1) can be divided evenly into both the numerator and denominator.

Simplifying a fraction is sometimes called reducing a fraction.

EXAMPLE

$\frac{6}{15}$ is not in simplest form because 3 is a factor of both 6 and 15.

$\frac{6 \div 3}{15 \div 3} = \frac{2}{5}$ Simplify $\frac{6}{15}$ by dividing both top and bottom by 3.

PROBLEM 13 | Simplify each of the following fractions.

A $\frac{6}{8}$ **B** $\frac{8}{16}$ **C** $\frac{4}{12}$ **D** $\frac{5}{20}$ **E** $\frac{9}{15}$ **F** $\frac{12}{18}$

Fractions and Measurements

Fractions are commonly used when discussing other units of measure. "Half an hour" and "half a pound" are part of our everyday lives.

EXAMPLE A

8 inches is what fraction of a foot?

$$\frac{8}{12}$$ ← Let the denominator be the number of inches in a foot or minutes in an hour.

$$\frac{8 \div 4}{12 \div 4} = \frac{2}{3}$$ ← Simplify each fraction.

8 inches is $\frac{2}{3}$ of a foot.

EXAMPLE B

10 minutes is what fraction of an hour?

$$\frac{10}{60}$$

$$\frac{10 \div 10}{60 \div 10} = \frac{1}{6}$$

10 minutes is $\frac{1}{6}$ of an hour.

Refer to tables of equivalent measures on p. 295 in the Appendix if needed.

PROBLEM 14 | What fractional part of a foot is

Ⓐ 3 inches?   Ⓑ 4 inches?   Ⓒ 9 inches?   Ⓓ 15 inches?

PROBLEM 15 | What fractional part of an hour is

Ⓐ 15 minutes?   Ⓑ 20 minutes?   Ⓒ 40 minutes?   Ⓓ 90 minutes?

Fractions and Simple Probability

Probability is the study of the chance or likelihood of an event happening. Probability is always expressed as a number between 0 and 1 and is often written as a simplified fraction.

Probability of an event happening $= \dfrac{\text{number of favorable outcomes}}{\text{total number of outcomes}}$

If an event is impossible, the probability of that event happening is 0.

If an event is certain, the probability of that event happening is 1.

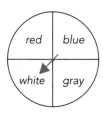

The circle is divided into 4 equal wedges starting at the center. The wedges are called **sectors** of the circle.

The spinner is just as likely to stop in one sector as another.

The probability (P) that the spinner will stop in the red sector is "one out of four," or $\frac{1}{4}$.

$$P(\text{red}) = \frac{\text{red area}}{\text{total area}} = \frac{1}{4}$$

There are six sides to a number cube. On a fair number cube, each side is equally likely to be turned up after the number cube is tossed.

The probability that the side with 3 dots lands up is $\frac{1}{6}$.

$$P(3) = \frac{\text{number of sides with 3 dots}}{\text{total number of sides}} = \frac{1}{6}$$

number cube

PROBLEM 16 | When rolling a number cube, what is the probability of getting

Ⓐ a 6?

Ⓑ an odd number?

Ⓒ a number less than 7?

Ⓓ a 0?

Ⓔ a number less than 3?

17 | In the spinner on page 158, what is the probability of landing in

Ⓐ a gray area?

Ⓑ an area whose color is in the U.S. flag?

Ⓒ a yellow area?

CALCULATOR EXPLORATION

How Can the Calculator Help?

You can find answers to some problems in this lesson by using the $\boxed{\text{a }^{b/c}}$ key on your calculator.

Convert a fraction to a mixed number and vice versa.

EXAMPLES Enter $\frac{9}{5}$: $\boxed{9}$ $\boxed{\text{a }^{b/c}}$ $\boxed{5}$ The display reads $\boxed{9 \lrcorner 5.}$.
Press the $\boxed{=}$ key. The display reads $\boxed{1 \lrcorner 4 \lrcorner 5.}$, or $1\frac{4}{5}$.

To go back to a fraction, you need to access the [d/c] key written above the $\boxed{\text{a }^{b/c}}$ key.
Leave $\boxed{1 \lrcorner 4 \lrcorner 5.}$ in the display. Press the [SHIFT] or $\boxed{\text{2}^{nd}}$ key and then the [d/c] key.
The display reads $\boxed{9 \lrcorner 5.}$ again.

To enter a mixed number, press the $\boxed{\text{a }^{b/c}}$ key between each of the numbers.
Enter $4\frac{3}{5}$: $\boxed{4}$ $\boxed{\text{a }^{b/c}}$ $\boxed{3}$ $\boxed{\text{a }^{b/c}}$ $\boxed{5}$ The display reads $\boxed{4 \lrcorner 3 \lrcorner 5.}$.

Simplify a fraction, or change a decimal to a fraction.

EXAMPLES Enter $\frac{12}{16}$: $\boxed{1}$ $\boxed{2}$ $\boxed{\text{a }^{b/c}}$ $\boxed{1}$ $\boxed{6}$ $\boxed{=}$ The display reads $\boxed{3 \lrcorner 4.}$.

Enter 0.35 as a fraction: $\boxed{3}$ $\boxed{5}$ $\boxed{\text{a }^{b/c}}$ $\boxed{1}$ $\boxed{0}$ $\boxed{0}$ $\boxed{=}$ The display reads $\boxed{7 \lrcorner 20.}$.

Find the decimal equivalent of a fraction or a mixed number.

(**Note:** This does not work on all calculators.)

EXAMPLE Enter $1\frac{3}{8}$: $\boxed{1}$ $\boxed{\text{a }^{b/c}}$ $\boxed{3}$ $\boxed{\text{a }^{b/c}}$ $\boxed{8}$ $\boxed{=}$ and $\boxed{\text{a }^{b/c}}$ again. The display reads $\boxed{1.375}$.

Use your calculator. Write the simplest single fraction that is equivalent to each of the following.

Ⓐ $\frac{27}{45}$ **Ⓑ** $7\frac{7}{9}$ **Ⓒ** 0.56 **Ⓓ** 0.6875 **Ⓔ** $\frac{64}{132}$ **Ⓕ** $40\frac{7}{8}$

CHECK YOUR UNDERSTANDING

You may use your calculator on any problem except where noted by this symbol:

1. Which of the common fractions below is a good estimate of a basketball player's performance if she made

   Ⓐ 5 of 9 shots? (**Hint:** $\frac{5}{9} \approx \frac{5}{10}$)

   Ⓑ 11 of 30 shots? (**Hint:** $\frac{11}{30} \approx \frac{10}{30}$)

   Ⓒ 15 of 21 shots?

   $$\frac{1}{2}, \frac{1}{3}, \frac{2}{3}, \frac{1}{4}, \frac{3}{4}, \frac{1}{5}, \frac{2}{5}$$

   Which would be a good estimate of a baseball player's performance if he hit

   Ⓓ 9 of 28 times at bat?
   Ⓔ 4 of 19 times at bat?
   Ⓕ 12 of 49 times at bat?

   Which would be a good estimate of a quarterback's performance if he completed

   Ⓖ 7 of 20 passes?
   Ⓗ 15 of 31 passes?
   Ⓘ 11 of 53 passes?

2. Arrange the following numbers in order from *least to greatest*. Use your calculator to change fractions to decimals.

   $0.6, \frac{1}{2}, 0.2, \frac{5}{8}, \frac{1}{4}, 0.58$

3. Gloria found two fabric remnants that she liked at the store. One remnant was marked $\frac{1}{2}$ yard, and the other was marked $\frac{3}{8}$ yard. Which piece is longer?

4. English wrench sizes are given in fraction form. Which fraction in each pair is *greater*?

   Ⓐ $\frac{3}{16}$ or $\frac{1}{4}$ Ⓓ $\frac{7}{8}$ or $\frac{3}{4}$

   Ⓑ $\frac{5}{8}$ or $\frac{1}{2}$ Ⓔ $\frac{13}{16}$ or $\frac{3}{4}$

   Ⓒ $\frac{5}{16}$ or $\frac{1}{4}$ Ⓕ $\frac{9}{16}$ or $\frac{1}{2}$

5. The following fractions all have applications in money or on a ruler. Complete each statement to make equivalent fractions.

   Ⓐ $\frac{1}{2} = \frac{}{100}$ Ⓓ $\frac{1}{10} = \frac{}{100}$

   Ⓑ $\frac{1}{4} = \frac{}{16}$ Ⓔ $\frac{3}{4} = \frac{}{16}$

   Ⓒ $\frac{2}{5} = \frac{}{10}$ Ⓕ $\frac{3}{5} = \frac{}{100}$

6. What is the length of the shaded region?

7. What fractional part of the circle is each sector?

   Ⓐ
   Ⓑ
   Ⓒ
   Ⓓ

8. What fractional part of a pound is

   Ⓐ 4 ounces?
   Ⓑ 2 ounces?
   Ⓒ 12 ounces?
   Ⓓ 24 ounces?

9. There are 20 marbles, all the same size and weight, in a bag. There are 5 red, 3 blue, 10 white, and 2 clear marbles. If you reach into the bag without looking and choose one marble, what is the probability that the marble is

   Ⓐ white?
   Ⓑ clear?
   Ⓒ blue?

TEST-TAKING PRACTICE

You may use your calculator on any problem except where noted by this symbol:

1. The circle graph below shows the results when a group of adults were asked if they were smokers. What fraction of the total said they were non-smokers?

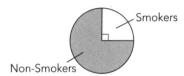
- Smokers
- Non-Smokers

Mark your answers in the circles in the grid.

2. When cutting a recipe in half, Laura found that she needs $\frac{3}{8}$ cup of sugar. This amount is halfway between

(1) 0 and $\frac{1}{4}$

(2) $\frac{1}{4}$ and $\frac{1}{2}$

(3) $\frac{1}{2}$ and $\frac{3}{4}$

(4) $\frac{1}{2}$ and 1

(5) Not enough information is given.

3. A piece of wire that measures 20 inches is what part of a yard?

(1) $\frac{1}{20}$

(2) $\frac{1}{2}$

(3) $\frac{3}{4}$

(4) $\frac{5}{9}$

(5) $\frac{10}{13}$

4. In one precinct, 95 out of 387 voters voted against the bond issue. Which fraction below is a good estimate of the size of this fractional part?

(1) $\frac{1}{4}$

(2) $\frac{1}{3}$

(3) $\frac{1}{2}$

(4) $\frac{2}{5}$

(5) $\frac{2}{9}$

5. A teacher uses a 10-sided die for classroom demonstrations. Each side is marked with one number, from 0 to 9. If she rolls the die, what is the probability that the number rolled is less than or equal to 5?

(1) $\frac{1}{5}$

(2) $\frac{1}{6}$

(3) $\frac{3}{5}$

(4) $\frac{1}{2}$

(5) $\frac{3}{10}$

MENTAL MATH

Which is greater?

1. $\frac{1}{3}$ or $\frac{1}{5}$

2. $\frac{5}{7}$ or $\frac{5}{8}$

3. $\frac{1}{4}$ or $\frac{3}{16}$

4. $\frac{1}{2}$ or $\frac{7}{15}$

In this lesson, you will learn how to add and subtract fractions using common fractions. You will also learn strategies to help you estimate the answers to other addition and subtraction problems.

Picturing Fractions

One important part of adding and subtracting fractions is to be able to rename one fraction with another that is equal to it. The fraction table below will help you to picture which of the common fractions are equal. Each line in the fraction table is a **number line** marked off in fractions having the same denominator. The fractions that are in line vertically are equal to each other.

FRACTION TABLE

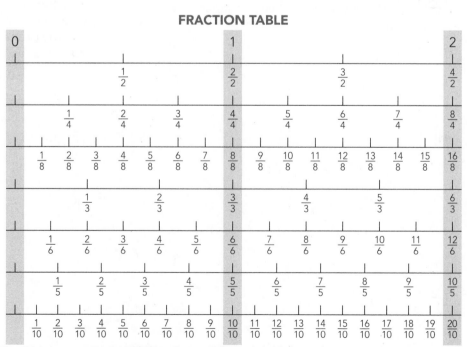

PROBLEM 1 | Use the fraction table on page 162 to find which fractions are equal to each other. Use the straight edge of your paper for accuracy.

EXAMPLE $\frac{1}{4} = \frac{2}{8}$

Ⓐ Name all the fractions shown that are equal to $\frac{1}{2}$.

Ⓑ Name all the fractions shown that are equal to $\frac{2}{3}$.

Ⓒ Name all the fractions shown that are equal to 1. What do they all have in common?

PROBLEM 2 | Use the fraction table to determine which fraction is greater than the other. (Again use a straight edge.) Place a > (greater than) or < (less than) sign to make the following true.

Ⓐ $\frac{1}{4}$ —— $\frac{1}{5}$ 　Ⓒ $\frac{1}{4}$ —— $\frac{1}{10}$ 　Ⓔ $\frac{1}{6}$ —— $\frac{1}{3}$ 　Ⓖ $\frac{1}{2}$ —— $\frac{3}{5}$

Ⓑ $\frac{5}{6}$ —— $\frac{7}{8}$ 　Ⓓ $\frac{7}{8}$ —— $\frac{9}{10}$ 　Ⓕ 1 —— $\frac{11}{10}$ 　Ⓗ $\frac{15}{10}$ —— $\frac{10}{8}$

PROBLEM 3 | Find these fractions on the fraction table and rename them as mixed numbers.

EXAMPLE $\frac{6}{5} = 1\frac{1}{5}$

Ⓐ $\frac{5}{4}$ 　　Ⓑ $\frac{5}{3}$ 　　Ⓒ $\frac{13}{8}$ 　　Ⓓ $\frac{19}{10}$ 　　Ⓔ $\frac{15}{8}$

Renaming Fractions

One step involved with adding and subtracting fractions is to rename a fraction with an equivalent one. Remember from the last lesson that you can use the Fundamental Principle of Fractions to find equivalent fractions if you do not have the fraction table at hand for reference.

To find a fraction that is equal to another, multiply (or divide) both the numerator and denominator by the same non-zero number.

EXAMPLE A

Rename $\frac{3}{4}$ so that it has a denominator of 8.

THINK: 4 times what number equals 8?

DO: Multiply both top and bottom by 2.

$$\frac{3}{4} = \frac{3 \times 2}{4 \times 2} = \frac{6}{8}$$

Multiplying by 1 results in an equal number.

EXAMPLE B

Rename $\frac{2}{5}$ so that it has a denominator of 15.

THINK: To get 15, multiply 5 by 3.

DO: Multiply both top and bottom by 3.

$$\frac{2}{5} = \frac{2 \times 3}{5 \times 3} = \frac{6}{15}$$

PROBLEM 4 | Rename these fractions with the denominators shown. Show the multiplication involved.

Ⓐ $\frac{2}{3} = \frac{}{6}$ 　Ⓑ $\frac{5}{6} = \frac{}{18}$ 　Ⓒ $\frac{3}{5} = \frac{}{20}$ 　Ⓓ $\frac{1}{4} = \frac{}{32}$ 　Ⓔ $\frac{5}{8} = \frac{}{16}$ 　Ⓕ $\frac{3}{16} = \frac{}{32}$

You also *rename* a fraction when you write it in simplest terms. You are finding an equivalent representation of the same value.

PROBLEM 5 | Find the simplest representation of these fractions by dividing the top and bottom by the same non-zero number. Show the division involved.

Ⓐ $\frac{4}{6}$ Ⓑ $\frac{4}{12}$ Ⓒ $\frac{12}{16}$ Ⓓ $\frac{16}{32}$ Ⓔ $\frac{5}{10}$ Ⓕ $\frac{5}{20}$

PROBLEM 6 | Can you rename $\frac{1}{4}$ as a fraction that has a denominator of 7? Why or why not?

Adding Fractions

Use the ruler to picture the problem.

Toni sewed two pieces of ribbon next to each other to make a stripe on a place mat. One ribbon is $\frac{1}{2}$ inch wide, and the other is $\frac{1}{8}$ inch wide. What is the total width of the stripe?

$\frac{1}{2}$ in.

$\frac{1}{8}$ in.

?

To find the answer, you must add two fractions. Picture the stripe next to the ruler and measure it.

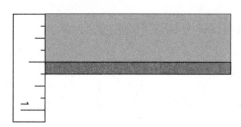

The final ruler mark is one of the "eighth" marks.

Count the number of eighths *down* to this mark.

The width of the stripe is $\frac{5}{8}$ in.

PROBLEM 7 | Use this picture of a ruler to determine the sum of the following fractions. You may find it helpful to mark off the lengths on a piece of paper.

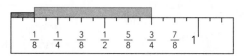

$\frac{1}{8}$ $\frac{1}{4}$ $\frac{3}{8}$ $\frac{1}{2}$ $\frac{5}{8}$ $\frac{3}{4}$ $\frac{7}{8}$ 1

EXAMPLE $\frac{1}{8} + \frac{5}{8} = \frac{3}{4}$ (shown by the shading on the ruler)

Ⓐ $\frac{1}{4} + \frac{1}{4}$ Ⓒ $\frac{1}{4} + \frac{1}{8}$ Ⓔ $\frac{5}{8} + \frac{1}{8}$ Ⓖ $\frac{1}{2} + \frac{1}{16}$ Ⓘ $\frac{3}{16} + \frac{1}{2}$

Ⓑ $\frac{1}{4} + \frac{1}{2}$ Ⓓ $\frac{3}{8} + \frac{1}{8}$ Ⓕ $\frac{5}{8} + \frac{1}{4}$ Ⓗ $\frac{1}{16} + \frac{1}{4}$ Ⓙ $\frac{3}{16} + \frac{1}{4}$

Use a picture to make sense of the rule for addition of fractions.

ADDITION OF FRACTIONS	To add two fractions with the same denominator, add only the numerators. $\frac{a}{c} + \frac{b}{c} = \frac{a+b}{c}$ $(c \neq 0)$

EXAMPLE

$\frac{1}{2} + \frac{1}{8}$

① Find a number that is divisible by both denominators. This will be the common denominator.

Both 2 and 8 divide evenly into 8.

② Rewrite the problem so that both fractions have the same denominator.

Rename $\frac{1}{2}$ as $\frac{4}{8}$: $\frac{4}{8} + \frac{1}{8}$

③ Add the numerators of the two fractions and place the sum over the same denominator.

$\frac{4}{8} + \frac{1}{8} = \frac{5}{8}$

Sometimes you need an additional step:

④ Write the answer in simplest terms.

$\frac{1}{8} + \frac{5}{8} = \frac{6}{8}$ $\frac{6}{8} = \frac{6 \div 2}{8 \div 2} = \frac{3}{4}$

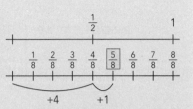

When both fractions have the same denominator, both are on the same number line where all the intervals are the same length.

Review the four steps in the process. There are two that require you to know about equivalent fractions. Which are they?

In many problems you will need to rename *both* fractions so they have the common denominator. To discover a denominator that will work for both fractions, you can "build" equivalent fractions.

EXAMPLE

$\frac{1}{5} + \frac{2}{3}$

Build equivalent fractions by multiplying each fraction in turn by $\frac{2}{2}, \frac{3}{3}, \frac{4}{4}, \frac{5}{5}$, and so on. Watch for the same denominator to occur.

$\frac{1}{5} \times \frac{2}{2} = \frac{2}{10}$ $\frac{2}{3} \times \frac{2}{2} = \frac{4}{6}$

$\frac{1}{5} \times \frac{3}{3} = \frac{3}{15}$ $\frac{2}{3} \times \frac{3}{3} = \frac{6}{9}$

$\frac{1}{5} \times \frac{4}{4} = \frac{4}{20}$ $\frac{2}{3} \times \frac{4}{4} = \frac{8}{12}$

$\frac{1}{5} \times \frac{5}{5} = \frac{5}{25}$ $\frac{2}{3} \times \frac{5}{5} = \frac{10}{15}$

Use $\frac{3}{15} + \frac{10}{15}$ as the problem, and you get $\frac{13}{15}$ as the answer.

PROBLEM 8 | Find the answers to the following problems, using the techniques above.

Ⓐ $\frac{3}{8} + \frac{1}{8}$ Ⓒ $\frac{1}{4} + \frac{1}{16}$ Ⓔ $\frac{5}{8} + \frac{1}{16}$ Ⓖ $\frac{2}{5} + \frac{3}{10}$ Ⓘ $\frac{1}{4} + \frac{2}{5}$

Ⓑ $\frac{1}{2} + \frac{1}{4}$ Ⓓ $\frac{3}{8} + \frac{1}{16}$ Ⓕ $\frac{3}{8} + \frac{3}{16}$ Ⓗ $\frac{1}{2} + \frac{1}{5}$ Ⓙ $\frac{2}{3} + \frac{1}{4}$

PROBLEM 9 | Jack spent $\frac{1}{3}$ of an hour on the phone in the morning and $\frac{1}{2}$ of an hour on the phone in the afternoon. What fraction of an hour did he spend on the phone altogether?

PROBLEM 10 | Tracy ate 3 slices of this pizza and Brian ate 2 slices. Altogether, what fraction of the pizza did they eat?

Subtracting Fractions

Use a ruler to picture the problem.

A seamstress normally makes seams that are $\frac{5}{8}$ inch wide. A seam $\frac{3}{4}$ inch wide is required on a tailoring job. How much wider is this than the normal seam?

Locate these two fractions on a ruler.
It is easy to see the difference between them.

$\frac{3}{4} - \frac{5}{8} = \frac{1}{8}$

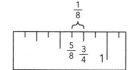

PROBLEM 11 | Sketch a ruler and picture the following problems on it to find the answers.

Ⓐ $\frac{1}{2} - \frac{1}{4}$ Ⓒ $\frac{3}{4} - \frac{5}{8}$ Ⓔ $\frac{3}{4} - \frac{1}{2}$ Ⓖ $\frac{3}{4} - \frac{3}{8}$ Ⓘ $\frac{7}{8} - \frac{3}{8}$

Ⓑ $\frac{3}{8} - \frac{1}{8}$ Ⓓ $\frac{7}{8} - \frac{3}{4}$ Ⓕ $\frac{3}{4} - \frac{5}{8}$ Ⓗ $\frac{9}{16} - \frac{1}{2}$ Ⓙ $\frac{11}{16} - \frac{7}{16}$

Use a picture to make sense of the rule.

SUBTRACTION OF FRACTIONS	To subtract fractions with the same denominator, subtract the numerators only. $\frac{a}{c} - \frac{b}{c} = \frac{a-b}{c}$ $(c \neq 0)$

EXAMPLE

$\frac{7}{10} - \frac{1}{5}$

① Find a common denominator.   10 is divisible by both 10 and 5.

② Write both fractions with the same denominator. $\frac{7}{10} - \frac{2}{10}$

③ Subtract the numerators only. Place the answer above the same denominator. $\frac{7}{10} - \frac{2}{10} = \frac{5}{10}$

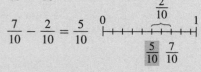

④ Write the answer in simplest terms. $\frac{5}{10} = \frac{1}{2}$

PROBLEM 12 | Follow the steps on page 166 to find the answers to these problems.

Ⓐ $\frac{1}{2} - \frac{1}{8}$ Ⓒ $\frac{3}{4} - \frac{3}{16}$ Ⓔ $\frac{3}{4} - \frac{3}{8}$ Ⓖ $\frac{1}{4} - \frac{1}{5}$ Ⓘ $\frac{2}{3} - \frac{1}{2}$

Ⓑ $\frac{1}{2} - \frac{1}{16}$ Ⓓ $\frac{5}{8} - \frac{5}{16}$ Ⓕ $\frac{7}{10} - \frac{1}{2}$ Ⓗ $\frac{1}{3} - \frac{1}{4}$ Ⓙ $\frac{2}{3} - \frac{3}{5}$

What part is left?

When a part is taken from the whole, you often need to know how much is left. Mathematically, we think of this as subtracting a fraction from 1.

 $1 - \frac{1}{4}$ $1 - \frac{1}{6}$ $1 - \frac{7}{10}$

$\frac{4}{4} - \frac{1}{4} = \frac{3}{4}$ $\frac{6}{6} - \frac{1}{6} = \frac{5}{6}$ $\frac{10}{10} - \frac{7}{10} = \frac{3}{10}$

Use whichever name for 1 that the problem suggests.

PROBLEM 13 | Find the answers.

Ⓐ $1 - \frac{3}{5}$ Ⓑ $1 - \frac{3}{8}$ Ⓒ $1 - \frac{6}{11}$ Ⓓ $1 - \frac{11}{12}$ Ⓔ $1 - \frac{13}{20}$

Complementary Probabilities

The idea that you used in finding what part is left is also used when discussing the probability of some event NOT occurring. Remember that the probability of an event that is certain to happen is 1, while the probability of an event that is impossible to happen is 0. All other probabilities are between 0 and 1.

EXAMPLE

When you roll a number cube, the probability of rolling a 5 is $\frac{1}{6}$. What is the probability of NOT rolling a 5?

The event of rolling a 5 will either happen or it won't happen. The two probabilities must add to 1 because one or the other is certain to occur. We say that they are **complementary**.

$P(5) + P(\text{not } 5) = 1$

So, $P(\text{not } 5) = 1 - P(5)$

$P(\text{not } 5) = 1 - \frac{1}{6} = \frac{5}{6}$

PROBLEM 14 | Pick a card from a deck of 52 cards. What is the probability that it is NOT

Ⓐ the 3 of clubs?   Ⓒ lower than a 4? (2s are the smallest cards)
Ⓑ a 3?   Ⓓ a face card?

Adding and Subtracting Mixed Numbers

Look at the number lines to get a picture of what the problems are asking and what the steps are doing.

Remember that 1 can be named by any fraction whose numerator and denominator are the same non-zero number ($\frac{2}{2}, \frac{4}{4}, \frac{5}{5}, \frac{8}{8}, \frac{10}{10}$, and so on).

EXAMPLE

On one day of training, Jamie swam $\frac{1}{2}$ mile, and on the next day he swam $\frac{3}{4}$ mile. How many miles did he swim over the 2 days?

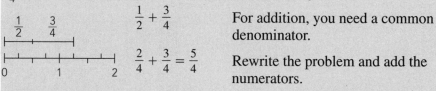

$\frac{1}{2} + \frac{3}{4}$ For addition, you need a common denominator.

$\frac{2}{4} + \frac{3}{4} = \frac{5}{4}$ Rewrite the problem and add the numerators.

$\frac{5}{4} = 1\frac{1}{4}$ miles Think: $1 = \frac{4}{4}$, so $\frac{5}{4} = \frac{4}{4} + \frac{1}{4}$ or $1 + \frac{1}{4}$.

EXAMPLE

Ron ran $1\frac{1}{2}$ miles on one day and ran $\frac{7}{8}$ mile the next day. How much farther did he run the first day than the second?

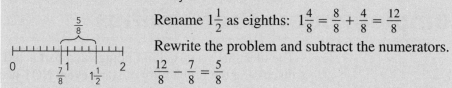

Rename $1\frac{1}{2}$ as eighths: $1\frac{4}{8} = \frac{8}{8} + \frac{4}{8} = \frac{12}{8}$

Rewrite the problem and subtract the numerators.

$\frac{12}{8} - \frac{7}{8} = \frac{5}{8}$

When the problems get more complex, remember that the commutative and the associative properties of addition allow you to **change the order and grouping of numbers when you add.**

EXAMPLE

$3\frac{1}{2} + 5\frac{5}{8}$

$(3 + \frac{1}{2}) + (5 + \frac{5}{8})$ This is the meaning of mixed numbers.

$(3 + 5) + (\frac{1}{2} + \frac{5}{8})$ The properties allow adding the whole numbers together and the fractions together.

$8 + \frac{9}{8}$

$8 + 1\frac{1}{8} = 9\frac{1}{8}$ Rename in simplest form.

> This same problem can be written in a vertical format.
>
> $3\frac{1}{2} = \quad 3\frac{4}{8}$
>
> $+ 5\frac{5}{8} = + 5\frac{5}{8}$
>
> $8\frac{9}{8} = 9\frac{1}{8}$

Subtracting can be just as easy for some problems.

$21\frac{7}{8} = \quad 21\frac{7}{8}$

$- 16\frac{1}{4} = - 16\frac{2}{8}$

$\rule{2cm}{0.4pt}$

$5\frac{5}{8}$

But it can get more complicated when you have to "borrow."

$10\frac{1}{4} = 10\frac{2}{8} = 9 + \frac{8}{8} + \frac{2}{8} = 9\frac{10}{8}$

$- 3\frac{5}{8} = \qquad\qquad\qquad\qquad - 3\frac{5}{8}$

$\rule{2cm}{0.4pt}$

$6\frac{5}{8}$

PROBLEM 15 | Use any of the methods discussed on page 168 to solve the following problems.

A $\frac{3}{4} + \frac{3}{4}$ **D** $3\frac{1}{8} + 5\frac{3}{4}$ **G** $7\frac{1}{10} + 4\frac{3}{5}$ **J** $10 - 5\frac{3}{4}$

B $1\frac{1}{4} - \frac{7}{8}$ **E** $4\frac{5}{16} - 2\frac{1}{4}$ **H** $9 - 2\frac{1}{8}$ **K** $66\frac{2}{3} + 12\frac{1}{2}$

C $5\frac{1}{2} - \frac{3}{4}$ **F** $8\frac{1}{32} + 10\frac{1}{4}$ **I** $3\frac{7}{8} + 8\frac{1}{4}$ **L** $37\frac{1}{2} - 16\frac{2}{3}$

Adding and Subtracting Measurements

Look for the similarities in the ideas and techniques that you used in adding and subtracting mixed numbers and those you need to add and subtract measurements. Refer to page 295 in the Appendix for the necessary equivalents.

EXAMPLE

A book weighing 3 pounds 10 ounces is put into a book bag that already weighed 8 pounds 12 ounces. What is the new weight of the book bag?

3 lb 10 oz	Add pounds to pounds and ounces to ounces.
+ 8 lb 12 oz	
11 lb 22 oz	Simplify 11 lb 22 oz because 22 oz is more than 1 lb.

11 lb + 1 lb + 6 oz   (There are 16 oz in 1 lb.)
12 lb 6 oz

PROBLEM 16 | **A** If 4 gallons 2 quarts of water are used to dilute 8 gallons 3 quarts of acid, how much is in the mixture?

B A piece of wire 5 feet 8 inches long was cut from a 100-foot coil. How long is the wire that remains on the coil?

C A bicycle deliveryman began his rounds with a load weighing 12 pounds 5 ounces. At his first stop he delivered a package that weighed 4 pounds 10 ounces. How heavy was the remaining load?

D Pieces of the following lengths were cut from a 10-foot rod of bar stock: 3 feet 2 inches, 2 feet 8 inches, and 1 foot 5 inches. What is the length of the remaining rod?

How Can the Calculator Help?

Adding and subtracting fractions and mixed numbers is easy to do on a calculator with a fraction key.

Enter the fractions or mixed numbers using the [a b/c] key on your calculator.

Use the operation keys ([+] and [−]) in the same way as with whole numbers and decimals. The answer in the display will be in fraction form.

EXAMPLE $15\frac{5}{9} - 8\frac{5}{6}$

ENTER   [1] [5] [a b/c] [5] [a b/c] [9] [−] [8] [a b/c] [5] [a b/c] [6] [=]
   [6 ⌐ 13 ⌐ 18.]

You read the display as 6 and $\frac{13}{18}$.

Use the calculator to find the answers.

Ⓐ $\frac{11}{12} + \frac{5}{8}$ **Ⓑ** $5\frac{7}{12} - 3\frac{2}{3}$ **Ⓒ** $7\frac{3}{5} + 3\frac{7}{8}$ **Ⓓ** $100 - 87\frac{5}{16}$

Class discussion topic: Finding the answers with the calculator is easy. Why should we learn how to find the answers without the calculator?

Estimating When Adding and Subtracting Fractions

It is important to estimate an answer when you are using a calculator so that you know if the answer on the display is reasonable. Moreover, in many situations, an estimate of an answer is often all you need to make decisions. The following strategies can get you started thinking about estimating with fractions.

1 Compare to an easy problem with 0, $\frac{1}{2}$, or 1.

Some of the easiest problems involve 0, $\frac{1}{2}$, and 1. By rounding other fractions to one of these, you can make estimating simple as well.

PROBLEM 17 | Decide whether each of these fractions is close to 0, $\frac{1}{2}$, or 1.

Ⓐ $\frac{1}{9}$ **Ⓒ** $\frac{21}{20}$ **Ⓔ** $\frac{14}{15}$ **Ⓖ** $\frac{9}{11}$ **Ⓘ** $\frac{2}{15}$ **Ⓚ** $\frac{6}{11}$ **Ⓜ** $\frac{10}{21}$ **Ⓞ** $\frac{5}{89}$

Ⓑ $\frac{3}{8}$ **Ⓓ** $\frac{3}{50}$ **Ⓕ** $\frac{9}{17}$ **Ⓗ** $\frac{27}{50}$ **Ⓙ** $\frac{43}{40}$ **Ⓛ** $\frac{2}{150}$ **Ⓝ** $\frac{9}{14}$ **Ⓟ** $\frac{5}{12}$

When you estimate, round the fractions to 0, $\frac{1}{2}$, or 1. Then add or subtract mentally.

EXAMPLES

$$\frac{9}{10} + \frac{5}{11} \approx 1\frac{1}{2}$$

$$1 + \frac{1}{2}$$

Exact: $1\frac{39}{110}$

$$\frac{9}{16} - \frac{1}{11} \approx \frac{1}{2}$$

$$\frac{1}{2} - 0$$

Exact: $\frac{83}{176}$

$$2\frac{11}{13} + 6\frac{4}{9} \approx 9\frac{1}{2}$$

$$(2 + 1) + \left(6 + \frac{1}{2}\right)$$

Exact: $9\frac{34}{117}$

PROBLEM 18

Estimate, rounding each fraction to 0, $\frac{1}{2}$, or 1. Use your calculator to verify that your estimate is close to the exact answer.

EXAMPLE $\frac{1}{7} + \frac{4}{9} \approx 0 + \frac{1}{2} = \frac{1}{2}$ Exact answer: $\frac{37}{63}$

Ⓐ $\frac{8}{9} + \frac{1}{11}$

Ⓑ $\frac{11}{12} - \frac{6}{7}$

Ⓒ $\frac{4}{9} + \frac{7}{15}$

Ⓓ $\frac{25}{49} + \frac{1}{15}$

Ⓔ $\frac{5}{6} + \frac{19}{20}$

Ⓕ $\frac{5}{7} + \frac{6}{11}$

Ⓖ $3\frac{2}{3} + 9\frac{7}{8}$

Ⓗ $6\frac{1}{5} + 3\frac{1}{4}$

Ⓘ $9\frac{11}{12} - 3\frac{1}{5}$

2 Look for other easy problems to use as references when estimating.

EXAMPLE A

What is an estimate of $\frac{1}{5} + \frac{1}{4}$?

$$\frac{1}{4} + \frac{1}{4} = \frac{1}{2}$$

Since $\frac{1}{5}$ is less than $\frac{1}{4}$, the actual answer is less than the estimate $\frac{1}{2}$.

① Think of an easy problem that is similar.

② Use common sense to adjust the estimate.

EXAMPLE B

What is an estimate of $10\frac{3}{8} - 3\frac{5}{6}$?

$$10\frac{3}{8} - 4 = 6\frac{3}{8}$$

Since $3\frac{5}{6}$ is less than 4, the difference is greater than the estimate $6\frac{3}{8}$.

PROBLEM 19

Compare these to easy problems so that you can refine the estimates.

Ⓐ $\frac{1}{4} + \frac{2}{3}$, (greater or less) than 1?

Ⓑ $\frac{3}{4} + \frac{1}{5}$, (greater or less) than 1?

Ⓒ $\frac{1}{5} + \frac{1}{6}$, (greater or less) than $\frac{1}{2}$?

Ⓓ $\frac{5}{8} - \frac{1}{10}$, (greater or less) than $\frac{1}{2}$?

Ⓔ $\frac{13}{15} - \frac{1}{2}$, (greater or less) than $\frac{1}{2}$?

Ⓕ $\frac{3}{16} + \frac{1}{10}$, (greater or less) than $\frac{1}{4}$?

PROBLEM 20 | *Estimate* the following answers. Compare your estimates to the exact answers found with a calculator.

A $\frac{8}{17} + \frac{1}{4}$ **C** $\frac{1}{2} - \frac{11}{40}$ **E** $11\frac{3}{4} - 7\frac{7}{8}$

B $\frac{9}{10} + \frac{1}{16}$ **D** $10\frac{1}{2} + 3\frac{5}{9}$ **F** $20\frac{3}{5} - 5\frac{1}{2}$

Adding and Subtracting Fractions in Real Situations

The situations that require you to add and subtract fractions are likely to be ones that involve measurement. Some will require an exact answer. In other situations, an estimate is all you need to proceed.

EXAMPLE

What is the total length of the bolt in the drawing?

To add, all fractions must have a common denominator. $\left(\frac{1}{4} = \frac{2}{8}\right)$

$\frac{2}{8} + \frac{7}{8} + \frac{3}{8} = \frac{12}{8} = 1\frac{4}{8} = 1\frac{1}{2}$ in.

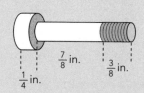

$\frac{7}{8}$ in. $\frac{3}{8}$ in. $\frac{1}{4}$ in.

EXAMPLE

Franco has a piece of PVC pipe that is 10 inches long. Is that long enough to cut two pieces, one $5\frac{3}{8}$ inches and the other $4\frac{1}{2}$ inches?

Add the whole numbers first. $5 + 4 = 9$

Are the fractions greater than or less than 1? $\frac{3}{8}$ is less than $\frac{1}{2}$, so the total is less than 1.

Yes, the 10-inch pipe is long enough.

In the problem below, decide whether an *exact answer* or an *estimate* is appropriate for the situation. Then find the necessary value.

PROBLEM 21 | How much sugar does Mabel need to bake both a batch of cookies that requires $\frac{3}{4}$ cup sugar and a loaf of banana bread that requires $\frac{1}{2}$ cup sugar?

PROBLEM 22 | In the deli section of a supermarket at the beginning of the day, a round of salami weighed $5\frac{5}{8}$ pounds. At inventory time at the end of the day, the remaining salami weighed $1\frac{1}{4}$ pounds. How much salami was sold that day?

PROBLEM 23 | On her tiptoes, Veda can reach to a height of 5 feet 8 inches. If she stands on a stepstool $1\frac{1}{4}$ feet high, will she be able to reach to 7 feet? Explain.

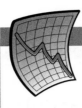

Use the table titled *Selected Measurements Used in Home Construction* on page 294 in the Appendix to answer the following problems. Use a calculator if necessary.

A What is the thickness of a countertop made of $\frac{5}{8}$-inch plywood and a covering of Formica?

B An outside wall is made of thick studs and covered on the inside with dry wall and on the outside with a layer of stucco and plywood. What is the total thickness of the wall?

C A tiled foyer (tile plus backer board) adjoins a room with hardwood laminate flooring. What is the difference in thickness of these two floor coverings?

D Quarter round molding is added to the bottom of the baseboard. What is the combined width of these two trim pieces?

E How tall will the cabinets be after a layer of $\frac{5}{8}$-inch plywood and granite countertops have been added?

F Using a carbide tip blade, Dennis wants to cut 3 pieces of molding of lengths $4\frac{3}{8}$ inches, $4\frac{3}{8}$ inches, and $3\frac{1}{4}$ inches from a 12-inch strip. Is that possible? Explain.

✓ CHECK YOUR UNDERSTANDING

You may use your calculator on any problem except where noted by this symbol:

1. Find an *exact answer* for each of the following problems. Try to "see" the problem and the answer on a number line or ruler.

   Ⓐ $\frac{1}{2} + \frac{3}{8}$ Ⓕ $\frac{1}{2} - \frac{3}{10}$

   Ⓑ $\frac{3}{4} + \frac{1}{2}$ Ⓖ $\frac{2}{5} + \frac{7}{10}$

   Ⓒ $\frac{7}{8} - \frac{1}{4}$ Ⓗ $\frac{2}{3} - \frac{1}{4}$

   Ⓓ $\frac{5}{8} + \frac{13}{16}$ Ⓘ $\frac{2}{3} + \frac{3}{5}$

   Ⓔ $\frac{1}{2} + \frac{15}{16}$

2. *Estimate* an answer for each of the following problems. Then use a calculator to find the exact answer.

   Ⓐ $\frac{3}{7} + \frac{4}{5}$

   Ⓑ $\frac{11}{12} + \frac{13}{15}$

   Ⓒ $\frac{1}{5} + \frac{1}{4}$

   Ⓓ $\frac{15}{16} - \frac{1}{20}$

   Ⓔ $\frac{15}{16} - \frac{2}{5}$

3. How much rope is left on a 50-feet coil after $4\frac{1}{3}$ feet is cut off?

4. A wrench is marked $\frac{5}{8}$ on one end and $\frac{21}{32}$ on the other. Which end is larger?

5. During one week, Juana worked these times on a specific project. What is the total time she should record on her time sheet?

   $2\frac{1}{4}$ hours, $1\frac{1}{2}$ hours, $5\frac{3}{4}$ hours, 3 hours 20 minutes

6. The drapes made for Elaine's window will extend 1 feet 4 inches on each side of the window frame. If the window frame measures 6 feet 6 inches, how long should the drapery rod be?

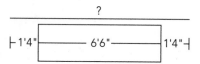

7. *Estimate* an answer for each of the following problems. Then use a calculator to find the exact answer.

   Ⓐ $7\frac{1}{4} + 4\frac{1}{3}$

   Ⓑ $10\frac{1}{3} - 5\frac{13}{16}$

   Ⓒ $4\frac{8}{9} + 2\frac{5}{11}$

   Ⓓ $6\frac{2}{3} + \frac{5}{16}$

   Ⓔ $30\frac{2}{5} - 10\frac{7}{12}$

8. Use the information in the chart below to estimate the total number of inches of wire used to assemble circuit board A.

ASSEMBLY SPECIFICATIONS

circuit board A	
Side 1	$21\frac{3}{4}$ in.
Side 2	$19\frac{1}{16}$ in.
Side 3	$12\frac{7}{8}$ in.
Side 4	$11\frac{2}{5}$ in.

TEST-TAKING PRACTICE

You may use your calculator on any problem except where noted by this symbol:

1. Thomas, a painter, can reach to a height of $7\frac{3}{4}$ feet while he is painting with a roller. How high will he be able to reach if an extension of $2\frac{1}{2}$ feet is added to the handle of his roller?

   (1) $3\frac{3}{4}$ ft

   (2) $5\frac{1}{4}$ ft

   (3) $9\frac{1}{4}$ ft

   (4) $10\frac{1}{4}$ ft

   (5) 14 ft

2. Find the perimeter of the figure below.

   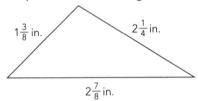

   (1) $4\frac{21}{64}$ in.

   (2) $5\frac{11}{20}$ in.

   (3) $6\frac{1}{4}$ in.

   (4) $6\frac{1}{2}$ in.

   (5) $9\frac{1}{16}$ in.

3. What is the diameter of the hole in the gasket below?

   (1) $1\frac{1}{2}$ in.

   (2) $3\frac{1}{2}$ in.

   (3) 5 in.

   (4) $6\frac{3}{4}$ in.

   (5) $8\frac{1}{2}$ in.

   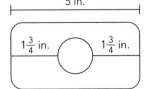

4. If all the letters in the word DECEMBER were placed in a container and one letter was picked at random, what is the probability that it would NOT be an E?

   Mark your answer in the circles in the grid.

5. Which of the following represents the order of the distances listed below, from *greatest* to *least*?

   (1) D, A, B, C
   (2) A, D, B, C
   (3) B, A, D, C
   (4) D, B, C, A
   (5) D, B, A, C

A	0.2 mile
B	$\frac{3}{8}$ mile
C	$\frac{1}{4}$ mile
D	0.5 mil

6. For a test on Friday, Jorge studied 2 hours 30 minutes on Monday, 1 hour 45 minutes on Wednesday, and 3 hours 20 minutes on Thursday. Altogether, how long did Jorge study for the test?

   (1) 6 hours 45 minutes
   (2) 6 hours 55 minutes
   (3) 7 hours 5 minutes
   (4) 7 hours 35 minutes
   (5) 8 hours 5 minutes

Multiplying and Dividing Fractions

Greater than or less than 1?

1. $\frac{1}{2} + \frac{2}{3}$ **3.** $\frac{1}{4} + \frac{5}{8}$

2. $\frac{2}{3} + \frac{1}{4}$ **4.** $\frac{5}{8} + \frac{3}{16}$

Finding a Fraction of a Fraction

When using fractions, *of* means "times."

What does *half of* something mean? Is it different from something *divided in half?* When you *divide something in thirds,* are you doing the same thing as when you find *a third* of something? If they are the same, what operation are you using—multiplication or division?

Finding *half of* 30 means *multiplying* $\frac{1}{2}$ by 30. However, remember from Lesson 8 that this also means the same as dividing 30 by 2. This lesson will show how these two ideas are related.

$\frac{1}{2}$ of $\frac{1}{4}$ means $\frac{1}{2} \times \frac{1}{4}$ $\frac{3}{4}$ of $\frac{2}{3}$ means $\frac{3}{4} \times \frac{2}{3}$

    ↑— original number   ↑— original number

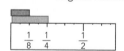

$\frac{1}{2}$ of $\frac{1}{4} = \frac{1}{2} \times \frac{1}{4} = \frac{1 \times 1}{2 \times 4} = \frac{1}{8}$ $\frac{3}{4}$ of $\frac{2}{3} = \frac{3}{4} \times \frac{2}{3} = \frac{3 \times 2}{4 \times 3} = \frac{6}{12} = \frac{1}{2}$

Note in the sketches above that the answers are *less than* the original numbers. This is an expected result because you were multiplying by numbers whose value was less than 1. (Refer to Lesson 9, page 96.)

TO MULTIPLY FRACTIONS	Multiply the numerators, multiply the denominators, and write the answer in simplest terms. $\frac{a}{b} \times \frac{c}{d} = \frac{ac}{bd}$ $(b \neq 0, d \neq 0)$

The procedure is easy because it follows what you might do naturally. No common denominator is required. *Just multiply.*

PROBLEM 1 | Multiply these fractions. Assure yourself that the answer is less than the original number.

A $\frac{1}{2}$ of $\frac{3}{4}$ **C** $\frac{1}{4}$ of $\frac{3}{4}$ **E** $\frac{1}{2}$ of $\frac{2}{3}$ **G** $\frac{3}{4}$ of $\frac{1}{8}$

      ⌐ original number

B $\frac{1}{3}$ of $\frac{5}{8}$ **D** $\frac{2}{3}$ of $\frac{4}{5}$ **F** $\frac{3}{4}$ of $\frac{1}{5}$ **H** $\frac{1}{8}$ of $\frac{4}{5}$

PROBLEM 2 | Bring recipes from home and calculate the amounts needed for each ingredient if you halve the recipe or if you double it for a larger group.

Finding a Fraction of a Whole Number and Canceling

Almost every day, you will be asked to find a fractional part of a number. It happens so often that you already know the answers to these problems.

- What is $\frac{1}{2}$ of an hour?

- What is $\frac{3}{4}$ of an hour?

- What is $\frac{3}{4}$ of a dollar?

Even though you know the answer, notice how the procedure of multiplying fractions is applied.

$\frac{1}{2}$ of 60 means $\frac{1}{2} \times 60$.

To write 60 as a fraction, write it as $\frac{60}{1}$. ⟵ (Dividing by 1 does not change the value.)

$\frac{1}{2} \times \frac{60}{1} = \frac{1 \times 60}{2 \times 1} = \frac{60}{2} = 30$ minutes

Compare methods. The technique of **canceling** allows you to compute with smaller numbers.

ORIGINAL

$\frac{3}{4} \times 100 = \frac{3 \times 100}{4 \times 1} = \frac{300}{4} = 75$

CANCELING

$$\frac{3}{\cancel{4}_{1}} \times \frac{\overset{25}{\cancel{100}}}{1} = \frac{3 \times 25}{1} = 75$$

Here, the top and bottom numbers were divided by 4.

The Fundamental Principle of Fractions says that you can divide both numerator and denominator by the same non-zero number without changing the value of the fraction. You have used it before when you simplified fractions; here it allows you to cancel during a multiplication problem.

EXAMPLES

$$\frac{2}{3} \text{ of } 60 = \frac{2 \times \overset{20}{\cancel{60}}}{\cancel{3} \times 1}_{1} = 40 \qquad\qquad \frac{3}{10} \text{ of } 150 = \frac{3 \times \overset{15}{\cancel{150}}}{\cancel{10} \times 1}_{1} = 45$$

(Both top and bottom are divided by 3.)   (Both top and bottom are divided by 10.)

PROBLEM 3 | Find the following fractional parts. Cancel when possible.

Ⓐ $\frac{1}{2}$ of 48   Ⓓ $\frac{2}{3}$ of 12   Ⓖ $\frac{1}{8}$ of 56   Ⓙ $\frac{1}{5}$ of 60

Ⓑ $\frac{1}{4}$ of 48   Ⓔ $\frac{2}{3}$ of 24   Ⓗ $\frac{3}{8}$ of 56   Ⓚ $\frac{1}{10}$ of 60

Ⓒ $\frac{1}{3}$ of 48   Ⓕ $\frac{2}{3}$ of 48   Ⓘ $\frac{5}{8}$ of 56   Ⓛ $\frac{3}{5}$ of 60

When you cancel, you make the multiplication problem easier in two ways: The numbers that you multiply are smaller and you eliminate the simplifying step at the end.

Compare these methods of multiplying two fractions.

EXAMPLES

WITHOUT CANCELING (NEED TO SIMPLIFY)	WITH CANCELING (SIMPLIFY EARLY)
$\frac{2}{5}$ of $\frac{7}{8} = \frac{2 \times 7}{5 \times 8} = \frac{14 \div 2}{40 \div 2} = \frac{7}{20}$	$\frac{2}{5}$ of $\frac{7}{8} = \frac{\overset{1}{\cancel{2}} \times 7}{5 \times \underset{4}{\cancel{8}}} = \frac{7}{20}$
$\frac{2}{3}$ of $\frac{9}{10} = \frac{2 \times 9}{3 \times 10} = \frac{18 \div 6}{30 \div 6} = \frac{3}{5}$	$\frac{2}{3}$ of $\frac{9}{10} = \frac{\overset{1}{\cancel{2}} \times \overset{3}{\cancel{9}}}{\underset{1}{\cancel{3}} \times \underset{5}{\cancel{10}}} = \frac{3}{5}$

CAUTION: Cancel ONLY when you are *multiplying*.

PROBLEM 4 | Multiply these fractions using canceling.

Ⓐ $\frac{3}{5}$ of $\frac{1}{6}$ Ⓒ $\frac{1}{2}$ of $\frac{4}{5}$ Ⓔ $\frac{3}{4}$ of $\frac{8}{9}$ Ⓖ $\frac{2}{5}$ of $\frac{3}{8}$

Ⓑ $\frac{2}{3}$ of $\frac{1}{4}$ Ⓓ $\frac{1}{3}$ of $\frac{3}{4}$ Ⓕ $\frac{5}{6}$ of $\frac{9}{10}$ Ⓗ $\frac{2}{3}$ of $\frac{3}{8}$

USING DATA

Use the *Investment Advice for a Lifetime* graphs on page 293 in the Appendix to answer the following questions.

Ⓐ According to the graphs, a 30-year-old with $7,500 to invest, should invest how much in stocks?

Ⓑ A couple in the 46 to 60 age range has $150,000 invested. How much of their investment should be in stocks if they follow this advice?

Ⓒ A retired man 70 years old has accumulated $375,000 in his savings. If he follows the advice in the graph, how much of his savings should be invested in bonds?

Probability: Independent and Dependent Events

PROBABILITY PRINCIPLE	To find the probability of two events happening in succession (one after another), *multiply* the probabilities of each.

EXAMPLE

When throwing a number cube, what is the probability of throwing 2 sixes in a row?

When throwing 2 number cubes, what is the probability of getting 2 sixes?

Since each throw of a number cube is **independent** of another, both probabilities would be $\frac{1}{6} \times \frac{1}{6} = \frac{1}{36}$.

EXAMPLE

What is the probability of drawing 2 aces in a row from a deck of cards?

This is an example of **dependent** events. After drawing 1 ace from the deck of 52 cards, there are only 3 aces left among the remaining 51 cards.

$P(\text{first ace}) = \frac{4}{52}$

$P(\text{second ace}) = \frac{3}{51}$

$P(\text{2 in a row}) = \frac{4}{52} \times \frac{3}{51} = \frac{12}{2,652} = \frac{1}{221}$

PROBLEM 5 | What is the probability of getting 3 heads in a row when flipping coins?

PROBLEM 6 | If a coin has been tossed 9 times, and each time it has landed on heads, what is the probability of the tenth toss coming up tails? Why?

PROBLEM 7 | An assortment of bills, two $20s, five $10s, and three $1s, are arranged randomly. What is the probability of first choosing (without looking) a $20 bill, keeping it, and then choosing the other $20 bill?

PROBLEM 8 | Throughout the season, Pat has made 3 out of every 5 free throw attempts. What is the probability that she will make both of her next two free throws?

Multiplying Mixed Numbers

When multiplying mixed numbers, it is often easiest to **rename** them first as single fractions and then multiply the fractions as before. Check the answers by estimating.

EXAMPLE A   **EXAMPLE B**

$2\frac{1}{2} \times 1\frac{3}{4}$ $4\frac{2}{3} \times 1\frac{1}{8}$

$\left(\frac{4}{2} + \frac{1}{2}\right) \times \left(\frac{4}{4} + \frac{3}{4}\right)$ Rename as single fractions. $\left(\frac{12}{3} + \frac{2}{3}\right) \times \left(\frac{8}{8} + \frac{1}{8}\right)$

$\frac{5}{2} \times \frac{7}{4} = \frac{35}{8} = 4\frac{3}{8}$ $\frac{14}{3} \times \frac{9}{8} = \frac{126}{24} = 5\frac{1}{4}$

Estimate: $2\frac{1}{2} \times 2 = 5$ Estimate: $5 \times 1 = 5$

Both exact answers are close to your estimates.

In other problems, you can choose to separate the whole number and fraction parts of the mixed number and multiply them separately.

EXAMPLE C   **EXAMPLE D**

$24 \times 3\frac{1}{2}$ $4\frac{2}{3} \times 10$

$24 \times \left(3 + \frac{1}{2}\right)$ $\left(4 + \frac{2}{3}\right) \times 10$

$(24 \times 3) + \left(24 \times \frac{1}{2}\right)$ Use the Distributive Property. $(4 \times 10) + \left(\frac{2}{3} \times 10\right)$

$72 + 12 = 84$ $40 + \frac{20}{3} = 40 + 6\frac{2}{3} = 46\frac{2}{3}$

Reasonable, less than 96 (24×4).   Reasonable, between 40 and 50 (5×10).

PROBLEM 9

Multiply using one of the methods above. Check your answers for reasonableness.

   Ⓐ $3\frac{1}{3} \times \frac{3}{4}$ **Ⓒ** $1\frac{4}{5} \times 3\frac{1}{3}$ **Ⓔ** $7\frac{1}{8} \times 16$ **Ⓖ** $90 \times 3\frac{3}{4}$

   Ⓑ $\frac{7}{8} \times 3\frac{1}{5}$ **Ⓓ** $2\frac{5}{8} \times 1\frac{1}{2}$ **Ⓕ** $24 \times 5\frac{5}{6}$ **Ⓗ** $7\frac{7}{8} \times 20$

PROBLEM 10

Refer to p. 295 in the Appendix to find the measurement equivalents that you need for these problems.

   Ⓐ How many inches are there in $3\frac{1}{2}$ feet?

   Ⓑ How many inches are there in $2\frac{1}{4}$ yards?

   Ⓒ How many ounces are there in $5\frac{3}{4}$ pounds?

   Ⓓ How many minutes are there in $3\frac{3}{4}$ hours?

   Ⓔ How many weeks are there in $2\frac{1}{4}$ years?

   Ⓕ How many cups are there in $10\frac{1}{8}$ gallons?

   Ⓖ Explain how you would recognize that these problems require you to multiply. Refer to p. 141 in Lesson 13 for help.

Estimating Fractional Parts

If you can make good estimates of the answers to problems like the ones below, you will know what kind of number to expect when a cashier rings up a sale.

DELICATESSEN

Corned Beef $5.75/lb	Salami $3.69/lb	Pepperoni $4.18/lb
Honey Ham $4.80/lb	Bologna $3.89/lb	Cheddar $3.99/lb

EXAMPLE A

How much would you expect to pay for $\frac{1}{4}$ pound of honey ham?

$$\frac{1}{4} \text{ of } \$4.80 = \frac{1 \times 4.80}{4 \times 1} = \$1.20$$

EXAMPLE B

About how much would you expect to pay for $\frac{3}{4}$ pound of salami?

$$\frac{3}{4} \text{ of } \$3.69 = \frac{3 \times 3.69}{4 \times 1} \approx$$

Look at the denominator before you round!

$$\frac{3 \times 3.60}{4 \times 1} = \$2.70$$

PROBLEM 11

Estimate how much would you expect to pay for

Ⓐ $\frac{3}{8}$ pound of pepperoni

Ⓒ $\frac{3}{4}$ pound of bologna

Ⓑ $\frac{1}{8}$ pound of corned beef

Ⓓ 4 ounces of cheddar

PROBLEM 12

The following sign appears on the window of a hardware store that is going out of business.

$\frac{1}{3}$ **Off All Marked Prices**

Round each dollar amount to *estimate* how much you would save on the following items.

Ⓐ a blender marked at $23.95

Ⓑ an outdoor thermometer marked at $8.25

Ⓒ a trash can marked at $16.95

Ⓓ a faucet replacement set marked at $126.75

Ⓔ a lawn mower marked at $207.25

Practice estimating like this every time this kind of situation comes up in your life. It's important to know what size number to expect.

Dividing Fractions

EXAMPLE

The problem $6 \div \frac{1}{4}$ asks, "How many $\frac{1}{4}$s are there in 6?"

Picture the problem first.

four $\frac{1}{4}$s

| 1 | 2 | 3 | 4 | 5 | 6 |

$6 \div \frac{1}{4} = \frac{6}{1} \times \frac{4}{1} = 24$

$\left(\frac{4}{1} \text{ is the } \mathbf{reciprocal} \text{ of } \frac{1}{4}.\right)$

You know that there are four $\frac{1}{4}$s in 1. It makes sense to multiply 6×4 to find the answer, 24.

Why is the answer so large?

Your answer is *greater* than either of the numbers because you are finding how many quarter-inches there are in 6 inches.

Analyze what you did. To divide by $\frac{1}{4}$, you multiplied by 4.

TO DIVIDE FRACTIONS   To divide by a fraction, multiply by its reciprocal.

You find the **reciprocal** of a fraction by simply turning it over. The reciprocal of $\frac{2}{3}$ is $\frac{3}{2}$, the reciprocal of $\frac{3}{4}$ is $\frac{4}{3}$, and the reciprocal of 3 is $\frac{1}{3}$.

> You can find the reciprocal of any number except 0.

EXAMPLE A

$\frac{1}{4} \div \frac{3}{4}$ asks,

"How many $\frac{3}{4}$s are in $\frac{1}{4}$?"

$\frac{1}{4} \div \frac{3}{4} = \frac{1}{\overset{}{\underset{1}{4}}} \times \frac{\overset{1}{4}}{3} = \frac{1}{3}$

EXAMPLE B

$20 \div \frac{5}{8}$ asks,

"How many $\frac{5}{8}$s are in 20?"

$20 \div \frac{5}{8} = \frac{\overset{4}{20}}{1} \times \frac{8}{\underset{1}{5}} = 32$

PROBLEM 13 | For each problem below, insert the numbers into this question: "How many _____s are there in _____?" Picture the answer first. Then find the answer as shown above. Ask yourself if your answer is reasonable.

EXAMPLE $6 \div \frac{2}{3}$ Ask: "How many $\frac{2}{3}$s are in 6?" $6 \div \frac{2}{3} = \frac{\overset{3}{6}}{1} \times \frac{3}{\underset{1}{2}} = 9$

Ⓐ $\frac{7}{8} \div \frac{1}{8}$ **Ⓓ** $\frac{3}{4} \div \frac{1}{2}$ **Ⓖ** $10 \div \frac{5}{6}$

Ⓑ $8 \div \frac{1}{3}$ **Ⓔ** $\frac{3}{4} \div \frac{1}{8}$ **Ⓗ** $3 \div \frac{3}{4}$

Ⓒ $8 \div \frac{2}{3}$ **Ⓕ** $\frac{3}{4} \div \frac{7}{8}$ **Ⓘ** $20 \div \frac{2}{3}$

How Can the Calculator Help?

To multiply and divide with your calculator, enter the fractions and mixed numbers using the a b/c key and use the operation keys (× , ÷) as usual. The answers will appear in fraction form.

While the calculator will carry out the computation, you need to pay attention to two other components of problem solving: deciding which operation to use and verifying that the answer in the display is reasonable. When you use the fraction key, there is a greater possibility that you might make an error while entering the numbers.

In this lesson we learned to use multiplication, not only when combining equal groups, but also when finding a fractional part of something.

EXAMPLE   A survey found that $\frac{7}{8}$ of employed young people own a VCR. Of these, $\frac{1}{2}$ also own a video camera. What fraction of employed young people own both a VCR and a video camera?

You need to find $\frac{1}{2}$ *of* $\frac{7}{8}$. This means $\frac{1}{2} \times \frac{7}{8}$, which equals $\frac{7}{16}$.

Is this reasonable? The situation makes it clear that the answer should be less than $\frac{7}{8}$ and it is.

Often you can decide whether a situation requires you to divide. Ask whether the question can be answered by finding, "how many _____s there are in _____."

EXAMPLE   A manufacturer has 30 yards of batik fabric. It takes $\frac{3}{4}$ yard to trim the front of one shirt. How many shirts can he trim with the fabric he has?

Does the question "How many $\frac{3}{4}$s are there in 30?" capture what this problem is asking? Yes, so enter it as $30 \div \frac{3}{4}$. The answer is 40.

Is it reasonable that the answer is greater than 30? Yes, you are dividing by a number less than 1.

Use the calculator to find each answer and check to see that it is reasonable.

Ⓐ $\frac{5}{8}$ of 45   **Ⓑ** $\frac{3}{4}$ of $7\frac{1}{2}$ **Ⓒ** 15 divided by $\frac{7}{8}$ **Ⓓ** 90 divided by $5\frac{1}{4}$

Decide whether to multiply or divide to find the answer to the following real-life problems. Write the problem. Use your calculator to find the answer and then assure yourself that the answer is reasonable.

Ⓔ If you maintain a speed of 60 mph for $3\frac{3}{4}$ hours, how far have you traveled in that time?

Ⓕ A stack of plywood measures 24 inches high. Each sheet of plywood is $\frac{5}{8}$ inch thick. How many sheets are in the stack?

Ⓖ The gasoline tank in Barry's car holds $16\frac{1}{2}$ gallons. When it is $\frac{3}{4}$ full, how many gallons does it contain?

Ⓗ If $\frac{5}{8}$ of a class is female and $\frac{2}{3}$ of the women are married, what fraction of the class is married women?

Ⓘ A filet of salmon weighing $2\frac{1}{2}$ pounds is divided into thirds. How much does each portion weigh?

✓ CHECK YOUR UNDERSTANDING

You may use your calculator on any problem except where noted by this symbol:

1. Find the following fractional parts.

   Ⓐ $\frac{1}{5}$ of 120   Ⓓ $\frac{5}{6}$ of 66

   Ⓑ $\frac{1}{8}$ of 96   Ⓔ $\frac{9}{10}$ of 80

   Ⓒ $\frac{2}{3}$ of 45   Ⓕ $\frac{3}{8}$ of 120

2. An after-Christmas sale advertised $\frac{1}{4}$ off the marked prices of all Christmas decorations.

   Estimate how much was saved on each of the following items.

   Ⓐ a tinsel garland marked $1.99
   Ⓑ a wreath marked $5.79
   Ⓒ a tree ornament marked $9.59
   Ⓓ a box of cards marked $12.75
   Ⓔ a treetop ornament marked $19.50

3. The recipe for Betty's seafood casserole says that it will serve 12 people. Donna needed to make enough to serve 4 people, so she had to find $\frac{1}{3}$ of each of the amounts in the recipe. The recipe called for the following amounts of ingredients (among others). How much of each should Donna put in?

   Ⓐ 1 cup mayonnaise

   Ⓑ $1\frac{1}{2}$ cups finely chopped celery

   Ⓒ 2 cups crushed potato chips

   Ⓓ $\frac{1}{2}$ cup chopped green pepper

   Ⓔ $\frac{3}{4}$ pound each of lobster, crab, and shrimp

4. Write the answers in simplest terms. Check for reasonableness.

   Ⓐ $4\frac{1}{10} + 6\frac{4}{7}$

   Ⓑ $7\frac{1}{2} \times 4\frac{5}{6}$

   Ⓒ $33\frac{1}{3} - 12\frac{1}{2}$

   Ⓓ $15\frac{3}{4} \div \frac{1}{2}$

   Ⓔ $9\frac{7}{8} \times 12\frac{1}{5}$

5. Solve the following equations. Write the answer in simplest terms.

   Ⓐ $x - \frac{2}{3} = 4\frac{2}{3}$

   Ⓑ $\frac{4}{5}x = \frac{9}{10}$

   Ⓒ $\frac{9}{16} = \frac{5}{32} + x$

   Ⓓ $8\frac{1}{3} = \frac{3}{4}x$

   Ⓔ $21\frac{3}{5} = \frac{1}{5}x$

6. Ⓐ How many minutes are there in $5\frac{1}{2}$ hours?

   Ⓑ How many hours are there in $2\frac{1}{3}$ days?

   Ⓒ How many feet are there in $4\frac{1}{3}$ yards?

   Ⓓ How many inches are there in $2\frac{1}{4}$ yards?

   Ⓔ How many cups are there in $1\frac{3}{4}$ gallons?

7. A rule of thumb says that you can predict the adult height of a person by doubling his or her height as a 2-year-old child. Dija is 2 feet 10 inches on her second birthday. Use the rule to predict how tall she will be as an adult.

TEST-TAKING PRACTICE

You may use your calculator on any problem except where noted by this symbol:

1. A developer intends to partition 36 acres into home lots. Each lot must be at least $\frac{3}{4}$ acre. How many homes can be built on this parcel?

   (1)   9
   (2) 12
   (3) 27
   (4) 48
   (5) 72

2. How many ounces of hamburger remain if $1\frac{1}{4}$ pounds are taken from a 5-pound package?

Mark your answers in the circles in the grid.

3. Every month, $\frac{2}{5}$ of the Lees' total income is spent on their mortgage payment. This year, $\frac{7}{8}$ of that amount pays interest on the loan. What fraction of their income is spent on home loan interest each month?

   (1) $\frac{2}{5}$
   (2) $\frac{3}{4}$
   (3) $\frac{7}{8}$
   (4) $\frac{7}{20}$
   (5) Not enough information is given.

Problems 4 and 5 refer to the following information.

A bag of fertilizer weighs $15\frac{1}{2}$ pounds. The instructions say to use $\frac{1}{2}$ pound per square yard of garden.

4. Larry loaded 30 bags onto a truck. How many pounds did he lift doing that job?

   (1) $14\frac{1}{2}$
   (2) $45\frac{1}{2}$
   (3) 465
   (4) $565\frac{1}{2}$
   (5) Not enough information is given.

5. How many square yards of garden can be fertilized with 1 bag?

   (1) $7\frac{1}{4}$
   (2) $7\frac{3}{4}$
   (3) 31
   (4) $46\frac{1}{2}$
   (5) 62

6. A ribbon $20\frac{1}{4}$ inches long is to be cut into 9 equal pieces. How long, in inches, will each piece be?

   (1) $2\frac{1}{4}$
   (2) $4\frac{1}{2}$
   (3) 10
   (4) $11\frac{1}{4}$
   (5) $29\frac{1}{4}$

Making Connections

MENTAL MATH

1. $\frac{1}{2}$ of $\frac{1}{4}$

2. $\frac{1}{2}$ of $\frac{1}{8}$

3. $\frac{1}{2}$ of $\frac{1}{3}$

4. $\frac{1}{2}$ of $\frac{3}{5}$

5. $\frac{1}{2}$ of $\frac{3}{10}$

6. $\frac{1}{2}$ of $\frac{2}{6}$

Did you notice a pattern while doing the mental math exercises? Did you notice that when you multiplied a fraction by $\frac{1}{2}$, the denominator was doubled? Noticing patterns and relationships is an important part of mathematics. The focus of this lesson is to point out some of the connections between things you have already learned, particularly with fractions and decimals.

Decimals and Fractions

Throughout this chapter, you have learned the decimal equivalents of fractions that are commonly used with measurements and money.

PROBLEM 1 | Use the fraction table in Lesson 16, page 162, to review fraction and decimal equivalents. Quiz yourself to see if you can write the decimal equivalent for each fraction. Check by using your calculator.

PROBLEM 2 | Finding the average of two numbers is the same as finding the value of the number that is halfway between them. Find the decimal value of the numbers halfway between the decimal equivalent of each of the following.

Ⓐ 0 and $\frac{1}{4}$

Ⓑ $\frac{1}{4}$ and $\frac{1}{2}$

Ⓒ $\frac{1}{2}$ and $\frac{3}{4}$

Ⓓ $\frac{3}{4}$ and 1

Ⓔ The problems above suggest another method to figure out the decimal values of the eighths in the table. Explain the pattern.

USING DATA

In the National Football League, quarterbacks are rated according to a complex formula that considers many aspects of the game. The formula was used to determine the top ten quarterbacks for the 2001 season, listed in the Appendix (p. 283). The formula and the resultant ratings are controversial, but rather than debate them, use the data to create your own ratings. Use your calculator.

Ⓐ To complete the first three columns of the table below, consider the number of completed passes (Cmp) compared to the number of attempted passes (Att).
Column 1: Form a fraction, Cmp/Att, for each of the 10 quarterbacks.
Column 2: Find the decimal equivalent (round to 3 places) of each fraction.
Column 3: Rank the quarterbacks, 1 through 10, using only your column 2 results.

Ⓑ To complete the next three columns of the table, consider the number of interceptions (Ints) compared to the number of touchdowns (TDs). Repeat the three steps of part Ⓐ with the fractions, Ints/TDs. When ranking, you need to decide whether the best performance is the least or greatest decimal value.

Ⓒ To complete the last column, compare the decimal values of Ints/TDs (from part Ⓑ) to the decimal values you found for problem 1 on page 186. Find a common fraction that would be a good estimate of the relationship.

EXAMPLE Kurt Warner $0.611 \approx 0.600 = \frac{3}{5}$

A TV announcer could say that Warner's record, an average of only 3 interceptions for every 5 touchdown passes, is a good indication of his performance under pressure.

Player	Cmp/Att	Decimal	Rank	Ints/TDs	Decimal	Rank	Common fraction Ints/TDs
Kurt Warner							
Peyton Manning							
Brett Favre							
Aaron Brooks							
Rich Gannon							
Trent Green							
Kerry Collins							
Jake Plummer							
Jeff Garcia							
Doug Flutie							

Solving Problems with Decimals and Fractions

Now that you know the decimal equivalents of many fractions, you can choose whether you want to use the **fraction** or **decimal form** when solving problems.

Sometimes using fractions is the easiest.

EXAMPLE

After purchasing $\frac{7}{8}$ yard of handwoven fabric, Doreen realizes that she can make two place mats from $\frac{1}{2}$ yard. How much fabric will she have left?

$\frac{7}{8} - \frac{1}{2}$

$\frac{7}{8} - \frac{4}{8} = \frac{3}{8}$ yd

Other situations can be more easily solved using decimals.

EXAMPLE

The odometer in George's car reads 44,322.4 miles after he has already traveled $10\frac{1}{2}$ miles on a trip. What should he record as the beginning odometer reading for this trip?

Odometer readings are expressed in decimals. Change $10\frac{1}{2}$ to 10.5.

$44,322.4 - 10.5 = 44,311.9$ miles

Sometimes a combination works well. Use fractions for estimating, then decimals and your calculator if you need a precise answer.

EXAMPLE

Hard salami costs \$3.49 a pound at the deli. What would you pay for $\frac{3}{4}$ of a pound?

Estimate: $\frac{3}{4}$ of \$3.49 $\approx \frac{3}{1\overset{}{4}} \times \frac{\overset{9}{\cancel{\$3.60}}}{1} = \$2.70$

With calculator: $\$3.49 \times 0.75 = \$2.6175 \approx \$2.62$

PROBLEM 3

First solve these problems *without* a calculator using the fraction form. Then solve them using the decimal form *with* a calculator. Compare the answers and the methods. For which problems do you prefer using fractions?

Ⓐ Roger has two lengths of pipe; one is $13\frac{3}{4}$ inches long, and the other is $9\frac{1}{2}$ inches long. What is their total length?

Ⓑ A bolt whose shaft is $4\frac{1}{2}$ inches long is placed through a beam $3\frac{3}{8}$ inches thick. How far does the bolt extend on the other side of the beam?

Ⓒ A coil of rope 50 feet long is to be cut into pieces $4\frac{1}{2}$ feet long. How many pieces of this length can be cut?

Ⓓ Marnie earns \$64 a day. If she works only $\frac{5}{8}$ of the day, what will she earn?

Ⓔ Cheddar cheese costs \$2.35 per pound. What is the price of $\frac{7}{8}$ of a pound? (Estimate the price using fractions.)

Fraction and Decimal Operations

Are there similarities in the methods you have learned to carry out the operations with fractions and the methods you use for decimals? A careful examination of the procedures and rules can help to show *why* they work and to demonstrate that everything "fits" or connects in mathematics.

Decimal fractions are special fractions whose denominators are powers of 10.

$0.7 = \frac{7}{10}$

$0.003 = \frac{3}{1,000}$

$135.3 = 135\frac{3}{10}$

Equivalent Fractions and Equivalent Decimals

Why is 0.5 equal to 0.50 and 0.500? What allows you to add (or ignore) the trailing zeros in a decimal?

$$\frac{5}{10} = \frac{(5 \times 100)}{(10 \times 100)} = \frac{500}{1,000} \qquad\qquad \frac{50 \div 10}{100 \div 10} = \frac{50}{100} = \frac{5}{10}$$

$$0.5 = 0.500 \qquad\qquad\qquad\qquad 0.50 = 0.5$$

The Fundamental Principle of Equal Fractions allows you to multiply or divide both numerator and denominator by the same non-zero number.

Adding and Subtracting

Before you add or subtract fractions, the denominators have to be the same.

$$\frac{1}{8} + \frac{1}{2} = \frac{1}{8} + \frac{4}{8} = \frac{5}{8} \qquad\qquad \frac{3}{4} + \frac{1}{5} = \frac{15}{20} + \frac{4}{20} = \frac{19}{20}$$

When adding and subtracting decimals, the decimal points have to be lined up when you write the problem down.

$$8.03 + 9.165 = \begin{array}{r} 8.03 \\ +9.165 \\ \hline 17.195 \end{array} \qquad\qquad 35.01 + 4{,}040 + 3.78 = \begin{array}{r} 35.01 \\ 4{,}040. \\ +\quad 3.78 \\ \hline 4{,}078.79 \end{array}$$

When the decimal points are lined up, the digits in each column have the same denominator.

Multiplying

When you are multiplying with decimals, the number of decimal places in the answer is the sum of the number of decimal places in the multipliers.

Explore the similarities between the rule for multiplying decimals and the rule for multiplying fractions.

PROBLEM 4 | When multiplying fractions, you multiplied *both* the numerators and denominators. Use the problem 0.07×0.003 to show how the fraction rule explains the rule for multiplying decimals. Begin by writing the problem in fraction form.

Dividing with Decimals

The steps in the traditional rule for division of decimals can be explained by writing the problem as a fraction.

EXAMPLE

One wooden pencil costs 8¢ ($.08). How many can you buy with $3.20?

① Move the decimal point of the *divisor* (denominator) to the end of the number.

$\frac{3.20}{.08}$ By moving the decimal point 2 places, we are multiplying by 100.

② Move the decimal point of the *dividend* (numerator) the same number of places.

$\frac{3.20}{08}$ We multiply the numerator by 100, the same number.

③ Now divide.

$\frac{320}{8} = 40$ pencils

PROBLEM 5

Each of these everyday problems requires you to add, subtract, multiply, or divide. Use the formulas on page 280 if necessary.

Ⓐ The side of a square measures 0.6 meter. What is the area of the square?

Ⓑ How much change would you expect from $5 when your purchase totaled $3.12?

Ⓒ After a 7.1-meter length of rope is cut from a 15-meter coil, how much is left?

Ⓓ A pork roast weighing 3.5 pounds costs $7.35. How much does it cost per pound?

Ⓔ What is the area of a triangle whose height is 0.6 meter and base is 1.5 meters?

Ⓕ Each aluminum can weighs 0.04 pound. How many cans would you need in order to have 5 pounds of cans to recycle?

Ⓖ One nail weighs 0.025 ounce. How many of these nails are there in 1 pound?

Multistep Problems

Everyday situations demonstrate how important it is to be able to work with fractions and decimals.

Discount and Sale Price

EXAMPLE

A certain model of TV set is marked $\frac{1}{4}$ off during a clearance sale. The original price was $240. What is the sale price of this TV set?

What is the relationship between the important words in this problem?

original price (or marked price) = sale price + discount

Often this needs to be rearranged to say,

sale price = original price − discount

Method 1: Find the amount of discount and subtract.

HOW TO PLAN IT:

First, find the discount $\left(\frac{1}{4} \text{ of } \$240\right)$.

Subtract to find the sale price.

HOW TO WRITE IT:

sale price = original price − discount

$s = 240 - \left(\frac{1}{4} \times 240\right)$ (Do what is in the parentheses first!)

$s = 240 - 60$

$s = \$180$

There is **another way to find the answer.** Examine the relationship again.

Think of the original price as being this rectangle.

Picture the discount as part of this rectangle.

The remainder of the rectangle must be the sale price.

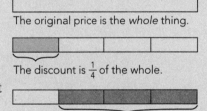

The original price is the *whole* thing.

The discount is $\frac{1}{4}$ of the whole.

The sale price is $\frac{3}{4}$ of the whole.

Method 2: Find the sale price directly.

HOW TO PLAN IT:

If the discount is $\frac{1}{4}$ of the original price, the sale price must be $\frac{3}{4}$, the remaining part. $\left(1 - \frac{1}{4} = \frac{3}{4}\right)$ To find the sale price, find $\frac{3}{4}$ of $240.

HOW TO WRITE IT:

sale price $= \left(1 - \frac{1}{4}\right) \times$ original price

$s = \frac{3}{4} \times 240$ (Find $\frac{3}{4}$ mentally.)

$s = \frac{3}{\overset{1}{\cancel{4}}} \times \frac{\overset{60}{\cancel{240}}}{1} = \$180$

PROBLEM 6 | *Estimate* the price someone would have to pay for the following articles during the sale advertised here. The prices shown are the original prices.

One Day Sale − $\frac{1}{4}$ off Everything	
Ⓐ student desk	$119.97
Ⓑ table lamp	18.88
Ⓒ electric shaver	47.88
Ⓓ tea kettle	31.99
Ⓔ hair dryer	14.94

PROBLEM 7 | Use your calculator to find the precise amount the store would charge for the articles listed in problem 6. Round to the nearest cent.

PROBLEM 8 | Which of the following equations could be used to find the sale price (on the day of the sale above) of a washing machine marked at $400?

(1) $s = \frac{1}{4} \times 400$

(2) $s = 400 - \frac{1}{4}$

(3) $s = 400 - \frac{1}{4}(400)$

(4) $s = \frac{1}{4}(400) + 400$

(5) $s = (1 + \frac{1}{4})400$

A different situation arises when you know the sale price and want to find the original price.

EXAMPLE

During the sale in problem 6, Jana paid $456 for a dinette set. What was the original price?

SALE PRICE

Picture the situation.

$456

Write an equation to describe the situation.	$\frac{3}{4}x = 456$
Divide both sides by $\frac{3}{4}$, that is, multiply by $\frac{4}{3}$.	$\frac{4}{3} \times \frac{3}{4}x = \frac{4}{3} \times 456$ $x = 608$

The original price is $608.

Caution: Many people make the following error on this kind of problem.

They multiply $\frac{1}{4} \times 456 = 114$. Then they add $456 + 114 = 570$. However, the sketch above clearly shows that they are finding $\frac{3}{4}$ of the wrong number.

PROBLEM 9 | During the $\frac{1}{4}$-off sale, what was the original price of

   Ⓐ a pillow whose sale price is $6.60?

   Ⓑ a plastic storage box whose sale price is $3.96?

   Ⓒ an ice chest whose sale price is $9.72?

Other Multistep Problems

EXAMPLE

The bus traveling the interstate highway averaged 63 mph for 2 hours 20 minutes. How far did the bus travel in that time?

HOW TO PLAN IT:	HOW TO WRITE IT:
To find the distance, multiply rate by time.	distance = rate × time ($d = rt$)
First, change the minutes to a fraction of an hour.	$d = 63 \times 2\frac{1}{3}$ (2 hours 20 minutes = $2\frac{20}{60} = 2\frac{1}{3}$)
Then find the distance.	$d = \frac{63}{1} \times \frac{7}{3} = 147$ miles

EXAMPLE

The gas tank on Portia's car holds 16.3 gallons. When the gas gauge reads $\frac{1}{4}$ full, how many gallons should be necessary to fill it up?

HOW TO PLAN IT:	HOW TO WRITE IT:
Portia needs to fill $(1 - \frac{1}{4})$ or $\frac{3}{4}$ of the tank.	$n = \frac{3}{4}$ of 16.3 (estimate: $\frac{3}{4} \times 16 = 12$)
	$n = 0.75 \times 16.3 = 12.225$ gal

PROBLEM 10 | Write a single equation to solve each of the following problems. Then solve. Use your calculator if necessary.

   Ⓐ How much change would you receive from a $10 bill if you purchased $1\frac{1}{2}$ pounds of corned beef priced at $5.60 a pound?

   Ⓑ Ronald stopped to fill the gas tank of his car when the gauge indicated that the tank was about $\frac{1}{8}$ full. If the tank holds 15.2 gallons, how many gallons should Ronald need in order to fill the tank?

   Ⓒ A truck driver noted that he had driven 144 miles in 2 hours 15 minutes. What rate of speed did he average during that period of time?

   Ⓓ A circular flower bed measuring 7 yards in diameter is to be edged with material that sells for $1.69 a yard. How much will the material cost for this job? (Use $\pi \approx \frac{22}{7}$.)

CHECK YOUR UNDERSTANDING

You may use your calculator on any problem except where noted by this symbol:

Problems 1–3 are based on the following information.

Batting averages in baseball are figured by dividing

$$\frac{\text{number of hits}}{\text{number of times at bat}}$$

This fraction is then converted into a 3-decimal-place number. So, if someone made 1 hit in 4 times at bat, the player's average would be $\frac{1}{4} = .250$.

1. Coming into the All-Star game of the 2002 season, Ichiro Suzuki of the Seattle Mariners had 124 hits in 347 at-bats. What was his batting average?

2. *Estimate* whether Alex Rodriguez' record of 100 hits in 328 at-bats resulted in an average that was higher than .333.

3. One player's contract states that he will earn a bonus if he has a batting average of .300 or higher for the season. What is the *least* number of hits he can have if he has 630 at-bats?

4. Which is greater?

   Ⓐ $\frac{1}{8}$ of a pound or 3 ounces

   Ⓑ 0.6 of a pound or $\frac{5}{8}$ of a pound

   Ⓒ $2\frac{1}{4}$ feet or 30 inches

   Ⓓ $\frac{2}{3}$ of an hour or 45 minutes

   Ⓔ $3\frac{1}{2}$ quarts or 15 cups

5. A triangle has a base of 5 feet and a height of $3\frac{1}{4}$ feet. What is the area of this triangle?

6. A rectangle measures 2 feet 4 inches in width and 5 feet in length. How many square feet are in the area of this rectangle?

7. Mrs. Hall divided a cake into three parts so that each of her sons would get an equal share. Paul ate half of his share in one day. What fractional part of the cake did Paul eat that one day?

8. During a white sale at a department store, all prices were $\frac{1}{3}$ off. What was the sale price of each item below?

   Ⓐ bath towel $8.99
   Ⓑ hand towel $6.79
   Ⓒ washcloth $4.39

9. A finished piece of cross-stitch (a form of needlework) is 10 inches wide. If each stitch is $\frac{1}{11}$ inch wide, how many stitches are in each row?

10. If two number cubes are thrown, what is the probability that

    Ⓐ one is a 6 and the other is a 1?
    Ⓑ both are 6s?
    Ⓒ one is a 6 and the other at least a 4?
    Ⓓ one is a 6 and the other is not?

11. Is the expression below *always true*, *never true*, or *sometimes true* for each set of values? Show an example.

    $$n^2 > n$$

    Ⓐ All values less than 0 ($n < 0$)
    Ⓑ All values between 0 and 1 ($0 < n < 1$)
    Ⓒ All values greater than 1 ($n > 1$)

TEST-TAKING PRACTICE

You may use your calculator on any problem except where noted by this symbol:

1. A group of 6 people ate 2 large pizzas. If each person ate the same amount, what fractional part of a pizza did each eat?

(1) $\frac{1}{12}$

(2) $\frac{1}{8}$

(3) $\frac{1}{6}$

(4) $\frac{1}{3}$

(5) $\frac{1}{2}$

2. Assuming that it is equally likely for a couple to conceive a boy or a girl, what is the probability that a couple's three children will all be girls?

(1) $\frac{1}{3}$

(2) $\frac{1}{4}$

(3) $\frac{1}{6}$

(4) $\frac{1}{8}$

(5) $\frac{3}{8}$

3. How many 37-cent stamps can be purchased for $15?

(1) 55
(2) 45
(3) 41
(4) 40
(5) 20

4. What is the weight of each portion if a $4\frac{1}{2}$-pound package of hamburger is divided into thirds?

(1) $13\frac{1}{2}$

(2) $3\frac{1}{2}$

(3) $2\frac{1}{4}$

(4) $1\frac{3}{4}$

(5) $1\frac{1}{2}$

5. A serving of punch is $\frac{3}{4}$ cup and there are 4 cups in a quart. A serving of punch is what fractional part of a quart?

Mark your answers in the circles in the grid.

	/	/	/	
.	.	.	.	.
0	0	0	0	0
1	1	1	1	1
2	2	2	2	2
3	3	3	3	3
4	4	4	4	4
5	5	5	5	5
6	6	6	6	6
7	7	7	7	7
8	8	8	8	8
9	9	9	9	9

6. During a $\frac{1}{4}$-off sale, a rug was sold for $144. What was the original price, in dollars, of the rug?

(1)   36
(2)   108
(3)   169
(4)   180
(5)   192

--It is time for a checkup again. This test-taking tip lesson contains problems covering all the concepts that you have learned so far in the book. However, since this one comes immediately after the fraction lessons, it contains more fraction problems than a typical test.

Multistep Problems

On good multiple-choice tests, the answer choices that are given for each item correspond to mistakes that students tend to make. A common mistake that is made on problems requiring more than one step is that students often stop after they finish only the first step. For this reason, expect to see the intermediate answers in the list of answer choices—ready to tempt you to make this error.

EXAMPLE

A refrigerator is priced at $1,150. The dealer offers a time payment plan under which Raul and Julia can pay $300 as a down payment and then make monthly payments of $90 a month for 12 months. How much more will Raul and Julia pay if they choose the time payment plan instead of paying the full price in cash?

(1) $1,380
(2) $1,080
(3) $ 850
(4) $ 230
(5) $ 70

Caution! Do not pick the first answer that appears in your work!

Ask the question in your own words, "How much more will the time payment plan cost?"

First, multiply to find the total monthly payments.

$90 × 12 months = $1,080

This intermediate answer is choice **(2)**.

Next, add the total monthly payments to the down payment.

$1,080 + $300 = $1,380

This intermediate answer is choice **(1)**.

Finally, subtract the cash price from the total cost of the time payment plan.

$1,380 − $1,150 = $230

The final answer is choice **(4)**.

One way to avoid choosing intermediate answers as the solution is to write a multistep problem as a single equation, as you learned in Lesson 10. For the problem above, you could have written:

difference = (300 + 90 × 12) − 1,150

After you have found an answer, *check* to see that it answers the question that is asked and is a reasonable solution.

✓ CHECK YOUR SKILLS

For problems 1–11, you may use a calculator. You may use the formulas (page 280) and the number grid directions (page 281) whenever you wish. On the test below, try to solve as many problems as possible with mental math and estimation.

1. Which expression below shows how many *square feet* make up the area of a sidewalk that is 3 feet wide and *m* yards long?

3 ft [   ]
          m yd

(1) $\frac{3}{m}$

(2) *m*

(3) 3*m*

(4) 9*m*

(5) $\frac{9}{m}$

2. How much change would you expect from a $10 bill if you purchased 5 rolls of paper towels at $1.19 each?

(1) $4.05
(2) $4.95
(3) $5.05
(4) $5.95
(5) $8.81

3. Which value of *p* makes the following equation true?

$3p - 10 = 77$

Mark your answer in the circles in the grid.

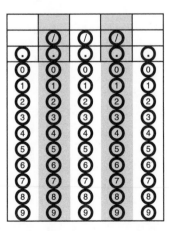

4. The automotive industry spent $889 million in TV advertising for the first half of the year. Which of the following gives this number in scientific notation?

(1) 8.89×10^2
(2) 8.89×10^5
(3) 8.89×10^6
(4) 8.89×10^8
(5) 8.89×10^{10}

Problems 5 and 6 refer to the following diagram.

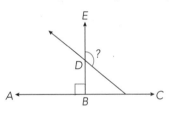

5. If angle *BCD* measures 45°, what is the measure of angle *EDC*?

(1) 45°
(2) 90°
(3) 120°
(4) 135°
(5) Not enough information is given.

6. What kind of angle is angle *ABD*?

(1) left
(2) right
(3) acute
(4) obtuse
(5) straight

7. In a sample of cross-stitch on gingham, each stitch is $\frac{1}{8}$ inch wide. How many stitches will there be across a border that is $2\frac{1}{2}$ inches wide?

(1) 20

(2) $3\frac{1}{5}$

(3) $2\frac{5}{8}$

(4) $2\frac{3}{8}$

(5) $\frac{5}{16}$

8. A 40-acre parcel of land is being developed for housing. Roads will take up 8 acres, and 4 acres of parkland are planned. Into how many $\frac{2}{3}$-acre home sites can the remaining acreage be divided?

(1) 18
(2) 21
(3) 28
(4) 32
(5) 42

9. For 1 hour 10 minutes, a cyclist maintained an average pace of 30 kilometers per hour. How far, in kilometers, did she travel in that time?

Mark your answer in the circles in the grid.

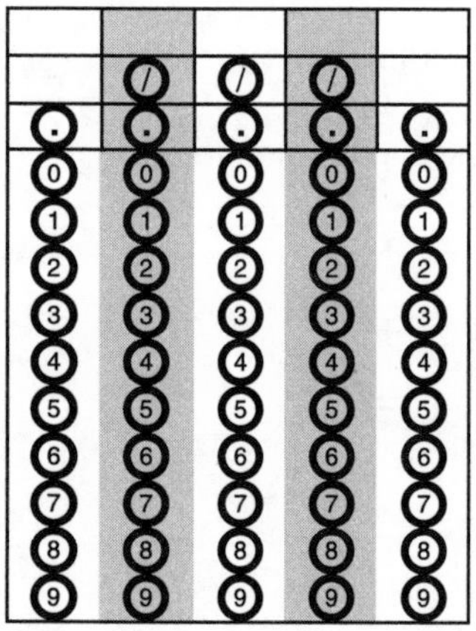

10. For each hour that Linda works at her part-time job, she earns $8.50. On Monday she worked $4\frac{1}{2}$ hours, on Tuesday she worked $1\frac{1}{2}$ hours, and on Wednesday she worked 3 hours. Which of the following expressions shows the number of dollars she earned during those 3 days?

(1) $(4\frac{1}{2} \times 1\frac{1}{2} \times 3)(\$8.50)$

(2) $9(\$8.50)$

(3) $3(\$8.50)(10)$

(4) $10(\$8.50)$

(5) $4.5(\$8.50) \times 1.5(\$8.50) \times 3(\$8.50)$

11. The heights of 3 children were reported as $3\frac{1}{2}$ feet, 40 inches, and 2 feet 8 inches. What is the mean (average) of these three heights?

(1) 3 ft
(2) 3 ft 2 in.
(3) 39 in.
(4) $3\frac{1}{2}$ ft
(5) 44 in.

You may NOT use a calculator for problems 12–22.

12. Which of the following drill bit sizes would you choose to drill a hole 0.125 inch in diameter?

(1) $\frac{1}{16}$ in.

(2) $\frac{1}{8}$ in.

(3) $\frac{3}{8}$ in.

(4) $\frac{1}{2}$ in.

(5) $\frac{9}{16}$ in.

13. Attendance figures showed that the stadium was filled to only $\frac{3}{5}$ its capacity for the 35 weeknight games during the season. How many seats were empty at each game?

(1)   14
(2)   21
(3) 12,000
(4) 16,000
(5) Not enough information is given.

14. How many yards of fabric are needed to make 5 cheerleaders' skirts if one skirt requires $1\frac{1}{4}$ yards?

(1) $3\frac{3}{4}$

(2) 4

(3) $5\frac{1}{20}$

(4) $6\frac{1}{4}$

(5) $9\frac{1}{5}$

Problems 15 and 16 refer to the following information.

An isosceles triangle has two sides that are equal. The two angles that are opposite these sides also are equal to each other.

15. What is the measure of the equal angles at *X* and *Z*?

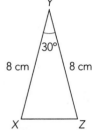

(1) 16°
(2) 50°
(3) 75°
(4) 150°
(5) Not enough information is given.

16. Find the intersection on the grid where point *C* must be located so that triangle *ABC* is an isosceles triangle.

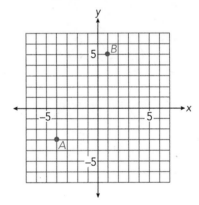

(1) (−4, 5)
(2) (6, −3)
(3) (5, −3)
(4) (−4, 6)
(5) (4, −1)

17. The process of choosing straws will be used to determine which one of a group of 5 people will have to perform a task. The person who chooses the one short straw from a group of 5 similar-looking straws is selected. What is the probability that Jasmine, the first in the group to choose, will NOT be selected?

Mark your answer in the circles in the grid.

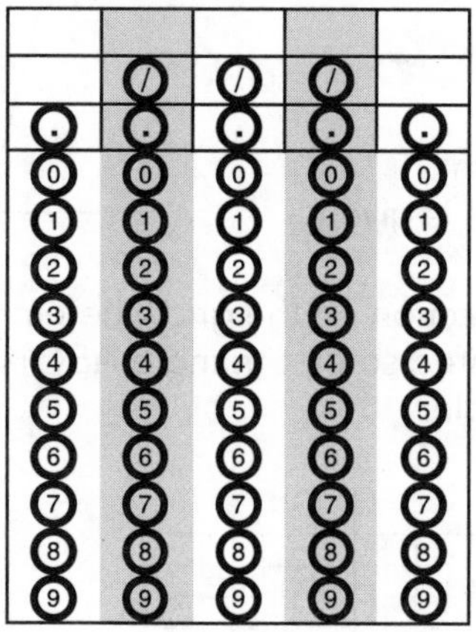

18. A rice and sauce mix weighs 127 grams. The nutrition information on the package says that it contains 100 grams of carbohydrates. Approximately what fractional part of the mix is carbohydrates?

(1) $\frac{1}{27}$

(2) $\frac{1}{5}$

(3) $\frac{4}{5}$

(4) $\frac{6}{5}$

(5) $\frac{27}{10}$

19. During a time trial, Uri cycled 5.25 kilometers in 10 minutes. During the same period, Sergio cycled $\frac{1}{10}$ of a kilometer farther than Uri. How far, in kilometers, did Sergio cycle?

(1) 52.5
(2) 5.35
(3) 5.26
(4) 5.15
(5) 0.525

20. The following amounts are interest rates on savings offered by various investments. Which is the highest rate?

(1) $7\frac{3}{4}\%$

(2) 7.46%

(3) $7\frac{7}{8}\%$

(4) 7.77%

(5) $7\frac{1}{2}\%$

Problems 21 and 22 refer to the following information.

The graph below shows the relationship between the number of pounds of aluminum cans submitted for recycling and the amount paid for them at a recycling center. That relationship is also shown by the formula $d = 0.25n$.

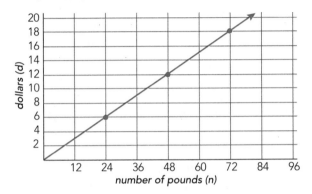

21. How much is paid for 20 pounds of cans?

   (1) $80
   (2) $40
   (3) $10
   (4) $ 5
   (5) Not enough information is given.

22. How many pounds of cans are needed to have a value of $10?

   (1) 40
   (2) 36
   (3) 30
   (4) 25
   (5) $2\frac{1}{2}$

SELF-EVALUATION CHART

Check your answers and compare your solutions with those given in the answer key. When you compare solutions, you can learn another way to do the problem and adopt the new way if you like it better than yours.

1. How many questions could you solve by estimating?

2. For which questions did you use a calculator?

3. Can you identify areas that you need to review?

problems	skill	lessons
1, 9	Measurement	8, 15
13	Not enough information	6, 9
2, 10, 11	Multistep problems	10
3	Solving equations	11
4	Scientific notation	13
5, 6, 15	Angles and triangles	4
7, 8, 14	Multiply and divide fractions	17
12, 18, 19, 20	Fractions and decimals	15, 18
16, 21, 22	Coordinate plane	5
17	Probability	16

Comparisons: Fractions as Ratios

MENTAL MATH

Are the two fractions equal?

1. $\frac{1}{2}$ and $\frac{5}{10}$ **3.** $\frac{1}{4}$ and $\frac{25}{100}$ **5.** $\frac{1}{5}$ and $\frac{5}{20}$

2. $\frac{1}{3}$ and $\frac{2}{9}$ **4.** $\frac{1}{8}$ and $\frac{8}{32}$ **6.** $\frac{1}{10}$ and $\frac{5}{50}$

To compare the fractions in the Mental Math exercise, you may have simplified one fraction. In this lesson, you will learn another way to decide when two fractions are equal.

Using Ratios (or Fractions) to Compare

A **ratio** compares two numbers by division, so it can be written as a fraction. You can also write ratios in other formats.

EXAMPLES

Ratios compare *two* numbers so they are not written as mixed numbers. Do *not* write the ratio $\frac{19}{12}$ as $1\frac{7}{12}$

There are twice as many men as women in this class.
The ratio of men to women is 2 to 1, 2:1, or $\frac{2}{1}$.

A bottle of juice contains 19 fluid ounces and a can contains 12 fluid ounces.
The ratio of the weight of a bottle to a can is 19 to 12, 19:12, or $\frac{19}{12}$.

7 out of the 20 candies are red.
The ratio of red candies to the total is 7 to 20, 7:20, or $\frac{7}{20}$.

You need two numbers to write a ratio. When you are comparing two numbers that have the same units of measure, for example, ounces to ounces, you do not need to mention them in the ratio. But take care to put the numbers in the fraction in the same order as the words in the statement.

EXAMPLE

There are 11 married students and 5 single students in a class of 16.

The ratio of *married students* to *single students* is 11 to 5, or $\frac{11}{5}$.

The ratio of *single students* to *married students* is 5 to 11, or $\frac{5}{11}$.

The ratio of *single students* to the *total number of students* is 5 to 16, or $\frac{5}{16}$.

PROBLEM 1 | Write each of the following comparisons using a ratio (fraction).

Ⓐ 212 miles in the morning and 341 miles in the afternoon: Write the ratio of *morning miles* to *afternoon miles*.

Ⓑ 25 miles on a bike and 7 miles on foot: Write the ratio of *miles on the bike* to *miles on foot*. (Leave as an improper fraction.)

Ⓒ 23 calories from fat out of a total of 180 calories in an energy bar: Write the ratio of *calories from fat* to the *total number of calories*.

Ⓓ Length of 10 meters compared to a width of 7 meters: Write the ratio of *width* to *length*.

Ⓔ One cup of oil and 20 cups of gas in a mixture: Write the ratio of *oil* to *total cups*.

Ⓕ One pound of cashews in 10 pounds of mixed nuts: Write the ratio of *cashews* to *other nuts* in the mixture.

Rates

When the two quantities being compared have different units of measure, the ratio is called a **rate**.

EXAMPLES

A city ordinance requires 3 parking spaces for each 100 square feet of retail floor area.

The required rate is $\frac{3 \text{ spaces}}{100 \text{ sq ft}}$.

A nursing home staffing policy requires 3 nurses' aides for every 10 residents.

The required rate is $\frac{3 \text{ aides}}{10 \text{ residents}}$.

In Lesson 9, you learned about the rate called **speed**: $\text{rate} = \frac{\text{distance}}{\text{time}}$.

When the distance is measured in miles and the time in hours, this becomes $\frac{\text{miles}}{\text{hour}}$ (miles per hour, or mph).

EXAMPLES

Cheryl can walk 4 miles in an hour.

Her *rate* of speed is $\frac{4 \text{ miles}}{1 \text{ hour}}$ (4 miles per hour), or simply 4 mph.

An average person's heart beats 72 times a minute.

This heart *rate* is $\frac{72 \text{ beats}}{1 \text{ minute}}$ (72 beats per minute).

When rates are given in terms of 1 unit of measure (that is, when the denominator is 1), they are called **unit rates**.

34 miles per gallon $= \frac{34 \text{ miles}}{1 \text{ gallon}}$ or $\frac{34}{1}$

PROBLEM 2 | Write each statement as a rate, first as a fraction and then using the word *per* to express the comparison.

EXAMPLE Bart can type 35 words in a minute.

$\frac{35 \text{ words}}{1 \text{ minute}}$ or 35 words per minute

Ⓐ 400 square feet of wall area is covered by one gallon of paint.

Ⓑ There are 4 glasses of milk in each quart.

Ⓒ The speed limit on some interstate highways is 65 miles an hour.

Ⓓ Warren earns $9.50 for each hour that he works.

Ⓔ A cyclist travels 25 miles in 3 hours.

Ⓕ The bank charges a monthly fee of $3.00.

Ⓖ Jennifer pays $32 for each concert ticket.

Ⓗ Each can of soda costs $.75 from the vending machine.

CALCULATOR EXPLORATION

Using Unit Rates to Compare

Which is faster:
132 miles in 2 hours or 332 miles in 5 hours?

Which is the better buy:
a package of paper towels with 240 sheets for $3.64, or a package of the same brand towels with 192 sheets for $3.16?

One way to find the answers is to find the unit rates or unit prices (using your calculator to divide) and then compare.

$\frac{132}{2}$ = 66 miles in 1 hour

$\frac{332}{5}$ = 66.4 miles in 1 hour

The faster rate is 332 miles in 5 hours.

$\frac{3.64}{240}$ = 0.015

$\frac{3.16}{192}$ = 0.016

The better buy is the one that costs the least for one sheet—$3.64 for 240 sheets.

Ⓐ Which represents the better gas mileage, 356 miles on 12 gallons of gas or 616 miles on 22 gallons?

Ⓑ Who has the faster production rate, shift A with 504 articles in 8 hours or shift B with 620 articles in 10 hours?

Ⓒ Which is the higher salary, $3,400 a month or $44,000 a year?

Ⓓ Which is the better buy, a dozen eggs for $.75 or 18 eggs for $1.08?

Ⓔ Which is the better buy, a package of 42 diapers for $8.97 or a package of 120 diapers for $25.97?

Ⓕ Which is the better buy, $9.44 for a 4-pack of audio tapes or $4.94 for a package of 2?

Ⓖ The hotel gave 190 Mexican pesos for $20 while the store gave 475 pesos for $50. Which transaction gave the higher exchange rate?

USING DATA

In this activity, you will use the data found on the nutrition labels in the Appendix (page 286) to discover the **unit rate**, calories per gram of fat. In other words, you will be looking for how many calories one gets from each gram of fat that is eaten. This rate should be the same, regardless of where the fat is found, but since the food companies report their data in slightly different ways, the rates will vary a little.

Ⓐ Find the data from the nutrition labels and calculate the unit rate for each. The first one has been done as an example.

food (1 serving)	calories from fat in 1 serving	grams of fat in one serving	unit rate: calories per gram of fat
muffin	210	23	9.13
peanut butter cookies			
potato chips			
blue corn chips			
vegetable chips			
granola bar			

Ⓑ Plot the position of the six data points (grams of fat, calories from fat), on the following graph, making a scatter plot. The point for the muffin (23, 210) has already been plotted.

A linear function describes a constant rate. When it is graphed, it is a straight line.

If the unit rates in the table were exactly the same for each food, the data points that you plotted would fall on a single straight line and represent a linear function. The unit rates were not identical, but they seem to be clustered around 9. Consequently, the points that you plotted do not fall on a straight line but they do cluster around a trend line, or a "line of best fit."

Ⓒ Draw a trend line. Use a straightedge to carefully draw a line from (0, 0) through the point (10, 90) that you plotted for the potato chips and extend it all the way to the edge of the graph. Notice that the other points are all close to the line that you have drawn.

You can conclude, from your data in the table and the graph, that there are 9 calories in each gram of fat in foods.

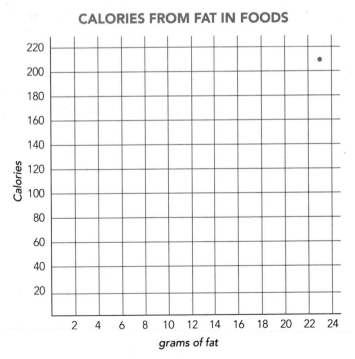

CALORIES FROM FAT IN FOODS

Calories (y-axis): 20, 40, 60, 80, 100, 120, 140, 160, 180, 200, 220

grams of fat (x-axis): 2, 4, 6, 8, 10, 12, 14, 16, 18, 20, 22, 24

Slopes: Picturing Rates on a Graph

Rates are represented on a graph by the steepness of the line.

The competitors in the 2002 Escape from Alcatraz triathlon swam 1.5 miles through the frigid waters of the San Francisco Bay, biked 18 miles through the hills and coastal roads of San Francisco, and ran 8 miles through the Presidio and along Baker Beach. This is the approximate data from one competitor's race.

activity	swim	transition	bike	transition	run	total
time	30 min	5 min	60 min	1 min	50 min	146 min
rate: miles per minute	0.05	0	0.3	0	0.16	Avg: 0.17

The following graph pictures the various rates throughout the race. Each line segment represents a different activity, and thus, a different rate of speed. Since the rates change, the overall graph does NOT picture a linear function.

PROBLEM 3

Ⓐ What is happening in the race during the times when the graph line is horizontal?

Ⓑ From the table, determine during which race mode, swimming, biking, or running, the competitor was traveling at the fastest rate. What do you notice about the steepness of the line segment on the graph for this activity?

Ⓒ During which of the three race modes was the competitor traveling most slowly? How is that pictured?

Ⓓ Make a rule: A faster rate will be pictured by a line that is _____.

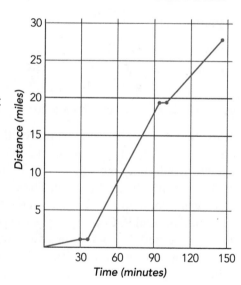

TRIATHLON PERFORMANCE

Examining the definition of **slope** and looking at some examples will help to see the reason behind the rule you made in problem 3Ⓓ connecting rates and steepness.

The ratio, $\frac{rise}{run}$, compares how far up (or down) the line goes to how far across it goes from left to right.

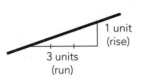

Sketching a right triangle under this line makes it easy to see that the line **rises** 1 unit while it **runs** 3 units.

The slope of this line is $\frac{rise}{run} = \frac{1}{3}$.

PROBLEM 4 | Find the slope of these lines. Use the ratio $\frac{rise}{run}$.

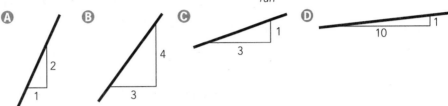

PROBLEM 5 |
Ⓐ Find the decimal equivalent of each slope that you found in problem 4 and arrange them in order from least to greatest. Verify that the greater the slope, the steeper the line.

Ⓑ What is the slope of the trend line that you drew in the Using Data activity on page 205?

Expressing Ratios in Simplest Form

There are 8 red candies out of 24.

What is the ratio of red candies to the total? $\frac{8}{24} = \frac{1}{3}$ The ratio is 1:3 or $\frac{1}{3}$.

Once a ratio is expressed as a fraction, you can apply the Fundamental Principle of Fractions to write that fraction (ratio) in its simplest form. It is in simplest form when no number (other than 1) can be divided into *both* the numerator and the denominator.

$$\frac{5}{20} = \frac{5 \div 5}{20 \div 5} = \frac{1}{4} \qquad \frac{15}{21} = \frac{15 \div 3}{21 \div 3} = \frac{5}{7} \qquad \frac{90}{120} = \frac{90 \div 30}{120 \div 30} = \frac{3}{4}$$

PROBLEM 6 | Write each of these comparisons as ratios in simplest terms.

Ⓐ Franz drove 360 kilometers in 3 hours.

Ⓑ 250 people out of 1,000 surveyed favored the proposition.

Ⓒ Naomi earned $80 for working 8 hours.

Ⓓ Al paid $100 for 5 tickets.

Ⓔ One box weighs 14 ounces, and the other weighs 7 ounces.

Ⓕ Of 80 kernels in the bag, 12 remained unpopped.

Equal Ratios Are Proportions

A statement that says two ratios are equal is called a **proportion**. A proportion uses the same reasoning that was used when we said that two fractions are equivalent; their values or decimal equivalents are equal even though the two numbers making up the fraction or ratio are not.

When solving problems using proportions, you need to think of the four numbers that are involved. There are interesting patterns to notice in proportions.

① First notice the relationship you used when you expressed the ratios in simplest terms.

$\dfrac{16}{20} = \dfrac{4}{5}$

proportion

Look **across** the proportion from numerator to numerator and denominator to denominator. Notice that $16 \div 4 = 4$ and $20 \div 4 = 5$. This is the pattern you have learned as the Fundamental Principle of Fractions.

$$\frac{16 \div 4}{20 \div 4} = \frac{4}{5}$$

Use this relationship to build equal ratios the way you built equivalent fractions in Lesson 16.

A recycling center pays 5¢ for 2 aluminum cans.

cans	2	4	6	8	10	12	14
cents	5	10	15	20	25	30	35

The table is filled in by building equal fractions, using the Fundamental Principle of Fractions. This ensures that the same rate, 5 cents for every 2 cans, is applied in every case and the table represents a constant rate.

$\dfrac{2}{5} \times \dfrac{2}{2} = \dfrac{4}{10}$ $\dfrac{2}{5} \times \dfrac{5}{5} = \dfrac{10}{25}$

$\dfrac{2}{5} \times \dfrac{3}{3} = \dfrac{6}{15}$ $\dfrac{2}{5} \times \dfrac{6}{6} = \dfrac{12}{30}$

$\dfrac{2}{5} \times \dfrac{4}{4} = \dfrac{8}{20}$ $\dfrac{2}{5} \times \dfrac{7}{7} = \dfrac{14}{35}$

PROBLEM 7 For $2, you can buy a package of 3 rolls of paper towels. Complete the table.

$	2			8	10	12
rolls	3	6	9			

PROBLEM 8 The ratio of length to width of certain rectangles is 5 to 3. Complete the table.

length	5			20	25	30
width	3	6	9			

② The second pattern in proportions is apparent when a proportion is written in the manner of an analogy (a statement that tells that two relationships are equal.) To notice the pattern, look **within**, from top to bottom of the same fraction.

The statement
6:12 :: 3:6 is read as
"6 is to 12 as 3 is to 6."

1 is to 5 as 3 is to 15

1:5 :: 3:15

$$\frac{1}{5} = \frac{3}{15}$$

Whatever you did (× or ÷) to 1 to get 5, do the same to 3 to get 15.

8 is to 80 as 3 is to 30

8:80 :: 3:30

$$\frac{8}{80} = \frac{3}{30}$$

The relationship (× or ÷) between 8 and 80 is the same as between 3 and 30.

PROBLEM 9 | Complete the following statements.

Ⓐ 9 is to 1 as _____ is to 2.

Ⓑ 8 is to 16 as _____ is to 10.

Ⓒ 4 is to 5 as 400 is to _____.

Ⓓ 5 is to 50 as 10 is to _____.

Ⓔ 9 is to 45 as 12 is to _____.

Ⓕ 100 is to 25 as _____ is to 15.

③ The third pattern in proportions is less apparent than the other two, but it can be applied in all proportion situations. When a pattern is so dependable that you can always fall back on it, it becomes a mathematical principle or law.

LAW OF PROPORTIONALITY | If $\frac{a}{b} = \frac{c}{d}$, then $ad = bc$.

In words, the Law of Proportionality says that if two ratios (fractions) are equal, their cross-products are equal. The **cross-products** are the answers you get when you multiply the numerator of each fraction by the denominator of the other.

$$\frac{2}{3} \times \frac{8}{12}$$

$2 \times 12 = 3 \times 8$
$24 = 24$

$$\frac{3}{5} \times \frac{9}{15}$$

$3 \times 15 = 5 \times 9$
$45 = 45$

Like some other laws you have learned, this one works both ways. That is, if the cross products are equal, the ratios (fractions) are equal. You can use this fact as a test to determine whether or not two ratios (fractions) are equal.

$\frac{5}{6} \overset{?}{=} \frac{25}{36}$

$5 \times 36 \overset{?}{=} 6 \times 25$
$180 \neq 150$

No, they are not equal.

(≠ means "is not equal to.")

$\frac{9}{12} \overset{?}{=} \frac{15}{20}$

$9 \times 20 \overset{?}{=} 15 \times 12$
$180 = 180$

Yes, they are equal.

PROBLEM 10 | Use the Law of Proportionality to determine whether or not each pair of ratios is equal. Then look for one of the other patterns, either *across* or *within* (top to bottom) the ratios, to verify your answer.

Ⓐ $\frac{3}{4} \overset{?}{=} \frac{9}{16}$

Ⓑ $\frac{4}{5} \overset{?}{=} \frac{12}{15}$

Ⓒ $\frac{3}{4} \overset{?}{=} \frac{15}{20}$

Ⓓ $\frac{3}{5} \overset{?}{=} \frac{9}{25}$

Ⓔ $\frac{2}{6} \overset{?}{=} \frac{5}{9}$

Ⓕ $\frac{5}{10} \overset{?}{=} \frac{22}{44}$

Ⓖ $\frac{3}{21} \overset{?}{=} \frac{12}{84}$

Ⓗ $\frac{8}{3} \overset{?}{=} \frac{72}{27}$

Ⓘ $\frac{3}{4} \overset{?}{=} \frac{9}{25}$

Ⓙ $\frac{3}{4} \overset{?}{=} \frac{75}{100}$

Ⓚ $\frac{3}{5} \overset{?}{=} \frac{60}{100}$

Ⓛ $\frac{5}{20} \overset{?}{=} \frac{20}{100}$

When to Use Ratios and Proportions in Problems

Remember that ratios and rates compare two quantities by using division as the basis for the comparison. How can you tell that a real situation is using division to compare two numbers?

Division and multiplication are the operations that involve equal groups. Look for clues that indicate this relationship. When the word *per* (meaning "for each") is used to describe a relationship, it means that the quantity is being considered in equal groups.

EXAMPLES

Use 3 tablespoons of flour for each tablespoon of butter.

The ratio of *flour* to *butter* is 3:1, or $\frac{3}{1}$.

The window's width is twice its height.

The ratio of *width* to *height* is 2 to 1, or $\frac{2}{1}$.

However, you *cannot* use ratios when things are being compared by subtraction.

EXAMPLE

Martha finished the assignment in 2 hours less time than it took Harry.

This comparison does not use division; it uses subtraction to compare. If Harry took h hours, Martha took $h - 2$ hours to finish. For example, if Harry took 5 hours, Martha took 3 hours.

PROBLEM 11

Decide whether or not each of the following relationships can be described using a ratio or a rate. If it can, write the ratio or rate in fraction form.

EXAMPLE   Ramona painted 4 rooms in 3 hours. $\frac{4}{3}$

Ⓐ It is 4 miles farther to Grove City than it is to Raymond.

Ⓑ The solar car was able to go 40 miles in one hour.

Ⓒ The height of the triangle was 5 times the length of its base.

Ⓓ The height of the triangle was 5 inches longer than its base.

Ⓔ Add 3 parts red pigment to 2 parts yellow pigment.

Ⓕ Add 3 cups more cereal than peanuts.

Ⓖ Duane is 5 years older than his sister, Luann.

Ⓗ Thomas is 5 times as old as his son, Ted.

Ⓘ 9 out of 10 doctors use this product.

Ⓙ The vote count in the council was 19 for, 10 against the measure.

You can use a proportion to solve a problem if the situation describes one ratio or rate and asks you to complete an equal ratio or rate. Separate the information into two fractions, one for each occurrence of the ratio or rate.

Make sure to set up the two ratios or rates in the same order. One way is to let the numerators both represent the same units of measure and also let the denominators both represent the same units. If you label them, it is easier to keep track of their position.

> **A proportion states that two ratios or two rates are equal.**

EXAMPLES

How much money would you receive for 100 cans if you get 5 cents for 2 cans?

$$\frac{5 \text{ cents}}{2 \text{ cans}} = \frac{x \text{ cents}}{100 \text{ cans}}$$

At 55 miles per hour, how long would it take to travel 500 miles?

$$\frac{55 \text{ miles}}{1 \text{ hour}} = \frac{500 \text{ miles}}{t \text{ hours}}$$

Use a variable in place of the missing value.

PROBLEM 12

The questions below have two parts. First, decide whether or not a proportion can be used to solve the problem. If yes, set up a proportion to represent the problem. Label the units in the numerator and denominator. **Do not solve.**

EXAMPLE Sarah bought a rug that measures 4 feet by 7 feet. What total area does the rug cover?
A ratio is given but the problem does not ask you to make a comparison. You would choose a different method of solution.

Ⓐ Andy has made 9 of 12 free-throw attempts. If he continues at this rate, how many shots will he make in 50 attempts?

Ⓑ A cake takes 45 minutes to bake. If the cake was put in the oven at 2:00, at what time was it done?

Ⓒ Tess noted that she had read 14 pages of her history assignment in 1 hour. At that rate, how long will it take her to read the entire assignment of 49 pages?

Ⓓ The standard dose of a medicine is 2 cc (cubic centimeters) for every 25 pounds of body weight. What should the dose be for a 130-pound woman?

Ⓔ One window measures 3 feet by 5 feet. Another measures 2 feet by 6 feet. What is the difference in their area?

> **Often a problem will state "at this rate" to indicate that the ratios are equal and a proportion is appropriate.**

PROBLEM 13

Four out of 5 doctors surveyed recommend Brand Y aspirin. This was based on a survey of 200 doctors. Which of the proportions below could be used to find the number of doctors who recommended Brand Y? (More than one answer choice is possible.)

Ⓐ $\frac{4}{5} = \frac{d}{200}$

Ⓒ $\frac{5}{4} = \frac{200}{d}$

Ⓔ $\frac{4}{d} = \frac{5}{200}$

Ⓑ $\frac{4}{5} = \frac{200}{d}$

Ⓓ $\frac{5}{4} = \frac{d}{200}$

✓ CHECK YOUR UNDERSTANDING

You may use your calculator on any problem except where noted by this symbol:

1. The following people were in a classroom one evening:

1 teacher, male
8 students, 3 male, 5 female

What is the ratio (in fraction form)

Ⓐ of students to teachers?
Ⓑ of male students to female students?
Ⓒ of male students to total students?
Ⓓ of female students to total students?
Ⓔ of males (total) to females?

2. Write each of the following rates as a unit rate or unit price.

Ⓐ Willie used 10 gallons of gasoline for a trip of 250 miles. What is the mpg?
Ⓑ The balloon rose 2,400 feet in 30 seconds. How many feet per second?
Ⓒ A package of 18 muffins costs $11.34. What is the price per muffin?
Ⓓ A 19-ounce can of soup costs $2.85. What is the price per ounce?
Ⓔ A telemarketer with 32 employees made 384 phone calls in one hour. How many calls were made per person?

3. In one game, Byron attempted 12 free throws and made 10 of them. Write the ratio of free throws missed to those attempted.

4. A driver's manual recommends certain distances to maintain between your car and the one ahead so that there is room to stop if necessary. It recommends that you leave 1 car length for every 10 mph of speed at which you are driving. Complete this table.

speed (mph)	20	30	40	50	60
car lengths					

5. In one high school graduating class, 140 out of 210 class members immediately went on to further schooling. Simplify this ratio.

6. What is the slope of the line shown below?

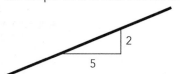

7. The ratio between the circumference and the diameter of every circle is the same:

$$\frac{\text{circumference}}{\text{diameter}} = \pi \approx \frac{22}{7}$$

Complete the following table.

c	22			88
d	7	14	21	

8. Complete the following statements.

Ⓐ 4 is to 20 as 20 is to _____.
Ⓑ 2 is to 12 as 12 is to _____.
Ⓒ 5 is to 25 as 11 is to _____.
Ⓓ 8 is to 11 as 80 is to _____.
Ⓔ 99 is to 9 as _____ is to 2.
Ⓕ 6 is to 42 as _____ is to 49.

9. Use the Law of Proportionality to determine which of the following ratios are equal.

Ⓐ $\frac{7}{8} \overset{?}{=} \frac{56}{64}$
Ⓑ $\frac{5}{9} \overset{?}{=} \frac{25}{81}$
Ⓒ $\frac{4}{5} \overset{?}{=} \frac{45}{55}$
Ⓓ $\frac{10}{15} \overset{?}{=} \frac{24}{36}$
Ⓔ $\frac{3}{8} \overset{?}{=} \frac{31}{81}$

10. Which package of batteries is the better buy, 4 batteries for $4.29 or 10 batteries for $10.79?

TEST-TAKING PRACTICE

You may use your calculator on any problem except where noted by this symbol:

1. 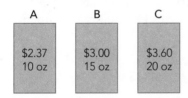 The Indianapolis 500 is a race that runs for 200 laps of the track. Al Unser, Sr., won the race in 1970 and led for 190 laps. He also won in 1987 but led for only 18 laps of the race. What is the ratio of the number of laps in which Unser led in 1970 to the total number of laps?

   (1) 18:190
   (2) 18:1970
   (3) 19:50
   (4) 19:1970
   (5) 19:20

2. What exchange rate $\left(\frac{\$CAN}{\$US}\right)$ was given when Lashunda received 60 Canadian dollars for 40 U.S. dollars?

   (1) $\frac{1.5}{1}$

   (2) $\frac{0.67}{1}$

   (3) $\frac{1}{0.67}$

   (4) $\frac{1}{1.5}$

   (5) $\frac{0.75}{1}$

3. Which of the following statements about the prices of these boxes of cereal is true?

A	B	C
$2.37	$3.00	$3.60
10 oz	15 oz	20 oz

   (1) The best price per ounce is Box A.
   (2) The best price per ounce is Box C.
   (3) Boxes B and C are the same price per ounce.
   (4) Boxes A and C are the same price per ounce.
   (5) The price per ounce for Box B is $.02.

Problems 4 and 5 refer to the following information and graph.

The Lee family saved for 5 years to make a down payment of $20,000 for a house. At the end of each year, Mr. Lee figured the total amount they had saved to that date and made the following graph.

SAVINGS FOR A DOWN PAYMENT

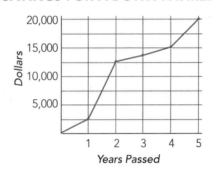

4. How much, in dollars, did the Lee family save the first year?

   Mark your answers in the circles in the grid.

5. In which year did the Lee family save the most money?

   (1) year 1
   (2) year 2
   (3) year 3
   (4) year 4
   (5) year 5

Are the fractions equivalent?

1. $\frac{1}{3}$ and $\frac{3}{15}$ **3.** $\frac{3}{5}$ and $\frac{10}{15}$ **5.** $\frac{9}{11}$ and $\frac{18}{33}$

2. $\frac{1}{2}$ and $\frac{60}{120}$ **4.** $\frac{3}{4}$ and $\frac{16}{20}$ **6.** $\frac{4}{5}$ and $\frac{16}{25}$

Seeing Proportions in Situations

When you learn more than one way to solve problems, you become a flexible thinker. You become the *master* with a choice of options, rather than being at the mercy of a single prescribed method.

Your daily experiences are full of situations that require you to decide whether or not two rates or ratios are equal. In the last lesson, you used the calculator to find unit rates to compare. In this lesson, you'll apply the Law of Proportionality to check if rates are equal. Either method will work for all problems, but sometimes one is easier than the other.

EXAMPLE

An over-the-counter cold medication is available in 2 package sizes. A package of 25 tablets costs $3.75, while a package of 12 tablets costs $1.80. Are both packages the same price per tablet?

There are many ways to set up a proportion for problems like this. There are two package sizes (large and small) and two characteristics (price and number of tablets) to consider. These boxes help to organize them.

	large	small
price	$3.75	$1.80
# of tablets	25	12

	price	no. of tablets
large	$3.75	25
small	$1.80	12

You can choose the format (and order) that makes the most sense to you, but in all cases you must be sure that the order is the same in both ratios. Writing the labels will help to keep the order straight.

$$\underset{\text{large}}{\frac{\$3.75}{25 \text{ tablets}}} \overset{?}{=} \underset{\text{small}}{\frac{\$1.80}{12 \text{ tablets}}} \qquad\qquad \underset{\text{prices}}{\frac{\$3.75 \text{ (lg)}}{\$1.80 \text{ (sm)}}} \overset{?}{=} \underset{\text{tablets}}{\frac{25 \text{(lg)}}{12 \text{(sm)}}}$$

To decide whether these are **true proportions**, that is, whether the ratios are indeed equal, find the cross-products. For each setup above, the multiplication is the same.

$$25 \times 1.80 = 3.75 \times 12$$
$$45 = 45 \text{ (a true proportion; the ratios are equal)}$$

PROBLEM 1 | Set up a proportion that fits each situation. Then test to see if it is true. You can use your calculator to multiply.

Ⓐ Javier traveled 165 miles in 3 hours. Is this an average speed of 55 mph?

Ⓑ Oranges are priced at 2 for $.35. Will 8 oranges cost $1.50?

Ⓒ Each table seats 6 people. To seat 64 people, 16 tables are needed.

Ⓓ At the recycling center, 5¢ is paid for 2 aluminum cans. To get $10.00, you need to have 200 cans.

Ⓔ To mix the fuel for a 2-cycle engine, you combine 1 part oil with 20 parts gasoline. If you start with 10 cups of gasoline, you need 2 cups of oil.

Ⓕ A recipe serving 6 people asks for 2 pounds of ground beef. To serve 24 people, you need 8 pounds of ground beef.

Ⓖ In a cereal bar, 75 of the 300 total calories come from fat. Is this the same rate as 40 out of 175 calories?

Ⓗ If 2 out of 5 students are men, you would expect 12 women in a class of 20.

Ⓘ If the ratio of men to women in a class is 2 to 3, you would expect 8 men in a class of 20. (Remember to label the ratios.)

Finding a Missing Number in a Proportion

Before going on to solve proportions, take time to review how you solved equations involving variables earlier in the book.

Sometimes you could guess the correct answer.

$3c = 18$ says that *something* times 3 is 18. What is that something? It is 6.

Other times you wrote an equivalent equation in which the variable was alone. Often you could think of "fact families" to do this.

$3n = \boxed{81}$ can also be written as $n = \frac{81}{3}$, and this equals 27.

The product (answer to multiplication) becomes the top number of the division problem.

And sometimes you used the algebraic properties of equality to write an equivalent equation.

$35x = 770$ To isolate *x*, divide both sides of the equation by 35.

$$\frac{35x}{35} = \frac{770}{35}$$

$$x = 22$$

PROBLEM 2 | Solve these equations using either the "fact families" or the algebraic properties.

Ⓐ $4 \cdot b = 240$ Ⓒ $7x = 357$ Ⓔ $25s = 454$

Ⓑ $5 \cdot t = 400$ Ⓓ $10d = 754$ Ⓕ $11y = 1,430$

Now, on to solving proportions using the Law of Proportionality. A typical situation that is described in a problem where proportions can be used involves two identical rates or ratios. You are given three of the numbers in the proportion and are asked to find the fourth one. Use a variable for the missing number, apply the techniques that you practiced in Problem 2, and find which value makes the proportion true.

EXAMPLE

$\frac{n}{5} = \frac{12}{20}$

$20n = 5 \cdot 12$ **STEP 1** Cross multiply. You get an equation with a variable in it.

$n = \frac{5 \cdot 12}{20} = \frac{60}{20}$ **STEP 2** Get n alone on its side of the equation.

$n = 3$ **STEP 3** Carry out the division.

$\frac{3}{5} = \frac{12}{20}$ **STEP 4** Check your answer. Replace n in the original with your answer, 3. Look for relationships (*across* or *within*) that allows you to check mentally.

$\frac{3 \times 4}{5 \times 4} = \frac{12}{20}$

$\frac{12}{20} = \frac{12}{20}$

Compare Method 1 and Method 2 below. Method 2 is easier because you cancel before multiplying the numbers.

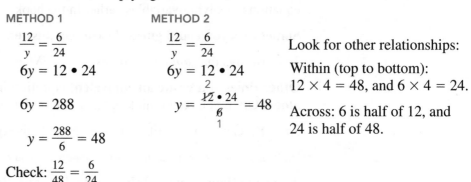

METHOD 1

$\frac{12}{y} = \frac{6}{24}$

$6y = 12 \cdot 24$

$6y = 288$

$y = \frac{288}{6} = 48$

Check: $\frac{12}{48} = \frac{6}{24}$

METHOD 2

$\frac{12}{y} = \frac{6}{24}$

$6y = 12 \cdot 24$

$y = \frac{\overset{2}{\cancel{12}} \cdot 24}{\underset{1}{\cancel{6}}} = 48$

Look for other relationships:

Within (top to bottom): $12 \times 4 = 48$, and $6 \times 4 = 24$.

Across: 6 is half of 12, and 24 is half of 48.

PROBLEM 3

Solve these proportions. Be sure to check your answers.

Ⓐ $\frac{c}{5} = \frac{24}{30}$ **Ⓒ** $\frac{5}{8} = \frac{p}{88}$ **Ⓔ** $\frac{t}{9} = \frac{10}{6}$ **Ⓖ** $\frac{6}{15} = \frac{10}{w}$

Ⓑ $\frac{8}{m} = \frac{20}{30}$ **Ⓓ** $\frac{4}{15} = \frac{20}{b}$ **Ⓕ** $\frac{10}{c} = \frac{25}{100}$ **Ⓗ** $\frac{3}{11} = \frac{k}{121}$

Fractions and Mixed Numbers in Proportions

Fractions and mixed numbers can be terms of a proportion. The solutions will not always be whole numbers.

$$\frac{1}{6} = \frac{b}{3}$$

$6b = 3$

$b = \frac{3}{6} = \frac{1}{2}$

Check:

$$\frac{1}{6} = \frac{\frac{1}{2}}{3}$$

Look across the example:
$6 = 2 \times 3$, and
$1 = 2 \times \frac{1}{2}$

$$\frac{\frac{1}{4}}{3} = \frac{v}{36}$$

$3v = \frac{1}{4} \cdot 36$

$3v = 9$

$v = 3$

Check:

$$\frac{\frac{1}{4}}{3} = \frac{3}{36}$$

Look across the example:
$3 \times 12 = 36$,
and $\frac{1}{4} \times 12 = 3$

This method of solving proportions (using the Law of Proportionality and cross multiplication) works in every case, with all numbers. However, that does not mean that you *must* use it every time. If you recognize another **pattern** in the proportion and can solve it mentally, the problem becomes easier.

LOOK WITHIN EACH FRACTION.

Take time to examine the relationships.

14 is 2×7, $\longleftarrow \frac{7}{14} = \frac{12}{s} \longrightarrow$ so s is 2×12.

The bottom number is 2 times the top. Therefore,
$$s = 24.$$

This completes the pattern, since
$$24 = 2 \times 12.$$

LOOK ACROSS THE PROPORTION.

Can you simplify the ratio first?

$$\frac{12 \div 4}{20 \div 4} = \frac{3}{5} \longrightarrow \frac{12}{20} = \frac{9}{d}$$

Both 12 and 20 are divisible by 4.

Now, look across $\longrightarrow \frac{3}{5} = \frac{9}{d}$

The pattern across is apparent:
3×3 is 9, so $5 \times 3 = d$.
$$d = 15$$

PROBLEM 4 | Solve these proportions using the method that seems best for the problem.

Ⓐ $\frac{4}{5} = \frac{12}{b}$

Ⓑ $\frac{k}{12} = \frac{6}{8}$

Ⓒ $\frac{3}{8} = \frac{r}{64}$

Ⓓ $\frac{3}{v} = \frac{7}{28}$

Ⓔ $\frac{8}{32} = \frac{n}{100}$

Ⓕ $\frac{3}{7} = \frac{d}{28}$

Ⓖ $\frac{n}{25} = \frac{48}{100}$

Ⓗ $\frac{3}{7} = \frac{r}{10}$

Ⓘ $\frac{44}{4} = \frac{d}{11}$

Ⓙ $\frac{5}{8} = \frac{n}{100}$

Ⓚ $\frac{1.2}{z} = \frac{4.8}{8}$

Ⓛ $\frac{1.5}{9} = \frac{s}{12}$

Ⓜ $\frac{\frac{1}{4}}{6} = \frac{\frac{1}{8}}{n}$

Ⓝ $\frac{\frac{1}{5}}{20} = \frac{c}{4}$

Ⓞ $\frac{2\frac{1}{2}}{5} = \frac{100}{a}$

Using Proportions to Solve Real Problems

There are so many interesting situations in which the underlying connection between the numbers is proportional. In some cases, you have already learned one other way to solve the problems.

EXAMPLE

The GED Testing Service reports that approximately 1 out of every 7 high school diplomas awarded in the United States each year is based on the GED Test. About 500,000 GED credentials were issued per year in the U.S. between 1991 and 2000. About how many high school diplomas were awarded in the United States per year during those years?

STEP 1 Set up the proportion.

$$\frac{GED}{total} : \frac{1}{7} = \frac{500{,}000}{n}$$

STEP 2 Cross multiply.

$$n = 7 \bullet 500{,}000 = 3{,}500{,}000$$

(*n* means the same thing as 1 • *n*)

STEP 3 Check:

$$\frac{1}{7} = \frac{500{,}000}{3{,}500{,}000}$$

In Lesson 7, you may have had trouble deciding whether to multiply or divide in problems like this.

EXAMPLE

How many feet are there in 7 yards? (There are 3 feet in 1 yard.)

$$\frac{3 \text{ ft}}{1 \text{ yd}} = \frac{f \text{ ft}}{7 \text{ yd}}$$

As the given ratio, use the equivalency 3 ft = 1 yd.

Cross multiplying leaves $f = 21$ feet. Check it.

Instead of using the formulas $c = nr$ and $d = rt$, you can arrange the information into a proportion.

EXAMPLE

It is 350 miles on the interstate from Chicago to Des Moines. If Miriam can average 56 mph, how long will it take to make the trip?

$$\frac{56 \text{ mi}}{1 \text{ hr}} = \frac{350 \text{ mi}}{h \text{ hr}}$$

$$56h = 350$$

$$h = \frac{350}{56} = 6.25 \text{ hours}$$

PROBLEM 5 | Use proportions to solve the following problems.

Ⓐ Of the 12 people in one department, 7 are women. If this ratio holds true for the entire company, how many women work in this company of 96 people?

Ⓑ Oranges are priced at 2 for $.35. How much will it cost for a dozen oranges?

Ⓒ A recipe that calls for $\frac{1}{2}$ cup of sugar makes 4 servings. How many cups of sugar would you need to make 10 servings?

Ⓓ How many feet are there in a mile and a half? (1 mi = 5,280 ft)

Ⓔ At the exchange rate of 11 pesos to the U.S. dollar, how many dollars would it cost to buy an ceramic bowl priced at 473 pesos?

Ⓕ The manufacturer of a compact car states that the car can average 52 miles per gallon in highway driving. At that rate, how much gas will it take to travel 611 miles?

USING DATA

Movie buffs often use the box-office receipts that movies generate to determine the most popular movies. However, since ticket prices have gone up over the years, a simple comparison of dollar amounts collected over the years does not tell the whole picture. The listing of the top 6 movies in the Appendix (page 283) has tried to tell a truer story by adjusting the receipts for ticket price inflation. The final column of numbers is an estimate of how much each movie would have generated at the box office if the tickets had cost the same as they do in 2002. Use the data in the table to imagine what the price of other things might have been years ago.

If the price of everything increased at the same rate that movie tickets did, what would have been the price (rounded to the nearest dollar) of

Ⓐ a car in 1939 that costs $25,000 in 2002?

Ⓑ a house in 1982 that costs $175,000 in 2002?

Ⓒ a lawn mower in 1956 that costs $150 in 2002?

Ⓓ a dinette set in 1997 that costs $475 in 2002?

Ⓔ Did you use the numbers of dollars as they were given in the table or did you add the zeroes that would make them millions of dollars? Would it make a difference? Why or why not?

Ⓕ From your own experience, discuss examples of items that did not follow the same pattern of price change as movie tickets over the years.

Similar Triangles

When two geometric figures are exact copies of one another, they are **congruent**.

Since $\triangle ABC \cong$ (is congruent to) $\triangle DEF$, all the corresponding parts are also congruent.

$\angle A \cong \angle D, \angle B \cong \angle E, \angle C \cong \angle F$

side $AB \cong$ side DE, side $AC \cong$ side DF, side $BC \cong$ side EF

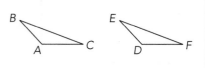
$\triangle ABC$ is **congruent** to $\triangle DEF$.

When two triangles have the same shape but different sizes, they are **similar**.

Since $\triangle KLM \sim$ (is similar to) $\triangle OPQ$, the corresponding angles are congruent:

$\angle K \cong \angle O, \angle L \cong \angle P, \angle M \cong \angle Q$

The lengths of the corresponding sides are **proportional**.

$\dfrac{\text{side } KL}{\text{side } OP} = \dfrac{\text{side } KM}{\text{side } OQ} = \dfrac{\text{side } LM}{\text{side } PQ}$

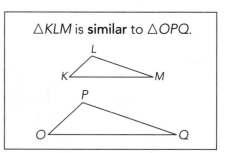
$\triangle KLM$ is **similar** to $\triangle OPQ$.

EXAMPLE

If the length of *KL* is 5 inches and the length of *LM* is 8 inches, while in the other triangle the length of *OP* is 15 inches, what is the length of *PQ*?

Here are two ways that you can set up the proportion:

$\dfrac{\text{side } KL}{\text{side } LM} = \dfrac{\text{side } OP}{\text{side } PQ}$ or $\dfrac{\text{side } KL}{\text{side } OP} = \dfrac{\text{side } LM}{\text{side } PQ}$

$\dfrac{5}{8} = \dfrac{15}{s}$ $\dfrac{5}{15} = \dfrac{8}{s}$

From either proportion, the answer is $s = 24$ inches.

The next example shows how knowing about similar triangles allows you to find the length of a side of a triangle that you cannot measure directly.

EXAMPLE

At the same time that a tall tree cast a shadow of 80 feet, a 6-foot post casts a shadow of 10 feet. How tall is the tree?

$\dfrac{\text{tree}}{\text{post}} : \dfrac{t}{6} = \dfrac{80}{10}$

$10t = 80 \cdot 6$

$t = \dfrac{\overset{8}{\cancel{80}} \cdot 6}{\cancel{10}} = 48 \text{ ft}$

Check: $\dfrac{\overset{}{48}}{6} = \dfrac{80}{10}; \dfrac{8}{1} = \dfrac{8}{1}$

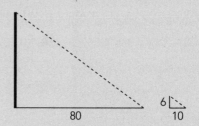

PROBLEM 6 | △DON ~ △KEY

       Ⓐ Find the length of side DN.

       Ⓑ If ∠D = 35° and ∠N = 75°, what is the measure of ∠O?

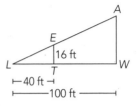

PROBLEM 7 | △LET ~ △LAW

What is the length of side AW?

(Look carefully for the similar triangles.)

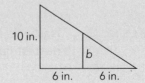

PROBLEM 8 | Which two of the triangles pictured are similar to each other?

   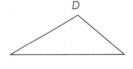

    (1) A and D
    (2) A and C
    (3) B and D
    (4) B and C
    (5) C and D

Using Similar Figures

The idea of similarity between figures is not only for triangles. Any figure is similar to another if their corresponding sides are in proportion.

When a drawing is enlarged or reduced in size, the figures are **similar.**

EXAMPLE A

A drawing that is 3 inches high and 5 inches wide will be blown-up in size so that it is 8 inches wide. How high will the enlarged drawing be?

$$\frac{5" \text{ wide}}{3" \text{ high}} = \frac{8" \text{ wide}}{h" \text{ high}}$$

$$5h = 24$$

$$h = \frac{24}{5} = 4\frac{4}{5} \text{ inches}$$

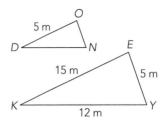

Scale drawings such as blueprints for construction projects are *similar* to the actual object.

EXAMPLE B

The following notation is found on a blueprint for a warehouse: 1 in. = $1\frac{1}{2}$ ft

Ⓐ A warehouse door is to be 12 ft. wide. How wide should it be on the blueprint?

$$\frac{\text{blueprint}}{\text{warehouse}} : \frac{1 \text{ in.}}{\frac{3}{2} \text{ ft}} = \frac{b}{12} \text{ ft}$$

$$\frac{3}{2}b = 12$$

$$b = 12 \div \frac{3}{2} = 12 \times \frac{2}{3} = 8 \text{ in.}$$

Ⓑ If a wall on the blueprint is 9 inches long, how long will it be in the warehouse?

$$\frac{\text{blueprint}}{\text{warehouse}} : \frac{1 \text{ in.}}{\frac{3}{2} \text{ ft}} = \frac{9 \text{ in.}}{w}$$

$$w = \frac{3}{2} \cdot \frac{9}{1} = \frac{27}{2} = 13\frac{1}{2} \text{ ft}$$

A map is a special kind of scale drawing. Since lines for highways are rarely straight, you need to estimate when using maps.

EXAMPLE C

One United States road map has the following scale: 1 in. ≈ 135 mi or 215 km

Ⓐ On the map, Albuquerque is about 2 inches from Amarillo. Approximately how many miles apart are they?

$$\frac{\text{map}}{\text{actual}} \cdot \frac{1 \text{ in.}}{135 \text{ mi}} = \frac{2}{m}$$

$$m = 2 \cdot 135 = 270 \text{ mi}$$

Ⓑ Dallas is 403 miles from Jackson, Mississippi. Approximately how many inches, to the nearest inch, apart will they be on the map?

$$\frac{\text{map}}{\text{actual}} \cdot \frac{1 \text{ in.}}{135 \text{ mi}} = \frac{n}{403}$$

$$135n = 403$$

$$n = 2.985 \approx 3 \text{ in.}$$

PROBLEM 9 | A 3 × 4-inch snapshot is enlarged so that its shorter side is 9 inches. How long will the longer side be?

PROBLEM 10 | On the warehouse blueprint in Example B, a window is 4 inches wide. How wide will it be in the warehouse?

PROBLEM 11 | A plot map, whose scale is 1 in. = 100 ft, shows the length of a lot to be $3\frac{1}{2}$ inches. How long is the actual lot?

PROBLEM 12 | Nashville is 208 miles from Memphis. How many inches apart, to the nearest half inch, would they be on the map in Example C?

Unit Rates Revisited

In the last lesson, you used your calculator to find unit prices and then compared them to find the better buy between two prices. You should also be prepared to use the idea of unit rates when you don't have a calculator handy or when the prices are not displayed. Try some strategies for estimating so that you can mentally make the economical choice.

EXAMPLE

It costs 73¢ for a 10-oz box of frozen cut corn. A 16-oz bag of the same brand of frozen cut corn is 89¢. Which has the lower unit price?

Round to compatible numbers for dividing, and estimate the unit prices.

Since the box contains 10 oz, you divide by 10. Move the decimal point 1 place to the left. $\frac{73}{10} = 7.3$¢ per oz

The bag contains 16 oz. Round 89 to 90 and 16 to 15 so that you can divide mentally. $\frac{89}{16} \approx \frac{90}{15} = 6$¢ per oz

The 16-oz bag is slightly less expensive according to the estimation.

PROBLEM 13

Try to decide which is the better buy by *estimating*. (Check yourself by finding the unit prices with your calculator.)

Ⓐ A bottle of 24 pain-reliever tablets costs $2.79. Compare this to a bottle containing 100 tablets, which is marked $6.49.

Ⓑ Dishwashing liquid in the 22-ounce container costs $1.59, while the 32-ounce container costs $2.49.

Ⓒ A box of 30 disposable diapers costs $10.99, while a box of 64 costs $19.99.

Ⓓ An 8-ounce container of yogurt costs $.63, while a 32-ounce container costs $1.79.

Ⓔ A special promotion of snack packs of raisins offers a package of six $1\frac{1}{2}$-ounce boxes for $.88. The regular price of a 9-ounce box is $1.09.

Ⓕ Discuss some reasons for choosing to buy a package that has the *higher* unit price.

CHECK YOUR UNDERSTANDING

You may use your calculator on any problem except where noted by this symbol:

1. Find the missing number in these proportions using a method that fits the problem. Mentally check your answer for reasonableness.

    A $\dfrac{x}{18} = \dfrac{4}{3}$ **E** $\dfrac{9}{54} = \dfrac{n}{30}$

    B $\dfrac{15}{x} = \dfrac{5}{7}$ **F** $\dfrac{4.5}{x} = \dfrac{0.03}{0.06}$

    C $\dfrac{9}{3} = \dfrac{12}{n}$ **G** $\dfrac{6}{1.5} = \dfrac{x}{3}$

    D $\dfrac{\frac{1}{2}}{8} = \dfrac{\frac{1}{4}}{x}$ **H** $\dfrac{\frac{1}{5}}{10} = \dfrac{\frac{1}{10}}{x}$

2. Kiwi fruit are on sale at 4 for $1.00. How much would 10 kiwi cost?

3. How many ounces are there in $3\frac{1}{2}$ pounds? (1 lb = 16 oz)

4. During the first game of the season, LaTanya made 6 of the 9 free throws she tried. If she continues at this rate, how many shots does she have to try in order to make 100 of them?

5. The record distance jumped by a frog in the Calaveras County Frog Jumping Jubilee was $21\frac{1}{2}$ feet. This distance was covered in 3 jumps. If a frog could keep up this rate, how far would it travel in 12 jumps?

6. Bob Barber set the land speed record for steam-powered vehicles, 145.6 mph, in 1985. At that rate, how far, to the nearest mile, will the vehicle travel in 10 minutes?

7. A dip recipe calls for a 3-ounce package of cream cheese and 2 teaspoons of dill weed. How much dill weed would you add if you used an 8-ounce package of cream cheese?

8. A marathon runner finished the race (a distance of about 26 miles) in $3\frac{1}{4}$ hours. How many miles per hour did she average?

9. The slope of this ramp is $\frac{1}{20}$. How far does it rise for each 50 feet that it crosses?

> 1 ft
> 20 ft

10. The quarterback from State U completed 20 out of 32 passes in a game against Crimson College. The quarterback from Crimson completed 6 fewer passes than his opponent. How many passes did he complete?

11. Juanita inspects parts on an assembly line. On the average, 1 out of 16 parts she inspects is defective. On a day that she inspects 800 parts, how many of them are *acceptable*?

12. The shadow of a light pole is 55 feet long at the same time that the shadow of a fence post is 11 feet long. What is the ratio of the length of the light pole to the length of the fence post?

13. A photo that measures 5 by 7 inches is in a frame that is 8 by 10 inches. Are the two rectangles *similar*?

> 8 in.
> 10 in.   7 in.
> 5 in.

14. Which is the better buy, a package of 2 rolls of paper towels at $1.99 or a package of 3 rolls (of the same kind) for $2.67?

15. How many hours are there in 200 minutes? (1 hr = 60 min)

16. On Wednesdays, tacos are 2 for $.99. On other days, each taco is $.59. Approximately how much do you save per taco on Wednesdays?

TEST-TAKING PRACTICE

You may use your calculator on any problem except where noted by this symbol:

1. 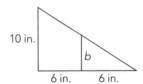 A map has the scale of 2 in. = 75 mi. How many actual miles apart are 2 cities that are 10 inches apart on the map?

    (1) 750
    (2) 375
    (3) 150
    (4) 100
    (5) Not enough information is given.

2. The aspect ratio (width to height) of the high-definition television (HDTV) screens is 16:9. What is the approximate height, in inches, of an HDTV screen whose width is 25 inches?

    (1) 44
    (2) 41
    (3) 34
    (4) 16
    (5) 14

3. What is the length, in inches, of the brace, *b*, in the triangular support shown below?

    10 in.

    b

    6 in.   6 in.

    Mark your answer in the circles in the grid.

4. Below is a table of U.S. toll roads and the cost for using each road.

road	miles	cost
Richmond (VA) Expressway	6.3	$.50
Dulles Toll Road	13	$.85
Holland East-West Expressway (Orlando, FL)	13.8	$.50
Dallas North Tollway	17	$1.00
Sawgrass Expressway (FL)	23	$1.50

Which toll road is the most expensive per mile?

   (1) Richmond Expressway
   (2) Dulles Toll Road
   (3) Holland East-West Expressway
   (4) Dallas North Tollway
   (5) Sawgrass Expressway

5. A pre-election poll of voters indicates that they will vote against the school bond issue 5 to 2. How many of the county's 35,700 voters are expected to vote for the bond issue?

   (1) 10,200
   (2) 14,280
   (3) 21,420
   (4) 25,500
   (5) 30,600

6. A nutrition label on White Cheddar Cheese Popcorn says that in one serving, 90 out of the 170 calories come from fat. It is known that each gram of fat produces 9 calories. How many grams of fat are in one serving of this popcorn?

   (1) 10
   (2) 17
   (3) 19
   (4) 72
   (5) 81

Percent I

Which common fraction equals

1. 0.50? **5.** 0.60?

2. 0.75? **6.** 0.40?

3. 0.20? **7.** $0.33\frac{1}{3}$?

4. 0.10? **8.** $0.12\frac{1}{2}$?

Each decimal in the exercises above has 2 decimal places; the decimals are *hundredths*. **Percent** also means hundredths. It is a ratio between some number and 100. The word *percent* literally means "per hundred" or "for each hundred." Two-place decimals can serve as the link between common fractions and percents. Replace "hundredths" with "percent" by removing 2 decimal places.

$$\frac{1}{2} = 0.50 = 50\% \qquad \frac{3}{4} = 0.75 = 75\% \qquad \frac{1}{5} = 0.20 = 20\% \qquad \frac{1}{10} = 0.10 = 10\%$$

50 hundredths 50 percent

Getting Comfortable with Percents

Before you concentrate on the procedures to calculate with percents, you should feel comfortable with percent relationships and find some answers mentally.

The percent ratio is used nearly every day in nearly every aspect of our lives. It is so common because it provides a standard way to compare ratios between quantities, in much the same way that unit rates do. With percent, you express a comparison in terms of the standard 100, or, out of a hundred.

A 6% sales tax means that for every $100 you spend, you pay $6 in tax.

6% is expressed as the ratio $\frac{6}{100}$ (6 out of 100).

A 9% interest rate means that $100 in savings will earn $9 a year in interest.

The ratio $\frac{9}{100}$ (9 out of 100) is the same as 9%.

PROBLEM 1 | Fill in the missing values in the table.

fraction	2-place decimal	percent	fraction	2-place decimal	percent
$\frac{3}{10}$				1.00	
	0.25		$\frac{1}{3}$		
		40%			7%

PROBLEM 2 | In a typical paragraph written in the English language, the letter *e* occurs most frequently. The table at the right gives the frequency, in percent, of some letters in ordinary English passages. Find the answers to the questions mentally.

letter	frequency
e	13%
t	9%
a, o	9%
n	7%
i, r	6.5%
s, h	6%

A How many *t*'s would you expect to find in a passage containing 100 letters?

B How many *e*'s would you expect to find in a passage containing 100 letters?

C How many *n*'s in 100 letters?

D How many *n*'s in 200 letters?

E How many *s*'s in 100 letters? in 300 letters? in 1,000 letters?

Benchmark Percents

100% of a number is *all* of it.		**0% is *none* of it.**
$100\% = \frac{100}{100} = 1$ or 1.00		$0\% = \frac{0}{100} = 0$
100% of 30 $\frac{100}{100}$ of 30 = 30	If 100% of a number *equals* the number, any percent less than 100% of it will be less than the number.	0% of 56 $0 \times 56 = 0$

10% of a number is $\frac{1}{10}$ of it.

$$10\% = \frac{10}{100} = \frac{1}{10} \text{ or } 0.10$$

To find 10% of a number, you can divide it by 10.

| 10% of 50
$\frac{1}{10}$ of 50 = 5
or
$0.10 \times 50. = 5$ | Remember that you can divide by 10 easily by moving the decimal point 1 place to the left.

The digits remain the same. | 10% of 155
$\frac{1}{10}$ of 155 = 15.5
or
$0.10 \times 155. = 15.5$ |

> **1% of a number is $\frac{1}{100}$ of it.**

$$1\% = \frac{1}{100} \text{ or } 0.01$$

To find 1% of a number, you can divide it by 100.

1% of 20

$\frac{1}{100}$ of 20 = 0.2

or

$0.01 \times 20. = 0.2$

Remember that you can divide by 100 easily by moving the decimal point 2 places to the *left*.

1% of 511

$\frac{1}{100}$ of 511 = 5.11

or

$0.01 \times 511. = 5.11$

PROBLEM 3 | Solve the following equations mentally.

40

A 100% of 40 = 40

10% of 40 = ____

1% of 40 = ____

80

C ____% of 80 = 80

____% of 80 = 8

____% of 80 = 0.8

500

E 100% of 500 = ____

10% of 500 = ____

1% of 500 = ____

300

B 100% of ____ = 300

10% of ____ = 30

1% of ____ = 3

2,000

D 100% of 2,000 = ____

10% of 2,000 = ____

1% of 2,000 = ____

1,500

F 100% of 1,500 = ____

____% of 1,500 = 150

1% of 1,500 = ____

PROBLEM 4 | Refer to the patterns shown above to mentally solve the following equations.

A 10% of 90 = x

B 10% of 91 = g

C 10% of 89 = p

D 1% of 70 = n

E 1% of 71 = h

F 1% of 69 = k

G x% of 250 = 25

H n% of 25 = 25

I p% of 900 = 9

More Percent Benchmarks

> **50% of a number is $\frac{1}{2}$ of it.**

$$50\% = \frac{50}{100} = \frac{1}{2}$$

To find 50% of a number, you can divide it by 2.

50% of 32

$\frac{1}{2}$ of $\overset{16}{\cancel{32}}$ = 16
 1

or

$0.5 \times 32 = 16$

Multiplying a number by $\frac{1}{2}$ is the same as dividing it by 2.

50% of 800

$\frac{1}{2}$ of $\overset{400}{\cancel{800}}$ = 400
 1

or

$0.5 \times 800 = 400$

25% of a number is $\frac{1}{4}$ of it.

$$25\% = \frac{25}{100} = \frac{1}{4}$$

To find 25% of a number, you can divide it by 4 or divide by 2 twice.

25% of 80	Multiplying a number by $\frac{1}{4}$ is the same as dividing it by 4 (or dividing by 2 twice).	25% of 420
$\frac{1}{\overset{1}{\cancel{4}}}$ of $\overset{20}{\cancel{80}} = 20$		$\frac{1}{\overset{1}{\cancel{4}}}$ of $\overset{105}{\cancel{420}} = 105$
or		or
$\frac{1}{2}\left(\frac{1}{2} \text{ of } 80\right) = \frac{1}{2}(40) = 20$		$\frac{1}{2}\left(\frac{1}{2} \text{ of } 420\right) = \frac{1}{2}(210) = 105$

20% of a number is $\frac{1}{5}$ of it.

$$20\% = \frac{20}{100} = \frac{1}{5}$$

To find 20% of a number, you can divide it by 5 or find 10% of the number and double it.

20% of 30	Multiplying a number by $\frac{1}{5}$ is the same as dividing it by 5 or dividing by 10 and doubling that.	20% of 105
$\frac{1}{\overset{1}{\cancel{5}}}$ of $\overset{6}{\cancel{30}} = 6$		$\frac{1}{\overset{1}{\cancel{5}}}$ of $\overset{21}{\cancel{105}} = 21$
or		or
$2\left(\frac{1}{10} \text{ of } 30\right) = 2(3) = 6$		$2\left(\frac{1}{10} \text{ of } 105\right) = 2(10.5) = 21$

PROBLEM 5 | Solve the following equations mentally.

20	**120**	
Ⓐ 100% of 20 = _____	**Ⓑ** 100% of 120 = _____	**Ⓒ** 50% of _____ = 40
50% of 20 = _____	_____% of 120 = 60	25% of _____ = 20
25% of 20 = _____	25% of 120 = _____	20% of _____ = 16

PROBLEM 6 | Mentally solve the following equations by using the patterns shown above.

Ⓐ 25% of 16 = x	**Ⓓ** 20% of 40 = c	**Ⓖ** x% of 30 = 15
Ⓑ 50% of 16 = b	**Ⓔ** 50% of t = 20	**Ⓗ** n% of 60 = 15
Ⓒ 50% of 12 = n	**Ⓕ** 50% of w = 30	**Ⓘ** p% of 500 = 100

More than 100% of a number	
$200\% = \frac{200}{100} = 2$	$300\% = \frac{300}{100} = 3$
To find 200% of a number, multiply it by 2.	To find 300% of a number, multiply it by 3.

PROBLEM 7 | Complete the following equations mentally.

Ⓐ 100% of 30 = _____   Ⓑ 100% of _____ = 9   Ⓒ 100% of 150 = _____

200% of 30 = _____   200% of 9 = _____   _____% of 150 = 300

300% of 30 = _____   _____% of 9 = 27   _____% of 150 = 450

Other common fractions		
$33\frac{1}{3}\% = \frac{1}{3}$	$30\% = \frac{300}{100} = \frac{3}{10}$	$75\% = \frac{75}{100} = \frac{3}{4}$
$33\frac{1}{3}\%$ of 15 = _____	30% of 60 = _____	75% of 48 = _____
$\frac{1}{3}$ of 15 = 5	$\frac{3}{10}$ of 60 = 18	$\frac{3}{4}$ of 48 = 36
	$\left(\frac{1}{10} \times 60 = 6 \,;\, 6 \times 3 = 18\right)$	$\left(\frac{1}{4} \times 48 = 12 \,;\, 12 \times 3 = 36\right)$

PROBLEM 8 | Using the patterns shown above, solve these equations mentally.

Ⓐ 100% of 32 = 32

50% of 32 = c

25% of 32 = d

75% of 32 = n

200% of 32 = t

400% of 32 = x

Ⓑ 100% of 60 = 60

_____% of 60 = 6

_____% of 60 = 12

_____% of 60 = 18

_____% of 60 = 30

_____% of 60 = 15

_____% of 60 = 45

Ⓒ 100% of 20 = 20

10% of 20 = m

20% of 20 = b

110% of 20 = p

120% of 20 = s

Ⓓ 100% of 300 = 300

$33\frac{1}{3}\%$ of 300 = _____

$66\frac{2}{3}\%$ of 300 = _____

300% of 300 = _____

600% of 300 = _____

Percent Equations as Proportions

So far you have been able to solve many percent problems mentally by noticing patterns. You should always look first for patterns. When the numbers are "nice" and the patterns are obvious, you can find the answer without using pencil and paper. However, you do need a method to solve more difficult percent problems. The good news is that you already know the method: using proportions.

Writing the Percent Proportion

A percent equation involves 3 numbers.

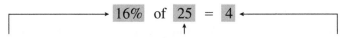

16% of 25 = 4

The percent is easily recognized by the % sign. It tells the **rate** (number per 100).

Another number is the **base** or "whole." It is the number that comes after the word *of* because it is what the percent is based on.

The third number is difficult to label. In some cases, it is the **part**, but we will call it the **amount**.

Make a proportion from these 3 numbers by setting up 2 equal ratios.

$$\text{rate} \left[\frac{\text{percent}}{100} = \frac{\text{amount}}{\text{base}} \right.$$

① One fraction comes from the **rate**. Place the percent over 100 to make a fraction.

$$\frac{16}{100}$$

② The other 2 numbers make up the second fraction. The **base** or "whole" goes on the bottom to correspond with the 100.

$$\overset{\text{rate}}{\underset{\downarrow}{}}$$
$$\frac{16}{100} = \frac{4}{25} \leftarrow \text{amount} \atop \leftarrow \text{base}$$

③ Check the proportion to see if it is true. First try to find patterns.

$$\frac{16 \div 4}{100 \div 4} = \frac{4}{25}$$

- Can you simplify either fraction?

- Look across the proportion as well as within each ratio to locate a pattern.

$$\frac{16}{100} = \frac{4}{25}$$
true proportion

- If you can't find a pattern, cross multiply and compare the products. If the cross products are equal, the fractions are equal; it is a true proportion.

PROBLEM 9 | Write these percent sentences as proportions. Check to see if they are true or false. Look for patterns before you cross multiply.

Ⓐ 90% of 10 is 9

Ⓔ 2% of 90 is 18

Ⓑ 75% of 96 is 70

Ⓕ 110% of 40 is 50

Ⓒ 6 is 15% of 40

Ⓖ 200% of 40 is 20

Ⓓ 30 is 40% of 75

Ⓗ 36 is 300% of 12

Solving the Percent Proportion

A percent problem is a **percent sentence** with one of the three numbers missing. If you know two of the numbers, you can find the third one. Use a variable in place of the missing number when you set up the proportion. Then solve the proportion just as you did in the last lesson.

30% of 80 = ____	55% of ____ = 33	100 = ____ % of 80
↑	↑	↑
80 is the base.	The base is missing.	The base is after *of.*

$$\frac{30}{100} = \frac{p}{80}$$

$$100p = 2{,}400$$

$$p = 24$$

$$\frac{55}{100} = \frac{33}{n}$$

$$55n = 3{,}300$$

$$n = 60$$

$$\frac{x}{100} = \frac{100}{80}$$

$$80x = 10{,}000$$

$$x = 125;$$
the rate is 125%.

Always put your answer back into the percent sentence. Use the benchmark percents you learned earlier to judge whether or not the answers are reasonable.

30% of 80 = <u>24</u>

Since 80 is less than 100, 30% of it should be less than 30.

55% of <u>60</u> = 33

The part, 33, should be a little more than half of the base, 60.

100 = <u>125%</u> of 80

100 is $\frac{1}{4}$ more than 80.

Look for ways that will make solving the proportion easier. But remember that you can *always* solve a proportion by cross-multiplying.

PROBLEM 10 | Write each of these percent sentences as a proportion. Use your calculator, if necessary, to solve for the missing value. Then put your answer back into the original problem to see if it makes sense.

Ⓐ 65% of 120 is what?

Ⓑ 70 is what % of 105?

Ⓒ 75% of what is 45?

Ⓓ 35% of 80 is what?

Ⓔ 105% of what is 42?

Ⓕ 9 is what % of 72?

Ⓖ 52% of 150 is what?

Ⓗ 250% of what is 10?

Ⓘ 252 is 36% of what?

Ⓙ 200 is what % of 125?

Writing the Percent Equation for a Situation

Before you can actually use what you have learned about percent to solve real problems, you need to know how to write the **percent equation** from the words that describe the problem situation. If a situation gives enough information, you will be able to place two numbers into the equation and then find the third one.

____ % of	____ =	____	or	____	= ____	% of ____
rate	base	amount		amount	rate	base

EXAMPLE

To earn a C on a certain test, Miguel needs to answer at least 70% of the questions correctly. If there are 40 questions on the test, what is the least number of correct answers that will earn him a C?

Which of the three numbers is missing: the rate, the base, or the amount?

The *rate* is easiest to spot, since it has a % sign.   70% of _____ = _____
                                                          rate   base   amount

The *base* is the number of questions.   70% of _40_ = _____
("70% of the questions")   rate   base   amount

The percent equation that represents this situation is **70% of 40 = *n*.**

EXAMPLE

On a test that had 25 questions, Marla answered 16 correctly. What percent of the questions did she get right?

You can see immediately that it is the *rate* that is missing. To place the other two numbers properly, determine which one is the *base*.

Look at the second sentence of the problem.   ___% of _25_ = ____
"What percent *of* the questions…" How   rate   base   amount
many questions were there on the test?
25 is the base.

That leaves the 16 to be the amount.   ___% of _25_ = _16_
                                         rate   base   amount

The percent equation for this situation is **what % of 25 = 16**
or **16 = what % of 25.**

EXAMPLE

Mannie answered 45 questions correctly on a test. This was 60% correct. How many questions were on the test?

You can see that the rate is given.   60% of ____ = ____
                                        rate   base   amount

Is 45 the base or the amount?   60% of ____ = _45_
                                  rate   base   amount

Percent correct on tests is based on the total number of questions, which is what the problem asks for. The base is missing. 45 is the amount.

The percent equation for this situation is **60% of *w* = 45** or **45 = 60% of *w*.**

PROBLEM 11 | Write the percent equation for each of the following situations. Use one of these formats as a guide. **Do not solve yet.**

_____ % of _____ = _____   or   _____ = _____ % of _____
  rate   base   amount   amount   rate   base

Ⓐ A 46-ounce can of fruit drink is labeled "10% fruit juice." How many ounces of real fruit juice are in that can?

Ⓑ Jesse paid $1.47 sales tax on a shirt that cost $21.00. What is the sales tax rate?

Ⓒ The newspaper reports that 11% of the working-age population of the city is unemployed. Later in the same article, it says that 2,200 people in the city are unemployed. What is the working-age population of the city?

Ⓓ To purchase a home for $150,000, the Jacobs were required to make a down payment of $22,500. The down payment was what percent of the total?

Ⓔ An electronics store advertised a discount of 20% off on all merchandise. How much discount would you get on a telephone that was priced at $85?

Ⓕ What percent of his basketball shots did Anthony make if he made 12 out of 30 attempts?

Solving Percent Equations Directly

Instead of setting up proportions, you can solve percent equations directly. Again, the good news is that you already know how to do this using algebraic principles.

EXAMPLE

Examine a percent equation: 60% of 95 = 57

Percent problems arise if any one of the three numbers is missing.

STEP 1 Write the percent equations using a variable in place of the missing number.

$$60\% \text{ of } 95 = m \qquad 60\% \text{ of } n = 57 \qquad \text{what } \% \text{ of } 95 = 57$$
    amount missing   base missing   rate missing

STEP 2 Write the percent as a fraction or a decimal. Replace *of* with *times*.

$$\frac{3}{5} \times 95 = m \qquad 0.60 \cdot n = 57 \qquad x \cdot 95 = 57$$

STEP 3 Use regular equation-solving methods. Use the algebraic rules to get the variable alone.

$$m = \frac{3}{\cancel{5}} \times \frac{\overset{19}{\cancel{95}}}{1} = 57 \qquad n = \frac{57}{0.60} = 95 \qquad x = \frac{57}{95} = 0.60 \text{ or } 60\%$$

STEP 4 Check by replacing the variable with your answer in the original equation.

$$60\% \text{ of } 95 = 57 \qquad 60\% \text{ of } 95 = 57 \qquad 60\% \text{ of } 95 = 57$$

Some people like the algebraic method because it seems shorter than using proportions. Others like the proportion method because the procedure is always the same.

PROBLEM 12 | Use the algebraic equation-solving method to solve these percent problems.

Ⓐ 90% of 150 = c

Ⓑ 125% of 48 = x

Ⓒ 55 = what % of 88

Ⓓ 2,000 = what % of 1,600

Ⓔ 80 = $33\frac{1}{3}$% of y

Ⓕ 250% of b = 50

CALCULATOR EXPLORATION

What Does the % Key Do?

Many calculators offer a [%] function, often written above the working keys as a 2nd function. To access the [%] function, press the **2nd** or the [SHIFT] key first and then press the working key just under the [%].

The [%] key places the decimal point in the correct place for you. You still need to enter the numbers and the operation to use.

STEP 1 Write the percent equation so that the variable is alone on its side of the equation. Do NOT change the rate (percent) to a decimal or a fraction.

STEP 2 Enter the numbers and operation sign.

STEP 3 Press the [SHIFT] or **2nd** key and the [%] key and the key if necessary.

EXAMPLES

54% of 860 = n

| 8 | 6 | 0 | × | 5 | 4 | 2nd | [%] | = | 464.4 |

85% of c = 136

$c = \frac{136}{85\%}$

| 1 | 3 | 6 | ÷ | 8 | 5 | 2nd | [%] | = | 160. |

36 = what % of 90

$x = \frac{36}{90}$

| 3 | 6 | ÷ | 9 | 0 | 2nd | [%] | = | 40. |

Use your calculator to find the answers to problem 11 **Ⓐ**–**Ⓕ** on page 234.

USING DATA

A **circle graph** (or **pie chart**) is used to picture data that shows how a total is divided up into portions. The whole circle represents 100%, or the entire amount. The relative size of each portion is represented by the size of the wedge, or sector, of the circle. The size of a sector is determined by the size, in degrees, of the central angle that defines it.

EXAMPLE A survey asked 1,200 people how many hours of sleep they typically get each night. The responses were the following:

no. of hours	percent	degrees
5 or less	15%	
6 hours	25%	
7 hours	30%	108°
8 hours	25%	
9 or more	5%	

To construct a circle graph that shows this data, start with a circle that has one radius drawn (Figure 1). Since the entire circle contains 360 degrees, the size of the central angle of each sector will be a percentage of 360. For example, the largest sector, representing 7 hours of sleep, will have a central angle that is 30% of 360 or 108 degrees (Figure 2).

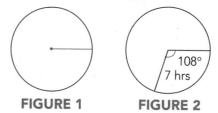

FIGURE 1   **FIGURE 2**

Ⓐ Find the number of degrees in the other sectors of the circle graph.

Ⓑ Use an existing radius as the base for drawing in the next sector in Figure 3. Use a protractor to measure the angle accurately. When all the sectors are drawn, label them appropriately.

Look at one of the sectors that represents 25% of the circle. Every part of that sector is 25% of the entire circle. Its area is 25% of the area of the entire circle and the length of the arc is 25% or $\frac{1}{4}$ of the circumference of the circle.

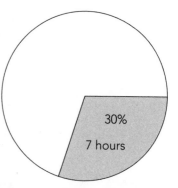

30%
7 hours

FIGURE 3

Ⓒ The diameter of the circle graph is about 5 cm. How much area is enclosed in the sector that represents 7 hours of sleep? How long is the arc (portion of the curve) for that sector? Round each answer to the nearest tenth of a cm.

More Applications

PROBLEM 13

When a used car is bought from a private citizen rather than an established business, the state collects sales tax when the car is registered to the new owner. In one state, where the tax rate is 5.25% for private car sales, the basis for the tax is determined by a complex depreciation formula based on the original price of the car.

For tax purposes, a new vehicle depreciates 15% of the original price the first year, an additional 10% of the original price the next year, and then 5% each following year.

Ⓐ A car that originally cost $22,000 is sold privately. According to the formula, how much did it depreciate over 2 years? What percent of the original price is this?

Ⓑ What is the tax basis for the 2-year-old car from part **Ⓐ**? How much tax would be assessed on it?

Ⓒ In how many years would the tax basis for a car be zero?

Ⓓ How much tax would someone pay if he bought a 7-year-old car that originally sold for $15,000?

PROBLEM 14

Department stores have sales to clear their seasonal inventory. The initial discounts are often made larger by using coupons. For example, the sale advertises a 15% discount on men's suits. The coupon from the newspaper says, "An extra 10% off the sale price of men's suits."

Ⓐ Without a coupon, what is the discount, in dollars, that would be taken off the price of a suit originally priced at $200? What is the sale price?

Ⓑ With a coupon, what additional discount, in dollars, would apply? Then what would the sale price be?

Ⓒ Do the two discounts add up to 25% of the original price of $200? If not, what percent of $200 is the total discount?

Ⓓ Explain the difference between this problem and part **Ⓐ** of problem 13.

✓ CHECK YOUR UNDERSTANDING

You may use your calculator on any problem except where noted by this symbol:

1. Try to solve these equations mentally (or with the least amount of paper and pencil work).

   Ⓐ 100% of 35 = _____
   Ⓑ 25% of 48 = _____
   Ⓒ 50% of 150 = _____
   Ⓓ $33\frac{1}{3}$% of 60 = _____
   Ⓔ 0% of 67 = _____
   Ⓕ 500% of 25 = _____
   Ⓖ 1% of 450 = _____
   Ⓗ 10% of 450 = _____
   Ⓘ 20% of 400 = _____
   Ⓙ 75% of 16 = _____

2. Which is greater?

   Ⓐ $25 or 25% of $110
   Ⓑ 10% of 30 or 15% of 20?
   Ⓒ 50% of 90 or 40% of 100?
   Ⓓ 200 or 25% of 1,000?
   Ⓔ $10 or 10% of $95?
   Ⓕ 20% of 25 or 25% of 20?

3. Set up each of these percent equations as a proportion. Decide whether each equation is true or false.

   Ⓐ $4 \overset{?}{=} 20\%$ of 20
   Ⓔ $30 \overset{?}{=} 250\%$ of 12
   Ⓑ $9 \overset{?}{=} 30\%$ of 30
   Ⓕ 1% of $3{,}000 \overset{?}{=} 3$
   Ⓒ 80% of $45 \overset{?}{=} 35$
   Ⓖ 110% of $85 \overset{?}{=} 95$
   Ⓓ 10% of $215 \overset{?}{=} 2.15$
   Ⓗ $8 \overset{?}{=} 75\%$ of 12

For problems 4–11, write a percent equation that describes the situation. Then solve the equation using whichever method seems best to you.

4. The Jacksons had to pay 6% of the selling price of their home as commission to their real estate broker. If they sold their home for $130,000, how much commission did they owe?

5. During a sale where all merchandise was discounted by 25%, Thomasina bought a dress whose original price was $78.00. How much discount was taken?

6. By getting 20 answers correct on a test, Bob got a score of 80%. How many questions were on the test?

7. Rosie works as a sales representative and gets paid a commission of 5% of the amount of merchandise that she sells. How much does she have to sell in order to earn $200 in commissions?

8. A survey of 250 people found that 175 of them wished that they had a better education. What percent of those surveyed was this?

9. Each week, $88 of Rich's pay is deducted for taxes. If his salary is $400 a week, what percent of his pay is deducted?

10. A builder estimates that Pat would save 40% of her heating costs if she installed new insulation. He estimates that he could do the job for $5,000. Pat's present heating costs are about $900 per year.

    Ⓐ At her present heating cost, how much could she expect to save this year?
    Ⓑ After how many years would Pat actually be saving money?

11. Kobe's free-throw percentage for the preseason was 90%. If he *made* 36 free throws, how many did he attempt?

TEST-TAKING PRACTICE

You may use your calculator on any problem except where noted by this symbol:

Problems 1 and 2 refer to the following information and graph.

A lighting store stocks three major kinds of fixtures: ceiling-mounted, wall-mounted, and free-standing lamps. The owners try to maintain the following distribution between these kinds of fixtures to result in the highest sales.

LIGHTING INVENTORY

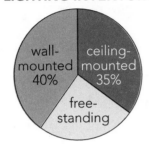

1. What percent of the total is allocated to free-standing lamps?

Mark your answer in the circles in the grid.

2. The owners strive to keep a total of 3,200 fixtures in stock. Approximately how many of them would be ceiling-mounted?

(1)   800
(2) 1,120
(3) 1,280
(4) 2,240
(5) 2,400

3. A city park was designed so that 65% of its area is planted with native vegetation, 20% is devoted to sports fields and 10% is reserved for trails and parking spaces. How many more acres are used for native vegetation than are used for sports fields?

(1) 650
(2) 200
(3)   55
(4)   45
(5) Not enough information is given.

4. Financial planners recommend that families save about 5% of their take-home pay. Ed and Sherrie save $90 each week from their combined paychecks, which total $1,200. What percent do Ed and Sherrie save?

(1)   1%
(2)   5%
(3)   7.5%
(4) 10%
(5) 90%

5. A survey was taken to discover what motorists thought of plans to install traffic circles at intersections on a busy street. Of those asked, 9 approved and 12 disapproved. Approximately what percentage of the participants approved of the traffic circles?

(1) 75%
(2) 67%
(3) 57%
(4) 43%
(5) 25%

6. A machine part is usable if the variation from its specified size is less than 3%. Which of the following lengths, in centimeters, is NOT acceptable for a part that was intended to be 32 centimeters long?

(1) 32.35
(2) 31.35
(3) 32.77
(4) 31.03
(5) 32.87

Part One

Before going on further to the last section in this book, use the following exercise to maintain your skills. If you are having difficulty, go back and review the topics in the last few lessons.

You may use your calculator on any problem except where noted by this symbol:

PROBLEM 1

At Hitech Corporation, there are 120 employees—45 women and 75 men. Twenty percent of the employees are at the executive level. Thirty percent of the employees are minorities. Two out of every three employees favor a new insurance plan.

Ⓐ What is the ratio, in fraction form, of women to men at Hitech?

Ⓑ What is the ratio, in fraction form, of women to total employees?

Ⓒ How many minority employees are there at Hitech?

Ⓓ How many executives are there?

Ⓔ What is the ratio, in fraction form, of executives to total employees?

Ⓕ How many employees favor a new insurance plan?

PROBLEM 2

Fill in the equivalent measurements below. Use the standard equivalents charts on page 295 in the Appendix whenever needed.

Ⓐ $1\frac{1}{2}$ cups = _____ fl oz

Ⓑ 3 cups = _____ pints

Ⓒ 40 oz = _____ lb

Ⓓ 36 fl oz = _____ cups

Ⓔ 2 pints = _____ cups

Ⓕ 22 cups = _____ qt

PROBLEM 3

Circle T (true) or F (false) for each of the following percent equations.

Ⓐ 10% of 250 = 25   T   F

Ⓑ 30 = 15% of 200   T   F

Ⓒ 24 = 25% of 6   T   F

Ⓓ 80% of 60 = 48   T   F

PROBLEM 4

The graph shows the performance of two different part-making machines on one day. Machine A ran perfectly for a while, but then was stopped for maintenance.

Ⓐ How many parts per hour did machine B produce?

Ⓑ For how many hours was Machine A idle?

Ⓒ On a day when Machine A runs perfectly for 8 hours, how many parts will it produce?

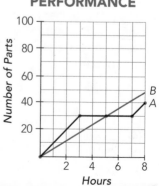

PERFORMANCE

Part Two

Now practice your test-taking skills with the following problems.

You may use your calculator on any problem except where noted by this symbol:

1. The measurement scale on a builder's blueprint reads $\frac{1}{2}$ in. $\doteq$ 1 ft. If the blueprint shows a foyer that is 3 inches wide, how many feet wide will the foyer actually be?

   (1) $\frac{3}{2}$
   (2) 3
   (3) 4
   (4) 6
   (5) 8

2. An army unit has a total of 120 enlisted personnel and officers. Which of the following is the ratio of enlisted people to officers if there are 20 officers in the unit?

   (1) 1:6
   (2) 5:1
   (3) 1:5
   (4) 1:7
   (5) 140:20

3. A quality-control check reveals that there is an average of 1 malfunctioning transistor in every 35 that come off the assembly line. How many defective transistors are produced in a day when 7,700 transistors come off the line?

   (1)   1
   (2)   29
   (3)   35
   (4)   220
   (5) 277,200

4. If 3 pounds of tomatoes cost $2.88, choose an equation that could be used to find the price of 5 pounds of tomatoes.

   (1) $\frac{3}{5} = \frac{x}{\$2.88}$
   (2) $\frac{3}{5} = \frac{\$2.88}{x}$
   (3) $\frac{5}{8} = \frac{x}{\$2.88}$
   (4) $\frac{3}{8} = \frac{x}{\$2.88}$
   (5) $\frac{3}{8} = \frac{\$2.88}{x}$

5. The Clemsons' real estate agent agreed to a 4% commission. If the selling price of a house was $110,000, how much did the agent collect?

   (1) $ 400
   (2) $ 4,000
   (3) $ 4,400
   (4) $ 6,600
   (5) $27,500

6. Thirty factory employees belong to a union. If the factory employs 250 people, what percent of the employees belong to the union?

   (1)   12%
   (2)   75%
   (3)   83%
   (4)   120%
   (5) 7,500%

7. When estimating a bid for landscaping a property, a landscaper distributes the costs according to the following graph.

COSTS FOR LANDSCAPING

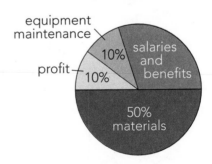

For a $36,000 job, how much does the landscaper allocate for salaries and benefits?

   (1) $ 3,000
   (2) $ 3,600
   (3) $10,800
   (4) $12,000
   (5) Not enough information is given.

Percent II

1. 25% of 40 = x

4. 10% of 75 = m

2. 50% of 20 = k

5. 200% of 25 = p

3. 20% of 35 = n

6. $33\frac{1}{3}$% of 90 = k

Estimating Using Benchmark Percents

The mental math exercises reviewed the work you did with benchmark percents in the last lesson. You can also use the benchmarks as a basis for estimating percentages. Keep the fractional equivalents of the benchmarks in mind and look for opportunities to round to compatible numbers.

25% of 41

Think: 40 is compatible with $\frac{1}{4}$.

$$\frac{1}{4} \text{ of } 40 = 10$$

25% of 41 ≈ 10

49% of 220

Think: 50% is close.

$$\frac{1}{2} \text{ of } 220 = 110$$

49% of 220 ≈ 110

PROBLEM 1

Write an estimate of each problem, then *estimate* the answer. Your estimates may be different from the ones on the answer page.

Ⓐ 11% of 90 = p

Ⓕ 9% of 1,099 = n

Ⓑ 27% of 120 = m

Ⓖ 48% of 64 = w

Ⓒ 20% of 37 = b

Ⓗ 32% of 66 = v

Ⓓ 98% of 67 = x

Ⓘ 0.8% of 400 = d

Ⓔ 296% of 500 = k

Ⓙ 25% of 45 = c

PROBLEM 2

Use your calculator to find the precise answers to the equations in problem 1. Discuss some everyday situations where estimating percents would be good enough and the exact answer is not necessary.

Tipping

You can estimate the amount to leave as a tip at a restaurant. It is common for people to leave at least a 15% tip if they are satisfied with the service. Here is an easy way to find an estimate of 15%.

EXAMPLE A		EXAMPLE B
The total bill of $8.13 ≈ $8.00	**STEP 1** Round the total to the nearest dollar.	The total of $24.67 ≈ $25.00
10% is $.80	**STEP 2** Find 10% by moving the decimal point 1 place to the left.	10% is $2.50
5% is + .40	**STEP 3** Find 5% by taking half of 10%.	5% is + 1.25
15% is $1.20	**STEP 4** Add the two amounts to find 15%.	15% is $3.75

PROBLEM 3 | Estimate the 15% tip for each of the following totals.

Ⓐ $4.88   Ⓑ $11.31   Ⓒ $17.65   Ⓓ $24.05   Ⓔ $31.72

PROBLEM 4 | A group of 6 friends shared pizzas and pitchers of drinks. The total bill was $41.45. Estimate a tip to leave and the amount that each person should contribute if they share the bill equally.

Estimating the Rate

When the number that is missing from a percent equation is the **rate** (the number with the % sign), both the **proportion** and the **equation** method lead to the same ratio.

When estimating, make the numbers compatible so that you have an easy fraction to simplify.

EXAMPLE

Find the rate in 66 = what % of 88.

USING PROPORTIONS		USING EQUATION SOLVING
$\frac{x}{100} = \frac{66}{88}$	Simplify the fraction before you divide. $\frac{66}{88} = \frac{3}{4} = 75\%$	$x = \frac{66}{88}$

EXAMPLES

29 = what % of 90	78 = what % of 20
$\frac{x}{100} = \frac{29}{90}$	$x = \frac{78}{20}$
How can this be changed to be an easy fraction?	What number is compatible with 20?
$\frac{29}{90} \approx \frac{30}{90} = \frac{1}{3} = 33\frac{1}{3}\%$	$\frac{78}{20} \approx \frac{80}{20} = 4 = 400\%$

PROBLEM 5 | *Estimate* the missing rate using the methods shown on page 243. Your estimates may differ from those on the answer page.

Ⓐ 102 = *what* % of 400   **Ⓕ** 398 = *what* % of 500

Ⓑ 30 = *what* % of 147   **Ⓖ** 52 = *what* % of 75

Ⓒ 95 = *what* % of 50   **Ⓗ** $1.00 = *what* % of $9.95

Ⓓ 8 = *what* % of 83   **Ⓘ** $1.50 = *what* % of $3.09

Ⓔ 0.9 = *what* % of 100   **Ⓙ** $19 = *what* % of $98.59

Simple Interest

Interest is a fee paid for the use of money. (Think of it as rent for money used.) If you use the bank's money, you pay interest to the bank. If the bank uses your money, the bank pays you and you earn interest.

For a car loan of $6,000, Ruth ended up paying $8,160 over 3 years. She paid $2,160 in interest.

After leaving $1,000 in a savings account for one year, Raul now has $1,096 in the account. He was paid $96 in interest.

The amount of interest paid is usually a percentage (**rate**) of the amount borrowed. The amount borrowed is called the **principal** of the loan.

interest = _____ % of principal

The **length of time** the money is used is an additional factor in problems involving interest. Interest rates are usually annual rates so time is usually given in years.

If Raul had left his money in the bank for only 6 months $\left(\frac{1}{2}\text{ year}\right)$, he would have earned only half the interest. If he had left it in there for 2 years, he would have earned twice as much.

The formula for calculating interest is on the formulas page (page 280).

SIMPLE INTEREST	interest = principal × rate × time

The equation-solving method of finding percentages works well for this type of problem.

PROBLEM 6 | Complete the following table, finding the interest for 1 year.

EXAMPLE

$i = prt$

$i = \$500 \times \frac{6}{100} \times 1$

$i = \frac{\overset{5}{\cancel{\$500}} \times 6}{\underset{1}{\cancel{100}}} = \$30$

		Principal			
		$500	**$1,000**	**$1,500**	**$2,000**
Rate	**6%**	$30			
	12%				

PROBLEM 7 Complete the table again using a time of 6 months $\left(t = \frac{1}{2}\right)$.

	Principal			
Rate	**$500**	**$1,000**	**$1,500**	**$2,000**
6%	$15			
12%				

Interest rates often involve fractional or decimal parts of a percent. You will see rates such as these:

$$5.5\% \qquad 6\frac{1}{2}\% \qquad 8.75\% \qquad 10\frac{1}{4}\%$$

To solve problems with these rates, first write them as decimals. Replace the % sign with a decimal point 2 places to the left of its original place.

$3\% = 0.03$	So:	$8\% = 0.08$	So:
$3.5\% = 0.035$	$3\frac{1}{2}\% = 0.035$	$8.75\% = 0.0875$	$8\frac{3}{4}\% = 0.0875$
$4\% = 0.04$		$9\% = 0.09$	

PROBLEM 8 Write these percents as decimals. Then find how much interest would be earned by depositing $1,000 for 1 year at each rate.

Ⓐ 6.5%   Ⓑ $7\frac{1}{2}\%$ Ⓒ 10.25%   Ⓓ $8\frac{1}{4}\%$ Ⓔ 6.6%

Change

The topic of this section is **change** and how to describe change by using percents.

EXAMPLE

Joan bought a sweater originally priced at $48 on sale for $36. At another store, Joyce bought a sweater for $60 that was originally marked $75.

	original price	sale price
Joan	$48	$36
Joyce	$75	$60

Who saved more?

Joyce says that she saved $3 more because she saved $15 and Joan saved $12.

Joan says that in relation to the original price, she saved 5% more. She shows these calculations:

$$12 \text{ out of } 48 = \frac{12}{48} = \frac{1}{4} = 25\% \qquad 15 \text{ out of } 75 = \frac{15}{75} = \frac{1}{5} = 20\%$$

In their own ways, both Joyce and Joan are correct. There are two important principles to learn from this example:

There is a difference between actual change and relative change.
Joyce saved $3 more when you consider actual change.
Joan saved 5% more when you consider relative change.

Percent change compares the actual change to the original number. We say that it is *based* on the original number. Consider the original number to be 100%—the total.

PROBLEM 9

Ⓐ In a city with a population of 200,000, the number of violent crimes went down last year from 10,000 to 9,800. What is the actual change in the number of crimes?

Ⓑ In another city whose population is 60,000, the number of violent crimes went down last year from 400 to 200. What is the actual change in the number of crimes?

Ⓒ Find the percent change for both cities. Explain how the picture is incomplete when you only know either the actual or the relative change.

Ⓓ Students must score 500 on a mathematics proficiency test in order to be admitted to a certain college. Jack and Jill both took the test without any preparation. Jill's score was 340 and Jack's was 240. They both attended a preparation class and took the test again. On the retake, both their scores increased by 50%. What were their actual scores on the retake?

Ⓔ For part **Ⓓ**, which information was more significant, the actual change or the percent change? Discuss the importance of knowing the base of the percent when interpreting data.

Percent Decrease

Change in a negative direction—a decrease in value—is seen in the common practice of stores offering a discount that results in a sale price.

PROBLEM 10

Elmer's Electric Emporium is having a 30%-off sale. Complete the table below.

marked price ($)	discount ($)	sale price ($)
50	0.30 × 50 = 15	50 − 15 = 35
60		
70		
80		
p		

The last row of the table should be $0.30p$ for discount and $p - 0.30p$ for sale price. However, when you only need to know the sale price, there is a more direct method to find it.

The diagram at the right shows that the sale price of any item during this sale is 70% of the marked price, or $0.70p$. The base, the original number, is shaded.

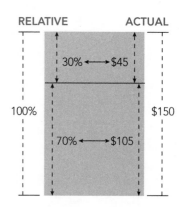

This means that you have two choices for finding the sale price.

EXAMPLE

Say that the marked price was $90.

YOU CAN FIND THE DISCOUNT FIRST:	OR YOU CAN SUBTRACT (MENTALLY) FIRST:
$0.30 \times \$90 = \$27$	$100\% - 30\% = 70\%$
Then subtract the discount from the marked price to get the sale price: $\$90 - \$27 = \$63$	Then multiply to find the sale price. $0.70 \times \$90 = \$63$
In a single equation: $\$90 - 0.30(\$90) = s$	In a single equation: $(1 - 0.30)\$90 = s$

For the problems on a test that ask how to set up an equation, you must recognize that both forms are correct.

PROBLEM 11

For some automobiles, the value *depreciates* (value is lost) 20% in the first year of ownership. Complete the table below in the manner shown.

original value ($)	depreciation ($)	value after 1 year ($)
8,000	$0.20 \times 8,000 = 1,600$	$8,000 - 1,600 = 6,400$
9,000		
10,000		
v		

PROBLEM 12

The value of the cars after 1 year is what % of the original value? Find the values in the last column of the table in problem 11 by using this rate directly instead of subtracting.

PROBLEM 13

The population of a city is expected to drop 6% in the next year. If the present population is 30,000, what is the expected population at the end of next year?

Percent Increase

You can work with change in a positive direction—an increase in value—in similar ways, either in steps or directly.

EXAMPLE

Eileen's salary is $22,000 per year. She has been promised a raise of 20% when she is promoted. What will her new annual salary be?

Eileen's old salary (the original number) is 100%. It is shaded in the diagram.

20% of the original number must be *added.*

Her new salary is 120% of the old salary.

Again, look at the two possible ways to solve this problem.

YOU CAN FIND THE RAISE FIRST:

$0.20 \times \$22,000 = \$4,400$

Then add the raise to the old salary:
$\$22,000 + \$4,400 = \$26,400$

As a single equation:
$\$22,000 + 0.20(\$22,000) = n$

OR YOU CAN ADD (MENTALLY) FIRST

$100\% + 20\% = 120\%$

Then find the new salary directly:
$1.20 \times \$22,000 = \$26,400$

As a single equation:
$1.20(\$22,000) = n$

PROBLEM 14 | The sales tax rate in a county is 7%. Complete the following table.

price ($)	sales tax ($)	total ($)
40.00	$0.07 \times 40.00 = 2.80$	$40.00 + 2.80 = 42.80$
60.00		
100.00		
1,000.00		
p		

PROBLEM 15 | Find each of the totals in the last column directly. (total = 107% of price)

PROBLEM 16 | If the rate of inflation is 4% per year, what would you expect to pay for a washing machine next year if it costs $350 this year?

PROBLEM 17 | Because of the construction of a new factory, the population of the city is expected to increase by 75% in the next 5 years. If the present population is 40,000, what is the expected population in 5 years?

PROBLEM 18 | To make a profit and to pay overhead costs, a furniture store sells furniture at a price that is 100% more than the store paid the manufacturer. What price would the store charge for a chair for which it paid $180?

How Can the % Key Help?

Calculators with % functions often have shortened procedures to find the new numbers after an increase or decrease. Two different orders in which to enter the information are shown below. Find the one that works for your calculator.

INCREASE EXAMPLE

What is the total amount to be paid after an $8\frac{3}{4}$% sales tax is added to a purchase price of $1,500?

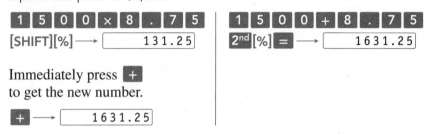

Immediately press **+** to get the new number.

+ ⟶ ⌐ 1 6 3 1 . 2 5 ⌐

The total is $1631.25.

DECREASE EXAMPLE

What is the sale price when a $775 washing machine is discounted by 15%?

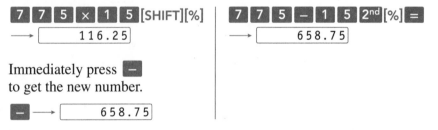

Immediately press **−** to get the new number.

− ⟶ ⌐ 6 5 8 . 7 5 ⌐

The sale price is $658.75.

Use your calculator to find each amount.

A With a sales tax rate of $7\frac{1}{4}$%, find the total bill for a purchase of supplies that cost $320.

B A dentist gives an 8% discount when the client pays cash at the time of service. How much will he charge for a $128 procedure when paid immediately?

C A flooring company adds an 18% waste allowance to the normal job requirement when the flooring is to be laid diagonally. How much should be ordered for a job that normally requires 1,800 board feet?

D After a year when the industry inflation rate averaged $3\frac{1}{2}$%, what price would be expected for a purchase that cost $572 the year before?

Finding the Rate of Increase and Decrease

The examples and problems on the last two pages showed that whether you are finding percent increase or decrease, the **base** of the percent is always the **original number**. Also, the **amount** in both is the amount of increase or decrease.

ORIGINAL PERCENT EQUATION   amount = rate × base

PERCENT CHANGE EQUATION   amount of increase or decrease =
rate × original number

When the rate is the number you need to find, rearrange the above equation to say:

$$\text{rate} = \frac{\text{amount of increase or decrease}}{\text{original number}}$$

Always divide by the original number when finding the rate of increase or decrease.

EXAMPLE

Theo paid $850 (total, including tax) for a stereo system that was marked $800. What is the sales tax rate that he paid?

The two numbers that you need are the amount of increase and the original number.

Find the actual amount of tax (increase).
$850 − $800 = $50

Now set up the ratio and solve.

$$\text{rate} = \frac{\text{amount of tax}}{\text{original number}} = \frac{50}{800} = 0.0625$$

$$\text{rate} = 6\frac{1}{4}\%$$

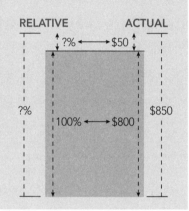

PROBLEM 19   Find the following amounts. You may want to use your calculator.

A Karen put $500 into a savings account. At the end of 1 year, the amount in the account was $542. What rate of interest was she paid on her money?

B Theresa bought a new car for $7,000. After owning it for a year, she sold it for $5,250. What was the rate of depreciation on her car?

C Pat received a raise in his salary. Before the raise, he was earning $320 a week. After the raise, he earned $380 a week. The raise was what percent of his salary?

D Laurinda bought a recliner that had a marked price of $480 and a sale price of $336. The discount was what percent of the original price?

E A parking lot near the airport raised its daily rates from $4 per day to $5 per day. By what percent were the rates raised?

F According to the census, a city's population went from 69,717 in 1980 to 76,838 in 1990. *Estimate* the percent of increase.

USING DATA

Refer to the Trends in GED Testing table and the Changes in a Decade bar graph on page 282 in the Appendix for the following questions. Round percentages to 1 decimal place.

Ⓐ From the trend table, determine the % decrease from 1991 to 2001 in the average age of the people taking the GED Tests.

Ⓑ From the trend table, determine the % increase from 1991 to 2001 in the total number tested.

Ⓒ From the trend table, determine the % increase from 1991 to 2001 in the percent who plan to do further study.

Ⓓ Examining the Changes in a Decade bar graph, notice that the amount of increase seems to be about the same in Area II, (Southern) and Area III, (Midwestern). Estimate this increase.

Ⓔ Find the % increase for Area II and for Area III.

Ⓕ In this case, which measure of change, actual or relative, would you consider to be more significant?

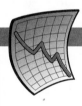

USING DATA

The Youth Risk Behavior Survey of 14,601 high school students shows a decline from 1997 to 2001 in smoking in this age group.

TEENS WHO SMOKE

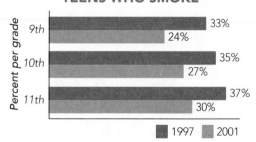

Source: Centers for Disease Control and Prevention

Ⓐ If the year 2001 trend from grade to grade continues, what percent of 12th graders would you expect to smoke?

Ⓑ What is the percent decrease in 9th grade smokers from 1997 to 2001? Round to the nearest percent.

✓ CHECK YOUR UNDERSTANDING

You may use your calculator on any problem except where noted by this symbol:

1. *Estimate* the following answers by finding compatible numbers. Any reasonable estimate is correct; yours does not have to be exactly the same as the one on the answer page.

   Ⓐ 48% of 32 = *n*

   Ⓑ 25% of 811 = *p*

   Ⓒ 98 = *what* % of 200

   Ⓓ 98 = *what* % of 498

   Ⓔ 19% of 75 = *m*

   Ⓕ 8.9% of 480 = *c*

   Ⓖ $2.99 = *what* % of $4.99

   Ⓗ $19.75 = *what* % of $58.67

   Ⓘ 38 = *what* % of 2000

   Ⓙ 6% of $47.50 = *t*

   Ⓚ 35 = *what* % of 700

2. Write the decimal equivalents of each percent.

   Ⓐ 3% = _____

   Ⓑ $3\frac{1}{2}$% = _____

   Ⓒ 30% = _____

   Ⓓ 35% = _____

   Ⓔ 350% = _____

   Ⓕ 1% = _____

   Ⓖ 0.5% = _____

   Ⓗ $\frac{1}{2}$% = _____

   Ⓘ 0.75% = _____

   Ⓙ $\frac{3}{4}$% = _____

   Ⓚ 7.3% = _____

   Ⓛ 800% = _____

3. On a recent trash-collecting day, 54% of the households of the city had separated their newspapers and glass from the rest of the trash for pickup. What percent of the households did *not* participate in the recycling efforts?

4. The sales tax for a county was $6\frac{1}{4}$% before a vote to raise the tax by $\frac{1}{2}$%. What was the sales tax rate after the vote?

5. Many credit card companies charge $1\frac{1}{2}$% interest *per month* on the unpaid balance. What is the annual (yearly) rate of interest that they charge?

6. Javi left a $4.00 tip for the server when the bill was $19.45. His tip was about what percent of the bill?

7. *Estimate* the sale price of a $188.88 camera when it is discounted 25%.

8. James completed 24 passes out of 35 attempts. Estimate the percent that he completed.

9. A living room furniture set is discounted from $800 to $560 during a sale. What is the rate of discount?

10. A T-shirt shop sells T-shirts at twice the price that it pays the supplier for them. Is this markup a percent increase of 50%, 100%, or 200%?

11. Terry's salary is $2,500 a month. If 21% of his pay is taken out in deductions, what is his take-home pay?

12. If you are charged $360 interest per year on a $3,000 loan, what rate of interest are you paying?

13. Total taxes on a gallon of gasoline in New York State adds $.50 to the price of every gallon of gasoline sold. If the before-tax price of gas in New York is $.80 a gallon, what is the percent increase caused by the taxes?

TEST-TAKING PRACTICE

You may use your calculator on any problem except where noted by this symbol:

Problems 1 and 2 refer to the following information and graph.

A local charity is proud of its efficiency in that it spent only 15% of the $600,000 in donations that it received last year on administrative and fund-raising costs. The remaining funds were devoted to the charity's activities.

DONATIONS

Program Activities

Administration and Fund-Raising

1. What percent of the donations was spent on the charity's activities?

Mark your answer in the circles in the grid.

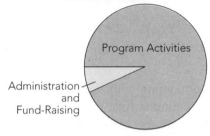

2. How many dollars did the charity spend on administrative and fund-raising costs?

(1) 510,000
(2) 150,000
(3) 90,000
(4) 60,000
(5) 9,000

3. Walter's promotion results in a 10% raise in his salary. If he was earning a salary of $21,000 a year before the promotion, which of the following expressions shows his new salary?

(1) 0.10($21,000)
(2) 0.90($21,000)
(3) $21,000 − 0.10($21,000)
(4) $21,000 + 0.10($21,000)
(5) 2.10($21,000)

4. During a special sale, you could buy one blanket at full price and get a second identical one at $\frac{1}{2}$ price. Emma wanted two blankets and bought them during this sale. What was the percent decrease in the price?

(1) 12.5
(2) 25
(3) 50
(4) 62.5
(5) 75

5. During a sale when all prices were reduced by 20%, Sunyun bought two sweaters, each marked $29.99, and three candles marked $19.59. If an 8% sales tax was added to the final purchase price, how much, in dollars, did she have to pay?

(1) 58.77
(2) 59.98
(3) 95.00
(4) 102.60
(5) 118.78

MENTAL MATH

1. $3 - 5 = x$

2. $-3 - 5 = y$

3. $4 - 7 = r$

4. $-4 - 7 = s$

5. $0 - 7 = t$

6. $7 - 0 = u$

7. $-7 - 0 = v$

8. $2 - 6 = m$

9. $-2 - 6 = n$

10. $6 - 2 = k$

You may have forgotten the rules for subtracting with signed numbers by now. Try picturing the first number on a number line, then moving to the left when you subtract. You will use negative numbers again in this lesson.

More About Slopes

Earlier you learned that the **slope** of line is defined by the ratio $\frac{\text{rise}}{\text{run}}$.

EXAMPLE

To find the slope of a line drawn on a grid, follow these steps.

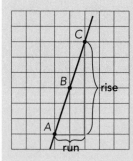

If a line leans **upward** from left to right, it has a **positive slope**.

STEP 1 Find two points on the line where there is an **intersection** of the grid lines.

STEP 2 Follow the grid lines to draw a triangle.

STEP 3 Count the number of units in the rise (6) and in the run (2).

STEP 4 Set up the ratio $\frac{\text{rise}}{\text{run}} = \frac{6}{2} = \frac{3}{1} = 3$

PROBLEM 1 | Slopes of straight lines are the same regardless of which two points you choose. Use point B and point C in the example above to find the slope.

PROBLEM 2 | Find the slopes of the lines drawn on the grid below. You may choose any two points and draw a rise and run. The first one is started for you.

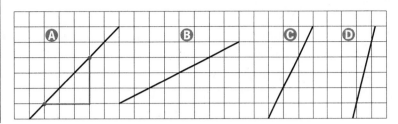

If a line leans **downward** from left to right, it has a **negative slope**.

Slopes of lines are not always positive numbers.

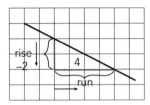 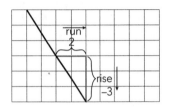

$$\frac{\text{rise}}{\text{run}} = \frac{-2}{4} = \frac{-1}{2} = -\frac{1}{2}$$

$$\frac{\text{rise}}{\text{run}} = \frac{-3}{2} = -\frac{3}{2}$$

The slope of a horizontal line is 0.

The slope of a vertical line is **undefined**. Remember about dividing by zero.

$$\frac{\text{rise}}{\text{run}} = \frac{0}{\text{any number}} = 0$$

$$\frac{\text{rise}}{\text{run}} = \frac{\text{any number}}{0} = \text{undefined}$$

PROBLEM 3 | Find the slopes of the following lines. Choose two points, and draw the rise and run as shown in 3Ⓐ.

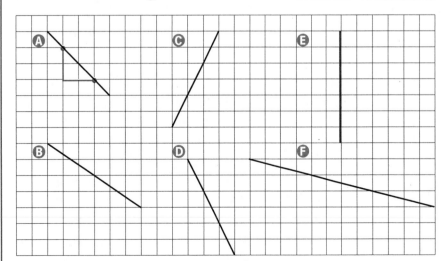

Finding Slopes from Coordinates

You should also be able to find the slope of a line if you are given 2 specific points on the line. Before you go on, you may need to review pages 52−55 of Lesson 5 to be clear on the (*x, y*) coordinates.

EXAMPLE

Find the slope of the line between points *A*(6, 3), and *B*(1, 2).

STEP 1
On a coordinate grid, locate points *A* and *B* and draw the line that includes them.

STEP 2
Proceed as before.

$$\frac{\text{rise}}{\text{run}} = \frac{1 \text{ unit}}{5 \text{ units}} = \frac{1}{5}$$

STEP 3

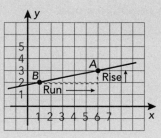

A second method corresponds to the formula for the slope of a line as given on the formulas page (page 280).

SLOPE OF A LINE	$\dfrac{y_2 - y_1}{x_2 - x_1}$ where (x_1, y_1) and (x_2, y_2) are two points on the line.

The **subscripts** (small numbers) make the slope formula look a lot more difficult than it actually is. There are two points:

P_1, (x_1, y_1) in this case is (1, 2). So x_1 is 1, and y_1 is 2.

P_2, (x_2, y_2) in this case is (6, 3). So x_2 is 6, and y_2 is 3.

The formula tells how to find the slope without a sketch. The steps below follow the formula. Use the sketch only to follow the logic of the steps.

STEP 1 $y_2 - y_1$ To find the **rise**, subtract the *y*-values from the points (*x*, **y**): (6, **3**) and (1, **2**). rise: 3 − 2 = 1

STEP 2 $x_2 - x_1$ To find the **run**, subtract the *x*-values from the points (**x**, *y*): (**6**, 3) and (**1**, 2). run: 6 − 1 = 5

STEP 3 Set up the ratio for slope. $\dfrac{\text{rise}}{\text{run}} = \dfrac{1}{5}$

You subtracted the *y*-values to find the rise and subtracted the *x*-values to find the run, then you set up the ratio $\dfrac{\text{rise}}{\text{run}}$.

$$m = \frac{y_2 - y_1}{x_2 - x_1} = \frac{3 - 2}{6 - 1} = \frac{1}{5}$$

The variable *m* is commonly used to indicate slope. Subscripts are used to make sure that you keep the *order* of subtraction the same for both the rise and the run. If you don't, your answer will have the opposite sign.

To find slopes, you can choose the method that best suits you and the problem. Either draw a sketch or use the formula. If you have time to do both when taking a test, use one method as a check of the other.

EXAMPLES

When you divide two numbers with the same sign, the answer is **positive**.

$\frac{1}{3} = \frac{1}{3}$ and $\frac{-1}{-3} = \frac{1}{3}$

When you divide two numbers with different signs, the answer is **negative**.

$\frac{-1}{3} = -\frac{1}{3}$ and $\frac{1}{-3} = -\frac{1}{3}$

Find the slope of the line between (9, 1) and (5, 3).

Let (9, 1) be point 2 and (5, 3) be point 1.

$$m = \frac{1-3}{9-5} = \frac{-2}{4} = \frac{-1}{2} \text{ or } -\frac{1}{2}$$

Since one number in the ratio is negative, the ratio is negative.

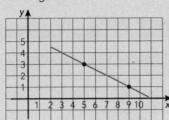

Find the slope of the line between (2, –2) and (7, 0).

Let (2, −2) be point 2 and (7, 0) be point 1.

$$m = \frac{-2-0}{2-7} = \frac{-2}{-5} = \frac{2}{5}$$

When 2 negatives are divided, the answer is positive.

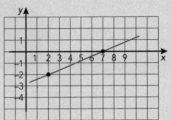

PROBLEM 4 | Switch the order of the points in the first example above. That is, let (5, 3) be point 2 and (9, 1) be point 1. Is the slope the same?

PROBLEM 5 | Find the coordinates of each point on the graph below.

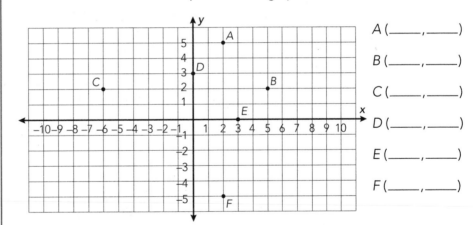

A (_____ , _____)

B (_____ , _____)

C (_____ , _____)

D (_____ , _____)

E (_____ , _____)

F (_____ , _____)

PROBLEM 6 | Use either the formula or the graph above (or both) to find the slope of the line between the following points. If you are using the formula, keep the points in the same order on the bottom as on the top.

Ⓐ points A and B　　Ⓒ points D and E　　Ⓔ points D and B

Ⓑ points C and B　　Ⓓ points A and F　　Ⓕ points C and A

PROBLEM 7 | The slope of a line from point D to point F is $\frac{-4}{1}$. Start at point D, go down 4 units (a rise of −4) and then go to the right 1 unit (a run of 1), and make a mark. Call it point G.

Ⓐ What are the coordinates of point G?

Ⓑ Use the slope formula to find the slope of the line between points G and F. Explain why you should have expected this number to be the answer.

Slopes from Informational Graphs

Slopes of lines have more meaning when they represent something real. Since a slope is a ratio, it can represent a **rate**—any common rate that defines the relationship between two quantities. Earlier in this book, you have seen examples of this: cost per apple, calories per gram of fat, miles per hour, and savings per year, to name a few. The next problems illustrate more ways that you can use the idea of slope to learn more from data in a graph.

USING DATA

After surveying the heads of urban households over the years, the following data has been compiled showing approximately how much an average family spends on food, eating in and eating out.

	eating in	eating out
1994	$2,700	$1,700
1997	$2,900	$1,900
2000	$3,100	$2,400

Ⓐ Plot the points that represent this data on the graph below. Use circles as the symbols for eating in and diamonds as symbols for eating out. Draw lines connecting the points in each category.

Ⓑ Find the annual (per year) increase in expenditures for *eating at home* by finding the slope of the line (ratio of the rise over the run) between two of the points indicated by circles. You can use the formula or you can draw the slope triangle.

Ⓒ From the graph, estimate the annual expenditure for food *at home* in 1999. Then use the slope that you found in part Ⓑ to find the value of the same point.

Ⓓ Extend the line for *eating at home* to the end of the graph. Use the graph to predict a number for annual expenditures in 2003. Verify it by using the slope.

Ⓔ Why would it be difficult to predict a number for annual *eating out* expenditures in 2003?

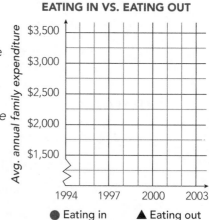

EATING IN VS. EATING OUT

● Eating in   ▲ Eating out

Graphs of Linear Functions

Most graphs that appear in newspapers and magazines picture a relationship between quantities that are established by collecting data. In contrast, the following examples and problems represent relationships between variables that are defined by mathematical rules. We will examine the problems in three ways: (1) by a table of values, (2) by a graph, and (3) by an equation. The goal is to see the connections between all three representations.

PROBLEM

Elena, a talented painter, is considering a moneymaking opportunity. She would buy clear bottles, hand paint a design on them, and sell them as salad-oil cruets at craft fairs. She would decorate just 250 bottles to sell.

Cost

Elena finds the bottles she wants at a craft supply store for $1.50 each. She estimates that she will have to spend $200 for paints and supplies. She would buy enough paints and supplies in advance to decorate all 250 bottles.

PROBLEM 8

Ⓐ Complete the table below. As you do, notice that the cost is *a function of* the number of bottles, that is, the cost depends on the number of bottles.

number of bottles	0	100	150	200
cost	200			

Ⓑ Use *x* as the variable for the number of bottles. Write an equation that could be used to find the cost (*y*) of any particular number of bottles.

$y = $ _____.

Ⓒ To make a graph from this table, treat each *pair* of numbers in the table as a *point* (*x*, *y*) on a graph. For example, 100 bottles and the cost $350 could be thought of as (100, 350).

Plot the points from the table onto the graph at the right. Draw a line through the points and extend it to the end of the graph.

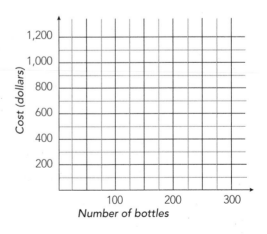

The line you drew is the graph of the equation in part Ⓑ. Any and all points on this line also satisfy the relationship between the cost (*y*) and the number of bottles (*x*); they all will make the equation true.

One point of special interest is the point that represents the cost before Elena buys any bottles. This is a **fixed cost** that does not depend on how many bottles she buys. In the equation, $y = 1.50x + 200$, the fixed cost is a constant. This point on the graph, (0, 200), is called the **y-intercept** because it falls on the y-axis.

In algebra, we commonly use the letter *b* to represent the value of *y* when *x* is 0. The point (0, *b*) is called the *y-intercept*.

PROBLEM 9

Use the equation from problem 8 to find the answers to the following. Verify your answers by checking the point on the graph.

Ⓐ How much would it cost Elena to buy and paint 50 bottles?

Ⓑ How much would it cost to buy and paint all 250 bottles?

Ⓒ Use algebraic principles to solve the equation and find how many bottles she would have purchased if she had spent a total of $650 for the project. Check your answer for reasonableness by finding the point on the graph.

> In algebra, we commonly use the letter *m* to represent the slope of a line, the amount of vertical change that corresponds to a horizontal change of 1.

Compare the graph and the equation from problem 8 to discover more connections.

PROBLEM 10

Ⓐ Choose two points on the line and use the slope formula to find the slope of the line.

Ⓑ The slope you found in part Ⓐ is the same as the cost of one bottle. Locate that number in the equation.

The general equation for any line is $y = mx + b$, where b represents the *y*-intercept and *m* represents the slope of the line.

PROBLEM 11

What if? What if the cost of each bottle, the unit rate, were $4?

Ⓐ What would the equation be?

Ⓑ Complete this table of values.

number of bottles	0	100	200
cost			

Ⓒ Plot these points on the graph on the preceding page and connect them with a line of a different color or pattern. Label it line 2.

Ⓓ Compare the two lines on the grid. What is the same, what is different?

PROBLEM 12

Another what if? What if the fixed cost of paint and supplies had been $400 and the bottles each cost $4?

Ⓐ What would the equation be?

Ⓑ Complete this table of values.

number of bottles	0	100	200
cost			

Ⓒ Plot these points on the graph on the preceding page and connect them with a line of a different color or pattern. Label it line 3.

Ⓓ Compare line 3 to line 2, the one you drew for problem 11. What is the same? What is different?

PROBLEM 13

Consider these equations. Answer the questions without graphing them or finding a table of values.

① $y = 35x + 60$ ② $y = 11x + 77$ ③ $y = 25x + 10$

Ⓐ Which equation would have the steepest slope when graphed?

Ⓑ Which equation would have the shallowest slope when graphed?

Ⓒ The point (0, 77) makes which equation true?

Ⓓ The point (0, 10) makes which equation true?

Revenue

Elena is sure that she will be able to sell all the salad oil cruets that she makes if she prices them at $5.50 each.

PROBLEM 14

Ⓐ Complete this equation so that it defines the relationship between the revenue (*r*) she would take in and the number of cruets (*x*) that she sells.

$r = $ _____.

Ⓑ Complete this table of values.

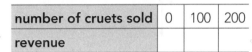

number of cruets sold	0	100	200
revenue			

Ⓒ Plot the points on this graph and connect them. This is the revenue function.

Ⓓ Approximately how much revenue would be generated if Elena sold 150 cruets?

Ⓔ Approximately how many cruets would Elena have to sell to generate revenue of $1,000?

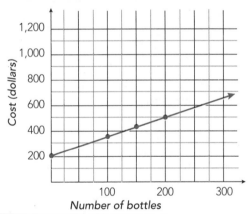

Break-even Point and Profit

Profit =
Revenue − Cost

Your graph above shows a line for cost and a line for revenue. Both cost and revenue are functions of *x*, the number of bottles that are made and sold. When the cost function is above the revenue function, Elena has spent more than she made. On the other hand, when the revenue function is above the cost function, she has made a profit.

PROBLEM 15

Ⓐ Use the graph to estimate how many cruets Elena has to sell in order to break even; that is, where the cost = revenue.

Ⓑ Verify your estimate by substituting your answer in the two functions.

PROBLEM 16

Ⓐ Use the graph to estimate the profit Elena would make if she made and sold 100 cruets.

Ⓑ Use the formula, Profit = Revenue − cost, to find Elena's profit if she sold 250 cruets.

CHECK YOUR UNDERSTANDING

You may use your calculator on any problem except where noted by this symbol:

To solve problems 1 and 2, use the graph from problem 1.

1. Label each of the points with its coordinates.

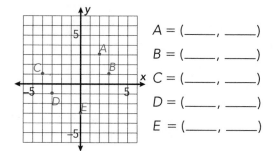

A = (_____ , _____)
B = (_____ , _____)
C = (_____ , _____)
D = (_____ , _____)
E = (_____ , _____)

2. Find the slope of each of the following lines.

Ⓐ point A to point B
Ⓑ point B to point A
Ⓒ point B to point C
Ⓓ point A to point C
Ⓔ point D to point B
Ⓕ point C to point E

3. Portia uses a subway fare card each day for her commute to and from work. The fare is subtracted after each ride. The graph shows the balance on her fare card after each work day.

Ⓐ How many dollars was the fare card worth before she used it?
Ⓑ How much does her commute cost each day?
Ⓒ How many days did it take for this fare card to have a zero balance?

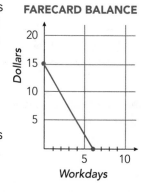

FARECARD BALANCE

Dollars / *Workdays*

4. A print shop charges $.05 a page to print a document. There is an added fee to spiral-bind a document.

The graph shows the cost of printing and binding a document with *p* pages.

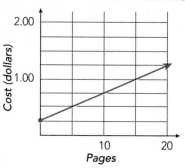

COST OF BINDING AND PRINTING

Cost (dollars) / *Pages*

Ⓐ How much does the print shop charge for binding the document?
Ⓑ Complete the equation of the line that is pictured. C = _____
Ⓒ How much do they charge for printing and binding a 16-page document?

5. Jerry and his mother both drove to the mall, which is 50 highway miles away. Jerry broke the speed limit and drove 70 mph, while his mother drove at 55 mph. The graph shows their progress.

Ⓐ Which line (top or bottom) pictures Jerry's trip?
Ⓑ How much time did he cut off the trip by speeding?
Ⓒ What is the slope of each of the lines?

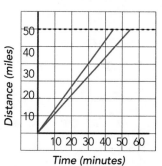

Distance (miles) / *Time (minutes)*

TEST-TAKING PRACTICE

You may use your calculator on any problem except where noted by this symbol:

1. 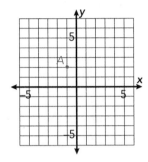 Imagine a line with a slope of −3 drawn from point *A*. Which point is on the line and has an *x*-value of 1?

   (1) (1, −3)
   (2) (1, −4)
   (3) (−3, 1)
   (4) (−4, 1)
   (5) (−6, 1)

2. Find the slope of the line between (0, 5) and (5, 0).

   (1) −5
   (2) −1
   (3) 0
   (4) 1
   (5) 5

Questions 3−4 refer to the following information and graph.

Surveys of heads of households in the U.S. show the following relationship between the annual amount spent on purchasing new cars and that spent on purchasing used cars.

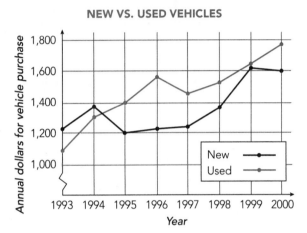

NEW VS. USED VEHICLES

Source: Bureau of Labor Statistics

3. During what year did the average household begin to spend more on buying used cars than on buying new cars?

   (1) 1994
   (2) 1995
   (3) 1996
   (4) 1999
   (5) 2000

4. During what year did spending on used cars increase the most over the prior year's spending?

   (1) 2000
   (2) 1999
   (3) 1996
   (4) 1994
   (5) 1993

Practice Test

Throughout this book, you have studied the topics that are likely to appear on standardized tests. Now you'll try a full-length, timed math proficiency test.

In the previous Test-Taking Tips lessons, we focused on the mathematical aspects of the items.

- Analyze the problem and ask yourself what you know about it.

- Decide what you need in order to find the answer. Is enough information given? Are extra numbers given that you don't need?

- Estimate an answer—it may be all you need to choose one of the answers.

- Be especially careful with multistep problems. Do not stop until you have completed all the steps.

- Ask whether or not the answer you have chosen is reasonable.

You may have noticed that there is more to a math test than just math. In this lesson, the test-taking tips will focus on other related skills and strategies.

Read the Problems Carefully

If you have completed this book, you will be familiar with most of the tasks that a test requires. However, many test-takers make the mistake of jumping quickly to do the math before really understanding what a particular problem asks. Take the time to read the problems carefully. Reread them until you are sure you understand what they ask. Do not assume anything.

Use a Variety of Strategies with Unfamiliar Problems

Expect to see some problems that are unfamiliar to you. Each form of a test is different and the choice of items is somewhat unpredictable. Don't spend a lot of time on these problems the first time through the test. When you come back to them, there are some things you can do to discover the path to the solution of these unusual items.

- Be confident that you can figure out a way to find the answer. Don't panic when you forget the "rules." Remember that there is usually more than one way to solve a problem.

- Look for relationships between the numbers or values in the problem. Can you see a "for each" relation? (multiplication) Is the problem asking how many of one thing fit into another? (division) Are the values proportional? Draw pictures of the relationships.

- Try to translate the words of the problem into the language of mathematics. On your scratch paper, write the parts of the problem that you know—for example, apples = 50 × number of trees.

- Substitute simpler numbers than the ones given in the problem so that you are comfortable seeing the relationship. For example, $\frac{422}{82}$ could be estimated as $\frac{400}{80}$.

Use the Formulas Page and Any Other Instructions Pages in the Test Booklet

The number grid directions show you how to use the grid for whole number, fraction, and decimal answers.

The page of formulas provides you not only with the familiar ones but also with some formulas that we have not used in this book. Check the formulas page to find a rule that connects the values given in an unfamiliar problem.

EXAMPLE

About how many cubic inches are in the cylindrical package shown in this diagram?

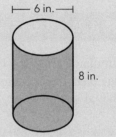

(1) 24
(2) 48
(3) 72
(4) 151
(5) 226

The words *cubic inches* tell you that the question is about volume. The formula for the volume of a cylinder is $V = \pi \times \text{radius}^2 \times \text{height}$.

Substitute the values into the formula.

$V = \pi \times (3)^2 \times 8$
$V \approx 226$ cu in.; choice (**5**) 226 is correct.

Use the Answer Choices

When all else fails, use the answer choices that are given. Substitute them, one by one, into the problem, and see which one is correct.

EXAMPLE

What value of x makes the following equation true?

$5x - 3 = 2x + 6$

(1) 1
(2) 2
(3) 3
(4) 4
(5) 5

You know that *x* is merely holding the place for a number. The question asks which number, used in place of *x*, will make a true statement. Try each one.

$x = 1;\quad 5(1) - 3 \neq 2(1) + 6$
$x = 2;\quad 5(2) - 3 \neq 2(2) + 6$
$x = 3;\quad 5(3) - 3 = 2(3) + 6$ Choice (**3**) is correct.
$x = 4;\quad 5(4) - 3 \neq 2(4) + 6$
$x = 5;\quad 5(5) - 3 \neq 2(5) + 6$

Final Test-Taking Hints

- Don't spend too much time on any one problem if you haven't finished the others. Be careful with your answer sheet if you skip a problem.

- Come back to the difficult problems after you are satisfied that you have done your best on the ones you understand.

- When time is running out, guess the answers to the problems you haven't finished. An unanswered question will always be counted wrong. Give yourself a chance with every problem.

PRACTICE TEST

To simulate actual test conditions, you should spend no more than 90 minutes on these questions. You may use the page of formulas (p. 280) and the number grid directions (p. 281). Similar pages may be included in the actual test as well.

You can use the calculator for Part 1: problems 1–25. Turn in the calculator after 45 minutes or when you finish Part 1, whichever comes first. After you turn in the calculator, you can start Part 2. If you have time, you can go back to Part 1, but you will not be able to use the calculator again.

Part 1

1. A video/DVD rental store counted the number of customers who came into the store during a 3-day holiday weekend. The count was 334 on Saturday, 157 on Sunday, and 265 on Monday. What was the mean (average) number of customers per day during the weekend?

- (1) 334
- (2) 265
- (3) 257
- (4) 252
- (5) 157

2. A bakery has eggs delivered 5 days a week. On Monday through Thursday, it has a standing order of n dozen eggs, and on Friday, it gets double that amount. Which of the following expressions shows the number of dozens of eggs the bakery gets each week?

- (1) $5n$
- (2) $5 + n$
- (3) $6(12n)$
- (4) $6 + n$
- (5) $6n$

3. At the end of the term, 35% of the students were still attending class. Which fraction is closest to this percentage?

- (1) $\frac{1}{2}$
- (2) $\frac{3}{4}$
- (3) $\frac{3}{8}$
- (4) $\frac{5}{8}$
- (5) $\frac{7}{8}$

4. A rectangular drawing that originally measured 16 cm × 21 cm was enlarged so that its longer side was 105 cm long. What is the length, in centimeters, of the shorter side of the enlarged drawing?

Mark your answer in the circles in the grid.

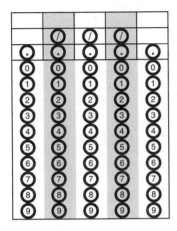

5. What is the value of the expression $3x^2 + 5x$ if $x = -2$?

Mark your answer in the circles in the grid.

6. Ricardo has a $20 dollar bill to buy gasoline. If it is priced at $1.39 per gallon, approximately how many gallons is the most he can buy?

(1) 13.9
(2) 14.4
(3) 18.6
(4) 21.4
(5) 27.8

7. During a clearance sale, a discount store will take 10% off the current price of an item each day until it is sold. On the third day of the sale, what is the price, in dollars, of an item whose original price was $150?

(1) 135.00
(2) 121.50
(3) 120.00
(4) 109.35
(5) 105.00

8. Debra received a $500 bonus at the end of the year. She bought a pair of roller skates for $169 and a leather chair for $283. Which expression shows how much of the bonus she has left?

(1) ($169 + $283) − $500
(2) $169 + $283 − $500
(3) $500 − $169 + $283
(4) $500 − ($169 + $283)
(5) $500 − ($169 − $283)

Problems 9–12 refer to the following information and graph.

Silvia's long distance phone carrier offers 3 pricing plans for long distance service. The monthly costs (excluding any taxes or other charges) for three plans are shown on the graph. The cost consists of a standard monthly fee plus a charge for each minute of long distance calls.

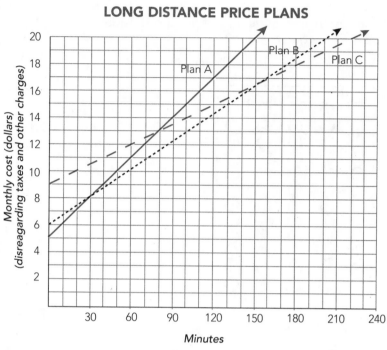

LONG DISTANCE PRICE PLANS

9. How much would it cost Silvia if she chose Plan B and did not make any long distance calls during one month?

(1) $15
(2) $ 9
(3) $ 6
(4) $ 5
(5) $ 3

10. How much would it cost (disregarding taxes and other charges) if Silvia had chosen Plan C and had an hour and a half of long distance calls in a month?

(1) $12.25
(2) $13.50
(3) $14.50
(4) $15.00
(5) $15.50

11. For approximately how many minutes a month of long-distance calls is Plan A the cheapest?

(1) ≤10
(2) ≤33
(3) ≤60
(4) ≤80
(5) ≤150

12. For $20 a month, how many more long-distance minutes would Silvia get with Plan C than with Plan A?

Mark your answer in the circles in the grid.

Problems 13 and 14 refer to the following graph.

PETE'S MONTHLY BUDGET

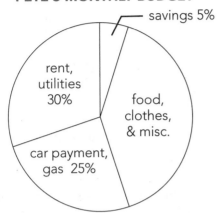

13. What percent of Pete's money is budgeted for food, clothes, and miscellaneous expenses?

Mark your answer in the circles in the grid.

14. If Pete's total monthly income is $2,850, how much money has he budgeted to save?

(1) $ 14.25
(2) $ 28.50
(3) $ 142.50
(4) $ 855.00
(5) $1,140.00

15. A survey reported that 3 out of 7 people in the county oppose raising the sales tax. Assuming this is true, how many from a diverse neighborhood of 245 people are likely to oppose raising the tax?

(1)   35
(2)   57
(3)   82
(4) 105
(5) 150

16. After a tune-up, the gas mileage on Oscar's car increased from 20 mpg to 24 mpg. What percent increase was that?

(1)   4%
(2)   8%
(3) 17%
(4) 20%
(5) 25%

17. Point A makes this equation true.

$$y = \frac{1}{3}x - 4$$

Which point also makes the equation true and has an x-value of 3?

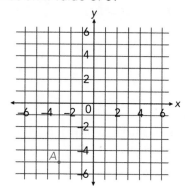

(1) (3, −4)
(2) (3, 1)
(3) (3, −3)
(4) (−3, 3)
(5) (1, 3)

18. The entrance to a banquet room is a doorway that is 6 feet across and 8 feet high. Workers carry circular tabletops through this doorway. What is the diameter, in feet, of the largest tabletop that will fit through this doorway at an angle?

(1) 6
(2) 8
(3) 10
(4) 12
(5) 14

6 ft
? 8 ft

Problems 19–21 refer to the following diagram.

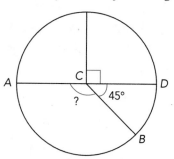

C is the center of this circle.
AD measures 20 cm.

19. Which of the following represents the area of the circle?

(1) 2(20)π
(2) $10^2\pi$
(3) 20π
(4) $20\pi^2$
(5) 10π

20. Approximately how long, in centimeters, is arc *BD*?

(1) 5
(2) 8
(3) 10
(4) 16
(5) 32

21. What is the measure, in degrees, of ∠ACB?

Mark your answer in the circles in the grid.

22. Vivian, a letter carrier, walks 9.7 miles on her postal route each working day. During one month of 31 days, there were 5 Sundays and 2 holidays on which she did not deliver the mail. How many miles did she walk on her route that month?

Mark your answer in the circles in the grid.

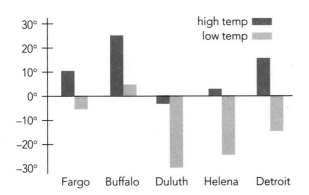

Problems 23–25 refer to the following table and graph.

The following high and low temperatures (°F) were recorded one day in January in these northern U.S. cities.

	Fargo	Buffalo	Duluth	Helena	Detroit
high	10°	25°	–3°	2°	15°
low	–5°	3°	–30°	–25°	–15°

23. In which city was the lowest low for the day recorded?

(1) Fargo
(2) Buffalo
(3) Duluth
(4) Helena
(5) Detroit

24. Which city had the greatest *range* of temperatures that day?

(1) Fargo
(2) Buffalo
(3) Duluth
(4) Helena
(5) Detroit

25. What is the difference, in degrees, between the high temperatures in Duluth and Detroit that day?

(1) 18
(2) 12
(3) 10
(4) 8
(5) 2

Part 2

You are not allowed to use a calculator for the remainder of the items.

26. A cookie recipe that yields 50 cookies calls for $1\frac{3}{4}$ cups flour. To make 100 cookies of the same size, how many cups of flour would be needed?

    (1) $\frac{7}{8}$

    (2) $\frac{7}{4}$

    (3) $2\frac{3}{8}$

    (4) $2\frac{3}{4}$

    (5) $3\frac{1}{2}$

27. Jorge arrived at the doctor's office at 8:45. He was finally called to see the doctor at 10:10. How long did Jorge wait?

    (1) 1 hr 10 min
    (2) 1 hr 25 min
    (3) 1 hr 40 min
    (4) 2 hr 10 min
    (5) 2 hr 25 min

28. A bank was charging its customers an interest rate of 9.85% on loans. If the bank lowered this interest rate by $\frac{1}{4}$%, what would the new rate be?

    (1) 9.35%
    (2) 9.6%
    (3) 9.9%
    (4) 10.1%
    (5) 10.35%

Problem 29 refers to the following diagram.

29. Which expression indicates the *perimeter* of the rectangle?

    (1) $3n^2$
    (2) $4n$
    (3) $4n^2$
    (4) $8n^2$
    (5) $8n$

30. The instructions for roasting a turkey say to roast it 20 minutes per pound. According to these instructions, how long should you roast a $10\frac{1}{2}$-pound turkey?

    (1) 2,000 minutes

    (2) 20 minutes

    (3) 2 hours

    (4) $3\frac{1}{2}$ hours

    (5) $4\frac{1}{5}$ hours

Problems 31 and 32 refer to the following diagram.

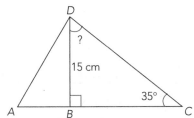

31. If the length of the line from point *A* to point *C* is 20 cm, how many square centimeters are in the area of △*ACD*?

Mark your answer in the circles in the grid.

32. If ∠*BCD* = 35°, which expression shows the measure of ∠*BDC*?

(1) 360° − 35°
(2) 180° − 35°
(3) 180° + 35°
(4) 180° − (90° + 35°)
(5) 180° − (90° − 35°)

33. A mail-order catalog charges $7 for shipping and handling on all orders. Jesse ordered 3 T-shirts at $12 each and 2 pairs of shorts at $24 each. Which of the following expressions equals the amount Jesse paid for this order?

(1) 5($12 + $24) + $7
(2) $12(36)
(3) (3 + $12)(2 + $24)($7)
(4) 3($12) + 2($24) − $7
(5) 3($12) + 2($24) + $7

34. The following table shows how the cost (*C*), in dollars, that an electrician will charge varies according to the number (*n*) of half-hours spent working.

n	0	1	2	3	4	5
C	40	60	80	100	120	140

Which of the following equations describes how the cost (*C*) is determined from *n*?

(1) $C = 20n + 40$
(2) $C = 40n + 20$
(3) $C = n(40 + 20)$
(4) $C = 2n(20)$
(5) $C = (n − 1)40$

35. During a sale where everything is discounted 25%, on which of the following items would you save more than $50?

a. a student desk marked $129.97
b. a microwave oven marked $288.96
c. a color TV marked $209.92

(1) a only
(2) b only
(3) c only
(4) a and b only
(5) b and c only

36. An observer who watched a fast-food counter for 60 minutes during a lunch period reported that the restaurant served an average of 2.7 people per minute. What was the total number of people served during the observed time?

(1)　22
(2)　122
(3)　162
(4)　182
(5)　Not enough information is given.

37. Figure *DEFG* is to be moved in the direction of the arrow until point *D* is located on (−3, −5). After the move, what is the location of point *F*?

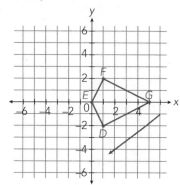

(1)　(3, −4)
(2)　(−1, −3)
(3)　(1, 2)
(4)　(−3, −1)
(5)　(−4, −3)

Problems 38 and 39 refer to the following information.

During a trial run of a 22-mile bicycle race, Tom recorded his progress every 15 minutes.

time (minutes)	0:15	0:30	0:45	0:60	0:75
total distance (miles)	5.4	7.4	12.8	18	22

38. How many miles did Tom travel in the last half-hour of his trial run?

(1)　10.8
(2)　10.2
(3)　　9.8
(4)　　9.2
(5)　　7.4

39. During the second 15-minute period, Tom was biking up a 2-mile uphill stretch of the course. What was his rate of speed on this portion of the course?

(1)　30 mph
(2)　　8 mph
(3)　　7.5 mph
(4)　　4 mph
(5)　Not enough information is given.

*Problems 40–42 refer to the following
information and graph.*

For exercise to be considered "aerobic," it must raise one's heart rate so that it is in the Target Heart Range that is illustrated in the graph below. The upper and lower limits of this range (percentages of one's maximum heart rate) vary with a person's age.

**TARGET HEART RATE FOR
AEROBIC EXERCISE**

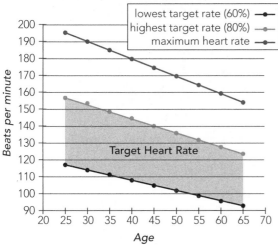

40. From the graph, estimate the least number of heartbeats per minute for a 33-year-old to be in the aerobic range.

   (1) 112
   (2) 133
   (3) 145
   (4) 150
   (5) 187

41. The maximum heart rate (*H*) is found by subtracting one's age (*a*) from 220.

$H = 220 - a$

What is the slope of the line that shows the Maximum Heart Rate?

   (1) −10
   (2) −1
   (3) 1
   (4) 10
   (5) Not enough information is given.

42. A rate of 130 beats per minute is within the target range until approximately what age?

   (1) 45
   (2) 52
   (3) 57
   (4) 60
   (5) 65

*Problems 43 and 44 refer to the following
information.*

As a fund-raising project, the Booster Club members sold raffle tickets for a new car whose selling price was $22,000. They sold a total of 6,500 tickets for $5 apiece. One ticket was chosen at a drawing to determine the winner of the car.

43. Theo bought 10 tickets, his sister bought 15 tickets, and their parents bought 25 tickets. What is the probability that a ticket from their family will be the winning ticket?

Mark your answer in the circles in the grid.

44. The car dealer charged the Booster Club only $18,550 for the car. Disregarding miscellaneous expenses, what was the net amount of funds that the club raised by this project?

   (1) $32,500
   (2) $22,000
   (3) $13,950
   (4) $12,050
   (5) $ 3,450

45. The floor area of a square platform is 110 square feet. Which is the best estimate of the length of each side?

(1) between 11 and 12 feet
(2) between 10 and 11 feet
(3) between 9 and 10 feet
(4) between 8 and 9 feet
(5) between 7 and 8 feet

Problem 46 refers to the following information and graph.

Two nationwide studies, one from 1960–1962 and another from 1988–1994, focused on the problem of obesity in the United States. The results, shown by the sex of the respondent, are in the graph below.

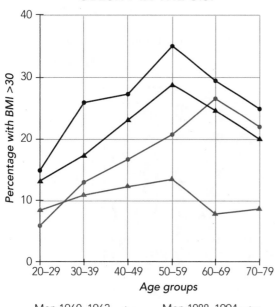

OBESITY IN THE U.S.

Men 1960–1962 ⟶ Men 1988–1994 ⟶
Women 1960–1962 ⟶ Women 1988–1994 ⟶

Source: Centers for Disease Control and Prevention

46. Which of the following statements would be accurate descriptions of the data that is pictured?

A. In both studies, in all age groups, the percentage of women who are obese is greater than the percentage of men.

B. In both studies for both men and women, the greatest percentage of obesity occurs in the age group 50–59.

C. In the most recent study, the percentage of obesity in both men and women is greater in all age groups than it was in the earlier study.

(1) All are true.
(2) Only A and B are true.
(3) Only B and C are true.
(4) Only C is true.
(5) None are true.

47. The following kinds of milk are available.

whole milk	3.3% fat
low-fat milk	2% fat
extra-light milk	1% fat

How many grams of fat are in a glass of low-fat milk?

(1) 1
(2) 2
(3) 3.3
(4) 98
(5) Not enough information is given.

48. Juin had only $20.00 with her on an errand to send an express mail letter and to buy stamps. Which equation below can be used to find the number of stamps (*n*) that she could buy if the express letter costs $13.95 and the stamps cost *x*¢?

(1) $n = \dfrac{\$20.00}{x}$

(2) $n = \dfrac{\$13.95}{x}$

(3) $n = \dfrac{(\$20.00 - \$13.95)}{x}$

(4) $n = (\$20.00 - \$13.95)x$

(5) $n = \$13.95x$

Problem 49 refers to the following diagram.

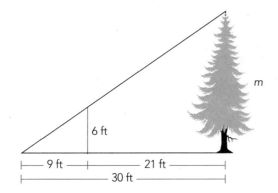

49. Which of the following proportions is the correct one for finding the height of the tree (*m*)?

(1) $\dfrac{6}{m} = \dfrac{9}{30}$

(2) $\dfrac{6}{m} = \dfrac{9}{21}$

(3) $\dfrac{6}{9} = \dfrac{m}{21}$

(4) $\dfrac{6}{9} = \dfrac{30}{m}$

(5) $\dfrac{6}{30} = \dfrac{9}{m}$

Problem 50 refers to the following diagram.

300 sq ft

50. To irrigate a circular area that is about 300 square feet, with the irrigation device pictured, approximately how long, in feet, should the rotating arm (*r*) of the sprinkler be?

(1) 100
(2)   50
(3)   17
(4)   10
(5)   7

Determine Your Mastery of Mathematical Problem Solving

STEP 1 Use the answer key on page 354 to check your answers.

STEP 2 Fill out the Practice Test Evaluation Chart on page 279.

- Put an X next to the items you answered correctly.

- Put a check mark (✓) next to the items you answered incorrectly.

STEP 3 Decide what material you need to review.

- Look at the check marks (✓) on your evaluation chart. You may see particular lessons that you need to review, or you may see a pattern that corresponds to particular sections of this book. (The table of contents divides this book into four sections.)

PRACTICE TEST EVALUATION CHART

Problems	Lessons	Problems	Lessons	Problems	Lessons
1 _____	10	18 _____	23	35 _____	22, 23
2 _____	7	19 _____	4	36 _____	10
3 _____	15,18	20 _____	12	37 _____	5
4 _____	21	21 _____	24	38 _____	10
5 _____	11	22 _____	5	39 _____	15
6 _____	10	23 _____	5	40 _____	*
7 _____	23	24 _____	5	41 _____	20, 24
8 _____	4	25 _____	11	42 _____	*
9 _____	24	26 _____	17	43 _____	18
10 _____	*	27 _____	* *	44 _____	9
11 _____	*	28 _____	23	45 _____	11
12 _____	*	29 _____	2	46 _____	*
13 _____	22	30 _____	17	47 _____	22
14 _____	22	31 _____	8	48 _____	10
15 _____	21	32 _____	4	49 _____	21
16 _____	10	33 _____	10	50 _____	11
17 _____	24	34 _____	24		

* Reading values from a graph was introduced in Lesson 1 and was revisited throughout the book.

* * Some problem topics are not discussed in this book. You should expect that a proficiency test will contain some items for which you have not practiced; that is why you have been building your reasoning power and "number sense" throughout this book.

Formulas

AREA of a:	
square	Area = side^2
rectangle	Area = length × width
parallelogram	Area = base × height
triangle	Area = $\frac{1}{2}$ × base × height
trapezoid	Area = $\frac{1}{2}$ × (base$_1$ + base$_2$) × height
circle	Area = π × radius^2; π is approximately equal to 3.14.
PERIMETER of a:	
square	Perimeter = 4 × side
rectangle	Perimeter = 2 × length + 2 × width
triangle	Perimeter = side$_1$ + side$_2$ + side$_3$
CIRCUMFERENCE of a **circle**	Circumference = π × diameter; π is approximately equal to 3.14.
VOLUME of a:	
cube	Volume = edge^3
rectangular solid	Volume = length × width × height
square pyramid	Volume = $\frac{1}{3}$ × (base edge)^2 × height
cylinder	Volume = π × radius^2 × height; π is approximately equal to 3.14.
cone	Volume = $\frac{1}{3}$ × π × radius^2 × height; π is approximately equal to 3.14.
COORDINATE GEOMETRY	distance between points = $\sqrt{(x_2 - x_1)^2 + (y_2 - y_1)^2}$ (x_1, y_1) and (x_2, y_2) are two points in a plane. slope of a line = $\frac{(y_2 - y_1)}{(x_2 - x_1)}$; (x_1, y_1) and (x_2, y_2) are two points on the line.
PYTHAGOREAN RELATIONSHIP	$a^2 + b^2 = c^2$; a and b are legs and c the hypotenuse of a right triangle.
MEASURES OF CENTRAL TENDENCY	**mean** = $\frac{x_1 + x_2 + \ldots + x_n}{n}$ where the x's are the values for which a mean is desired, and n is the total number of values for x. **median** = the middle value of an odd number of _**ordered**_ scores, and halfway between the two middle values of an even number of _**ordered**_ scores.
SIMPLE INTEREST	interest = principal × rate × time
DISTANCE	distance = rate × time
TOTAL COST	total cost = (number of units) × (price per unit)

Adapted from the GED Testing Service

Number Grid Directions

Mixed numbers, such as $3\frac{1}{2}$, cannot be entered in the alternate format grid. Instead, represent them as decimal numbers (in this case, 3.5) or fractions (in this case, $\frac{7}{2}$). No answer can be a negative number, such as –8.

To record your answer for an alternate format question

- begin in any column that will allow your answer to be entered
- write your answer in the boxes on the top row
- in the column beneath a fraction bar or decimal point (if any) and each number in your answer, fill in the bubble representing that character
- leave blank any unused column

EXAMPLE

The scale on a map indicates that $\frac{1}{2}$ inch represents an actual distance of 120 miles. In inches, how far apart on the map will two towns be if the actual distance between them is 180 miles?

The answer to the above example is $\frac{3}{4}$, or 0.75, inches. A few examples of how the answer could be gridded are shown below.

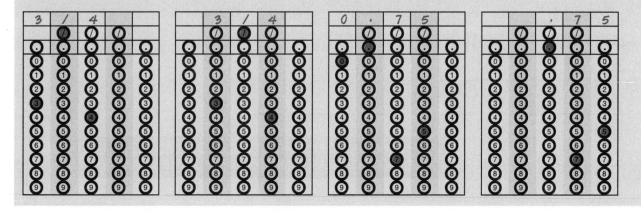

Points to remember:

- The answer sheet will be machine scored. **The circles must be filled in correctly.**
- Mark no more than one circle in any column.
- Grid only one answer even if there is more than one correct answer.
- Mixed numbers such as $3\frac{1}{2}$ must be gridded as 3.5 or $\frac{7}{2}$.
- No answer can be a negative number.

Adapted from the GED Testing Service

GED Stats

TRENDS IN GED TESTING 1991–2001

Year	Avg. Age	Planning Further Study	Total Number Tested
1991	26.4	58.6	806,038
1992	26.6	61.4	790,565
1993	26.0	61.7	790,165
1994	25.6	65.6	822,537
1995	25.3	63.7	829,904
1996	25.0	64.4	867,802
1997	24.7	65.4	827,105
1998	24.6	67.6	822,181
1999	24.6	65.0	860,079
2000	24.7	66.2	860,684
2001	25.2	65.5	1,069,899

Source: GED Testing Service, American Council on Education

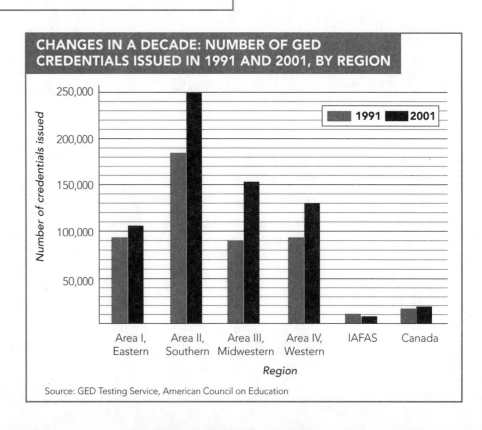

CHANGES IN A DECADE: NUMBER OF GED CREDENTIALS ISSUED IN 1991 AND 2001, BY REGION

Source: GED Testing Service, American Council on Education

Sports and Entertainment

NFL STATS 2001 REGULAR SEASON

Passing Yards

Player	Team	Yds	Att	Cmp	TDs	Ints	Long	Rating
Kurt Warner	STL	4830	546	375	36	22	65	101.4
Peyton Manning	IND	4131	547	343	26	23	86	84.1
Brett Favre	GB	3921	510	314	32	15	67	94.1
Aaron Brooks	NO	3832	558	312	26	22	63	76.4
Rich Gannon	OAK	3828	549	361	27	9	49	95.5
Trent Green	KC	3783	523	296	17	24	67	71.1
Kerry Collins	NYG	3764	568	327	19	16	76	77.1
Jake Plummer	ARI	3653	525	304	18	14	68	79.6
Jeff Garcia	SF	3538	504	316	32	12	61	94.8
Doug Flutie	SD	3464	521	294	15	18	78	72.0

Source: NFL.com

BOX OFFICE HIT MOVIES

(adjusted for ticket price inflation)

Movie	Year	North American box office (millions)	adjusted North American box office (millions)
1. Gone with the Wind	1939	198.7	1,187.7
2. Star Wars	1977	460.9	1,026.7
3. The Sound of Music	1965	163.2	824.1
4. E.T. The Extraterrestrial	1982	434.9	815.0
5. The Ten Commandments	1956	80.0	758.1
6. Titanic	1997	600.8	747.4

Source: www.the-movie-times.com

Health, Nutrition, and Fitness

BODY MASS INDEX (English and Metric)

Height (feet and inches)

Weight (pounds)	5'0"	5'1"	5'2"	5'3"	5'4"	5'5"	5'6"	5'7"	5'8"	5'9"	5'10"	5'11"	6'0"	6'1"	6'2"	6'3"	6'4"	Weight (kilograms)
100	20	19	18	18	17	17	16	16	15	15	14	14	14	13	13	12	12	45
105	21	20	19	19	18	17	17	16	16	16	15	15	14	14	13	13	13	47
110	21	21	20	19	19	18	18	17	17	16	16	15	15	15	14	14	13	50
115	22	22	21	20	20	19	19	18	17	17	17	16	16	15	15	14	14	52
120	23	23	22	21	21	20	19	19	18	18	17	17	16	16	15	15	15	54
125	24	24	23	22	21	21	20	20	19	18	18	17	17	16	16	16	15	57
130	25	25	24	23	22	22	21	20	20	19	19	18	18	17	17	16	16	59
135	26	26	25	24	23	22	22	21	21	20	19	19	18	18	17	17	16	61
140	27	26	26	25	24	23	23	22	21	21	20	20	19	18	18	17	17	63
145	28	27	27	26	25	24	23	23	22	21	21	20	20	19	19	18	18	66
150	29	28	27	27	26	25	24	23	23	22	22	21	20	20	19	19	18	68
155	30	29	28	27	27	26	25	24	24	23	22	22	21	20	20	19	19	70
160	31	30	29	28	27	27	26	25	24	24	23	22	22	21	21	20	19	72
165	32	31	30	29	28	27	27	26	25	24	24	23	22	22	21	21	20	75
170	33	32	31	30	29	28	27	27	26	25	24	24	23	22	22	21	21	77
175	34	33	32	31	30	29	28	27	27	26	25	24	24	23	22	22	21	79
180	35	34	33	32	31	30	29	28	27	27	26	25	24	24	23	22	22	82
185	36	35	34	33	32	31	30	29	28	27	27	26	25	24	24	23	23	84
190	37	36	35	34	33	32	31	30	29	28	27	26	26	25	24	24	23	86
195	38	37	36	35	33	32	31	31	30	29	28	27	26	26	25	24	24	88
200	39	38	37	35	34	33	32	31	30	30	29	28	27	26	26	25	24	91
205	40	39	37	36	35	34	33	32	31	30	29	29	28	27	26	26	25	93
210	41	40	38	37	36	35	34	33	32	31	30	29	28	28	27	26	26	95
215	42	41	39	38	37	36	35	34	33	32	31	30	29	28	28	27	26	98
220	43	42	40	39	38	37	36	34	33	32	32	31	30	29	28	27	27	100
225	44	43	41	40	39	37	36	35	34	33	32	31	31	30	29	28	27	102
230	45	43	42	41	39	38	37	36	35	34	33	32	31	30	30	29	28	104
235	46	44	43	42	40	39	38	37	36	35	34	33	32	31	30	29	29	107
240	47	45	44	43	41	40	39	38	36	35	34	33	33	32	31	30	29	109
245	48	46	45	43	42	41	40	38	37	36	35	34	33	32	31	31	30	111
250	49	47	46	44	43	42	40	39	38	37	36	35	34	33	32	31	30	114

| 150 | 152.5 | 155 | 157.5 | 160 | 162.5 | 165 | 167.5 | 170 | 172.5 | 175 | 177.5 | 180 | 182.5 | 185 | 187.5 | 190 |

Height (centimeters)

☐ Underweight   ☐ Weight appropriate   ☐ Overweight   ☐ Obese

Adapted from *Clinical Guidelines on the Identification, Evaluation, and Treatment of Overweight and Obesity in Adults: The Evidence Report*

OVERWEIGHT AND OBESITY IN THE U.S., 1960–1994

| | Overweight and Obesity[1] | | Obesity[2] | |
	1960–1962	1988–1994	1960–1962	1988–1994
Both Sexes	43.3%	54.9%	12.8%	22.3%
Men				
20–29	39.9%	43.1%	9.0%	12.5%
30–39	49.6	58.1	10.4	17.2
40–49	53.6	65.5	11.9	23.1
50–59	54.1	73.0	13.4	28.9
60–69	52.9	70.3	7.7	24.8
70–79	36.0	63.1	8.6	20.0
Women				
20–29	17.0%	33.1%	6.1%	14.6%
30–39	32.8	47.0	12.1	25.8
40–49	42.3	52.7	17.1	26.9
50–59	55.0	64.4	20.4	35.6
60–69	63.1	64.0	27.2	29.8
70–79	57.4	57.9	21.9	25.0

1. BMI greater than or equal to 25.
2. BMI greater than or equal to 30.

SOURCE: Centers for Disease Control and Prevention, 2000

WALKING SPEED CONVERSION CHART

Based on an average stride of 2.5 ft long

steps per minute	minutes per mile	miles per hour
70	30	2.0
90	24	2.5
105	20	3.0
120	17	3.5
140	15	4.0
160	13	4.5
175	12	5.0
190	11	5.5
210	10	6.0

WALKING VS. OTHER WORKOUTS

Calories burned by a 150-lb person per hour

exercise	calories
Brisk walking (4 mph)	350
Walking with a 15-lb backpack	410
Uphill walking (10% incline, 3 mph)	500
Racewalking	600
Slow running	550
Recreational tennis (singles)	430
Swimming (slow crawl)	400

NUTRITION LABELS FROM SELECTED SNACKS

MUFFIN

Nutrition Facts
Serving Size 1 muffin 4 oz (113g)
Servings Per Container 4

Amount per serving

Calories 460 Calories from Fat 210

	% Daily Value*
Total Fat 23g	**36%**
Saturated Fat 4.5g	**23%**
Cholesterol 85mg	**29%**
Sodium 380mg	**16%**
Total Carbohydrate 55g	**18%**
Dietary Fiber less than 1 gram	**4%**
Sugars 29g	
Protein 6g	

Vitamin A 2%	•	Vitamin C 6%
Calcium 2%	•	Iron 10%

*Percent Daily Values are based on a 2,000 calorie diet. Your daily values may be higher or lower depending on your calorie needs:

		Calories: 2,000	2,500
Total Fat	Less than	65g	80g
Sat Fat	Less than	20g	25g
Cholesterol	Less than	300mg	300mg
Sodium	Less than	2,400mg	2,400mg
Total Carbohydrate		300g	375g
Dietary Fiber		25g	30g

Calories per gram:
Fat 9 • Carbohydrate 4 • Protein 4

VEGETABLE CHIPS

Nutrition Facts
Serving 1 oz (28g/about 10 chips)
Servings Per Container about 8

Amount per serving

Calories 140 Calories from Fat 70

	% Daily Value*
Total Fat 7g	**11%**
Saturated Fat 1g	**6%**
Cholesterol 0mg	**0%**
Sodium 70mg	**3%**
Total Carbohydrate 18g	**6%**
Dietary Fiber 3g	**12%**
Sugars 1g	
Protein 1g	

Vitamin A 0%	•	Vitamin C 4%
Calcium 2%	•	Iron 2%

*Percent Daily Values are based on a 2,000 calorie diet. Your daily values may be higher or lower depending on your calorie needs:

		Calories: 2,000	2,500
Total Fat	Less than	65g	80g
Sat Fat	Less than	20g	25g
Cholesterol	Less than	300mg	300mg
Sodium	Less than	2,400mg	2,400mg
Total Carbohydrate		300g	375g
Dietary Fiber		25g	30g

Calories per gram:
Fat 9 • Carbohydrate 4 • Protein 4

PEANUT BUTTER COOKIES

Nutrition Facts
Serving Size 3 cookies (32/1.1oz)
Servings Per Container about 11

Amount per serving

Calories 160 Calories from Fat 80

	% Daily Value*
Total Fat 9g	**13%**
Saturated Fat 2g	**9%**
Cholesterol 5mg	**2%**
Sodium 125mg	**5%**
Total Carbohydrate 18g	**6%**
Dietary Fiber 1g	**5%**
Sugars 8g	
Protein 4g	

Vitamin A 0%	•	Vitamin C 0%
Calcium 0%	•	Iron 0%

*Percent Daily Values are based on a 2,000 calorie diet. Your daily values may be higher or lower depending on your calorie needs:

		Calories: 2,000	2,500
Total Fat	Less than	65g	80g
Sat Fat	Less than	20g	25g
Cholesterol	Less than	300mg	300mg
Sodium	Less than	2,400mg	2,400mg
Total Carbohydrate		300g	375g
Dietary Fiber		25g	30g

Calories per gram:
Fat 9 • Carbohydrate 4 • Protein 4

GRANOLA BAR

Nutrition Facts
Serv. Size 1 bar (37 g)
Calories 140
Fat Cal. 25

*Percent Daily Values (DV) are based on a 2,000 calorie diet.

Amount/serving	%DV*	Amount/serving	%DV*
Total Fat 3g	**5%**	**Total Carb.** 27g	**9%**
Sat. Fat 0.5g	**3%**	Fiber 1g	**4%**
Cholest. 0mg	**0%**	Sugars 13g	
Sodium 110mg	**5%**	**Protein** 2g	

Vitamin A 15% • Vitamin C 0% • Calcium 20% • Iron 10% • Thiamin 25% • Riboflavin 25% • Niacin 25% • Vitamin B6 25% • Folic Acid 10%• Zinc 10%

BLUE CORN CHIPS

Nutrition Facts
Serving Size 1oz (28g/About 16 chips)
Servings Per Container 9

Amount per serving

Calories 150 Calories from Fat 60

	% Daily Value*
Total Fat 7g	**10%**
Saturated Fat .5g	**4%**
Cholesterol 0mg	**0%**
Sodium 10mg	**0%**
Total Carbohydrate 18g	**6%**
Dietary Fiber 1 gram	**6%**
Sugars 0g	
Protein 2g	

Vitamin A 0%	•	Vitamin C 0%
Calcium 4%	•	Iron 4%

*Percent Daily Values are based on a 2,000 calorie diet.

POTATO CHIPS

Nutrition Facts
Serving Size 1oz (28g/About 20 chips)
Servings Per Container 3

Amount per serving

Calories 150 Calories from Fat 90

	% Daily Value*
Total Fat 10g	**15%**
Saturated Fat 3g	**15%**
Cholesterol 0mg	**0%**
Sodium 180mg	**8%**
Total Carbohydrate 15g	**5%**
Dietary Fiber 1g	**4%**
Sugars 0g	
Protein 2g	

Vitamin A 0%	•	Vitamin C 10%
Calcium 0%	•	Iron 0%

*Percent Daily Values are based on a 2,000 calorie diet.

Travel and Transportation

EXCHANGE RATES

Country	Currency	ISO	per 1 U.S. Dollar
Australia	Dollar	AUD	1.789974
Canada	Dollar	CAD	1.561176
European Union	Euro	EUR	1.015848
Japan	Yen	JPY	123.9290
Korea (South)	Won	KRW	1229.204
Mexico	Peso	MXN	10.00400
Russia	Ruble	RUB	31.75227
Saudi Arabia	Riyal	SAR	3.750519
South Africa	Rand	ZAR	10.07166
Taiwan	Dollar	TWD	34.79595
United Kingdom	Pound	GBP	0.641378
United States	Dollar	USD	1.000000

Source: ExchangeRate.com Inc.

POPULATION AND LAND AREA

region	population (millions)	area (square miles)
Africa	818	11,698,111
North America	316	7,699,508
Latin America and Caribbean	525	7,946,684
Asia	3,720	12,262,691
Europe	727	8,875,867
Oceania	31	3,306,741

Source: Population Reference Bureau

WHY DO GAS PRICES DIFFER ACROSS THE U.S.A.?

GASOLINE BY THE GALLON

In October 2001, the average price of a gallon of gasoline was $1.32. What that paid for, broken down:

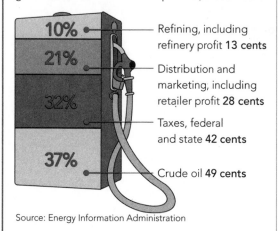

10% — Refining, including refinery profit **13 cents**

21% — Distribution and marketing, including retailer profit **28 cents**

32% — Taxes, federal and state **42 cents**

37% — Crude oil **49 cents**

Source: Energy Information Administration

HIGHEST AND LOWEST METRO AREAS GASOLINE PRICES, DEC 2001

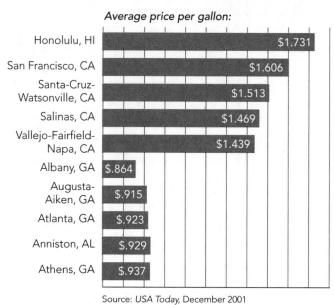

Average price per gallon:

Honolulu, HI	$1.731
San Francisco, CA	$1.606
Santa-Cruz-Watsonville, CA	$1.513
Salinas, CA	$1.469
Vallejo-Fairfield-Napa, CA	$1.439
Albany, GA	$.864
Augusta-Aiken, GA	$.915
Atlanta, GA	$.923
Anniston, AL	$.929
Athens, GA	$.937

Source: *USA Today*, December 2001

STATE GASOLINE TAX RATES

Gasoline taxes are roughly one-third the amount motorists pay for gas. In addition to 18.4 cents per gallon federal tax, consumers pay state and local taxes. This list shows the amount of state taxes being charged per gallon.

State	cents per gallon	rank	State	cents per gallon	rank	State	cents per gallon	rank
Alabama	16.00	41	Kentucky	15.00	46	North Dakota	21.00	25
Alaska	8.00	50	Louisiana	20.00	28	Ohio	22.00	20
Arizona	18.00	36	Maine	22.00	20	Oklahoma	16.00	41
Arkansas	21.50	24	Maryland	23.50	16	Oregon	24.00	14
California	25.94	7	Massachusetts	21.00	25	Pennsylvania	26.00	6
Colorado	22.00	20	Michigan	19.00	34	Rhode Island	28.00	3
Connecticut	25.00	9	Minnesota	20.00	28	South Carolina	16.00	41
Delaware	23.00	17	Mississippi	18.00	36	South Dakota	22.00	20
District of Columbia	23.00	17	Missouri	17.00	40	Tennessee	20.00	28
Florida	18.67	35	Montana	27.00	4	Texas	20.00	28
Georgia	11.19	49	Nebraska	24.50	11	Utah	24.50	11
Hawaii	NA	NA	Nevada	24.00	14	Vermont	20.00	28
Idaho	25.00	9	New Hampshire	18.00	36	Virginia	16.00	41
Illinois	26.80	5	New Jersey	14.50	47	Washington	23.00	17
Indiana	16.00	41	New Mexico	18.00	36	West Virginia	25.65	8
Iowa	20.00	28	New York	31.50	1	Wisconsin	30.30	2
Kansas	21.00	25	North Carolina	24.10	13	Wyoming	14.00	48

Source: *USA Today*

Science and Geography

HEAT INDEX TABLE

Air Temperature (°F)

	70	75	80	85	90	95	100	105	110	115	120
30	67	73	78	84	90	96	104	113	123	135	148
35	67	73	79	85	91	98	107	118	130	143	
40	68	74	79	86	93	101	110	123	137	151	
45	68	74	80	87	95	104	115	129	143		
50	69	75	81	88	96	107	120	135	150		
55	69	75	81	89	98	110	126	142			
60	70	76	82	90	100	114	132	149			
65	70	76	83	91	102	119	138				
70	70	77	85	93	106	124	144				
75	70	77	86	95	109	130					
80	71	78	86	97	113	136					
85	71	78	87	99	117						
90	71	79	88	102	122						
95	71	79	89	105							
100	72	80	91	108							

Relative Humidity (%) (vertical axis label)

Heat Index	affects on the human body
130 or above	heat stroke highly likely with continued exposure
105 to 130	heat stroke likely with prolonged exposure
90 to 105	heat stroke possible with prolonged exposure

Source: National Weather Service

NEW WIND CHILL CHART (2001)

Temperature (°F)

	30	25	20	15	10	5	0	−5	−10	−15	−20	−25
5	25	19	13	7	1	−5	−11	−16	−22	−28	−34	−40
10	21	15	9	3	−4	−10	−16	−22	−28	−35	−41	−47
15	19	13	6	0	−7	−13	−19	−26	−32	−39	−45	−51
20	17	11	4	−2	−9	−15	−22	−29	−35	−42	−48	−55
25	16	9	3	−4	−11	−17	−24	−31	−37	−44	−51	−58
30	15	8	1	−5	−12	−19	−26	−33	−39	−46	−53	−60
35	14	7	0	−7	−14	−21	−27	−34	−41	−48	−55	−62
40	13	6	−1	−8	−15	−22	−29	−36	−43	−50	−57	−64
45	12	5	−2	−9	−16	−23	−30	−37	−44	−51	−58	−65
50	12	4	−3	−10	−17	−24	−31	−38	−45	−52	−60	−67
55	11	4	−3	−11	−18	−25	−32	−39	−46	−54	−61	−68
60	10	3	−4	−11	−19	−26	−33	−40	−48	−55	−62	−69

Wind (mph) (vertical axis label)

Source: National Weather Service

■ Frostbite occurs in 15 minutes or less

U.S. HIGHPOINTS GUIDE

State	Peak	Height	Height Rank	State	Peak	Height	Height Rank
Alabama	Cheaha Mountain	2,407	35	Montana	Granite Peak	12,799	10
Alaska	Mount McKinley	20,320	1	Nebraska	Panorama Point	5,424	20
Arizona	Humphreys Peak	12,633	12	Nevada	Boundary Peak	13,143	9
Arkansas	Mount Magazine (Signal Hill)	2,753	34	New Hampshire	Mount Washington	6,288	18
California	Mount Whitney	14,494	2	New Jersey	High Point	1,803	40
Colorado	Mount Elbert	14,433	3	New Mexico	Wheeler Peak	13,161	8
Connecticut	Frissell–S. Slope	2,380	36	New York	Mount Marcy	5,344	21
Delaware	Ebright Azimuth	448	49	North Carolina	Mount Mitchell	6,684	16
Florida	Lakewood (Britton Hill)	345	50	North Dakota	White Butte	3,506	30
Georgia	Brasstown Bald	4,784	25	Ohio	Campbell Hill	1,550	43
Hawaii	Mauna Kea	13,796	6	Oklahoma	Black Mesa	4,973	23
Idaho	Borah Peak	12,662	10	Oregon	Mount Hood	11,239	13
Illinois	Charles Mound	1,235	45	Pennsylvania	Mount Davis	3,213	33
Indiana	Hoosier Hill	1,257	44	Rhode Island	Jerimoth Hill	812	46
Iowa	Hawkeye Point	1,670	42	South Carolina	Sassafras Mountain	3,560	29
Kansas	Mount Sunflower	4,039	28	South Dakota	Harney Peak	7,242	15
Kentucky	Black Mountain	4,145	27	Tennessee	Clingmans Dome	6,643	17
Louisiana	Driskill Mountain	535	48	Texas	Guadalupe Peak	8,749	14
Maine	Katahdin (Baxter Peak)	5,267	22	Utah	Kings Peak	13,528	7
Maryland	Backbone Mountain	3,360	32	Vermont	Mount Mansfield	4,393	26
Massachusetts	Greylock	3,491	31	Virginia	Mount Rogers	5,729	19
Michigan	Mount Arvon	1,979	38	Washington	Mount Rainier	14,411	4
Minnesota	Eagle Mountain	2,301	37	West Virginia	Spruce Knob	4,863	24
Mississippi	Woodall Mountain	806	47	Wisconsin	Timms Hill	1,951	39
Missouri	Taum Sauk	1,772	41	Wyoming	Gannett Peak	13,804	5

Source: americasroof.com

Consumer and Citizen

appliance	specs	usage	cost	cost per month
THE PRICE OF POWER				
KITCHEN				
Dishwasher	drying unit on	3 loads a week	12¢ a load	$1.44 a month
Refrigerator	20 cubic feet, top freezer, auto defrost, made in 1993	constant	25¢ a day	$6.99 a month
Microwave	1,500-watt	10 minutes a day, 7 days a week	4¢ a day	$1.01 a month
LAUNDRY				
Clothes washer	$\frac{1}{2}$-hp motor	3 loads a week	4¢ a load	48¢ a month
Clothes dryer, electric	$\frac{1}{2}$-hp motor, 5,000-watt	3 loads a week	66¢ a load	$7.92 a month
HOUSEHOLD				
Small electrical appliances	examples: clock, coffee maker, radio	2 hours a day, 7 days a week	1¢ a day	34¢
Color television	20 inches, 265-watt	21 hours a week	10¢ a day	$2.72 a month
Central air conditioner	3 ton	3 hours a day, 7 days a week	$1.29 a day	$36.19 a month
Ceiling fan	80-watt, without light	3 hours a day, 7 days a week	3¢ a day	81¢ a month
Light bulb	incandescent, 100-watt	6 hours a day, 7 days a week	7¢ a day	$2.02 a month
Personal computer and monitor	at low-power state	1 hour a day, 7 days a week	2¢ an hour	$0.44 a month
Electric blanket	queen-size, 100-watts	7 hours a day, 7 days a week	70¢ a day	$19.52 a month

Source: Pacific Gas and Electric; Southern California Edison

A DECADE OF CHANGE FOR THE USA

Data from Census 2000 reflect a nation that is better educated, more prosperous, and more diverse than in 1990.

VALUE OF HOMES

Less than $99,000

| 1990 | 63% |
| 2000 | 40% |

$100,000 – $199,999

| 1990 | 24% |
| 2000 | 38% |

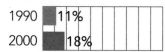

$200,000 – $499,999

| 1990 | 11% |
| 2000 | 18% |

$500,000 or more

| 1990 | 2% |
| 2000 | 3% |

Median value

| 1990 | $100,000 |
| 2000 | $119,600 |

LIVING IN POVERTY

All individuals

| 1990 | 13% |
| 2000 | 12% |

Under 18 yrs old

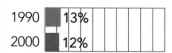

| 1990 | 18% |
| 2000 | 16% |

Age 65 and over

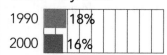

| 1990 | 13% |
| 2000 | 10% |

EDUCATION

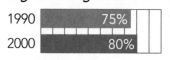

High school graduate or higher

| 1990 | 75% |
| 2000 | 80% |

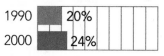

Bachelor's degree or higher

| 1990 | 20% |
| 2000 | 24% |

2000

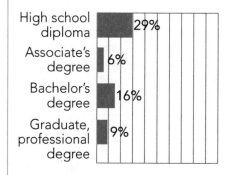

High school diploma	29%
Associate's degree	6%
Bachelor's degree	16%
Graduate, professional degree	9%

PEOPLE WHO LIVE IN THE USA

U.S. natives

| 1990 | 92% |
| 2000 | 89% |

Non-natives

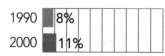

| 1990 | 8% |
| 2000 | 11% |

Birthplace of foreign-born (2000)

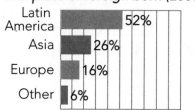

Latin America	52%
Asia	26%
Europe	16%
Other	6%

INCOME

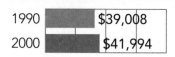

Median household income

| 1990 | $39,008 |
| 2000 | $41,994 |

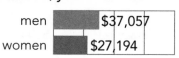

Median earnings in 2000 for full-time, year-round workers

| men | $37,057 |
| women | $27,194 |

Men earn 36% more than women.

MARITAL STATUS

2000

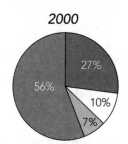

56% 27% 10% 7%

1990

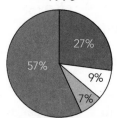

57% 27% 9% 7%

1950

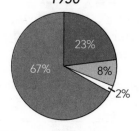

67% 23% 8% 2%

☐ Divorced ▨ Widowed
▨ Married ▨ Never married

Source: Census Bureau

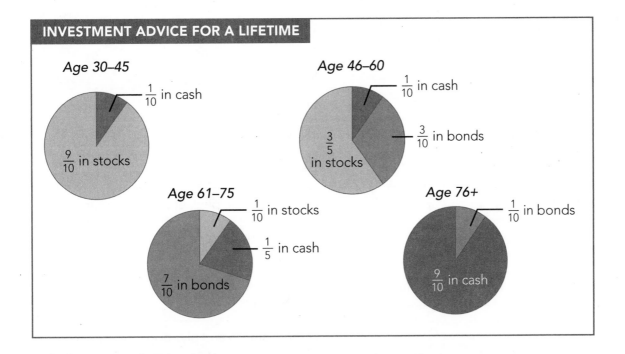

INVESTMENT ADVICE FOR A LIFETIME

Age 30–45

$\frac{1}{10}$ in cash

$\frac{9}{10}$ in stocks

Age 46–60

$\frac{1}{10}$ in cash

$\frac{3}{10}$ in bonds

$\frac{3}{5}$ in stocks

Age 61–75

$\frac{1}{10}$ in stocks

$\frac{1}{5}$ in cash

$\frac{7}{10}$ in bonds

Age 76+

$\frac{1}{10}$ in bonds

$\frac{9}{10}$ in cash

ELECTORAL COLLEGE VOTES FOR THE 2000 NATIONAL ELECTION

Allocation based on 1990 census

State	Electoral College Votes	State	Electoral College Votes	State	Electoral College Votes
Alabama	9	Kentucky	8	North Dakota	3
Alaska	3	Louisiana	9	Ohio	21
Arizona	9	Maine	4	Oklahoma	8
Arkansas	6	Maryland	10	Oregon	7
California	54	Massachusetts	12	Pennsylvania	23
Colorado	8	Michigan	18	Rhode Island	4
Connecticut	8	Minnesota	10	South Carolina	8
Delaware	3	Mississippi	7	South Dakota	3
District of Columbia	2	Missouri	11	Tennessee	11
		Montana	3	Texas	32
Florida	25	Nebraska	5	Utah	5
Georgia	13	Nevada	4	Vermont	3
Hawaii	4	New Hampshire	4	Virginia	13
Idaho	4	New Jersey	15	Washington	11
Illinois	22	New Mexico	5	West Virginia	5
Indiana	12	New York	33	Wisconsin	11
Iowa	7	North Carolina	14	Wyoming	3
Kansas	6				

SELECTED MEASUREMENTS USED IN HOME CONSTRUCTION

Floors

Floor tile	$\frac{3}{8}$ in.
Backer board underlayment	$\frac{1}{2}$ in.
Thin-set	$\frac{1}{16}$ in.
Hardwood laminate	$\frac{5}{8}$ in.

Cabinets

Unfinished height	$34\frac{1}{2}$ in.
Formica	$\frac{1}{16}$ in.
Granite	$\frac{3}{4}$ in.

Walls

Thin studs	$3\frac{5}{8}$ in.
Thick studs	$5\frac{5}{8}$ in.
Dry wall	$\frac{1}{2}$ in.
Texture (orange peel, etc)	$\frac{1}{16}$ in.
Quarter-round molding	$\frac{9}{16}$ in.
Wall tile	$\frac{1}{4}$ in.
Baseboard	$\frac{9}{16}$ in.
Exterior stucco and plywood	$1\frac{1}{16}$ in.

Cutting Allowance

Carbide tip blade	$\frac{1}{8}$ in.
Steel blade	$\frac{1}{16}$ in.

WOMEN'S SHOE SIZE CONVERSION CHART

United States	4	$4\frac{1}{2}$	5	$5\frac{1}{2}$	6	$6\frac{1}{2}$	7	$7\frac{1}{2}$	8	$8\frac{1}{2}$	9	$9\frac{1}{2}$	10	$10\frac{1}{2}$	11
Europe	34	34.5	35	36	36.5	37	38	38.5	39	40	40.5	41	42	42.5	43
Japan	22	22.5	23	23.5	24	24.5	25	25.5	26	26.5	27	27.5	28	28.5	29
United Kingdom	2	$2\frac{1}{2}$	3	$3\frac{1}{2}$	4	$4\frac{1}{2}$	5	$5\frac{1}{2}$	6	$6\frac{1}{2}$	7	$7\frac{1}{2}$	8	$8\frac{1}{2}$	9

Mathematics

Measurement Equivalents

	Customary Units	Metric Units
Length	12 inches (in.) = 1 foot (ft) 3 feet = 1 yard (yd) 5,280 feet = 1 mile (mi)	10 millimeters (mm) = 1 centimeter (cm) 100 centimeters = 1 meter (m) 1,000 meters = 1 kilometer (km)
Capacity	8 fluid ounces (fl oz) = 1 cup 2 cups = 1 pint (pt) 2 pints = 1 quart (qt) 4 quarts = 1 gallon	1,000 milliliters (mL) = 1 liter (L) 1,000 liters = 1 kiloliter (kL)
Weight (Mass)	16 ounces (oz) = 1 pound (lb) 2000 pounds = 1 ton (T)	1,000 milligrams (mg) = 1 gram (g) 1,000 grams = 1 kilogram (kg) 10,000 kilograms = 1 metric ton (T)
Temperature	32° F = freezing point of water 98.6° F = normal body temperature 212° F = boiling point of water	0° C = freezing point of water 37° C = normal body temperature 100° C = boiling point of water
Time	60 seconds = 1 minute 60 minutes = 1 hour 24 hours = 1 day 7 days = 1 week	

Other Ways to Compute

Some Other Ways to Add: Adding Without Carrying

FRONT-END ADDITION | 46 + 38 | | 34 + 57

Start from the left. Think:

40 + 30 is 70
6 + 8 is 14
70 + 14 is 84

Think: 30 + 50 is 80
4 + 7 is 11
80 + 11 is 91

BALANCING WITH ADDITION | 18 + 35 | | 49 + 56

Make it an easier problem:

Subtract the same thing that you add.

18 + 35 = 53
plus 2   minus 2   same
20 + 33 = 53

49 + 56 = 105
plus 1   minus 1   same
50 + 55 = 105

Try these without paper and pencil.

Ⓐ 23 + 18   Ⓓ 25 + 37   Ⓖ 57 + 27   Ⓙ 44 + 37

Ⓑ 34 + 27   Ⓔ 78 + 16   Ⓗ 27 + 18   Ⓚ 51 + 79

Ⓒ 69 + 24   Ⓕ 33 + 49   Ⓘ 35 + 56   Ⓛ 65 + 85

Another Way to Subtract: Subtracting Without Borrowing

BALANCING WITH SUBTRACTION 83 − 28

Make it an easier problem:

① Add to make the second number an even 10.
② Add the same amount to the first number.

The difference between the numbers remains the same.

83 − 28 = 55
plus 2   plus 2   same
85 − 30 = 55

| 73 − 47 | | 65 − 39

The difference 73 − 47 is the same as the difference 76 − 50, which is easy to see as 26.

What number should you add to both? 66 − 40 = 26
The same difference!

Change these to problems you can do in your head.

Ⓐ 44 − 18   Ⓓ 76 − 39   Ⓖ 55 − 38   Ⓙ 96 − 58

Ⓑ 35 − 16   Ⓔ 63 − 15   Ⓗ 60 − 24   Ⓚ 104 − 69

Ⓒ 51 − 33   Ⓕ 77 − 29   Ⓘ 52 − 26   Ⓛ 120 − 47

Another Way to Multiply: The Front-End Method

46 × 7

$$46 \quad (40 + 6)$$
$$\underline{\times\ 7} \quad \text{Start by multiplying 7 by 40 (the front end of the number).}$$
$$280 \leftarrow 7 \times 40$$
$$\underline{+\ 42} \quad \text{Next, multiply 7 by 6.}$$
$$322 \quad \text{Add the two partial products.}$$

Picture this problem as finding the area of two adjoining rectangles.

The same problem can be written as an exercise in using the distributive property.

	40	6
7	280	42

$$7(46) = 7(40 + 6) \quad \text{Expand 46 into its place values.}$$
$$= 7 \cdot 40 + 7 \cdot 6 \quad \text{Write in expanded form.}$$
$$= 280 + 42 \quad \text{Multiply first.}$$
$$= 322 \quad \text{Then add.}$$

One advantage of using this method is that the first partial product you find is a good estimate of the total answer.

EXAMPLE

When you are finding the answer to 762 × 8, the first partial product (700 × 8 = 5,600) gives you an idea of how big the answer will be. Look at the sketch of the rectangles involved.

	700	60	2
8	5,600	480	16

The first partial product (5,600) told you the most about the answer. In some situations (including the GED Test), the first front-end product may be all you need.

This method can also be used to multiply one 2-digit number by another. Just as in the traditional method, each digit of one number must be multiplied by each digit of the other. However, when you are using the front-end method, the order in which you multiply doesn't matter.

64 × 35

METHOD 1 (traditional)

$$64$$
$$\underline{\times\ 35}$$
$$320$$
$$\underline{1920}$$
$$2,240$$

METHOD 2 (front-end)

$$64 \quad (60 + 4)$$
$$\underline{\times\ 35} \quad (30 + 5)$$
$$1800 \leftarrow (60 \times 30)$$
$$120 \leftarrow (4 \times 30)$$
$$300 \leftarrow (60 \times 5)$$
$$\underline{+\ 20} \leftarrow (4 \times 5)$$
$$2,240$$

	60	4
30	1,800	120
5	300	20

Use the front-end method to multiply the following.

A 37 × 8   **C** 108 × 7   **E** 2,008 × 4   **G** 72 × 91

B 29 × 6   **D** 431 × 9   **F** 32 × 45   **H** 56 × 33

Another Way to Divide

Do you need to find the exact answer to a division problem, and you don't have a calculator? There are not a lot of rules involved in this method for long division. Just remember that division is repeated subtraction.

EXAMPLE A

The problem $\frac{385}{35}$ asks, "How many times can you subtract 35 from 385?"

First, estimate the number of times you can subtract 35 from 385. This estimate must be less than the actual answer, but does not necessarily have to be close.

To keep this easy, think about the multiples of 35 that you know mentally. Ask, "Can I subtract 100 35s? (3,500)." No. "Can I subtract 10 35s? (350)." Yes.

```
35)385
   350  | 10   Subtract 10 35s from 385 and keep track of the 10 off to the side.
    35  |      How many 35s can you subtract from the number remaining?
    35  | + 1  Again, subtract and then keep track of the number.
     0  |  11  When you cannot subtract any more 35s, add the numbers on the side for the answer.
```

EXAMPLE B

The problem $\frac{2,382}{22}$ asks, "How many times can you subtract 22 from 2,382?"

Estimate by thinking about multiplying 22 by powers of 10. You can subtract 22×100 (2,200).

```
22)2,382 |        Subtract 100 22s from 2,382.
   2200  | 100    Write this number on the side.
    182  |        Can you subtract 10 x 22 (220) from this? No.
     88  |  4     Estimate how many and multiply.
     94  |        Subtract and keep track of the number. (Your estimates may differ—see below).
     88  | + 4 r 6  You can subtract 4 22s again from the number remaining.
      6  | 108    You cannot subtract any more 22s. The number left is the remainder.
```

EXAMPLE C

Three solutions are shown. You may use different estimates from these, but your answer should be the same.

```
53)13,455 |          53)13,455 |          53)13,455 |
   5300   | 100        10600   | 200         10600   | 200
   8155    |            2855    |             2855    |
   5300   | 100         1590   | 30          2650    | 50
   2855    |            1265    |             205     |
   1060   | 20          1060   | 20          159     | + 3
   1795    |            205     |             46      | 253 r 46
   1060   | 20          159    | + 3
   735     |            46      | 253 r 46
   530    | 10
   205     |
   159    | + 3
   46      | 253 r 46
```

Find the exact answer by using the method shown above.

Ⓐ $\frac{288}{24}$ **Ⓑ** $\frac{1,452}{45}$ **Ⓒ** $\frac{4,680}{72}$ **Ⓓ** $\frac{5,955}{29}$

Answer Key

Lesson 1

"Seeing" Addition & Subtraction,
pages 2–12

1. **A** and **B** Pictures will vary.

2. **A**, **B** and **C** Pictures and problems will vary.

3. **A** $10 + 7$ or $7 + 10$ **B** $130 + 205$ or $205 + 130$

4. **A** $15 - 4$ **B** $450 - 250$

5. **A** $12 - 5$ **D** $11 - 2$
   B $10 + 3$ or $3 + 10$ **E** $4 + 5$ or $5 + 4$
   C $6 + 4$ or $4 + 6$ **F** $37 - 19$

6. **A** $3 + 8$ or $8 + 3$ **G** $18 - 10$
   B $n + 8$ or $8 + n$ **H** $12 - 4$
   C $9 + 2$ or $2 + 9$ **I** $t - 4$
   D $b + 2$ or $2 + b$ **J** $15 - 7$
   E $12 - 4$ **K** $b - 7$
   F $12 - x$

7. **A** 5,000   **C** 40; 400; 4,000
   B 150; 1,500; 15,000

8. **A** 540   **D** 1,010
   B 1,020   **E** 2,500
   C 120   **F** 8,100

9. **A** 134   **C** 33, 83, 103, 243
   B 54, 84, 94   **D** 69, 99, 549

10. The '5' in the place immediately to the right of the circled digit is exactly the same as the midpoint on the graph. Halfway between the 100s is 50; halfway between the 10s is 5, and so on.

    B $600 - 300 = 300$ **E** $1{,}100 - 900 = 200$
    C $100 + 600 = 700$ **F** $700 - 700 = 0$
    D $800 + 1{,}100 = 1{,}900$

11. **A** $60 + 30 = 90$ **D** $120 - 40 = 80$
    B $70 + 20 = 90$ **E** $100 - 60 = 40$
    C $80 + 40 = 120$ **F** $60 - 30 = 30$

USING DATA	
A Most: cheddar cheese, Least: low-fat yogurt	
B 100	**E** 25
C 50	**F** 45
D 20	**G** 105

CHECK YOUR UNDERSTANDING, page 11

1. $5 + 6$ or $6 + 5$ 19. 600
2. $8 + b$ or $b + 8$ 20. 7,500
3. $7 - 3$ 21. 5,800
4. $14 - 8$ 22. 540
5. $3 + 6$ or $6 + 3$ 23. 3,430
6. $x + 6$ or $6 + x$ 24. 795
7. $18 - 9$ 25. 805
8. $18 - x$ 26. 61
9. $54 - 10$ 27. 91
10. $x - 10$ 28. 101
11. $r + 0.3$ or $0.3 + r$ 29. 241
12. $l + 15$ or $15 + l$ 30. 65
13. $h - 8$ 31. 85
14. $b + 75$ or $75 + b$ 32. 95
15. $b - 25$ 33. 445
16. $7 + a$ or $a + 7$ 34. $23 + 59 \approx 20 + 60 = 80$
17. $a - 7$ 35. $37 + 78 \approx 40 + 80 = 120$
18. 1,300   36. $17 + 52 \approx 20 + 50 = 70$

37. $188 + 521 \approx 200 + 500 = 700$

38. $375 + 283 \approx 400 + 300 = 700$

39. $1{,}212 + 2{,}111 \approx 1{,}000 + 2{,}000 = 3{,}000$

40. $79 - 43 \approx 80 - 40 = 40$

41. $98 - 33 \approx 100 - 30 = 70$

42. $437 - 109 \approx 400 - 100 = 300$

43. $3{,}988 - 1{,}756 \approx 4{,}000 - 2{,}000 = 2{,}000$

44. $4{,}102 - 1{,}444 \approx 4{,}000 - 1{,}000 = 3{,}000$

45. $976 - 622 \approx 1{,}000 - 600 = 400$

46. $5{,}987 + 3{,}421 \approx 6{,}000 + 3{,}000 = 9{,}000$

47. $49{,}822 - 24{,}788 \approx 50{,}000 - 25{,}000 = 25{,}000$

TEST-TAKING PRACTICE, page 12

1. (3) 1,584
$671 + 913 = 1{,}584$

2. (2) $520
$815 - 295 = 520$

3. 102

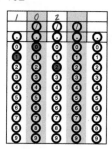

4. (2) 60

5. (5) 28
Minneapolis $132 -$ Reno $104 = 28$

Lesson 2

Grouping to Add More Than Two Numbers,
pages 13–24

MENTAL MATH			
1. 40		**4.** 90
2. 60		**5.** 70
3. 80		**6.** 40

1. Ⓐ $37 + (27 + 3)$
$37 + 30 = 67$

Ⓑ $(11 + 19) + 24$
$30 + 24 = 54$

Ⓒ $(6 + 14) + (13 + 7) + 56$
$(20 + 20) + 56 = 96$

2. Ⓐ $56 + (99 + 1)$
$56 + 100 = 156$

Ⓑ $(56 + 4) + 37$
$60 + 37 = 97$

Ⓒ $(17 + 3) + 24$
$20 + 24 = 44$

Ⓓ $15 + (9 + 21)$
$15 + 30 = 45$

Ⓔ $(15 + 5) + (26 + 4) + 32$
$20 + 30 + 32$
$50 + 32 = 82$

Ⓕ $(22 + 8) + (3 + 37) + 24$
$30 + 40 + 24$
$70 + 24 = 94$

3. Ⓐ $(23 + 7) + (9 + 11) + 42$
$30 + 20 + 42$
$50 + 42 = 92$

Ⓑ $(46 + 4) + (21 + 9) + 17$
$50 + 30 + 17$
$80 + 17 = 97$

Ⓒ $(12 + 18) + (4 + 26) + 53$
$30 + 30 + 53$
$60 + 53 = 113$

Ⓓ $(35 + 5) + (17 + 3) + 16$
$40 + 20 + 16$
$60 + 16 = 76$

4. Ⓐ $(6 + 4) + (5 + 9)$
$10 + 14 = 24$
  Ⓒ $(8 + 12) + 4 + x$
$20 + 4 + x = 24 + x$

Ⓑ $(7 + 3) + (5 + 4)$
$10 + 9 = 19$
  Ⓓ $(7 + 3) + 13 + x$
$10 + 13 + x = 23 + x$

5. Ⓐ $20 + 13 = 33$
  Ⓑ $20 + 18 = 38$

6. FIGURE A

Ⓐ $(12 + 13) + (6 + 6)$
$25 + 12 = 37$
  Ⓒ $(12 + 13) + (11 + 11)$
$25 + 22 = 47$

Ⓑ $(12 + 13) + (8 + 8)$
$25 + 16 = 41$

FIGURE B

Ⓐ $(6 + 6) + (6 + 6) + 6$
$12 + 12 + 6 = 30$

Ⓑ $(8 + 8) + (8 + 8) + 8$
$16 + 16 + 8 = 40$

Ⓒ $(11 + 11) + (11 + 11) + 11$
$22 + 22 + 11 = 55$

7. Ⓐ $x + y + 8$

Ⓑ $(4 + 6) + 8$
$10 + 8 = 18$

Ⓒ $5 + (7 + 8)$
$5 + 15 = 20$

USING DATA

Ⓐ The expression $x - 2$ represents the UK size.
$(12) - 2 = 10$

Ⓑ The expression $n - 18$ represents the U.S. size.
$(31) - 18 = 13$

8. Ⓐ

FRONT END:	$2 + $4 + $1 = $7
SECOND LOOK:	$2 + $4 + $1 = $7
CALCULATOR:	$7.83

Ⓑ

FRONT END:	$7 + $11 + 0 = $18
SECOND LOOK:	$7 + $12 + $1 = $20
CALCULATOR:	$20.14

Ⓒ

FRONT END:	$6 + $1 + $1 = $8
SECOND LOOK:	$6 + $2 + $2 = $10
CALCULATOR:	$10.27

9. Ⓐ about $5
$4.21 + $.84
$2.65 + $2.12

Ⓑ about $10
$9.15 + $.84
$4.21 + $5.89
$7.39 + $2.65
$7.68 + $2.12

Ⓒ about $15
$9.15 + $5.89
$12.30 + $2.65
$7.68 + $7.39
$11.09 + $4.21

CALCULATOR EXPLORATION

Ⓐ $.24, $0.01 + 0.01 + 0.01 + 0.01 + 0.1 + 0.1 = 0.24$

Ⓑ $.32, $0.1 + 0.1 + 0.1 + 0.01 + 0.01 = 0.32$

Ⓒ $.55, $0.5 + 0.01 + 0.01 + 0.01 + 0.01 + 0.01 = 0.55$

Ⓓ $.18, $0.05 + 0.05 + 0.05 + 0.01 + 0.01 + 0.01 = 0.18$

Ⓔ $.63, $0.5 + 0.05 + 0.05 + 0.01 + 0.01 + 0.01 = 0.63$

Ⓕ $.54, $0.25 + 0.25 + 0.01 + 0.01 + 0.01 + 0.01 = 0.54$

Ⓖ $.50, $0.1 + 0.1 + 0.1 + 0.1 + 0.05 + 0.05 = 0.50$

10.

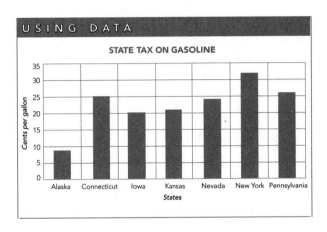

USING DATA

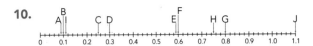

STATE TAX ON GASOLINE

11. Ⓐ 0.6   0.6**0** or 0.07? 60 is greater than 7.

Ⓑ 0.7   0.677 or 0.7**00**? 700 is greater than 677.

Ⓒ 0.2   0.04 or 0.2**0**? 20 is greater than 4.

Ⓓ 3.9   3.9**0** or 3.09? 390 is greater than 309.

Ⓔ 1.3   1.3**0** or 0.13? 130 is greater than 13.

Ⓕ 1.005   1.005 or 1.**000**? 1,005 is greater than 1,000.

Ⓖ 2   2.**00** or 0.50? 200 is greater than 50.

Ⓗ 70.8   70.8**0** or 7.08? 7,080 is greater than 708.

12. Ⓐ 8 is greater than 6   Ⓓ 10 is less than 40

Ⓑ 6 is less than 8   Ⓔ 1.6 is greater than 0.67

Ⓒ 40 is greater than 10   Ⓕ 7.2 is less than 10

13. Ⓐ $<$ Ⓔ $=$

Ⓑ $=$ Ⓕ $<$

Ⓒ $<$ Ⓖ $<$

Ⓓ $>$ Ⓗ $>$

14. Ⓑ $3.00 - 3.00 = 0$ Ⓕ $0.70 - 0.69 = 0.01$

Ⓒ $0.80 - 0.08 = 0.72$ Ⓖ $1.20 - 0.12 = 1.08$

Ⓓ $90.00 - 0.09 = 89.91$ Ⓗ $1.00 - 0.89 = 0.11$

Ⓔ $0.70 - 0.70 = 0$

CALCULATOR EXPLORATION

Ⓐ 5.04, −5.04   Ⓒ 2.2, −2.2

Ⓑ 0.15, −0.15   Ⓓ 0.17, −0.17

Using the calculator, subtract the two numbers. If the answer is positive, the first number that you entered is the greater one. If the answer is negative, the second number that you entered is greater.

15. Ⓐ Marcus
Ⓑ 25 miles
Ⓒ

Ben	Marcus
2	12
8	18
9	19
13	23
20	30

Ⓓ Pictures will vary
Ⓔ (3) $b + 10$

CHECK YOUR UNDERSTANDING, page 23

1. $(45 + 5) + (8 + 12) = 50 + 20 = 70$
2. $(21 + 9) + (3 + 17) + 16 = 30 + 20 + 16 = 66$
3. $(36 + 4) + (15 + 15) + 29 = 40 + 30 + 29 = 99$
4. $(19 + 11) + (8 + 32) + 56 = 30 + 40 + 56 = 126$
5. $(7 + 13) + 17 = 20 + 17 = 37$
6. $(27 + 23) + 35 + x = 50 + 35 + x = 85 + x$
7. $(4.5 + 4.5) + (3.1 + 6.9) = 9 + 10 = 19$
8. $(4.8 + 5.2) + 1.7 + x = 10 + 1.7 + x = 11.7 + x$
9. $22 + 18 + x = 40 + x$
10. Ⓐ $(22 + 18) + 16$
    $40 + 16 = 56$
    Ⓑ $(22 + 18) + 13$
    $40 + 13 = 53$
    Ⓒ $(22 + 18) + 17.7$
    $40 + 17.7 = 57.7$
11. $x + 3$
12. Ⓐ $24 + 3 = 27$ inches
    Ⓑ $32 + 3 = 35$ inches
    Ⓒ $18 + 3 = 21$ inches
13. All of the following estimates used rounding. You could also use front-end estimates.

    Ⓐ Estimate: ≈ $12.00
    $4 + $2 + $6 = $12
    Exact: $12.50

    Ⓑ Estimate: ≈ $43.00
    $15 + $23 + $5 = $43
    Exact: $42.99

    Ⓒ Estimate: ≈ $25.00
    $12 + $5 + $6 + $2 = $25
    Exact: $24.99

    Ⓓ Estimate: ≈ $24.00
    $3 + $13 + $7 + $1 = $24
    Exact: $24.14

14. Ⓐ ≈ 40 km (using rounding)
    $8 + 10 + 4 + 12 + 6 = 40$
    Ⓑ 39.85 km

15. Ⓐ >
Ⓑ <
Ⓒ >
Ⓓ =
Ⓔ >
Ⓕ >
Ⓖ <
Ⓗ >

16. Ⓐ $2 - 0.68 = 1.32$
Ⓑ $11 - 9.56 = 1.44$
Ⓒ $0.4 - 0.04 = 0.36$
Ⓓ $0.77 - 0.7 = 0.07$
Ⓔ $15 - 1.5 = 13.5$
Ⓕ $0.33 - 0.3 = 0.03$

TEST-TAKING PRACTICE, page 24

1. (5) $1.54
$1.47 + 0.03 + 0.04 = $1.54

2. 4.91
$20 - (4.79 + 2.95 + 7.35) = $4.91

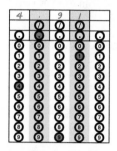

3. (4) 0.06, 0.2, 0.26, 6
0.06; 0.20; 0.26; 0.60

4. (4) $1.60

5. (5) 80
Honolulu $1.70 − Atlanta $.90 = $.80

Lesson 3

Equivalent Equations: Addition and Subtraction, pages 25–35

MENTAL MATH		
1. 59	4.	67
2. 46	5.	93
3. 39		

1. Ⓑ $9 + 3 = 12, 3 + 9 = 12, 12 - 3 = 9, 12 - 9 = 3$
   Ⓒ $6 + 7 = 13, 7 + 6 = 13, 13 - 6 = 7, 13 - 7 = 6$
   Ⓓ $7 + 9 = 16, 9 + 7 = 16, 16 - 7 = 9, 16 - 9 = 7$
2. Ⓐ $x + 9 = 17, 9 + x = 17, 17 - x = 9, 17 - 9 = x$
   Ⓑ $x + 7 = 12, 7 + x = 12, 12 - x = 7, 12 - 7 = x$
   Ⓒ $x + 8 = 13, 8 + x = 13, 13 - x = 8, 13 - 8 = x$
   Ⓓ $x + 6 = 14, 6 + x = 14, 14 - x = 6, 14 - 6 = x$
3. Ⓐ $12 - x = 8, 12 - 8 = x$
   Ⓑ $17 - x = 9, 17 - 9 = x$

$\quad$ C $\quad$ $15 - x = 12, 15 - 12 = x$
$\quad$ D $\quad$ $100 - x = 45, 100 - 45 = x$
$\quad$ E $\quad$ $30 - x = 29.9, 30 - 29.9 = x$
$\quad$ F $\quad$ $100 - x = 81, 100 - 81 = x$

4. A $\quad$ $17 - 9 = x, 9 + x = 17$
$\quad$ B $\quad$ $x = 20 - 15, 15 + x = 20$
$\quad$ C $\quad$ $x - 20 = 15, 20 + 15 = x$
$\quad$ D $\quad$ $x - 6 = 8, 8 + 6 = x$
$\quad$ E $\quad$ $x - 32 = 8, 32 + 8 = x$
$\quad$ F $\quad$ $75 - 40 = x, 40 + x = 75$

5. A $\quad$ $\$500 + x = \$1,125$ (Let x = what Andy needs to save)

$\quad$ B $\quad$ $\$100 - x = \$12$ (Let x = what LaTonya spent)

For problems 6 and 7, your equation does not have to be exactly the same as those given, but it must be equivalent.

6. A $\quad$ p = profit, $\$8 + p = \$49$
$\quad$ B $\quad$ m = miles of trip, $11,031.8 + m = 11,988.2$
$\quad$ C $\quad$ w = original weight, $w - 32 = 185$
$\quad$ D $\quad$ p = profit, $\$8,500 + p = \$9,999$

7. A $\quad$ $100 + 80 + x = 230$ $\quad$ B $\quad$ $567 = 121 + x$

8. A $\quad$ $x = 6$ $\qquad\qquad$ E $\quad$ $x = 8$
$\quad$ B $\quad$ $x = 60$ $\qquad\qquad$ F $\quad$ $n = 20$
$\quad$ C $\quad$ $x = 5$ $\qquad\qquad$ G $\quad$ $x = 11$
$\quad$ D $\quad$ $x = 75$ $\qquad\qquad$ H $\quad$ $p = 70$

9. A $\quad$ $100 + x = 125$ $\qquad$ D $\quad$ $x - 100 = 225$
$\qquad$ $125 - 100 = x$ $\qquad\quad$ $225 + 100 = x$
$\qquad$ $25 = x$ $\qquad\qquad\quad$ $325 = x$

$\quad$ B $\quad$ $100 - x = 70$ $\qquad$ E $\quad$ $p + 30 = 56$
$\qquad$ $100 - 70 = x$ $\qquad\quad$ $56 - 30 = p$
$\qquad$ $30 = x$ $\qquad\qquad\quad$ $26 = p$

$\quad$ C $\quad$ $x + 100 = 225$ $\qquad$ F $\quad$ $56 - p = 30$
$\qquad$ $225 - 100 = x$ $\qquad\quad$ $56 - 30 = p$
$\qquad$ $125 = x$ $\qquad\qquad\quad$ $26 = p$

10. These are solutions for problem 6.
$\quad$ A $\quad$ $p = \$49 - \$8$
$\qquad$ $p = \$41$

$\quad$ B $\quad$ $m = 11,988.2 - 11,031.8$
$\qquad$ $m = 956.4$ miles

$\quad$ C $\quad$ $w = 185 + 32$ $\qquad$ D $\quad$ $p = \$9,999 - \$8,500$
$\qquad$ $w = 217$ pounds $\qquad\quad$ $p = \$1,499$

These are solutions for problem 7.
$\quad$ A $\quad$ $x = 230 - 180$ $\qquad$ B $\quad$ $x = 567 - 121$
$\qquad$ $x = 50$ feet $\qquad\qquad$ $x = 446$ grams

11. A $\quad$ $x + 25 - 25 = 76 - 25$ $\;$ F $\quad$ $100 + 45 = x - 45 + 45$
$\qquad$ $x = 51$ $\qquad\qquad\qquad\qquad$ $145 = x$

$\quad$ B $\quad$ $y + 34 - 34 = 80 - 34$ $\;$ G $\quad$ $32 - 17 = 17 + x - 17$
$\qquad$ $y = 46$ $\qquad\qquad\qquad\qquad$ $15 = x$

$\quad$ C $\quad$ $51 + m - 51 = 99 - 51$ $\;$ H $\quad$ $y - 88 + 88 = 102 + 88$
$\qquad$ $m = 48$ $\qquad\qquad\qquad\qquad$ $y = 190$

$\quad$ D $\quad$ $x - 75 + 75 = 24 + 75$ $\;$ I $\quad$ $49 + 14 = n - 14 + 14$
$\qquad$ $x = 99$ $\qquad\qquad\qquad\qquad$ $63 = n$

$\quad$ E $\quad$ $m - 21 + 21 = 49 + 21$ $\;$ J $\quad$ $72 - 24 = b + 24 - 24$
$\qquad$ $m = 70$ $\qquad\qquad\qquad\qquad$ $48 = b$

12. (4) $\$109 - \$78 = p$

13. (4) $37 = 103 - m$

CHECK YOUR UNDERSTANDING, page 34

1. A $\quad$ $14.7 + 8 + x$

$\quad$ B $\quad$ $14.7 + 8 + x = 30$
$\qquad$ or $22.7 + x = 30$

$\quad$ C $\quad$ $x = 30 - 22.7$

$\quad$ D $\quad$ $x = 7.3$ inches

$\quad$ E $\quad$ $14.7 + 8 + 7.3 = 30$ true

2. A $\quad$ $x - 41 = 299$ $\qquad$ C $\quad$ 340 pounds $= x$
$\quad$ B $\quad$ $299 + 41 = x$ $\qquad$ D $\quad$ $340 - 41 = 299$ true

3. A $\quad$ $x - \$98 = \$64$ $\qquad$ C $\quad$ $x = \$162$
$\quad$ B $\quad$ $x = \$64 + \$98$ $\qquad$ D $\quad$ $\$162 - \$98 = \$64$ true

4. A $\quad$ $\$46,500 + p = \$90,000$
$\quad$ B $\quad$ $\$90,000 - \$46,500 = p$
$\quad$ C $\quad$ $\$43,500 = p$
$\quad$ D $\quad$ $46,500 + 43,500 = 90,000$ true

5. A $\quad$ $x = 15 - 4$ $\qquad$ C $\quad$ $x = 45 - 15$
$\quad$ B $\quad$ $y = 20 - 9$ $\qquad$ D $\quad$ $n = 35 - 30.5$

6. A $\quad$ $23 - 15 = a$ $\qquad$ D $\quad$ $t = 61 + 49$
$\qquad$ $8 = a$ $\qquad\qquad\qquad$ $t = 110$

$\quad$ B $\quad$ $x = 75 - 54$ $\qquad$ E $\quad$ $104 - 85 = p$
$\qquad$ $x = 21$ $\qquad\qquad\qquad$ $19 = p$

$\quad$ C $\quad$ $s = 68 - 39$ $\qquad$ F $\quad$ $138 + 32 = n$
$\qquad$ $s = 29$ $\qquad\qquad\qquad$ $170 = n$

7. A $\quad$ $62 + x - 62 = 81 - 62$
$\qquad$ $x = 19$

$\quad$ B $\quad$ $y + 47 - 47 = 55 - 47$
$\qquad$ $y = 8$

$\quad$ C $\quad$ $p - 66 + 66 = 15 + 66$
$\qquad$ $p = 81$

$\quad$ D $\quad$ $79 + 31 = m - 31 + 31$
$\qquad$ $110 = m$

TEST-TAKING PRACTICE, page 35

1. (4) $855 = 327 + x + 288$

2. (2) $15 = 5 + 7 + m$

3. 19

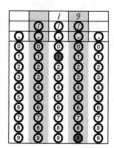

4. (2) 95

5. (3) $113 = 96 + d$

Skill Maintenance

Lessons 1–3, pages 36–37

Part One

1. Ⓐ $6 - 3$ Ⓓ $m + 1,250$
   Ⓑ $s + 23$ Ⓔ $f + 9$
   Ⓒ $p - 10$ Ⓕ $17 + n$

2. Ⓐ $(125 + 75) + (130 + 100)$
   $200 + 230 = 430$ ft

   Ⓑ $(12 + 8) + (10 + 6)$ Ⓒ $26 + 26 + 26$
   $20 + 16 = 36$ m $52 + 26 = 78$ in.

3. Ⓐ $1,000 - 650 = x$ Ⓒ $430 - 300 = x$
   Ⓑ $470 - 99 = y$

4. Ⓐ $675 + 300 = x$ Ⓒ $78 = x - 7$
   975 miles $= x$ $78 + 7 = x$
   $\$85 = x$

   Ⓑ $x + 200 = 925$ Ⓓ $20,320 = 5,910 + r$
   $x = 925 - 200$ $20,320 - 5,910 = r$
   $x = \$725$ $14,410$ ft $= r$

Part Two

1. (2) 0.15
   0.15; 0.17; 0.20; 1.10; 1.20

2. (4) $18
   Estimate: $14 + $3 + $1 = $18

3. 2,716
   $1,215 + 672 + 829 = 2,716$

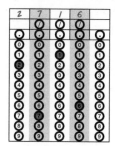

4. (4) 505
   Estimate: $1,200 - 700 = 500$
   Choice (4) 505 is closest to the estimate.

5. (5) 350
   The tip of the bar is halfway between 300 and 400.

6. (2) $433.00
   $233.12 - $980.12 + $1,180.00 = $433.00

7. (3) 557
   $150 + 150 + 100 + 157 = 557$ cm

Lesson 4

Geometry Topics, pages 38–47

MENTAL MATH	
1. $n = 140$	**4.** $n = 56$
2. $x = 145$	**5.** $c = 22$
3. $p = 95$	

1. Ⓐ right Ⓓ straight
   Ⓑ obtuse Ⓔ acute
   Ⓒ obtuse Ⓕ acute

2. acute

3. right

4. COMPLEMENT   SUPPLEMENT
   Ⓐ $20° + c = 90°$ $20° + s = 180°$
   $c = 90° - 20°$ $s = 180° - 20°$
   $c = 70°$ $s = 160°$

   Ⓑ $75° + c = 90°$ $75° + s = 180°$
   $c = 90° - 75°$ $s = 180° - 75°$
   $c = 15°$ $s = 105°$

   Ⓒ $115° + s = 180°$
   $s = 180° - 115°$
   $s = 65°$

D $42° + c = 90°$ $\qquad$ $42° + s = 180°$
$\quad c = 90° - 42°$ $\qquad$ $s = 180° - 42°$
$\quad c = 48°$ $\qquad\qquad$ $s = 138°$

5. $60°$

6. A $75°$ $\qquad\qquad$ **B** $65°$

7. $180° - m°$ or $180 - m$

CALCULATOR EXPLORATION

A $180 - (57 + 99) = 24$; $180 - 57 - 99 = 24$
$180 - 57 + 99 = 222$

B $180 - (11 + 47) = 122$; $180 - 11 - 47 = 122$
$180 - 11 + 47 = 216$

C $180 - 52 - 107 = 21$; $180 - (52 + 107) = 21$
$180 - 52 + 107 = 235$
$a - (b + c) = a - b - c$

---

8. $x + 90° + 30° = 180°$
$\quad x = 180° - 120°$
$\quad x = 60°$

9. A $m + 80° + 35° = 180°$
$\qquad m = 180° - 115°$
$\qquad m = 65°$

$\quad$ **B** $m + 110° + 22° = 180°$
$\qquad m = 180° - 132°$
$\qquad m = 48°$

$\quad$ **C** $m + 90° + 37° = 180°$
$\qquad m = 180° - 127°$
$\qquad m = 53°$

10. (3) $180° - (90° + x°)$

REASONING ACTIVITY

A $\angle BUV$ and $\angle AVC$

B $105°$, because together the two angles form a straight angle. $(105 + 75 = 180)$

C $105°$, because the angles are the three angles in a triangle. $(75 + 105 = 180)$; the answers are equal.

D $\angle BUV = 125°$ and $\angle 2 + \angle 3 = 125°$

E $\angle AVC = 130°$ and $\angle 1 + \angle 2 = 130°$

---

11. Answers will vary. One possible answer is the corner lines where the walls meet.

12. Answers will vary. One possible answer is a window frame.

13. A $\angle 1 \cong \angle 3$
$\qquad \angle 2 \cong \angle 4$

$\quad$ **B** $\angle 1 + \angle 2$
$\qquad \angle 2 + \angle 3$
$\qquad \angle 3 + \angle 4$
$\qquad \angle 4 + \angle 1$

$\quad$ **C** $35°$

14. A $\angle 2$ and $\angle 6$ $\qquad$ **C** $\angle 4$ and $\angle 8$
$\quad$ **B** $\angle 3$ and $\angle 7$

15. (2) $180° - 140°$

16. A $140°$ $\qquad\qquad$ **C** $40°$
$\quad$ **B** $40°$ $\qquad\qquad\;$ **D** $140°$

17. There are many different lines of reasoning possible to find these answers.
$\quad$ **A** $\angle 3 = 60°$ $\qquad$ **C** $\angle 8 = 25°$
$\quad$ **B** $\angle 4 = 95°$

CHECK YOUR UNDERSTANDING, page 46

1. $\angle MNO$, $\angle ONM$, $\angle N$

2. $\angle Q + \angle R = 180°$ and $\angle P + \angle O = 180°$

3. A $180° - 95° - 51° = \angle F$

$\quad$ **B** $34° = \angle F$

$\quad$ **C** $180° - 95° - x = \angle F$

$\quad$ **D** $180° - 90° - 27° = \angle E$
$\qquad 63° = \angle E$

$\quad$ **E** Both angles must be acute angles, and their measures must sum to $90°$.

4. corner $2 = 180° - 45° = 135°$

5. A $90° - 47° = x$ $\qquad$ **B** $180° - 47° = x$
$\qquad 43° = x$ $\qquad\qquad\qquad 133° = x$

6. $\angle 2 = 112°$

7. A $\angle 3 = 90°$
$\quad$ **B** $\angle 2 = 180° - 130° = 50°$
$\quad$ **C** $\angle 5 = 180° - (50° + 90°) = 40°$
$\quad$ **D** The sum of the angles in a triangle equal $180°$.
$\quad$ **E** Together, $\angle 4 + \angle 5 + \angle 6$ form a straight angle.

TEST-TAKING PRACTICE, page 47

1. (2) $67°$ $\quad$ The angles are supplementary angles.

2. (4) $45°$

3. (2) $\$642.25$

4. 88

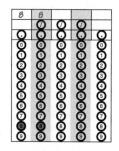

5. **(4)** $180 - (52 + x)$

Lesson 5

The Number Line and the Coordinate Grid,
pages 48–57

MENTAL MATH

1. less	**4.** greater
2. less	**5.** greater
3. greater	

1. Ⓐ 8   Ⓒ −25
     Ⓑ 0   Ⓓ −5.6

2. Ⓐ $-9 < -8$ Ⓔ $2 > -2$
     Ⓑ $5 < 6$ Ⓕ $5.4 < 5.5$
     Ⓒ $5 > -6$ Ⓖ $-5.4 > -5.5$
     Ⓓ $-5 > -6$ Ⓗ $-2 < -1.2$

3. Ⓐ $-15, -10, 3, 5, 9$ Ⓑ $-10, -9, -2, 0, 8$

4. Ⓐ $6 + 9 = 15$ Ⓒ $11 - 17 = -6$
     Ⓑ $15 - 9 = 6$ Ⓓ $(-6) - 9 = -15$

CALCULATOR EXPLORATION

$56 - (-43) = 99$	$(-16) - (-28) = 12$
$56 - 43 = 13$	$(-16) - 28 = -44$
$56 + 43 = 99$	$(-16) + 28 = 12$
$113 - (-176) = 289$	$45 - (-80) = 45 + 80 = 125$
$113 + 176 = 289$	
$113 - 176 = -63$	

5. Ⓐ 17°   Ⓒ 23°
     Ⓑ 22°   Ⓓ $-3° - 13° = x$
                               $-16° = x$

6. Ⓐ $15 - 27 = x$ Ⓓ $(-22) - 33 = k$
       $-12 = x$ $-55 = k$

     Ⓑ $(-34) + (-44) = n$ Ⓔ $-32 + 16 = b$
       $-78 = n$ $-16 = b$

     Ⓒ $47 + (-67) = x$ Ⓕ $(-18) - 4 = s$
       $-20 = x$ $-22 = s$

with a calculator:
     Ⓖ $x = -171$ Ⓙ $b = 430$
     Ⓗ $n = 138$ Ⓚ $m = -338$
     Ⓘ $y = 354$ Ⓛ $r = -102$

7.

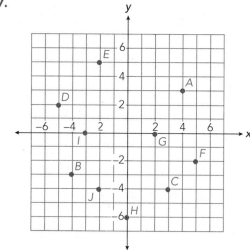

8. Ⓑ $(1, 9)$ Ⓘ $(-3, -4)$
     Ⓒ $(9, 1)$ Ⓙ $(3, -4)$
     Ⓓ $(6, 2)$ Ⓚ $(4, -3)$
     Ⓔ $(-3, 6)$ Ⓛ $(0, 5)$
     Ⓕ $(-5, 6)$ Ⓜ $(5, 0)$
     Ⓖ $(-6, 5)$ Ⓝ $(-6, 0)$
     Ⓗ $(-1, 3)$ Ⓟ $(0, -7)$

9. Ⓐ $(4, 0)$ Ⓒ $(-3, -2)$
     Ⓑ $(1, 4)$ Ⓓ $(-8, 5)$

10. $(1, 3)$

CHECK YOUR UNDERSTANDING, page 56

1. Ⓐ $7 > 2$ Ⓔ $-7 < -2$
     Ⓑ $-3 > -4$ Ⓕ $0 < 9$
     Ⓒ $0 > -9$ Ⓖ $7 > 6.5$
     Ⓓ $-7 < 6.5$ Ⓗ $-7 < -6.5$

2. Ⓐ $15° - 18° = x$ Ⓓ $-4° + 31° = x$
       $-3° = x$ $27° = x$

     Ⓑ 16°   Ⓔ $(-2°) - n°$

     Ⓒ 11°

3. Ⓐ $25 - 34 = k$
$-9 = k$

Ⓑ $57 + (-45) = m$
$12 = m$

Ⓒ $-75 + 21 = n$
$-54 = n$

Ⓓ $-39 + 103 = x$
$64 = x$

Ⓔ $48 - (-48) = n$
$96 = n$

Ⓕ $(-72) - 128 = p$
$-200 = p$

4. Ⓐ $(3, 4)$
Ⓑ $(0, 5)$
Ⓒ $(-3, 4)$
Ⓓ $(-4, 3)$
Ⓔ $(-5, 0)$

Ⓕ $(-3, -4)$
Ⓖ $(0, -5)$
Ⓗ $(4, -3)$
Ⓘ $(5, 0)$

5.

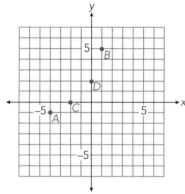

TEST-TAKING PRACTICE, page 57

1. **(5)** $-4 > -14$

2. **(3)** $(0, -4)$

3. **(3)** $-3°$
10°F is 13° higher than -3°F.

4. **(4)** $(3, -4)$

Lesson 6

Test-Taking Tips, pages 58–63

MENTAL MATH	
1. 1,300	**6.** -100
2. 78	**7.** 96
3. 84	**8.** -35
4. 140	**9.** 540
5. 296	**10.** -20

CHECK YOUR SKILLS

1. **(4)** 0.9, 0.95, 1.01, 1.11, 1.2
STEP 1 add zeros to give the numbers the same number of decimal places.
1.01, 0.90, 1.20, 0.95, 1.11
STEP 2 Order from least to greatest.
0.90, 0.95, 1.01, 1.11, 1.20

2. **(2)** April 25
$18 + 7$(days in one week) $= 25$

3. **(4)** $x - 35$
present weight – weight to lose

4. **(3)** 368
Estimate:
STEP 1 $331 + 37 \approx$
$330 + 40 = 370$ ft
STEP 2 370 is the closest
to answer choice **(3)** 368.

Picture the situation:

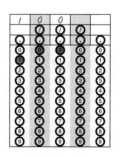

Use the calculator: $331 - (-37) = 368$

5. 100
$(29 + 11) + (25 + 35)$
$40 + 60 = 100$

6.

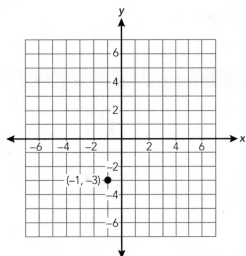

7. (3) 82°
180° − 45° − 53° = x (straight angle)
Estimate: 45° + 53° ≈ 100°
180° − 100° = 80°
Answer choice (3) 82° is the closest.
Or solve the equation:
180° − 98° = x
82° = x

8. (3) 74°
∠2 + ∠4 + ∠5 = 180°
53° + 53° + x = 180°
Estimate: 53° + 53° ≈ 100°
180° − 100° = 80°
Answer choice (3) 74° is the closest.
Or solve the equation:
106° + x = 180°
x = 180° − 106° = 74°

9. (3) 29

Lesson 7

"Seeing" Multiplication and Division,
pages 64–76

MENTAL MATH	
1. 8	**4.** 28
2. 15	**5.** 50
3. 20	

1. Answers will vary.

2. Answers will vary.

3. Ⓐ 8 × 6 or 6 × 8

Ⓑ 40 ÷ 20 or 20$\overline{)40}$ or $\frac{40}{20}$

Ⓒ 36 ÷ 4 or 4$\overline{)36}$ or $\frac{36}{4}$

Ⓓ 3 × 500 or 500 × 3

4. Ⓒ and Ⓓ had different answers.

5.

EQUIVALENT FORMS	NUMBERS AND WORDS
Ⓐ $\frac{21}{7}$ or 7$\overline{)21}$	21 divided by 7
Ⓑ 21 − 7	21 minus 7
Ⓒ 20 × x or 20(x) or 20 • x	20 times x
Ⓓ 3$\overline{)m}$ or m ÷ 3	m divided by 3
Ⓔ 4 + 15 or 15 + 4	4 plus 15
Ⓕ 36 ÷ 6 or $\frac{36}{6}$	36 divided by 6

6. Ⓐ 32 ÷ 8 or $\frac{32}{8}$ or 8$\overline{)32}$

Ⓑ 8 ÷ 32 or $\frac{8}{32}$ or 32$\overline{)8}$

Ⓒ 32 ÷ b or $\frac{32}{b}$ or b$\overline{)32}$

Ⓓ 8 ÷ x or $\frac{8}{x}$ or x$\overline{)8}$

Ⓔ 6 × 3 or 6(3)

Ⓕ 6 + 3 or 3 + 6

Ⓖ 6 ÷ 3 or $\frac{6}{3}$ or 3$\overline{)6}$

Ⓗ 6 − 3

Many people find it more difficult to write the mathematical expressions that have to be written in a different order than the words.

7.

EXPRESSION	REASON
Ⓐ 5 × 10	combining equal groups
Ⓑ 20 ÷ 5 or $\frac{20}{5}$	separating into equal groups
Ⓒ 36 ÷ 12 or $\frac{36}{12}$	separating into equal groups
Ⓓ 3y	combining equal groups
Ⓔ 2 × 12	combining equal groups
Ⓕ 12x	combining equal groups
Ⓖ 100 ÷ 25 or $\frac{100}{25}$	separating into equal groups
Ⓗ 125 ÷ 25 or $\frac{125}{25}$	separating into equal groups

8. Ⓐ 10,000   Ⓘ 0.0001
    Ⓑ 0   Ⓙ 0
    Ⓒ 10,000   Ⓚ 0
    Ⓓ 9,999   Ⓛ 10,000
    Ⓔ undefined   Ⓜ n
    Ⓕ 10,001   Ⓝ n
    Ⓖ 10,000   Ⓞ 0
    Ⓗ 10,000   Ⓟ 0

9. Ⓐ 1,200   Ⓖ 720,000
    Ⓑ 5,400   Ⓗ 1,700
    Ⓒ 3,200   Ⓘ 300
    Ⓓ 80   Ⓙ 7
    Ⓔ 300   Ⓚ 400,000
    Ⓕ 30,000   Ⓛ 500

CALCULATOR EXPLORATION

Ⓐ The numbers, 432 and 540 are divisible by 36.

Ⓑ The numbers 910, 990 and 300 are divisible by 10. If the last digit of a number is zero, the number is divisible by 10

Ⓒ The numbers 910, 345, 990 and 305 are multiples of 5.

    If the last digit of a number is 0 or 5, the number is divisible by 5.

Ⓓ The numbers 910, 996, 322, 308 and 144 are divisible by 2.

    If the last digit of a number is *even* (0, 2, 4, 6, 8), the number is a multiple of 2.

Ⓔ The numbers 345, 996, 144, 441, and 12,543 are divisible by 3.

Ⓕ The numbers 117, 144, 441, 585, 9,468 and 47,520 are divisible by 9.

---

10. Your estimated answers do not have to be exactly the same as those listed.

Ⓐ $3 \times 49 \approx 3 \times 50 = 150$, Exact: 147

Ⓑ $8 \times 411 \approx 8 \times 400 = 3,200$, Exact: 3,288

Ⓒ $769 \times 7 \approx 800 \times 7 = 5,600$, Exact: 5,383

Ⓓ $53 \times 78 \approx 50 \times 80 = 4,000$, Exact: 4,134

Ⓔ $92 \times 39 \approx 90 \times 40 = 3,600$, Exact: 3,588

Ⓕ $27 \times 63 \approx 30 \times 60 = 1,800$, Exact: 1,701

Ⓖ $\$6.18 \times 43 \approx \$6 \times 40 = \$240$, Exact: $265.74

Ⓗ $\$24.75 \times 105 \approx \$25 \times 100 = \$2,500$, Exact: $2,598.75

11. (4) 2,160

    Estimate: $20 \times 100 = 2,000$
    Choice (4) is the only close answer.

12. EASIER   SOLUTION

Ⓐ $\dfrac{200}{4}$ 50

Ⓑ $\dfrac{880}{8}$ 110

Ⓒ $\dfrac{1,200}{60}$ 20

Ⓓ $\dfrac{1,600}{40}$ 40

13. Ⓐ $\dfrac{418}{7} \approx \dfrac{420}{7} = 60$ Ⓕ $\dfrac{1,486}{500} \approx \dfrac{1,500}{500} = 3$

    Ⓑ $\dfrac{1,823}{3} \approx \dfrac{1,800}{3} = 600$ Ⓖ $\dfrac{1,221}{40} \approx \dfrac{1,200}{40} = 30$

    Ⓒ $\dfrac{537}{9} \approx \dfrac{540}{9} = 60$ Ⓗ $\dfrac{1,221}{400} \approx \dfrac{1,200}{400} = 3$

    Ⓓ $\dfrac{779}{4} \approx \dfrac{800}{4} = 200$ Ⓘ $\dfrac{12,211}{4,000} \approx \dfrac{12,000}{4,000} = 3$

    Ⓔ $\dfrac{1,486}{50} \approx \dfrac{1,500}{50} = 30$

14. PROBLEM   FACT

Ⓐ $\dfrac{230}{3} \approx \dfrac{240}{3} = 80$ $24 \div 3 = 8$

Ⓑ $\dfrac{621}{8} \approx \dfrac{640}{8} = 80$ $64 \div 8 = 8$

Ⓒ $\dfrac{1,853}{3} \approx \dfrac{1,800}{3} = 600$ $18 \div 3 = 6$

Ⓓ $\dfrac{2,234}{3} \approx \dfrac{2100}{3} = 700$ $21 \div 3 = 7$

Ⓔ $\dfrac{3,816}{6} \approx \dfrac{3,600}{6} = 600$ $36 \div 6 = 6$

Ⓕ $\dfrac{443}{5} \approx \dfrac{450}{5} = 90$ $45 \div 5 = 9$

Ⓖ $\dfrac{745}{9} \approx \dfrac{720}{9} = 80$ $72 \div 9 = 8$

15. (3) $1,254

    Estimate: $\dfrac{\$6,270}{5} \approx \dfrac{\$6,000}{5} = \$1,200$

    Choice (3) $1,254 is closest to the estimate.

CHECK YOUR UNDERSTANDING, page 75

1. Ⓐ 2(12) or 2 × 12 or 2 • 12

    Ⓑ $\dfrac{42}{3}$ or 42 ÷ 3

    Ⓒ 7 × 21 or 7 • 21 or 7(21)

    Ⓓ $\dfrac{104}{52}$ or 104 ÷ 52

    Ⓔ $\dfrac{72}{6}$ or 72 ÷ 6

    Ⓕ 100y or 100 × y or 100(y) or 100 • y

    Ⓖ 2p or 2 × p or 2(p) or 2 • p

2. Ⓐ $\dfrac{2,600,000}{10}$ Ⓑ $260,000

3. Ⓐ 500 × 8   Ⓑ 4,000 sheets

4. Ⓐ 450 + 350   Ⓑ 800 calories

5. Ⓐ $\dfrac{\$1,000}{\$200}$ Ⓑ 5 payments

6. 30*n*

7. Ⓐ 420
  Ⓑ 4,200
  Ⓒ 42,000
  Ⓓ 420,000
  Ⓔ 1,300
  Ⓕ 60
  Ⓖ 600
  Ⓗ 30
  Ⓘ 30
  Ⓙ 30
  Ⓚ 3,000
  Ⓛ 1,600
  Ⓜ 3,000
  Ⓝ 30,000

8. Ⓐ 140, 1,200
  Ⓑ 140, 765, 405, 1,200
  Ⓒ 140, 258, 602, 1,200
  Ⓓ 765, 258, 405, 1,200

9. Your estimated answers do not have to be exactly the same as those listed.

Ⓐ 7(683) ≈ 7(700) = 4,900

Ⓑ 3(926) ≈ 3(900) = 2,700

Ⓒ 43 × 68 ≈ 40 × 70 = 2,800

Ⓓ 92(79) ≈ 90(80) = 7,200

Ⓔ 98 × 438 ≈ 100 × 400 = 40,000

Ⓕ $\frac{566}{3} ≈ \frac{600}{3} = 200$

Ⓖ 4,188 ÷ 6 ≈ 4,200 ÷ 6 = 700

Ⓗ 733 + 319 ≈ 700 + 300 = 1,000

Ⓘ 1,010 − 397 ≈ 1,000 − 400 = 600

Ⓙ $\frac{532}{9} ≈ 540 ÷ 9 = 60$

Ⓚ $\frac{532}{8} ≈ 560 ÷ 8 = 70$

Ⓛ $\frac{532}{5} ≈ 550 ÷ 5 = 110$

10. Ⓐ 2,499; 1,500
  Ⓑ 2,049; 1,950

TEST-TAKING PRACTICE, page 76

1. (3) 1,296 miles
  Estimate: 27 miles per gallon × 48 gallons ≈ 30 × 50 = 1,500
  1,500 miles is closest to answer choice (3) 1,296.

2. (4) $\frac{2,000}{40}$
  2,000 pounds/40 pounds per carton = cartons

3. (4) $7.98
  5 fans × $.03 = $.15 × 7 days = $1.05
  1 air conditioner $1.29 × 7 days = $9.03
  9.03 − 1.05 = 7.98

4. 1,250
  250 × 5 = 1,250

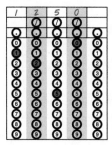

5. (3) 11
  2,750 ÷ 250 = 11

Lesson 8

Measurement: Multiplying More Than Two Numbers, pages 77–87

MENTAL MATH	
1. 589	**4.** 589
2. 589	**5.** undefined
3. 589	**6.** 1

1. Answers will vary.

2. Ⓐ miles
  Ⓑ feet or yards
  Ⓒ square yards
  Ⓓ cubic feet

3. Ⓐ 44 m² or 44 square meters
  Ⓑ 480 sq in.
  Ⓒ 27 cm² or 27 square centimeters
  Ⓓ 40 sq ft

REASONING ACTIVITY

Ⓐ Some possible rectangles would measure 12 by 2, 6 by 4, and 8 by 3.

Ⓑ Possible sentences: (1) 24 is divisible by each and every dimension, 2, 3, 4, 6, 8, and 12, as well as 24 and 1; or (2) All the dimensions, 2, 3, 4, 6, 8, and 12, are factors of 24 along with 24 and 1.

Ⓒ 5 is not a factor of 24.

Ⓓ There are many possibilities: 24 × 48, 24 × 72, 48 × 72. Both dimensions must be a multiple of both 8 and 12.

Ⓔ 63. Think of 20, the common multiple of 4 and 5. Count by 20s, looking for the one that, when you add 3, gives a multiple of 9.

4. The formula says to multiply the length (l) by the width (w) to find the area (A). This is what we have been doing in the previous problems when we found the number of squares.

5. ⓐ 2.9 ft × 19.5 ft ≈ 3 ft × 20 ft = 60 sq ft

   ⓑ 2.9 ft × 19.5 ft = 56.55 sq ft

   ⓒ In this case, you would probably use the estimate so you wouldn't take the chance of running short of tiles.

6. (4) $A = 2(5)$

   This expression represents multiplying the length by the width.

7. ⓐ 9 ft × 7 ft = 63 sq ft
   ⓑ 6 mm × 11 mm = 66 mm²
   ⓒ 7 m × 4 m = 28 m²
   ⓓ 5 in. × 8 in. = 40 sq in.

8. The formula says to multiply the base (b) by the height (h) to get the area (A). This is exactly what we have been doing.

9. (5) $(10 \times 7) - (10 \times 4)$

   This represents subtracting to find the difference between the areas.
   $(l \times w) - (b \times h)$
   $(10 \times 7) - (10 \times 4)$

10. ⓐ $A = \frac{1}{2}bh$
    $A = \frac{1}{2} \times 25 \times 12$
    $A = (\frac{1}{2} \times 12) \times 25$
    $A = 6 \times 25$
    $A = 150$ sq in.

    ⓒ $A = \frac{1}{2}bh$
    $A = \frac{1}{2} \times 12 \times n$
    $A = 6n$ sq ft

    ⓑ $A = \frac{1}{2}bh$
    $A = (\frac{1}{2} \times 20) \times 33$
    $A = 10 \times 33$
    $A = 330$ m²

11. ⓐ (2) 12 sq ft
    $A = \frac{1}{2} \times (6 \times 4)$
    $A = \frac{1}{2} \times 24 = 12$

    ⓑ (3) 16 ft
    $P = 5 + 5 + 6$
    $P = 16$

12. ⓐ A of rectangle = lw
    $A = 5 \times 2 = 10$ m²

    2 m
    5 m

    A of triangle = $\frac{1}{2}bh$
    $A = \frac{1}{2}(2 \times 1)$
    $A = \frac{1}{2}(2) = 1$ m²

    2 m
    |1 m|

    Total area: 10 m² + 1 m² = 11 m²

    ⓑ A of rectangle = lw
    $A = 11 \times 4 = 44$ sq in.

    4 in.
    11 in.

    A of triangle = $\frac{1}{2}bh$
    $A = \frac{1}{2}(11 \times 2) = 11$ sq in.

    11 in.
    2 in.

    Shaded area: 44 sq in. − 11 sq in. = 33 sq in.

    ⓒ A of first rectangle = lw
    $A = 12 \times 2 = 24$ sq in.

    12 in.
    2 in.

    A of second rectangle = lw
    $A = 10 \times 3 = 30$ sq in.

    2 in.
    3 in.
    10 in.

    Add: 24 sq in. + 30 sq in. = 54 sq in.

    ⓓ A of first rectangle = lw
    $A = 16 \times 10 = 160$ sq ft

    16 ft
    10 ft

    A of second rectangle = lw
    $A = 8 \times 12 = 96$ sq ft
    Subtract:
    160 sq ft − 96 sq ft = 64 sq ft

    16 ft
    2 ft
    10 ft
    2 ft   2 ft

13. ⓐ $11 \times (2 \times 4) = 88$ m³
    ⓑ $x \times (9 \times 5) = 45x$ cu ft
    ⓒ $9 \times (10 \times 3) = 270$ cm³
    ⓓ $(24 \times 10) \times n = 240n$ cu in.

14. (4) 7,776
    $18 \times (12 \times 36)$
    $18 \times 432 = 7,776$ cu in.

15. ⓐ $(2 \times 5) \times 57 = 570$
    ⓑ $(5 \times 6) \times 13 = 390$
    ⓒ $(4 \times 25) \times 89 = 8,900$
    ⓓ $(2 \times 50) \times 44 = 4,400$
    ⓔ $(4 \times 5) \times 41 = 820$
    ⓕ $(2 \times 15) \times 22 = 660$

16. **Ⓐ** $58 \times 2 = 116$

  double 50 = 100
  double 8 = + 16
     116

Ⓑ $\frac{58}{2} = 29$

  half of 50 = 25
  half of 8 = + 4
     29

Ⓒ $127 \times 2 = 254$

  double 100 = 200
  double 20 = 40
  double 7 = + 14
      254

Ⓓ $\frac{284}{2} = 142$

  half of 200 = 100
  half of 80 = 40
  half of 4 = + 2
      142

Ⓔ $177 \times 2 = 354$

  double 100 = 200
  double 70 = 140
  double 7 = + 14
      354

Ⓕ $\frac{76}{2} = 38$

  half of 60 = 30
  half of 16 = + 8
      38

CHECK YOUR UNDERSTANDING, page 86

1. **Ⓐ** 1 yd = 3 × 12 in. = 36 in.

  Ⓑ 1 mi = 5,280 ft ÷ 3 = 1,760 yd

  Ⓒ 1 sq ft = 12 in. × 12 in. = 144 sq in.

  Ⓓ 1 sq yd = 3 ft × 3 ft = 9 sq ft

2. **Ⓐ** $A = lw$
  $A = 12 \bullet 7 = 84 \text{ cm}^2$

  Ⓑ $A = \frac{1}{2}bh$

  $A = (\frac{1}{2} \times 8) \times 15$

  $A = 4 \times 15 = 60 \text{ sq in.}$

  Ⓒ $A = \frac{1}{2}bh$

  $A = \frac{1}{2}(11 \times 11)$

  $A = \frac{1}{2}(121)$

  $A = 60.5 \text{ m}^2$

Ⓓ total area =
  area of **1** + area of **2**
  = (15 × 7) + (4 × 5)
  = 105 + 20 = 125 m²

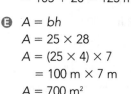

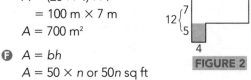

FIGURE 1

Ⓔ $A = bh$
  $A = 25 \times 28$
  $A = (25 \times 4) \times 7$
  $ = 100 \text{ m} \times 7 \text{ m}$
  $A = 700 \text{ m}^2$

FIGURE 2

Ⓕ $A = bh$
  $A = 50 \times n$ or $50n$ sq ft

Ⓖ $A = bh$
  $A = 9 \times 16$
  $A = 144 \text{ mm}^2$

Ⓗ total area = area of ☐ + area of △

  $= (20 \times 25) + (\frac{1}{2} \times 10 \times 25)$

  = 500 + 125

  = 625 sq ft

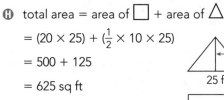

3. **Ⓐ** 3 + 3 + 1 = 7 yd

  Ⓑ $A = \frac{1}{2}bh$

  $A = \frac{1}{2} \bullet 1 \bullet 2.5 = 1.25 \text{ sq yd}$

4. **Ⓐ** $A = lw - lw$
  $A = (9 \times 5) - (3 \times 2) = 39 \text{ sq yd}$

  Ⓑ 9 cu yd

5. **Ⓐ** 24 + 10 + 24 + 10 = 68 cm

  Ⓑ $24 \times 10 = 240 \text{ cm}^2$

  Ⓒ $V = lwh$
  $V = (24 \times 10) \times 30$
  $V = 240 \times 30$
  $V = 7,200 \text{ cm}^3$

TEST-TAKING PRACTICE, page 87

1. 7
  $3 \times 4 \times 7 = 84$

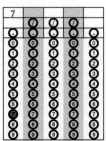

2. (3) $V = 9 \times 5 \times 2$

$V = lwh$

$V = (9 \text{ in.}) \times (5 \text{ in.}) \times (2 \text{ in.})$

3. (2) $(1, 4)$

4. (4) 21

$A = \frac{1}{2} \times b \times h$

$\frac{1}{2} \times 6 \times 7 = 21$

5. (1) 256

$lw - lw$

$(44 \times 24) - (20 \times 40)$

$1,056 - 800$

256 m^2

Lesson 9

Equivalent Equations:
Multiplication and Division, pages 88–99

MENTAL MATH	
1. 108	**4.** 800
2. 342	**5.** 700
3. 360	**6.** 2,900

1. Ⓐ $5 \times \$14 = \$70$

Ⓑ $10 \times \$14 = \$140$

Ⓒ $70 \times \$14 = \$980$

Ⓓ Multiply \$14 by the number of CDs.

2. Ⓐ About \$112 (a little above \$110)

Ⓑ 7 CDs

Ⓒ Since the problem asks how many 14s there are in \$100, you would divide: $\frac{100}{14}$.

Ⓓ Divide the total cost by 14.

3. Ⓐ $5 \times 250 = 1,250$ miles

Ⓑ $10 \times 250 = 2,500$ miles

Ⓒ Multiply 250 by the number of hours.

Ⓓ $250n$

4. Ⓐ 2,000 miles (move up from 8, then over to 2,000)

Ⓑ Since 1,500 falls between 1,400 and 1,600, start between those lines. Move over to the diagonal line, then down to 6 hours.

Ⓒ Since the problem asks how many 250s there are in 1,500, you would divide: $\frac{1,500}{250}$.

Ⓓ Divide the distance by 250.

5. Ⓐ $9 \times 6 = 54$, $6 \times 9 = 54$, $\frac{54}{9} = 6$, $\frac{54}{6} = 9$

Ⓑ $9x = 54$, $x(9) = 54$, $\frac{54}{9} = x$, $\frac{54}{x} = 9$

Ⓒ $20 \times 5 = 100$, $5 \times 20 = 100$, $\frac{100}{5} = 20$, $\frac{100}{20} = 5$

Ⓓ $20 \times 5 = n$, $5 \times 20 = n$, $\frac{n}{20} = 5$, $\frac{n}{5} = 20$

6. Ⓐ $6 \times n = 72$, $\frac{72}{6} = n$

Ⓑ $2t = 128$, $\frac{128}{t} = 2$

Ⓒ $5(600) = p$, $\frac{p}{600} = 5$

Ⓓ $24m = 1,200$, $\frac{1,200}{m} = 24$

7. Ⓐ $w = \frac{45}{9}$ Ⓕ $n = \frac{75}{15}$

Ⓑ $k = \frac{8}{96}$ Ⓖ $m = 125(10)$

Ⓒ $p = \frac{39}{13}$ Ⓗ $b = \frac{105}{21}$

Ⓓ $x = \frac{95}{5}$ Ⓘ $w = 6(9)$

Ⓔ $t = \frac{99}{11}$

8. Ⓐ $n = \frac{c}{r}$, $r = \frac{c}{n}$ Ⓒ $n = \frac{350}{14} = 25$

Ⓑ $n = \frac{280}{14}$

9. Ⓐ $r = \frac{d}{t}$, $t = \frac{d}{r}$ Ⓒ $t = \frac{1,500}{250} = 6$

Ⓑ $t = \frac{750}{250}$

10. Ⓐ $d = rt$ or $t = \frac{d}{r}$

$90 = 20t$ $t = \frac{90}{20}$

$t = \frac{90}{20}$ $t = 4.5$ hours

$t = 4.5$ hours

Check: $20 \times 4.5 = 90$

Ⓑ Not enough information is given. You could have figured how much time had passed, but not what time it was when he finished.

Ⓒ $c = nr$ or $r = \frac{c}{n}$

$69 = 25r$ $r = \frac{69}{25}$

$r = \frac{69}{25}$ $r = 2.8$¢

$r = 2.8$¢ or \$.028

Check: $25(\$.028) = \$.70$

Ⓓ $d = rt$

$d = 8.5(1.4)$

$d = 11.9$ km

Check: $8.5(1.4) = 11.9$

Ⓔ $r = \frac{c}{n}$ $\frac{1.00}{7} = 0.14$

F $n = \frac{c}{r}$ $\frac{10.00}{1.25} = 8$

  $8(2) = 16$

11. Ⓐ $5z = 60$

  $\frac{5z}{5} = \frac{60}{5}$

  $z = 12$

  Check: $5(12) = 60$

Ⓓ $15 = \frac{x}{30}$

  $30(15) = 30(\frac{x}{30})$

  $450 = x$

  Check: $15 = \frac{450}{30}$

Ⓑ $78 = 6y$

  $\frac{78}{6} = \frac{6y}{6}$

  $13 = y$

  Check: $78 = 6(13)$

Ⓔ $364 = 14t$

  $\frac{364}{14} = \frac{14t}{14}$

  $26 = t$

  Check: $364 = 14(26)$

Ⓒ $\frac{p}{7} = 14$

  $7(\frac{p}{7}) = 7(14)$

  $p = 98$

  Check: $\frac{98}{7} = 14$

Ⓕ $88x = 2,024$

  $\frac{88x}{88} = \frac{2,024}{88}$

  $x = 23$

  Check: $88(23) = 2,024$

12.

price per gallon (r)	total cost (c)
.50	$ 6.00
.75	$ 9.00
.85	$10.20
.99	$11.88
1.00	$12.00
1.50	$18.00
2.00	$24.00
3.00	$36.00

13. Ⓐ It increases.
 Ⓑ less than
 Ⓒ $12
 Ⓓ less than, greater than

14. Ⓐ greater than
 Ⓑ less than
 Ⓒ less than
 Ⓓ greater than
 Ⓔ greater than

15.

price per lb (r)	number of lb (n)
.50	24
.75	16
1.00	12
4.00	3
6.00	2
12.00	1
24.00	0.5

16. Ⓐ decreases
 Ⓑ greater
 Ⓒ less
 Ⓓ 1
 Ⓔ greater, less, 1

17. Ⓐ greater than
 Ⓑ less than
 Ⓒ less than
 Ⓓ greater than

18. Ⓐ −72
 Ⓑ −84
 Ⓒ 90
 Ⓓ 121
 Ⓔ 160
 Ⓕ −1,700

19. Ⓐ −25
 Ⓑ −8
 Ⓒ 24
 Ⓓ −50
 Ⓔ −25
 Ⓕ 21

20. Ⓐ (3) $6.00
 Ⓑ

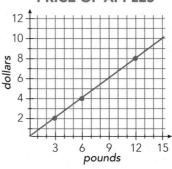

PRICE OF APPLES

Ⓒ 7.5 pounds; find $5 on the vertical axis, follow straight across to the line and then go straight down to halfway between 7 and 8.

Ⓓ $0.67; $c = .67n$

CHECK YOUR UNDERSTANDING, page 98

1. $\frac{40}{8} = 5$

  $\frac{40}{5} = 8$

2. Ⓐ $c = (6)($24.99)$
 Ⓑ $c = 149.94

3. Ⓐ $r = \frac{$186}{6}$
 Ⓑ $r = 31

4. Ⓐ $A = lw$
  $84 = 7w$
 Ⓒ $12 \text{ ft} = w$

 Ⓑ $\frac{84}{7} = w$

5. Ⓐ total savings = number of weeks × weekly savings
  $1,000 = w × 50

 Ⓑ $\frac{1,000}{50} = w$
  $20 \text{ weeks} = w$

6. Ⓐ $c = 1.2($2.45)$

 Ⓑ The cost will be greater than $2.45 because the package weighs more than 1 pound.

7. Ⓐ $d = rt$ Ⓒ $c = nr$
$d = 50t$ $\frac{c}{n} = r$
 $\frac{\$n}{12} = r$

Ⓑ $c = nr$
$\frac{c}{r} = n$
$\frac{\$12}{\$b} = n$

8. $\$19.95 \times 5 = \$99.75$

9. Ⓐ 120 Ⓔ −77
Ⓑ −80 Ⓕ 31
Ⓒ 4 Ⓖ −900
Ⓓ −18 Ⓗ −960

10. Ⓐ $t - 27 = 51$
$t - 27 + 27 = 51 + 27$
$t = 78$
Check: $78 - 27 = 51$

Ⓑ $14x = 210$
$\frac{14x}{14} = \frac{210}{14}$
$x = 15$
Check: $14(15) = 210$

Ⓒ $m + 25 = 25$
$m + 25 - 25 = 25 - 25$
$m = 0$
Check: $0 + 25 = 25$

Ⓓ $t + 30 = 25$
$t + 30 - 30 = 25 - 30$
$t = -5$
Check: $(-5) + 30 = 25$

Ⓔ $\frac{n}{17} = 17$
$17(\frac{n}{17}) = 17(17)$
$n = 289$
Check: $\frac{189}{17} = 17$

Ⓕ $\frac{y}{17} = -1$
$17(\frac{y}{17}) = 17(-1)$
$y = -17$
Check: $\frac{-17}{17} = -1$

Ⓖ $12x = -108$
$\frac{12x}{12} = \frac{-108}{12}$
$x = -9$
Check: $12(-9) = -108$

Ⓗ $36d = -1,800$
$\frac{36d}{36} = \frac{-1,800}{36}$
$d = -50$
Check: $36(-50) = -1,800$

TEST-TAKING PRACTICE, page 99

1. 7
$\frac{3,640}{520} = 7$ hours

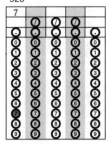

2. (4) $\frac{\$49.95 \leftarrow \text{total cost}}{x \leftarrow \text{number of items}}$

3. (2) $(0.8)(2)(5)$
Tracy walks 0.8 of a mile each way,
5 times a week.

4. (4) 28
$\frac{1,000}{36} = 27.8$.
You need 28 boxes to ship them all.

5. (2) $100 - 70 \leftarrow$ distance to Gary
$\uparrow$ distance to Chicago

6. (3) $1\frac{1}{2}$ hours
$t = \frac{d}{r}$; $t = \frac{100}{65} \approx 1.5$ or $1\frac{1}{2}$ hours

Lesson 10

Multistep Problems, pages 100–111

MENTAL MATH	
1. no	**4.** no
2. yes	**5.** yes
3. yes	

1. Ⓐ 5, 11, 21, 2 Ⓒ 260, 36, 15, 49
Ⓑ 13, 13, 4, 30

2. Ⓐ $12 - 6 \div 2$ $(12 - 6) \div 2$
$12 - 3 = 9$ $6 \div 2 = 3$

Ⓑ $3 + 12 \times 2$ $(3 + 12) \times 2$
$3 + 24 = 27$ $15 \times 2 = 30$

Ⓒ $6 \times 3 + 2$ $6 \times (3 + 2)$
$18 + 2 = 20$ $6 \times 5 = 30$

Ⓓ $\frac{12 - 7}{(-5)} = \frac{5}{(-5)} = -1$

E $\dfrac{21 - 7}{7 - 5} = \dfrac{14}{2} = 7$

F $15 \div (6 - 4 + 1)$
$15 \div 3 = 5$

3. **A** $8(2) + 8(5)$ **F** $8k - 3k$
   B $34(21) + 34(19)$ **G** $33m + 15$
   C $12(10) - 12(5)$ **H** $80y - 80$
   D $5(4) + 5(3) + 5(8)$ **I** $30 - 3x$
   E $13x + 39$

4. **A** $6(8 + 5)$ **F** $(13 - 9)n$ or $4n$
   B $12(7 - 3)$ **G** $25m + 22p$
   C $10(d + 2)$ **H** $(15 + 1)x = 16x$
   D $6(b - 5)$ **I** $(1 + 8 - 3)y = 6y$
   E $(7 + 6)x$ or $13x$

5. **(3)** $6(7 + 3)$

CALCULATOR EXPLORATION

A $256 \div 32 \times 4 = 32$, no parentheses

B $(437 + 78) \times 31 = 15{,}965$, parentheses

C $2{,}604 - 45 \times 32 = 1{,}164$, no parentheses

D $(650 + 376) \div 3 = 342$, parentheses

E $30 \times 72 + 25 \times 43 = 3{,}235$, no parentheses

F $1{,}364 \div (45 + 79) = 11$, parentheses

---

6. **A** $P = 2(5.1) + 2(3.9)$ **C** $P = 2(9) = 18$ m
   B $P = 2(5.1 + 3.9)$

7. **A** Mean $= \dfrac{85 + 90 + 70 + 80 + 85}{5} = 82$
   B Median $= 85°$

8. **A** Mean $=$
   $\dfrac{90{,}000 + 250{,}000 + 125{,}000 + 1{,}600{,}000 + 95{,}000 + 300{,}000}{6}$
   $= \$410{,}000$
   B $\$187{,}500$

9. **A** Mean $= \$58{,}000$
   Median $= \$24{,}000$
   B Median
   C Mean
   D Both mean and median increase by $20,000.
   E The median remains the same, but the mean changes to $70,500.

10. **A** $3 + 4 \times 12$ **C** $5(2) + 3(4)$
    B $\$5 - (3 \times \$.25)$ **D** $5(2) + 8(2)$

11. **A** $6 + 3 \times 7$ **F** $5(\$.37) + 7(\$.21)$
    B $10(15 - 7)$ **G** $8(\$8) + 3(\$12)$
    C $6(5 + 8)$
    D $\dfrac{35 - 25}{2}$ or $\dfrac{1}{2}(35 - 25)$
    E $\dfrac{98.99}{4 + 3}$

12. **A** $50 - 12(3) = r$
    14 ft $= r$
    B $p = \dfrac{283 + 165}{4} = \dfrac{448}{4} = \$112$
    C $3(2.05 + .70 + .85) = t$
    $t = 3(3.60) = \$10.80$

13. **A** Equation: $x = \$2{,}000 - (\$17.95 \times 50)$
    Estimate: $x \approx \$2{,}000 - (\$20 \times 50) = \$1{,}000$
    Exact: $x = \$1{,}102.50$
    B Equation: $s = \dfrac{\$23{,}245 + \$10{,}755}{12}$

    Estimate: $s \approx \dfrac{\$24{,}000 + \$12{,}000}{12} = \dfrac{36{,}000}{12} = \$3{,}000$
    Exact: $s = \$2{,}833.33$
    C Equation: $d = (8 \times \$6.25) + (3.5 \times \$10)$
    Estimate:
    $d \approx (8 \times \$6) + (4 \times \$10) = \$48 + \$40 = \$88$
    Exact: $d = \$85$

CHECK YOUR UNDERSTANDING, page 110

1. **A** No, 21 and 11 **G** Yes, 38
   B Yes, $8 + k$ **H** Yes, 150
   C Yes, 8 **I** No, $9x$ and $9x^2$
   D Yes, $4m + 2$ **J** Yes, $36x - 60$
   E Yes, 35 **K** Yes, $17y$
   F No, 50 and 98

2. **A** 18 **E** 16
   B 19 **F** 36
   C 7 **G** 152
   D 3 **H** 4

3. **A** 145 **D** 946
   B 288 **E** 139
   C 32 **F** 24

4. **A** $5(9) - 3$ **D** $\dfrac{12 + m}{15}$
   B $10(30 + 8)$ **E** $\dfrac{78}{(18 - 5)}$
   C $4b + 6$ **F** $\dfrac{(62 + 68)}{2}$ or $\dfrac{1}{2}(62 + 68)$

5. $P = 2(l + w)$
   $= 2(7 + 13)$
   $= 40$ in.
   $A = lw = 7 \bullet 13 = 91$ sq in.

6. **Ⓐ** $x = \$10 - 5(\$.65)$
   Ⓑ Estimate: $x = \$10 - \$3.50 = \$6.50$
   Ⓒ $x = \$6.75$

7. **Ⓐ** $p = 40(\$7.20) + 5(1.5)(\$7.20)$
   Ⓑ Estimate: $\$280 + 10(\$7) =$
   $\$280 + \$70 = \$350$
   Ⓒ $p = \$342$

8. **Ⓐ** $r = 2(\$24) + 200(\$.15)$
   Ⓑ Estimate: $\$50 + \$30 = \$80$
   Ⓒ $r = \$78$

9. **Ⓐ** $m = \dfrac{23 + 20 + 27 + 21}{4}$
   Ⓑ Estimate: pick a number in the middle—23
   Ⓒ $m = 22.75$ mpg

10. **Ⓐ** $c = 2(26) + 3(43)$
    Ⓑ Estimate: $50 + 120 = 170$
    Ⓒ $c = 181$ mg

TEST-TAKING PRACTICE, page 111

1. **(2)** $5(\$3.95 + \$.50)$

2. **(3)** 144
   $$A = \frac{1}{2} \times (b_1 + b_2) \times h$$
   $$\frac{1}{2} \times (12 + 24) \times 8$$
   $$\frac{1}{2}(36)(8)$$
   $$18(8) = 144 \text{ sq in.}$$

3. **(4)** $2(1.5 + 2.5)$

4. 1,542
   $$\frac{1,509 + 1,575}{2} = 1,542$$

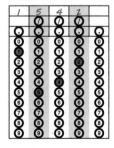

5. **(2)** 7
   $$\frac{225}{7 \times 5} = 6.4 \approx 7$$

6. **(5)** $s = 3(.55) - 1$

Skill Maintenance

Lessons 7–10, pages 112–113

Part One

1. **Ⓐ** bh **Ⓒ** lwh
   25×18 $10 \times 5 \times h$

   Ⓑ $2l + 2w$ or $2(l + w)$
   $2(8) + 2(n)$ $2(8 + n)$

2. **Ⓐ** $\dfrac{344}{4}$ or $\$344 \div 4$ or $4\overline{)344}$
   $\dfrac{344}{4} = \$86$

   Ⓑ $\$.43\ (2 \times 12)$ or $\$.43 \times 2 \times 12$
   $\$.43 \times 24 = \$10.32$

   Ⓒ $50 \times y$ seats
   $50y$ seats

   Ⓓ $\dfrac{30}{4 + 6} = \dfrac{30}{10} = 3$ balloons

3. Your estimates should be *similar* to the ones below. All *reasonable estimates* are acceptable.

   Ⓐ $2,073/500 \approx 2,000/500 = 4$
   Ⓑ $8 \times 189 \approx 8 \times 200 = 1,600$
   Ⓒ $99(12) \approx 100(12) = 1,200$
   Ⓓ $\dfrac{187}{90} \approx \dfrac{180}{90} = 2$
   Ⓔ $\dfrac{403}{7} \approx \dfrac{420}{7} = 60$

4. $A = lw - lw$
   $A = (25 \times 12) - (3 \times 3)$
   $A = (25 \times 4 \times 3) - 9$
   $A = (100 \times 3) - 9$
   $A = 300 - 9 = 291 \text{ m}^2$

5. This problem could be solved several different ways. You could use $6 \times$ the price for 1 cu ft, or $3 \times$ the price for 2 cu ft, or even $2 \times$ the price for 3 cu ft because the pattern is *$22.50 for each cubic foot.* (Always check a chart to see if the pattern stays the same.)
   Use $3 \times$ the price for 2 cu ft (for easiest multiplication).

   $3 \times \$45 = (3 \times 40) + (3 \times 5) = 120 + 15 = \$135$

6. **Ⓐ** $20 - \underbrace{14 \div (2)}\ =$
   $20 - \quad 7 \quad = 13$

   Ⓑ $\dfrac{122 - 50}{(-8)} = \dfrac{72}{(-8)} = -9$

   Ⓒ $9(20 - 9) = 9(11) = 99$

   Ⓓ $(12 + 20) \div 4 + 102 =$
   $32 \div 4 + 102 =$
   $8 + 102 = 110$

E $\dfrac{(-10) + 2 + 7 + (-2) + 3}{5} = \dfrac{0}{5} = 0$

F $(5)(-4) + (5)(5) = (-20) + 25 = 5$

Part Two

1. (3) $4(1,119 + 689)$

2. (3) 70
Answer is from the graph, but check using the expression $3 + 70(0.10)$.

3. (3) 11.50
$3 + 85(0.10) = 11.50$

4. 260
$V = lwh$
$V = 13 \times (10 \times 2)$
$V = 13 \times 20 = 260$ cu ft

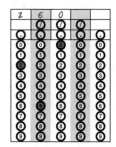

5. (2) 50
The perimeter does not change with the cut-out.

6. (5) Not enough information is given.
You need to know the size of the cut-out.

Lesson 11

Powers and Roots, pages 114–125

MENTAL MATH		
1. 64		**4.** 10
2. 6		**5.** 144
3. 16		

1. **D** 8×8; "8 squared" or "8 to the second power"; 64
  E $2 \times 2 \times 2 \times 2 \times 2$; 2^5; 32
  F 5^2; "5 squared" or "5 to the second power"; 25
  G $6 \times 6 \times 6$; 6^3; 216
  H $8 \times 8 \times 8 \times 8$; "8 to the fourth power"; 4,096
  I $4 \times 4 \times 4 \times 4 \times 4 \times 4 \times 4 \times 4$; 4^8; 65,536
  J m^2; "m squared" or "m to the second power"

2. **A** $A = s^2 = 15^2 = 225$ mm^2
  B $A = 36^2 = 1{,}296$ sq in.
  C $A = 24^2 = 576$ sq in.
  D $A = 10^2 = 100$ mm^2
  E $A = 22^2 = 484$ cm^2

REASONING ACTIVITY
A $A = lw = 15(12) = 180$ sq ft
B 20 sq yd
C 9 sq ft = 1 sq yd
D Find the area in square feet and then divide by 9 $A = \dfrac{9(18)}{9} = 18$ sq yd or write the dimensions in yards first $A = 3 \times 6 = 18$ sq yd
E $A = \dfrac{8(10)}{9} = \dfrac{80}{9} = 8.9$ sq yd

3. **A** 4   **C** 10
  B 5   **D** 12

4. **A** $\sqrt{400} = 20$ **C** $\sqrt{225} = 15$
  B $25^2 = 625$ **D** $11^2 = 121$

5. $A = s^2$
  $81 = s^2$
  $s = \sqrt{81} = 9$ ft

6. **A** $5 + 3^2$ $(5 + 3)^2$ $5 + 3(2)$
       $5 + 9 = 14$ $8^2 = 64$ $5 + 6 = 11$
  B $2(3)^2$ $(2 \times 3)^2$ $2 \times 3(2)$
       $2(9) = 18$ $6^2 = 36$ $2 \times 6 = 12$
  C $5(6) + 4^2$ $5^2 - \sqrt{4}$ $\sqrt{16} + \sqrt{4}$
       $30 + 16 = 46$ $25 - 2 = 23$ $4 + 2 = 6$
  D $4(3) + 9^2$ $4(3 + 9)^2$ $4(3) + \sqrt{9}$
       $12 + 81 = 93$ $4(12)^2 = 576$ $12 + 3 = 15$

7.

x	5	2
$3x^2$	$3(5)(5) = 75$	$3(2)(2) = 12$

0	-2	-5
$3(0)(0) = 0$	$3(-2)(-2) = 12$	$3(-5)(-5) = 75$

8. **A** $9x + 10 - 10 = 145 - 10$
  $\dfrac{9x}{9} = \dfrac{135}{9}$
  $x = 15$

  B $14y - 6 + 6 = 50 + 6$
  $\dfrac{14y}{14} = \dfrac{56}{14}$
  $y = 4$

C $112 - 13 = 11n + 13 - 13$

$\dfrac{99}{11} = \dfrac{11n}{11}$

$9 = n$

D $87 + 3 = 5n - 3 + 3$

$\dfrac{90}{5} = \dfrac{5n}{5}$

$18 = n$

E $10b - 35 + 35 = -65 + 35$

$\dfrac{10b}{10} = \dfrac{-30}{10}$

$b = -3$

F $10b + 35 - 35 = -65 - 35$

$\dfrac{10b}{10} = \dfrac{-100}{10}$

$b = -10$

9. **A** no

$4^2 + 5^2 \neq 6^2$

$16 + 25 \neq 36$

$41 \neq 36$

B yes

$8^2 + 15^2 = 17^2$

$64 + 225 = 289$

$289 = 289$

C yes

$9^2 + 12^2 = 15^2$

$81 + 144 = 225$

$225 = 225$

D yes

$18^2 + 24^2 = 30^2$

$324 + 576 = 900$

$900 = 900$

E no

$6^2 + 11^2 \neq 12^2$

$36 + 121 \neq 144$

$157 \neq 144$

F yes

$12^2 + 16^2 = 20^2$

$144 + 256 = 400$

$400 = 400$

G yes

$5^2 + 12^2 = 13^2$

$25 + 144 = 169$

$169 = 169$

H yes

$7^2 + 24^2 = 25^2$

$49 + 576 = 625$

$625 = 625$

I yes

$15^2 + 20^2 = 25^2$

$225 + 400 = 625$

$625 = 625$

10. **(1)** 5 mi

$c^2 = a^2 + b^2$

$13^2 = 12^2 + b^2$

$13^2 - 12^2 = b^2$

$169 - 144 = b^2$

$25 = b^2$

$\sqrt{25} = b$

$5 = b$

11. **(2)** $30^2 - 10^2 = b^2$

This equation represents $c^2 - a^2 = b^2$.

12. **A** 7 (a little more than 7)

B between 8 and 9

C between 20 and 25

D between 30 and 40; closer to 30

E between 40 and 50; a good estimate is 45

F between 5 and 6; a good estimate is 5.5

G between 11 and 12; closer to 11

H between 8 and 9; a good estimate is 8.5

13. The Casio *fx-260* squares the 2 and then multiplies that product by 3. The calculator does not multiply 3 by 2 first. It follows the order of operations that you learned—exponents before multiplying.

14. $500 = s^2$

$s = \sqrt{500} \approx 22.4$ cm

15. $225 + 25 = c^2$

$c^2 = 250$

$c = \sqrt{250} \approx 15.8$ ft

16. $5(3 \cdot 55)^2 = A$

136,125 sq ft $= A$

CHECK YOUR UNDERSTANDING, page 124

1. **A** 225
B 64
C 6
D 11
E 11
F 17
G 144
H 76
I 300
J 100
K 44
L 2

2. **A** $9^2 = 81$
B $19^2 = 361$
C $45^2 = 2,025$

3. **A** no; $3^2 + 5^2 \neq 8^2$
B yes; $600^2 + 800^2 = 1,000^2$
C yes; $16^2 + 30^2 = 34^2$
D yes; $10^2 + 24^2 = 26^2$

4. **A** between 3 and 4; 3.16
B between 6 and 7; 6.32
C between 12 and 13; 12.25

5. **A** $5(10)(10) = 500$
B $5(3)(3) = 45$
C $5(0)(0) = 0$
D $5(-3)(-3) = 45$
E $5(-10)(-10) = 500$

6. $196 = s^2$

$s = \sqrt{196} = 14$ ft

7. **A** $3n - 7 + 7 = 59 + 7$

$\dfrac{3n}{3} = \dfrac{66}{3}$

$n = 22$

B $15x - 10 + 10 = -100 + 10$

$\dfrac{15x}{15} = \dfrac{-90}{15}$

$x = -6$

8. $a^2 + b^2 = c^2$
$3^2 + 4^2 = c^2$
$25 = c^2$
$c = \sqrt{25}$ = 5 blocks

9. obese
BMI = 703(220)/(70)^2
BMI = 31.6

10. BMI = 703(135)/(65)^2
BMI = 22.5

TEST-TAKING PRACTICE, page 125

1. **(5)** between 8 ft and 9 ft
$8^2 + 4^2 = c^2$
$64 + 16 = c^2$
$c = \sqrt{80}$ = just less than 9 ft

2. **(1)** 8.0
$4x - 2 + 2 = 30 + 2$
$\frac{4x}{4} = \frac{32}{4}$
$x = 8$

3. **(2)** $600
15 ft × 18 ft =
(15 ft ÷ 3) × (18 ft ÷ 3) =
5 yd × 6 yd = 30 sq yd
30 × $20 = $600

4. **(2)** $500^2 - 400^2 = a^2$
$c^2 = a^2 + b^2$
$500^2 = a^2 + 400^2$
$500^2 - 400^2 = a^2$

5. **(5)** 65
$r = 2\sqrt{5 \cdot 210} = 2\sqrt{1,050} = 64.8$

6. 170
$150^2 + 80^2 = p^2$
$28,900 = p^2$
$p = \sqrt{28,900}$
$p = 170$ ft

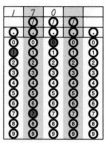

Lesson 12

Circles, pages 126–133

MENTAL MATH	
1. 10	**4.** 7
2. 100	**5.** 6.5
3. 6	

1. Ⓐ 5 m   Ⓒ 9 ft
   Ⓑ $d = 2r$ Ⓓ $d = 2r$
   $d = 2(1) = 2$ cm $d = 2(3) = 6$ in.

2. Ⓐ $r = \frac{1}{2}d$ Ⓒ $r = \frac{1}{2}d$
   $r = \frac{1}{2}(2) = 1$ ft $r = \frac{1}{2}(8) = 4$ m
   Ⓑ 2 ft   Ⓓ 7 in.

3. Ⓐ Estimate: $C = \pi d$
   $C \approx (3)(12) = 36$ m
   Using 3.14: $C \approx (3.14)(12) = 37.68$ m

   Ⓑ Estimate: $C = \pi d$
   $C \approx (3)(5) = 15$ in.
   Using 3.14: $C \approx (3.14)(5) = 15.7$ in.

   Ⓒ Estimate: $C = \pi d$ $d = 2r$
   $C \approx (3)(4.5)(2)$
   $C \approx 3(9) = 27$ ft
   Using 3.14: $C \approx (3.14)(4.5)(2) = 28.26$ ft

   Ⓓ Estimate: $C \approx (3)(10)(2)$
   $C \approx (30)(2) = 60$ in.
   Using 3.14: $C \approx (3.14)(10)(2) = 62.8$ in.

4. Ⓐ 37.69911184 m   Ⓒ 28.27433388 ft
   Ⓑ 15.70796327 m   Ⓓ 62.83185307 in.

5. When you find how far the bicycle travels when the wheel goes around once—you are finding the circumference of the wheel.

   Ⓐ Using 3: 3(2.25) = 6.75 ft
   Using 3.14: 3.14(2.25) = 7.065 ft
   Using π : 7.068583471 ft

   Ⓑ Using the π key on your calculator is easiest. Without a calculator, using 3 is easiest and will give an accurate enough answer.

CALCULATOR ACTIVITY

Measurements of the circumference and diameter of the various objects will vary, but $\frac{C}{d}$ should come close to 3.14159. It is likely that the most accurate answer will come with the larger objects when the measurement error does not have as much impact on the answer.

6. Ⓐ $C = \pi d$

$\frac{C}{\pi} = d$

$d \approx \frac{10}{3} = 3.3$ m

$d \approx \frac{10}{3.14} = 3.2$ m

$d \approx \frac{10}{\pi} = 3.2$ m

Ⓑ $r = \frac{1}{2}d$

$r = \frac{1}{2}(3.2) = 1.6$ m

7. Ⓐ $C = \pi d$

$C \approx (3.14)(9.5)$

Estimate: $C \approx (3)(10) = 30$ in.

Ⓑ Using 3.14: $(3.14)(9.5) = 29.83 = 30$ in.

Ⓒ You would need to *round* up to 30 inches. Since it is likely to be sold by the yard, you would probably buy a yard of it.

8. $\frac{C}{\pi} = d$

$d \approx \frac{20}{3.14} = 6.37$ in.

9. Ⓐ $C \approx 6$ cm

Ⓑ $d \approx \frac{6}{3} = 2$ cm

10. Ⓐ $A = \pi r^2$

$A = \pi (10)^2$

$A = \pi (100) \approx 314$ sq in.

Ⓑ $A = \pi r^2$

$A = \pi (5)^2$

$A = \pi (25) \approx 78.5$ cm^2

Ⓒ $A = \pi r^2$

$A = \pi (50)^2$

$A = \pi (2,500) \approx 7,850$ sq ft

Ⓓ $A = \pi r^2$

$A = \pi (25)^2$

$A = \pi (625) \approx 1,962.5$ m^2

11. $A = \pi r^2$

$\frac{A}{\pi} = r^2$

$\frac{50}{\pi} = r^2$

16 in. $\approx r^2$

4 in. $\approx r$

12. $C = \pi d$

$C = \pi(16) \approx 50.24$ or 50 in.

$A = \pi r^2$

$A = \pi(8)^2$

$A \approx 200.96$ or 201 sq in.

13.

The diagram below shows two figures.

$P = 2l + \pi d$

$P = (2 \bullet 20) + (\pi \bullet 4)$

$P \approx 40 + 12.56 = 52.56$ ft

14. (4) $\frac{\pi \times 4 \times 4}{3}$

$A = \frac{\pi r^2}{3}$

$A = \frac{\pi \times 4 \times 4}{3}$

REASONING ACTIVITY

shape	perimeter	dimensions	area formula	area
rectangle	100 ft	For example: $l = 30$, $w = 20$	$A = lw$	600 sq ft
square	100 ft	$s = 25$ ft	$A = s^2$	625 sq ft
circle	100 ft	$d = 100/\pi$ $r = 50/\pi$	$A = \pi r^2$	796 sq ft

CHECK YOUR UNDERSTANDING, page 132

1. Ⓐ Estimate: $C = \pi d$

$C \approx (3)(10) = 30$ cm

Using π: $C = \pi (9.8) \approx 30.79$ cm

Ⓑ Estimate: $C = \pi d$

$C \approx (3)(50) = 150$ ft

Using π: $C = \pi (47) \approx 147.65$ ft

Ⓒ Estimate: $C = \pi d$

$C \approx (3)(3 \times 2) = 18$ m

Using π: $C = \pi (3.1)(2) \approx 19.48$ m

Ⓓ Estimate: $C = \pi d$

$C \approx (3)(50 \times 2) = 300$ ft

Using π: $C = \pi (47)(2) \approx 295.31$ ft

2. $d = \frac{C}{\pi}$

$d = \frac{25,000}{\pi} \approx \frac{24,000}{3} = 8,000$ miles

3. $A = \pi r^2$

$A = \pi(3)^2$

$A \approx 28.26$ m^2

4. No, with a 10-mile radius they reached an area of about 300 sq miles but with a 20-mile radius they reach an area of about 1,200 sq miles. This is 4 times as much listening area.

5. They both leave the same amount of wasted cake. The area of the large circle is $\pi(4)^2 = 16\pi$. The area of each small circle is $\pi(1)^2 = 1\pi$, but there are 16 of them so the total area is also 16π.

6. $A = \pi r^2$

$\dfrac{A}{\pi} = r^2$

$\dfrac{75}{\pi} = r^2$

$25 \approx r^2$

$5 \text{ ft} \approx r$

7. Ⓐ Area of each plot $= \dfrac{\text{area of circle}}{6}$

$A = \dfrac{\pi(8)^2}{6} \approx 33.5 \text{ sq ft}$

Ⓑ $C = \pi d = \pi(16) \approx 50 \text{ ft}$

8. Large Pizza:

$A = \pi r^2 = \pi \cdot 8^2 \approx 201 \text{ sq in.}$

Medium Pizza:

$A = \pi r^2 = \pi \cdot 6^2 \approx 113 \text{ sq in.}$

Difference:

$201 - 113 = 88 \text{ sq in.}$

TEST-TAKING PRACTICE, page 133

1. (2) AD

A diameter must pass through the center of the circle.

2. (4) $(20)(20)\pi$

Area $= \pi r^2$

AC is a radius.

$\pi \cdot (20)(20)$ is the same as $(20)(20)\pi$

3. (2) 31.4

$d = 2r = 2 \cdot 5 = 10 \text{ inches}$

Estimate: $C = \pi d$

$C \approx (3)(10) = 30 \text{ inches}$

Exact: $C = \pi \cdot (10) \approx 31.4 \text{ inches}$

4. (2) 70

Area of square $= 18^2 = 324 \text{ sq in.}$

Area of circle $= \pi(9)^2 \approx 254 \text{ sq in.}$

Difference $\approx 70 \text{ sq in.}$

5. 775

$(310)(2.5) = 775 \text{ ft}$

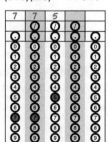

6. (2) 100

The circumference is about 3 times the diameter of any circle.

310 is about 3 times 100.

$\dfrac{310}{\pi} \approx \dfrac{300}{3} = 100$

7. (4) 3.14(7.5)(7.5)

diameter $= 15$

$r = \dfrac{1}{2}d = 7.5$

$A = \pi r^2 \approx (3.14)(7.5)(7.5)$

Lesson 13

More Powers—Powers of 10, pages 134–143

MENTAL MATH	
1. 350	**4.** 42,000
2. 600	**5.** 691,000
3. 9,250	

1. Ⓑ 10^1

Ⓒ 1,000,000 (6)

Ⓓ 10^9

Ⓔ The exponent (n) is the same as the number of zeros when you write the number the long way.

2. Ⓐ 10^3 **Ⓒ** 4 places, 10^4

Ⓑ 10^7

3. Ⓐ $3(10)^2 + 8(10)^1$ **Ⓓ** $2(10)^7 + 9(10)^6$

Ⓑ $5(10)^3 + 2(10)^{-2}$ **Ⓔ** $1(10)^2 + 4(10)^{-3}$

Ⓒ $6(10)^4 + 4(10)^2$

4. Ⓐ $5(10)^1$ **Ⓕ** $9(10)^3$

Ⓑ $5(10)^{-1}$ **Ⓖ** $3(10)^4$

Ⓒ $8(10)^4$ **Ⓗ** $6(10)^{-3}$

Ⓓ $8(10)^2$ **Ⓘ** $6(10)^8$

Ⓔ $9(10)^{-2}$ **Ⓙ** $3(10)^7$

5. Ⓐ 7,302; 0.7302; 730,200

Ⓑ 21.05; 0.002105; 2,105

Ⓒ 450; 0.045; 45,000

Ⓓ 0.8; 0.00008; 80

6. Ⓐ 7.5×10^4 **Ⓔ** 8×10^{-3}

Ⓑ 3.09×10^5 **Ⓕ** 3×10^{-5}

Ⓒ 8.7×10^8 **Ⓖ** 9.5×10^{-6}

Ⓓ 9.14×10^9 **Ⓗ** 2.8×10^{-7}

7. 7.6×10^7

8. 189,000,000,000

9. 4×10^{-4} m

10. 0.000001 m

Class Activity

Ⓐ $8{,}400{,}000 \times 200 = 1{,}680{,}000{,}000$

$8.4 \times 10^6 \times 2 \times 10^2 = 16.8 \times 10^8 = 1.68 \times 10^9$

Ⓑ $\dfrac{8{,}400{,}000}{200} = 42{,}000$

$8.4 \times 10^6 \div (2 \times 10^2) = 4.2 \times 10^4$

Ⓒ $10{,}000 \times 0.05 = 500$

$1 \times 10^4 \times 5 \times 10^{-2} = 5 \times 10^2$

Your answers may vary from these.

Check that your answers are reasonable.

11. Estimate: $200 \times 9{,}000 = 2 \times 10^2 \times 9 \times 10^3 =$
$18 \times 10^5 = 1{,}800{,}000$

12. Estimate: $\$3.58 \times 10^9 \div (\$2.85 \times 10^6) = \$1.3 \times$
$10^3 = \$1{,}300$

13. Estimate: $\$2.2 \times 10^7 \div (\$3 \times 10^4) = 0.7 \times 10^3 = 700$

USING DATA

Ⓐ Answers may vary because different scales may have been chosen.

WORLD POPULATION DISTRIBUTION

Ⓑ

POPULATION	AREA
1. Oceania	1. Oceania
2. North America	2. North America
3. Latin America and Caribbean	3. Latin America and Caribbean
4. Europe	4. Europe
5. Africa	5. Africa
6. Asia	6. Asia

Ⓒ Population

Africa	8.2×10^8
North America	3.2×10^8
Latin America and Caribbean	5.3×10^8
Asia	3.7×10^9
Europe	7.3×10^8
Oceania	3.1×10^7

Ⓓ Area

Africa	1.2×10^7
North America	7.7×10^6
Latin America and Caribbean	7.9×10^6
Asia	1.2×10^7
Europe	8.9×10^6
Oceania	3.3×10^6

Ⓔ Density
Asia has the highest density.
$3.7 \times 10^9 \div 1.2 \times 10^7 \approx 3 \times 10^2$

14. (2) $8 \times 120 \leftarrow$ calories
$\qquad\qquad\uparrow\qquad$ servings

15. (4) $\dfrac{522 \leftarrow \text{miles}}{9 \leftarrow \text{gallons}}$

16. (5) $\$27.75$
Estimate: $5 \times \$6 = \$30$

CHECK YOUR UNDERSTANDING, page 142

1. Ⓐ tens   Ⓓ ten thousands
Ⓑ tenths   Ⓔ hundredths
Ⓒ thousands

2. Ⓐ 10^5 Ⓒ 10^{-1}
Ⓑ 10^{-2} Ⓓ 10^6

3. Ⓐ $7(10)^1 + 8(10)^0$
Ⓑ $6(10)^4 + 2(10)^3$
Ⓒ $5(10)^3 + 3(10)^1 + 9(10)^{-1}$
Ⓓ $9(10)^7 + 3(10)^6$
Ⓔ $4(10)^1 + 7(10)^{-1} + 3(10)^{-2}$

4. Ⓐ 9×10^4 Ⓓ 2.9×10^{-5}
Ⓑ 7×10^{-3} Ⓔ 8.8×10^7
Ⓒ 4.5×10^6

5. 2.5×10^6

6. Estimate: $3 \times 10^7 \div 10^2 = 3 \times 10^5 = 300{,}000$

7. Ⓐ 5.88×10^{12}
Ⓑ Estimate: $6 \times 6 \times 10^{12} = 36 \times 10^{12}$
$= 3.6 \times 10^{13}$

8. $2 \times 10^5 \times 6 \times 10^9 = 12 \times 10^{14}$

9. Ⓐ $g = \dfrac{550}{8}$
Ⓑ Estimate: $\dfrac{560}{8} = 70$ gal
Ⓒ $g = 68.75$ gal

10. Ⓐ $c = 4(\$2.49)$
Ⓑ Estimate: $4(\$2.50) = \$10.00$
Ⓒ $c = \$9.96$

11. Ⓐ $c = \frac{\$4.95}{24}$
    Ⓑ Estimate: $\frac{\$4.80}{24} = \$.20$
    Ⓒ $c = \$.21$

12. Ⓐ $p = \frac{\$4.39}{6}$
    Ⓑ Estimate: $\frac{\$4.20}{6} = \$.70$
    Ⓒ $p = \$.73$

13. Ⓐ $g = \frac{100}{16}$
    Ⓑ Estimate: $\frac{100}{20} = 5$ gallons
    Ⓒ $g = 6.25$ gallons

14. Ⓐ $t = \frac{58}{12}$
    Ⓑ Estimate: $= \frac{60}{12} = 5$ minutes
    Ⓒ $t = 4.8$ minutes

TEST-TAKING PRACTICE, page 143

1. **(4)** 1,000,000
   1,000 thousands is 1,000,000

2. **(1)** 1996

3. **(2)** 400,000
   1,300 thousand − 900 thousand = 400 thousand

4. **(4)** $26,400
   $y = \$2,200 \times 12 = \$26,400$

5. **(3)** $481
   $d = \$18.50(\frac{1}{2} \cdot 52)$ weeks $= \$481$
   Estimate: $\$20 \times 25 = \$500$

6. 14
   $\frac{3.5 \times 10^5}{2.5 \times 10^4} = 1.4 \times 10 = 14$

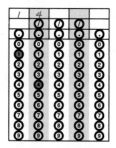

Lesson 14

Test-Taking Tips, pages 144–149

Check Your Skills

1. **(3)** 12 and 13
   $12^2 = 144$, $13^2 = 169$; 150 is between these.
   Estimate: $\sqrt{150}$ is between 12 and 13.

2. **(4)** 150
   $d = rt$
   $375 = 2.5r$
   $150 = r$
   Estimate: $r = \frac{375}{2.5} \approx$ more than 100 but less than 200
   This is closest to **(4)** 150.

3. **(4)** 6
   area of large rectangle − area of cutout
   $(55 \times 50) - (40 \times 15)$
   $2,750 - 600 = 2,150$ sq ft
   $\frac{2,150}{400} = 5.375$ (more than 5 gallons).
   6 gallons are necessary.

4. **(2)** $\frac{48}{7}$
   1,050 is extra information.

5. 100
   $V = lwh$
   $5 \times 5 \times 8 = 200$
   $200 \times \$.50 = \$100$

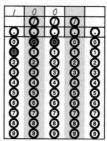

6. **(3)** 3.14×10
   $C = \pi d$; 10 is the diameter

7. **(3)** 65°
   $180° - 115° = 65°$
   The measure of angle *COD* is extra information.

8. (2) $1.10

total spent for coffee = $5.95 − 3($1.25)

$c = \frac{\$5.95 - 3(\$1.25)}{2} = \frac{\$2.20}{2} = \$1.10$

 9. (5) Not enough information is given.
To average over 5 days, you need to know the temperatures for each day.

10. (1) 28

$A = \pi r^2$

$A = \pi(3)^2 \approx 28$ square units

11. (2) (−2, 1)

12. (4) 25 + 4n

13. (4) 28,440

$y = (\$2,790 - \$420) \times 12$

Estimate: $y \approx \$2,400 \times 10 = 24,000$

Choice (4) is higher than but close to 24,000.

14. (2) 15

$a^2 + b^2 = c^2$

$9^2 + 12^2 = c^2$

$225 = c^2$

$\sqrt{225} = c$

$15 = c$

15. (5) 72

$h = 8^2 + 8 = 64 + 8 = 72$

16. (1) 100(6 + 3 + 7)

17. (3) 12

$A = \frac{1}{2}bh$

$30 = \frac{1}{2} \times 5 \times h$

$\frac{30}{5} = \frac{1}{2}h$

$6 = \frac{1}{2}h$

$12 = h$

18. (2) 1997

The line is steepest from 1996 to 1997.

19. (4) 60

$6x + 3x = 9x = 180°$

$x = 20°$

$3x = 60°$

20. (1) 4

The median will be between the 10th and 11th numbers when they are listed in order. Both of these numbers are 4.

Lesson 15

Size of Fractions, pages 150–161

MENTAL MATH		
1. 1		**4.** 4
2. 2		**5.** 6
3. 3		**6.** 12

1. Ⓐ 0.25   Ⓕ 0.2
Ⓑ 0.2   Ⓖ 2.4
Ⓒ 0.125   Ⓗ 1.5
Ⓓ 2.0   Ⓘ 0.8
Ⓔ 0.25

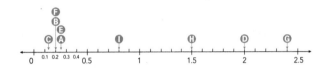

2. less or smaller

3. less than 1: Ⓐ, Ⓔ, Ⓕ, Ⓗ
greater than 1: Ⓑ, Ⓒ, Ⓓ
equal to 1: Ⓖ, Ⓘ

4. Your answers can match exactly or be close to these answers.

Ⓐ $\frac{11}{12}$ Ⓓ $\frac{6}{7}$
Ⓑ $\frac{5}{6}$ Ⓔ $\frac{13}{14}$
Ⓒ $\frac{19}{20}$ Ⓕ $\frac{9}{10}$

5. Ⓐ $\frac{4}{3} = \frac{3}{3} + \frac{1}{3} = 1\frac{1}{3}$ Ⓔ $\frac{14}{3} = \frac{12}{3} + \frac{2}{3} = 4\frac{2}{3}$

Ⓑ $\frac{5}{2} = \frac{4}{2} + \frac{1}{2} = 2\frac{1}{2}$ Ⓕ $\frac{11}{5} = \frac{10}{5} + \frac{1}{5} = 2\frac{1}{5}$

Ⓒ $\frac{7}{4} = \frac{4}{4} + \frac{3}{4} = 1\frac{3}{4}$ Ⓖ $\frac{17}{6} = \frac{12}{6} + \frac{5}{6} = 2\frac{5}{6}$

Ⓓ $\frac{10}{7} = \frac{7}{7} + \frac{3}{7} = 1\frac{3}{7}$ Ⓗ $\frac{20}{3} = \frac{18}{3} + \frac{2}{3} = 6\frac{2}{3}$

6. exactly $\frac{1}{2}$: Ⓑ, Ⓒ, Ⓖ
greater than $\frac{1}{2}$: Ⓐ, Ⓓ, Ⓔ, Ⓕ, Ⓗ

7. (3) $\frac{9}{16}$ yd

The only answer greater than $\frac{1}{2}$ is $\frac{9}{16}$.

8. Ⓐ $\frac{4}{5}$ (same numerator, smaller denominator)

Ⓑ $\frac{8}{11}$ (greater numerator, same denominator)

Ⓒ $\frac{5}{6}$ (same numerator, smaller denominator)

D $\frac{10}{9}$ $\left(\frac{10}{9} \text{ is greater than 1; } \frac{9}{10} \text{ is less than 1}\right)$

E $\frac{13}{5}$ (same numerator, smaller denominator)

F $\frac{6}{11}$ (greater numerator, same denominator)

G $\frac{11}{20}$ $\left(\frac{5}{10} \text{ is } \frac{1}{2}; \frac{11}{20} \text{ is greater than } \frac{1}{2}\right)$

H $\frac{5}{8}$ $\left(\frac{5}{8} \text{ is greater than } \frac{1}{2}; \frac{4}{9} \text{ is less than } \frac{1}{2}\right)$

I $\frac{5}{9}$ $\left(\frac{5}{9} \text{ is greater than } \frac{1}{2}; \frac{8}{17} \text{ is less than } \frac{1}{2}\right)$

9. A \$.30, 0.3   **E** \$.60, 0.6
B \$.70, 0.7   **F** \$.80, 0.8
C \$.90, 0.9   **G** \$.50, 0.5
D \$.40, 0.4   **H** \$.50, 0.5

10. A 0.8   **I** $\frac{1}{10}$
B 0.33 ... or $0.\overline{3}$ **J** $\frac{4}{10} = \frac{2}{5}$
C 0.3   **K** $\frac{2}{3}$
D 0.75   **L** $\frac{6}{10} = \frac{3}{5}$
E 0.5   **M** 0.9
F $\frac{2}{10} = \frac{1}{5}$ **N** 1.0
G $\frac{1}{4}$ **O** 1.1
H $\frac{7}{10}$

11. A $\frac{2}{8}$ **F** $\frac{3}{8}$
B $\frac{6}{8}$ **G** $\frac{10}{16}$
C $\frac{5}{4}$ **H** $\frac{10}{4}$
D $\frac{12}{8}$ **I** $\frac{20}{16}$
E $\frac{2}{16}$

12. A >   **D** <
B >   **E** <
C >   **F** <

13. A $\frac{3}{4}$ **D** $\frac{1}{4}$
B $\frac{1}{2}$ **E** $\frac{3}{5}$
C $\frac{1}{3}$ **F** $\frac{2}{3}$

14. A $\frac{3}{12} = \frac{1}{4}$ **C** $\frac{9}{12} = \frac{3}{4}$
B $\frac{4}{12} = \frac{1}{3}$ **D** $\frac{15}{12} = \frac{5}{4} = 1\frac{1}{4}$

15. A $\frac{15}{60} = \frac{1}{4}$ **C** $\frac{40}{60} = \frac{2}{3}$
B $\frac{20}{60} = \frac{1}{3}$ **D** $\frac{90}{60} = \frac{3}{2} = 1\frac{1}{2}$

16. A $\frac{1}{6}$ **D** 0 (impossible)
B $\frac{3}{6} = \frac{1}{2}$ **E** $\frac{2}{6} = \frac{1}{3}$
C 1 (a certainty)

17. A $\frac{1}{4}$ **C** 0 (impossible)
B $\frac{3}{4}$

CALCULATOR EXPLORATION

A $\frac{3}{5}$ **D** $\frac{11}{16}$
B $\frac{70}{9}$ **E** $\frac{16}{33}$
C $\frac{14}{25}$ **F** $\frac{327}{8}$

CHECK YOUR UNDERSTANDING, page 160

1. A $\frac{1}{2}$ $\left(\frac{5}{9} \text{ is a little more than } \frac{1}{2}.\right)$

B $\frac{1}{3}$ $\left(\frac{11}{30} \approx \frac{10}{30} \text{ or } \frac{1}{3}\right)$ **F** $\frac{1}{4}$ $\left(\frac{12}{49} \approx \frac{12}{48} \text{ or } \frac{1}{4}\right)$

C $\frac{3}{4}$ $\left(\frac{15}{21} \approx \frac{15}{20} \text{ or } \frac{3}{4}\right)$ **G** $\frac{1}{3}$ $\left(\frac{7}{20} \approx \frac{7}{21} \text{ or } \frac{1}{3}\right)$

D $\frac{1}{3}$ $\left(\frac{9}{28} \approx \frac{9}{27} \text{ or } \frac{1}{3}\right)$ **H** $\frac{1}{2}$ $\left(\frac{15}{31} \approx \frac{15}{30} \text{ or } \frac{1}{2}\right)$

E $\frac{1}{5}$ $\left(\frac{4}{19} \approx \frac{4}{20} \text{ or } \frac{1}{5}\right)$ **I** $\frac{1}{5}$ $\left(\frac{11}{53} \approx \frac{11}{55} \text{ or } \frac{1}{5}\right)$

2. $0.2; \frac{1}{4}; \frac{1}{2}; 0.58; 0.6; \frac{5}{8}$

First, compare as decimals from least to greatest.
0.200; 0.250; 0.500; 0.580; 0.600; 0.625
Then rename in their original form.

3. $\frac{1}{2}$ yd is longer because $\frac{3}{8}$ is less than $\frac{1}{2}$ $\left(\frac{4}{8}\right)$.

4. A $\frac{1}{4}$ **D** $\frac{7}{8}$
B $\frac{5}{8}$ **E** $\frac{13}{16}$
C $\frac{5}{16}$ **F** $\frac{9}{16}$

5. A $\frac{50}{100}$ **D** $\frac{10}{100}$
B $\frac{4}{16}$ **E** $\frac{12}{16}$
C $\frac{4}{10}$ **F** $\frac{60}{100}$

6. $2\frac{3}{8}$ in.

7. A $\frac{1}{2}$ **C** $\frac{1}{8}$
B $\frac{1}{4}$ **D** $\frac{1}{8}$

8. ⓐ $\frac{4}{16} = \frac{1}{4}$ ⓒ $\frac{12}{16} = \frac{3}{4}$

ⓑ $\frac{2}{16} = \frac{1}{8}$ ⓓ $\frac{24}{16} = \frac{3}{2} = 1\frac{1}{2}$

9. ⓐ $\frac{10}{20} = \frac{1}{2}$ ⓒ $\frac{3}{20}$

ⓑ $\frac{2}{20} = \frac{1}{10}$

TEST-TAKING PRACTICE, page 161

1. $\frac{3}{4}$

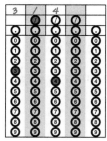

2. (2) $\frac{1}{4}$ and $\frac{1}{2}$

$\frac{1}{4} = \frac{2}{8}$ and $\frac{1}{2} = \frac{4}{8}$

$\frac{3}{8}$ is halfway between $\frac{2}{8}$ and $\frac{4}{8}$.

3. (4) $\frac{5}{9}$

$\frac{20}{36} = \frac{5}{9}$

4. (1) $\frac{1}{4}$

$\frac{100}{400} = \frac{1}{4}$

5. (3) $\frac{3}{5}$

$\frac{6}{10} = \frac{3}{5}$

Lesson 16

Adding and Subtracting Fractions,
pages 162–175

MENTAL MATH		
1. $\frac{1}{3}$	3. $\frac{1}{4}$
2. $\frac{5}{7}$	4. $\frac{1}{2}$

1. ⓐ $\frac{1}{2} = \frac{2}{4}, \frac{4}{8}, \frac{3}{6}, \frac{5}{10}$

ⓑ $\frac{2}{3} = \frac{4}{6}$

ⓒ $1 = \frac{2}{2}, \frac{4}{4}, \frac{8}{8}, \frac{3}{3}, \frac{6}{6}, \frac{5}{5}, \frac{10}{10}$

The numerator and the denominator are the same.

2. ⓐ $\frac{1}{4} > \frac{1}{5}$ ⓔ $\frac{1}{6} < \frac{1}{3}$

ⓑ $\frac{5}{6} < \frac{7}{8}$ ⓕ $1 < \frac{11}{10}$

ⓒ $\frac{1}{4} > \frac{1}{10}$ ⓖ $\frac{1}{2} < \frac{3}{5}$

ⓓ $\frac{7}{8} < \frac{9}{10}$ ⓗ $\frac{15}{10} > \frac{10}{8}$

3. ⓐ $\frac{5}{4} = 1\frac{1}{4}$ ⓓ $1\frac{9}{10} = 1\frac{9}{10}$

ⓑ $\frac{5}{3} = 1\frac{2}{3}$ ⓔ $\frac{15}{8} = 1\frac{7}{8}$

ⓒ $\frac{13}{8} = 1\frac{5}{8}$

4. ⓐ $\frac{2 \times 2}{3 \times 2} = \frac{4}{6}$ ⓓ $\frac{1 \times 8}{4 \times 8} = \frac{8}{32}$

ⓑ $\frac{5 \times 3}{6 \times 3} = \frac{15}{18}$ ⓔ $\frac{5 \times 2}{8 \times 2} = \frac{10}{16}$

ⓒ $\frac{3 \times 4}{5 \times 4} = \frac{12}{20}$ ⓕ $\frac{3 \times 2}{16 \times 2} = \frac{6}{32}$

5. ⓐ $\frac{4 \div 2}{6 \div 2} = \frac{2}{3}$ ⓓ $\frac{16 \div 16}{32 \div 16} = \frac{1}{2}$

ⓑ $\frac{4 \div 4}{12 \div 4} = \frac{1}{3}$ ⓔ $\frac{5 \div 5}{10 \div 5} = \frac{1}{2}$

ⓒ $\frac{12 \div 4}{16 \div 4} = \frac{3}{4}$ ⓕ $\frac{5 \div 5}{20 \div 5} = \frac{1}{4}$

6. No, because 7 is not a multiple of 4.

7. ⓐ $\frac{1}{2}$ ⓕ $\frac{7}{8}$

ⓑ $\frac{3}{4}$ ⓖ $\frac{9}{16}$

ⓒ $\frac{3}{8}$ ⓗ $\frac{5}{16}$

ⓓ $\frac{1}{2}$ ⓘ $\frac{11}{16}$

ⓔ $\frac{3}{4}$ ⓙ $\frac{7}{16}$

8. ⓐ $\frac{4}{8} = \frac{1}{2}$ ⓕ $\frac{6}{16} + \frac{3}{16} = \frac{9}{16}$

ⓑ $\frac{2}{4} + \frac{1}{4} = \frac{3}{4}$ ⓖ $\frac{4}{10} + \frac{3}{10} = \frac{7}{10}$

ⓒ $\frac{4}{16} + \frac{1}{16} = \frac{5}{16}$ ⓗ $\frac{5}{10} + \frac{2}{10} = \frac{7}{10}$

ⓓ $\frac{6}{16} + \frac{1}{16} = \frac{7}{16}$ ⓘ $\frac{5}{20} + \frac{8}{20} = \frac{13}{20}$

ⓔ $\frac{10}{16} + \frac{1}{16} = \frac{11}{16}$ ⓙ $\frac{8}{12} + \frac{3}{12} = \frac{11}{12}$

9. $\frac{5}{6}$ hour

$\frac{1}{2} + \frac{1}{3} = \frac{3}{6} + \frac{2}{6} = \frac{5}{6}$

10. $\frac{5}{8}$

$\frac{3}{8} + \frac{2}{8} = \frac{5}{8}$

11. (A) $\frac{1}{4}$

(F) $\frac{1}{8}$

(B) $\frac{2}{8} = \frac{1}{4}$

(G) $\frac{3}{8}$

(C) $\frac{1}{8}$

(H) $\frac{1}{16}$

(D) $\frac{1}{8}$

(I) $\frac{4}{8} = \frac{1}{2}$

(E) $\frac{1}{4}$

(J) $\frac{4}{16} = \frac{1}{4}$

12. (A) $\frac{4}{8} - \frac{1}{8} = \frac{3}{8}$

(F) $\frac{7}{10} - \frac{5}{10} = \frac{2}{10} = \frac{1}{5}$

(B) $\frac{8}{16} - \frac{1}{16} = \frac{7}{16}$

(G) $\frac{5}{20} - \frac{4}{20} = \frac{1}{20}$

(C) $\frac{12}{16} - \frac{3}{16} = \frac{9}{16}$

(H) $\frac{4}{12} - \frac{3}{12} = \frac{1}{12}$

(D) $\frac{10}{16} - \frac{5}{16} = \frac{5}{16}$

(I) $\frac{4}{6} - \frac{3}{6} = \frac{1}{6}$

(E) $\frac{6}{8} - \frac{3}{8} = \frac{3}{8}$

(J) $\frac{10}{15} - \frac{9}{15} = \frac{1}{15}$

13. (A) $\frac{2}{5}$

(D) $\frac{1}{12}$

(B) $\frac{5}{8}$

(E) $\frac{7}{20}$

(C) $\frac{5}{11}$

14. (A) $1 - \frac{1}{52} = \frac{51}{52}$

(B) $1 - \frac{4}{52} = 1 - \frac{1}{13} = \frac{12}{13}$

(C) $1 - \frac{8}{52} = 1 - \frac{2}{13} = \frac{11}{13}$

(D) $1 - \frac{12}{52} = 1 - \frac{3}{13} = \frac{10}{13}$

15. (A) $1\frac{1}{2}$

$\frac{3}{4} + \frac{3}{4} = \frac{6}{4} = 1\frac{2}{4} = 1\frac{1}{2}$

(B) $\frac{3}{8}$

$1\frac{1}{4} - \frac{7}{8} = \frac{5}{4} - \frac{7}{8} = \frac{10}{8} - \frac{7}{8} = \frac{3}{8}$

(C) $4\frac{3}{4}$

$5\frac{1}{2} - \frac{3}{4} = 5\frac{2}{4} - \frac{3}{4} =$

$\frac{22}{4} - \frac{3}{4} = \frac{19}{4} = 4\frac{3}{4}$

(D) $8\frac{7}{8}$

$3\frac{1}{8} + 5\frac{3}{4} = (3 + 5) + \left(\frac{1}{8} + \frac{6}{8}\right) = 8\frac{7}{8}$

(E) $2\frac{1}{16}$

$4\frac{5}{16} - 2\frac{1}{4} = 4\frac{5}{16} - 2\frac{4}{16} = 2\frac{1}{16}$

(F) $18\frac{9}{32}$

$8\frac{1}{32} + 10\frac{1}{4} =$

$(8 + 10) + \left(\frac{1}{32} + \frac{8}{32}\right) = 18\frac{9}{32}$

(G) $11\frac{7}{10}$

$7\frac{1}{10} + 4\frac{3}{5} =$

$(7 + 4) + \left(\frac{1}{10} + \frac{6}{10}\right) = 11\frac{7}{10}$

(H) $6\frac{7}{8}$

$9 - 2\frac{1}{8}$ or   First, subtract the 2.

$8\frac{8}{8} - 2\frac{1}{8} = 6\frac{7}{8}$ $9 - 2 = 7$

Then subtract $\frac{1}{8}$: $7 - \frac{1}{8} = 6\frac{7}{8}$

(I) $12\frac{1}{8}$

$3\frac{7}{8} + 8\frac{1}{4} =$

$(3 + 8) + \left(\frac{7}{8} + \frac{2}{8}\right) = 11\frac{9}{8} = 12\frac{1}{8}$

(J) $4\frac{1}{4}$

$10 - 5\frac{3}{4} =$ or   First, subtract the 5.

$9\frac{4}{4} - 5\frac{3}{4} = 4\frac{1}{4}$ $10 - 5 = 5$

Then subtract $\frac{3}{4}$: $5 - \frac{3}{4} = 4\frac{1}{4}$

(K) $79\frac{1}{6}$

$66\frac{2}{3} + 12\frac{1}{2} =$

$(66 + 12) + \left(\frac{4}{6} + \frac{3}{6}\right) = 78\frac{7}{6} = 79\frac{1}{6}$

(L) $20\frac{5}{6}$

$37\frac{1}{2} - 16\frac{2}{3} =$

$37\frac{3}{6} - 16\frac{4}{6} =$

$36\frac{6}{6} + \frac{3}{6} - 16\frac{4}{6} =$

$39\frac{9}{6} - 16\frac{4}{6} = 20\frac{5}{6}$

16. (A) 13 gal 1 qt

    4 gal 2 qt

  + 8 gal 3 qt

  12 gal 5 qt = 13 gal 1 qt

(B) 94 ft 4 in.

100 ft

− 5 ft 8 in.

First, subtract 5 ft from 100 ft to get 95 ft.

Then subtract 8 in. to get 94 ft 4 in.

C 7 lb 11 oz

$$12 \text{ lb } 5 \text{ oz} = 11 \text{ lb } 21 \text{ oz}$$
$$- \underline{\quad 4 \text{ lb } 10 \text{ oz} = \quad 4 \text{ lb } 10 \text{ oz}}$$
$$7 \text{ lb } 11 \text{ oz}$$

D 2 ft 9 in.

$$3 \text{ ft } 2 \text{ in.}$$
$$2 \text{ ft } 8 \text{ in.}$$
$$+ \underline{\quad 1 \text{ ft } 5 \text{ in.}}$$
$$6 \text{ ft } 15 \text{ in.} = 7 \text{ ft } 3 \text{ in.}$$

First, subtract 7 ft from 10 ft to get 3 ft. Then subtract 3 in. to get 2 ft 9 in.

CALCULATOR EXPLORATION

A $1\frac{13}{24}$ **C** $11\frac{19}{40}$

B $1\frac{11}{12}$ **D** $12\frac{11}{16}$

---

17. close to 0: **A**, **D**, **I**, **L**, **O**

close to $\frac{1}{2}$: **B**, **F**, **H**, **K**, **M**, **N**, **P**

close to 1: **C**, **E**, **G**, **J**

18. **A** $1 + 0 = 1$ Exact: $\frac{97}{99}$

B $1 - 1 = 0$ Exact: $\frac{5}{84}$

C $\frac{1}{2} + \frac{1}{2} = 1$ Exact: $\frac{41}{45}$

D $\frac{1}{2} + 0 = \frac{1}{2}$ Exact: $\frac{424}{735}$

E $1 + 1 = 2$ Exact: $1\frac{47}{60}$

F $1 + \frac{1}{2} = 1\frac{1}{2}$ Exact: $1\frac{20}{77}$

G $(3 + 1) + (9 + 1) = 14$ Exact: $13\frac{13}{24}$

H $(6 + 0) + (3 + 0) = 9$ Exact: $9\frac{9}{20}$

I $(9 + 1) - (3 + 0) = 7$ Exact: $6\frac{43}{60}$

19. Compare to:

A $\frac{1}{3} + \frac{2}{3}$ (since $\frac{1}{4}$ is less than $\frac{1}{3}$): less than 1

B $\frac{3}{4} + \frac{1}{4}$ (since $\frac{1}{5}$ is less than $\frac{1}{4}$): less than 1

C $\frac{1}{4} + \frac{1}{4}$ (since both are less than $\frac{1}{4}$): less than $\frac{1}{2}$

D $\frac{5}{8} - \frac{1}{8}$ (since $\frac{1}{10}$ is less than $\frac{1}{8}$): greater than $\frac{1}{2}$

E $1 - \frac{1}{2}$ (since $\frac{13}{15}$ is less than 1): less than $\frac{1}{2}$

F $\frac{3}{16} + \frac{1}{16}$ (since $\frac{1}{10}$ is greater than $\frac{1}{16}$): greater than $\frac{1}{4}$

20. **A** Estimate: $\frac{8}{17} + \frac{1}{4} \approx$

$$\frac{1}{2} + \frac{1}{4} = \frac{3}{4}$$
Exact: $\frac{49}{68}$

B Estimate: $\frac{9}{10} + \frac{1}{16} \approx$

$$\frac{9}{10} + \frac{1}{10} = 1$$
Exact: $\frac{77}{80}$

C Estimate: $\frac{1}{2} - \frac{11}{40} \approx$

$$\frac{1}{2} - \frac{1}{4} = \frac{1}{4}$$
Exact: $\frac{9}{40}$

D Estimate: $10\frac{1}{2} + 3\frac{5}{9} \approx$

$$10\frac{1}{2} + 4 \approx 14\frac{1}{2}$$
Exact: $14\frac{1}{18}$

E Estimate: $11\frac{3}{4} - 7\frac{7}{8} \approx$

$$11\frac{3}{4} - 8 = 3\frac{3}{4}$$
Exact: $3\frac{7}{8}$

F Estimate: $20\frac{3}{5} - 5\frac{1}{2} \approx$

$$20\frac{1}{2} - 5\frac{1}{2} = 15$$
Exact: $15\frac{1}{10}$

21. An estimate of $1\frac{1}{2}$ cups is probably adequate.

22. An estimate would be appropriate but since these are "nice" numbers, find the exact answer.

$$5\frac{5}{8} - 1\frac{2}{8} = 4\frac{3}{8} \text{ lb}$$

23. No, she will reach only 6 feet 11 inches.

5 ft 8 in. + 1 ft 3 in. = 6 ft 11 in.

USING DATA

A $\frac{5}{8} + \frac{1}{16} = \frac{10}{16} + \frac{1}{16} = \frac{11}{16}$ in.

B
stud	$5\frac{5}{8}$
dry wall	$\frac{1}{2}$
stucco	$+ 1\frac{1}{16}$
	$7\frac{3}{16}$ in.

C
tile	$\frac{3}{8}$ hardwood $\frac{5}{8}$
board	$+ \frac{1}{2}$
	$\frac{7}{8} - \frac{5}{8} = \frac{2}{8} = \frac{1}{4}$ in.

D quarter-round $\frac{9}{16}$

baseboard $+ \frac{9}{16}$

$\frac{18}{16} = 1\frac{1}{8}$ in.

E cabinet $34\frac{1}{2}$

plywood $\frac{5}{8}$

granite $+ \frac{3}{4}$

$35\frac{7}{8}$

F $4\frac{3}{8} + 4\frac{3}{8} + 3\frac{1}{4} = 12$

$12 + \frac{1}{8} + \frac{1}{8} = 12\frac{1}{4}$ inches

The three pieces would take all of the 12-inch strip. Because two cuts with the carbide tip blade would take another $\frac{1}{4}$ inch, Dennis could not cut these 3 pieces.

CHECK YOUR UNDERSTANDING, page 174

1. **A** $\frac{7}{8}$ **F** $\frac{2}{10} = \frac{1}{5}$

   B $\frac{5}{4} = 1\frac{1}{4}$ **G** $\frac{11}{10} = 1\frac{1}{10}$

   C $\frac{5}{8}$ **H** $\frac{5}{12}$

   D $\frac{23}{16} = 1\frac{7}{16}$ **I** $\frac{19}{15} = 1\frac{4}{15}$

   E $\frac{23}{16} = 1\frac{7}{16}$

2. **A** Estimate: $1\frac{1}{2}$ **D** Estimate: 1

   $\frac{3}{7} + \frac{4}{5} \approx \frac{1}{2} + 1 = 1\frac{1}{2}$ $\frac{15}{16} - \frac{1}{20} \approx 1 - 0 = 1$

   Exact: $1\frac{8}{35}$ Exact: $\frac{71}{80}$

   B Estimate: 2 **E** Estimate: $\frac{3}{5}$

   $\frac{11}{12} + \frac{13}{15} \approx 1 + 1 = 2$ $\frac{15}{16} - \frac{2}{5} \approx 1 - \frac{2}{5} = \frac{3}{5}$

   Exact: $1\frac{47}{60}$ Exact: $\frac{43}{80}$

   C Estimate: $\frac{1}{2}$

   $\frac{1}{5} + \frac{1}{4} \approx \frac{1}{4} + \frac{1}{4} = \frac{1}{2}$

   Exact: $\frac{9}{20}$

3. $45\frac{2}{3}$ ft

   $50 - 4\frac{1}{3} = 49\frac{3}{3} - 4\frac{1}{3} = 45\frac{2}{3}$

4. $\frac{21}{32}$ is larger $\left(\frac{5}{8} = \frac{20}{32}\right)$

5. $12\frac{5}{6}$ hr

   $(2 + 1 + 5 + 3) + \left(\frac{1}{4} + \frac{1}{2} + \frac{3}{4} + \frac{1}{3}\right) = 11 + 1\frac{5}{6} = 12\frac{5}{6}$ hr

   She would probably record 13 hours.

6. 9 ft 2 in.

   6 ft 6 in.

   1 ft 4 in.

   $+ $ 1 ft 4 in.

   8 ft 14 in. = 9 ft 2 in.

7. Your estimates should be close to the answers given.

   A $(7 + 4) + \left(\frac{1}{4} + \frac{1}{4}\right) = 11\frac{1}{2}$ Exact: $11\frac{7}{12}$

   B $10\frac{1}{3} - 6 = 4\frac{1}{3}$ Exact: $4\frac{25}{48}$

   D $5 + 2\frac{1}{2} = 7\frac{1}{2}$ Exact: $7\frac{34}{99}$

   D $6\frac{2}{3} + \frac{1}{3} = 7$ Exact: $6\frac{47}{48}$

   E $30\frac{1}{2} - 10\frac{1}{2} = 20$ Exact: $19\frac{49}{60}$

8. $65\frac{1}{2}$ in.

   $21\frac{3}{4} \approx 22$

   $19\frac{1}{16} \approx 19$

   $12\frac{7}{8} \approx 13$

   $11\frac{2}{5} \approx 11\frac{1}{2}$

   $65\frac{1}{2}$

TEST-TAKING PRACTICE, page 175

1. **(4)** $10\frac{1}{4}$ ft

   $(7 + 2) + \left(\frac{3}{4} + \frac{1}{2}\right) = 9 + 1\frac{1}{4} = 10\frac{1}{4}$

2. **(4)** $6\frac{1}{2}$ in.

   $(1 + 2 + 2) + \left(\frac{3}{8} + \frac{7}{8} + \frac{2}{8}\right)$

   $5 + \frac{12}{8} = 5 + \frac{8}{8} + \frac{4}{8} = 6\frac{1}{2}$

3. **(1)** $1\frac{1}{2}$ in.

   $5 - \left(1\frac{3}{4} + 1\frac{3}{4}\right) \approx$

   $5 - (2 + 2) = 1$

   The estimate of 1 is closest to choice (1) $1\frac{1}{2}$.

4. $\frac{5}{8}$

$1 - P(E) = 1 - \frac{3}{8} = \frac{5}{8}$

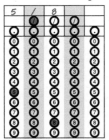

5. **(4)** D, B, C, A

Change to decimals with the same place value.

A: 0.2 = 0.200   ④

B: $\frac{3}{8}$ = 0.375   ②

C: $\frac{1}{4}$ = 0.250   ③

D: 0.5 = 0.500   ①

6. **(4)** 7 hours 35 minutes

2 hr 30 min
1 hr 45 min
+ 3 hr 20 min
_____
6 hr 95 min = 7 hr 35 min

Lesson 17

Multiplying and Dividing Fractions,
pages 176–185

MENTAL MATH

1. greater than	**3.** less than
2. less than	**4.** less than

1. Ⓐ $\frac{3}{8}$ Ⓔ $\frac{2}{6} = \frac{1}{3}$

Ⓑ $\frac{5}{24}$ Ⓕ $\frac{3}{20}$

Ⓒ $\frac{3}{16}$ Ⓖ $\frac{3}{32}$

Ⓓ $\frac{8}{15}$ Ⓗ $\frac{4}{40} = \frac{1}{10}$

2. Answers will vary.

3. Ⓐ $\frac{1}{2} \times \frac{\overset{24}{\cancel{48}}}{1} = 24$ Ⓖ $\frac{1}{8} \times \frac{\overset{7}{\cancel{56}}}{1} = 7$

Ⓑ $\frac{1}{4} \times \frac{\overset{12}{\cancel{48}}}{1} = 12$ Ⓗ $\frac{3}{8} \times \frac{\overset{7}{\cancel{56}}}{1} = 21$

Ⓒ $\frac{1}{3} \times \frac{\overset{16}{\cancel{48}}}{1} = 16$ Ⓘ $\frac{5}{8} \times \frac{\overset{7}{\cancel{56}}}{1} = 35$

Ⓓ $\frac{2}{3} \times \frac{\overset{4}{\cancel{12}}}{1} = 8$ Ⓙ $\frac{1}{5} \times \frac{\overset{12}{\cancel{60}}}{1} = 12$

Ⓔ $\frac{2}{3} \times \frac{\overset{8}{\cancel{24}}}{1} = 16$ Ⓚ $\frac{1}{10} \times \frac{\overset{6}{\cancel{60}}}{1} = 6$

Ⓕ $\frac{2}{3} \times \frac{\overset{16}{\cancel{48}}}{1} = 32$ Ⓛ $\frac{3}{5} \times \frac{\overset{12}{\cancel{60}}}{1} = 36$

4. Ⓐ $\frac{3}{5} \times \frac{1}{6} = \frac{1}{10}$ Ⓔ $\frac{3}{4} \times \frac{8}{9} = \frac{2}{3}$

Ⓑ $\frac{2}{3} \times \frac{1}{4} = \frac{1}{6}$ Ⓕ $\frac{5}{6} \times \frac{9}{10} = \frac{3}{4}$

Ⓒ $\frac{1}{2} \times \frac{4}{5} = \frac{2}{5}$ Ⓖ $\frac{2}{5} \times \frac{3}{8} = \frac{3}{20}$

Ⓓ $\frac{1}{3} \times \frac{3}{4} = \frac{1}{4}$ Ⓗ $\frac{2}{3} \times \frac{3}{8} = \frac{1}{4}$

USING DATA

Ⓐ $6,750 $\frac{9}{10} \times 7,500 = 6,750$

Ⓑ $90,000 $\frac{3}{5} \times 150,000 = 90,000$

Ⓒ $262,500 $\frac{7}{10} \times 375,000 = 262,500$

5. $P(\text{3 heads}) = \frac{1}{2} \times \frac{1}{2} \times \frac{1}{2} = \frac{1}{8}$

6. $P(\text{tail}) = \frac{1}{2}$; each toss is an independent event

7. $P(20) \times P(20) = \frac{2}{10} \times \frac{1}{9} = \frac{1}{45}$

8. $P(\text{make}) \times P(\text{make}) = \frac{3}{5} \times \frac{3}{5} = \frac{9}{25}$

9. The estimates below show one possible way to estimate.

Ⓐ Exact: $\frac{10}{3} \times \frac{3}{4} = \frac{5}{2} = 2\frac{1}{2}$

Estimate: $3 \times 1 = 3$

Ⓑ Exact: $\frac{7}{8} \times \frac{16}{5} = \frac{14}{5} = 2\frac{4}{5}$

Estimate: $1 \times 3 = 3$

Ⓒ Exact: $\frac{9}{5} \times \frac{10}{3} = 6$

Estimate: $2 \times 3 = 6$

Ⓓ Exact: $\frac{21}{8} \times \frac{3}{2} = \frac{63}{16} = 3\frac{15}{16}$

Estimate: $3 \times 1 = 3$

E Exact: $(7 \times 16) + \left(\frac{1}{8} \times 16\right) = 112 + 2 = 114$

Estimate: Should be less than $7 \times 20 = 140$

F Exact: $(24 \times 5) + \left(24 \times \frac{5}{6}\right) = 120 + 20 = 140$

Estimate: $25 \times 6 = 150$

G Exact: $(90 \times 3) + \left(90 \times \frac{3}{4}\right) = 270 + 67\frac{1}{2} = 337\frac{1}{2}$

Estimate: $90 \times 4 = 360$

H Exact: $(7 \times 20) + \left(\frac{7}{8} \times 20\right) = 140 + 17\frac{1}{2} = 157\frac{1}{2}$

Estimate: $8 \times 20 = 160$

10. **A** $3\frac{1}{2} \times 12 = 36 + 6 = 42$ in.

B $2\frac{1}{4} \times 36 = 72 + 9 = 81$ in.

C $5\frac{3}{4} \times 16 = 80 + 12 = 92$ oz

D $3\frac{3}{4} \times 60 = 180 + 45 = 225$ min

E $2\frac{1}{4} \times 52 = 104 + 13 = 117$ wk

F $10\frac{1}{8} \times 16 = 160 + 2 = 162$ cups

G Each problem asked us to combine a number of equal groups.

11. **A** $\frac{3}{8} \times \$4.18$: $\frac{3}{8} \times \$4.00 = \$1.50$

B $\frac{1}{8} \times \$5.75$: $\frac{1}{8} \times \$5.60 = \$.70$

C $\frac{3}{4} \times \$3.89$: $\frac{3}{4} \times \$4.00 = \$3.00$

D $\frac{1}{4} \times \$3.99$: $\frac{1}{4} \times \$4.00 = \$1.00$

12. Notice that all of the estimated numbers below are evenly divisible by 3.

A $\frac{1}{3} \times \$24 = \$8$ **D** $\frac{1}{3} \times \$120 = \$40$

B $\frac{1}{3} \times \$9 = \$3$ **E** $\frac{1}{3} \times \$210 = \$70$

C $\frac{1}{3} \times \$18 = \$6$

13. **A** $\frac{7}{8} \div \frac{1}{8} = \frac{7}{8} \times \frac{\overset{1}{8}}{1} = 7$

B $8 \div \frac{1}{3} = \frac{8}{1} \times \frac{3}{1} = 24$

C $8 \div \frac{2}{3} = \frac{\overset{4}{8}}{1} \times \frac{3}{2} = 12$

D $\frac{3}{4} \div \frac{1}{2} = \frac{3}{\underset{2}{4}} \times \frac{\overset{1}{2}}{1} = \frac{3}{2} = 1\frac{1}{2}$

E $\frac{3}{4} \div \frac{1}{8} = \frac{3}{\underset{1}{4}} \times \frac{\overset{2}{8}}{1} = 6$

F $\frac{3}{4} \div \frac{7}{8} = \frac{3}{\underset{1}{4}} \times \frac{\overset{2}{8}}{7} = \frac{6}{7}$

G $10 \div \frac{5}{6} = \frac{\overset{2}{10}}{1} \times \frac{6}{\underset{1}{5}} = 12$

H $3 \div \frac{3}{4} = \frac{3}{1} \times \frac{4}{\underset{1}{3}} = 4$

I $20 \div \frac{2}{3} = \frac{\overset{10}{20}}{1} \times \frac{3}{2} = 30$

CALCULATOR EXPLORATION

A $\frac{5}{8} \times 45 = 28\frac{1}{8}$

Estimate: The answer should be between $25 \left(\frac{5}{8} \times 40\right)$ and $30 \left(\frac{5}{8} \times 48\right)$.

B $\frac{3}{4} \times 7\frac{1}{2} = 5\frac{5}{8}$

Estimate: The answer should be a little less than $6 \left(\frac{3}{4} \times 8\right)$.

C $15 \div \frac{7}{8} = 17\frac{1}{7}$

Estimate: The answer should be greater than 15 because $\frac{7}{8}$ is less than 1.

D $90 \div 5\frac{1}{4} = 17\frac{1}{7}$

Estimate: The answer should be around 20 $(100 \div 5)$.

E 225 miles

$d = rt$

$d = (60)\left(3\frac{3}{4}\right)$

$d = 225$

Estimate: $60 \times 4 = 240$.

F 38 sheets

You are asking, "How many $\frac{5}{8}$s in 24?"

$24 \div \frac{5}{8} = 38\frac{2}{5}$ sheets

Estimate: The answer will be between 24 and 48.

G $12\frac{3}{8}$ gallons

You are asking, "What is $\frac{3}{4}$ of $16\frac{1}{2}$?"

$16\frac{1}{2} \times \frac{3}{4} = 12\frac{3}{8}$

Estimate: The answer will be around 12 $\left(\frac{3}{4} \text{ of } 16\right)$.

H $\frac{5}{12}$

You are asking, "What is $\frac{2}{3}$ of $\frac{5}{8}$?"

$\frac{2}{3} \times \frac{5}{8} = \frac{5}{12}$

Estimate: The answer should be less than $\frac{5}{8}$.

① $\frac{5}{6}$ pound

$2\frac{1}{2} \times \frac{1}{3} = \frac{5}{6}$

The words "divided into thirds" may be confusing, this asks you to find $\frac{1}{3}$ of $2\frac{1}{2}$, that is, multiply by $\frac{1}{3}$ (or divide by 3).

Estimate: The answer should be less than 1.

CHECK YOUR UNDERSTANDING, page 184

1. **Ⓐ** 24 **Ⓓ** 55

   Ⓑ 12 **Ⓔ** 72

   Ⓒ 30 **Ⓕ** 45

2. Estimates may vary.

   Ⓐ $\frac{1}{4}$ of \$2.00 = \$.50 **Ⓓ** $\frac{1}{4}$ of \$12.00 = \$3.00

   Ⓑ $\frac{1}{4}$ of \$5.60 = \$1.40 **Ⓔ** $\frac{1}{4}$ of \$20.00 = \$5.00

   Ⓒ $\frac{1}{4}$ of \$10.00 = \$2.50

3. **Ⓐ** $\frac{1}{3}$ cup $\left(1 \times \frac{1}{3} = \frac{1}{3}\right)$

   Ⓑ $\frac{1}{2}$ cup $\left(1\frac{1}{2} \times \frac{1}{3} = \frac{\overset{1}{\cancel{3}}}{2} \times \frac{1}{\cancel{3}} = \frac{1}{2}\right)$

   Ⓒ $\frac{2}{3}$ cup $\left(2 \times \frac{1}{3} = \frac{2}{3}\right)$

   Ⓓ $\frac{1}{6}$ cup $\left(\frac{1}{2} \times \frac{1}{3} = \frac{1}{6}\right)$

   Ⓔ $\frac{1}{4}$ pound each $\left(\frac{\overset{1}{\cancel{3}}}{4} \times \frac{1}{\cancel{3}} = \frac{1}{4}\right)$

4. **Ⓐ** $4\frac{1}{10} + 6\frac{4}{7} = 10\frac{47}{70}$ **Ⓓ** $15\frac{3}{4} \div \frac{1}{2} = 31\frac{1}{2}$

   Ⓑ $7\frac{1}{2} \times 4\frac{5}{6} = 36\frac{1}{4}$ **Ⓔ** $9\frac{7}{8} \times 12\frac{1}{5} = 120\frac{19}{40}$

   Ⓒ $33\frac{1}{3} - 12\frac{1}{2} = 20\frac{5}{6}$

5. **Ⓐ** $x = 4\frac{2}{3} + \frac{2}{3} = 5\frac{1}{3}$

   Ⓑ $x = \frac{9}{10} \div \frac{4}{5} = \frac{9}{10} \times \frac{5}{4} = 1\frac{1}{8}$

   Ⓒ $x = \frac{9}{16} - \frac{5}{32} = \frac{13}{32}$

   Ⓓ $x = 8\frac{1}{3} \div \frac{3}{4} = 8\frac{1}{3} \times \frac{4}{3} = 11\frac{1}{9}$

   Ⓔ $x = 21\frac{3}{5} \div \frac{1}{5} = 21\frac{3}{5} \times \frac{5}{1} = 108$

6. **Ⓐ** 330 min $(5 \times 60) + \left(\frac{1}{2} \times 60\right) = 300 + 30 = 330$

   Ⓑ 56 hr $(2 \times 24) + \left(\frac{1}{3} \times 24\right) = 48 + 8 = 56$

   Ⓒ 13 ft $(4 \times 3) + \left(\frac{1}{3} \times 3\right) = 12 + 1 = 13$

   Ⓓ 81 in. $(2 \times 36) + \left(\frac{1}{4} \times 36\right) = 72 + 9 = 81$

   Ⓔ 28 c $(1 \times 16) + \left(\frac{3}{4} \times 16\right) = 16 + 12 = 28$

7. **(3)** 5 ft 8 in.

$$\begin{array}{r} 2 \text{ ft } 10 \text{ in.} \\ \times \qquad 2 \\ \hline 4 \text{ ft } 20 \text{ in.} = 5 \text{ ft } 8 \text{ in.} \end{array}$$

TEST-TAKING PRACTICE, page 185

1. **(4)** 48

You are asking, "How many $\frac{3}{4}$s in 36?"

$36 \div \frac{3}{4} = \overset{12}{\cancel{36}} \times \frac{4}{\underset{1}{\cancel{3}}} = 48$

Since you divided by a number less than 1, your answer should be greater than 36.

2. 60

$5 - 1\frac{1}{4} = 3\frac{3}{4}$ lb = 48 oz + 12 oz = 60 oz

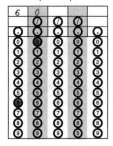

3. **(4)** $\frac{7}{20}$

$\underset{\underset{\uparrow}{\substack{\text{interest portion} \\ \text{of mortgage}}}}{\frac{7}{\underset{4}{\cancel{8}}}} \times \underset{\underset{\uparrow}{\substack{\text{fraction of} \\ \text{income going} \\ \text{to mortgage}}}}{\frac{\overset{1}{\cancel{2}}}{5}} = \underset{\underset{\uparrow}{\substack{\text{fraction of income} \\ \text{going to interest}}}}{\frac{7}{20}}$

4. **(3)** 465

$30 \times 15\frac{1}{2} = (30 \times 15) + \left(30 \times \frac{1}{2}\right) =$
$450 + 15 = 465$

5. **(3)** 31

$15\frac{1}{2} \div \frac{1}{2} = 15\frac{1}{2} \times 2 = 31$

6. **(1)** $2\frac{1}{4}$

$20\frac{1}{4} \div 9 = 2\frac{1}{4}$

Lesson 18

Making Connections, pages 186–195

1. $\frac{1}{8}$		**4.** $\frac{3}{10}$	
2. $\frac{1}{16}$		**5.** $\frac{3}{20}$	
3. $\frac{1}{6}$		**6.** $\frac{2}{12} = \frac{1}{6}$	

1. Check with your calculator.

2. Ⓐ $\dfrac{\left(0 + \frac{1}{4}\right)}{2} = \dfrac{1}{8}$ Ⓒ $\dfrac{\left(\frac{1}{2} + \frac{3}{4}\right)}{2} = \dfrac{5}{8}$

Ⓑ $\dfrac{\left(\frac{1}{4} + \frac{1}{2}\right)}{2} = \dfrac{3}{8}$ Ⓓ $\dfrac{\left(\frac{3}{4} + 1\right)}{2} = \dfrac{7}{8}$

Ⓔ The decimal values of the less-familiar eighths above can be found by finding the decimal value that is halfway between the fourths that you know.

Player	Cmp/Att	Decimal	Rank	Ints/TDs	Decimal	Rank	Common fraction Ints/TDs
Kurt Warner	$\frac{375}{546}$	0.687	1	$\frac{22}{36}$	0.611	4	$\frac{3}{5}$
Peyton Manning	$\frac{343}{547}$	0.627	3	$\frac{23}{26}$	0.885	8	$\frac{9}{10}$
Brett Favre	$\frac{314}{510}$	0.616	5	$\frac{15}{32}$	0.469	3	$\frac{1}{2}$
Aaron Brooks	$\frac{312}{558}$	0.559	10	$\frac{22}{26}$	0.846	7	$\frac{5}{6}$
Rich Gannon	$\frac{361}{549}$	0.658	2	$\frac{9}{27}$	0.333	1	$\frac{1}{3}$
Trent Green	$\frac{296}{523}$	0.566	8	$\frac{24}{17}$	1.412	10	$\frac{7}{5}$
Kerry Collins	$\frac{327}{568}$	0.576	7	$\frac{16}{19}$	0.842	6	$\frac{5}{6}$
Jake Plummer	$\frac{304}{525}$	0.579	6	$\frac{14}{18}$	0.778	5	$\frac{7}{9}$ or $\frac{3}{4}$
Jeff Garcia	$\frac{316}{504}$	0.627	4	$\frac{12}{32}$	0.375	2	$\frac{3}{8}$
Doug Flutie	$\frac{294}{521}$	0.564	9	$\frac{18}{15}$	1.200	9	$\frac{6}{5}$

3. Ⓐ $13\frac{3}{4} + 9\frac{1}{2} = 22 + 1\frac{1}{4} = 23\frac{1}{4}$ in.

$13.75 + 9.5 = 23.25$ in.

Ⓑ $4\frac{1}{2} - 3\frac{3}{8} = 1\frac{1}{8}$ in.

$4.5 - 3.375 = 1.125$ in.

Ⓒ $50 \div \frac{9}{2} = \frac{100}{9} = 11\frac{1}{9} \approx 11$ pieces

$50 \div 4.5 = 11.1... \approx 11$ pieces

Ⓓ $\frac{5}{8} \times \$64 = \$40$

$0.625 \times \$64 = \$40$

$\left(\frac{5}{8} = 0.625\right)$

Ⓔ $\frac{7}{8} \times \$2.35 \approx \frac{7}{8} \times \$2.40 = \$2.10$

$0.875 \times \$2.35 = \$2.05625 \approx \$2.06$

$\left(\frac{7}{8} = 0.875\right)$

4. $\frac{7}{100} \times \frac{3}{1,000} = \frac{21}{100,000}$ written as a decimal is 0.00021. Because you have to multiply the denominators as well as the numerators, the denominator increases to 10^5, a decimal with 5 (2 + 3) decimal places.

5. Ⓐ 0.36 m²

$A = s^2$

$A = (0.6)^2$ m

$A = 0.36$ m²

Ⓑ $1.88

$\$5.00 - \$3.12 = \$1.88$

Ⓒ 7.9 m

15 m $- 7.1$ m $= 7.9$ m

Ⓓ $2.10

$\frac{\$7.35}{3.5} = \$2.10$

Ⓔ 0.45 m²

$A = \frac{1}{2}(0.6)(1.5) = 0.45$

Ⓕ 125 cans

$\frac{5.00}{.04} = 125$

Ⓖ 640 nails

$\frac{16.000}{.025} = 640$

(1 lb = 16 oz)

6. Ⓐ $\$119.97 \times \frac{3}{4} \approx \$120 \times \frac{3}{4} = \$90$

Ⓑ $\$18.88 \times \frac{3}{4} \approx \$20 \times \frac{3}{4} = \$15$

Ⓒ $\$47.88 \times \frac{3}{4} \approx \$48 \times \frac{3}{4} = \$36$

Ⓓ $\$31.99 \times \frac{3}{4} \approx \$32 \times \frac{3}{4} = \$24$

Ⓔ $\$14.94 \times \frac{3}{4} \approx \$16 \times \frac{3}{4} = \$12$

Notice that the rounded numbers were chosen to be divisible by the 4 in $\frac{3}{4}$.

7. Ⓐ $89.98   Ⓓ $24.00
Ⓑ $14.16   Ⓔ $11.21
Ⓒ $35.91

8. (3) $s = 400 - \frac{1}{4}(400)$

9. Ⓐ $8.80

$$\frac{3}{4}x = 6.60$$

$$x = 6.60 \times \frac{4}{3} = 8.80$$

Ⓑ $5.28

$$\frac{3}{4}x = 3.96$$

$$x = 3.96 \times \frac{4}{3} = 5.28$$

Ⓒ $12.96

$$\frac{3}{4}x = 9.72$$

$$x = 9.72 \times \frac{4}{3} = 12.96$$

10. Ⓐ $1.60

$$10 - \left(\frac{3}{2} \times 5.60\right) = c$$

$$10 - \left(\frac{3}{2} \times \frac{5.6}{1}\right) = c$$

$$\$1.60 = c$$

Ⓑ 13.3 gal

$$g = \left(1 - \frac{1}{8}\right)15.2$$

$$g = \frac{7}{8} \times \frac{15.2}{1} = 13.3 \text{ gal}$$

Ⓒ 64 mph

$$\frac{d}{t} = r$$

$$144 \div 2\frac{1}{4} = r$$

$$144 \div \frac{9}{4} = 144 \times \frac{4}{9} = r$$

$$64 \text{ mph} = r$$

Ⓓ $37.18

$$C = \$1.69(\pi d)$$

$$C = \$1.69\left(\frac{22}{7} \times 7\right)$$

$$C = 1.69\left(\frac{22}{7} \times \frac{7}{1}\right)$$

$$C = 1.69(22)$$

$$C = \$37.18$$

CHECK YOUR UNDERSTANDING, page 194

1. $\frac{124}{347} = .357$

2. $\frac{100}{328}$ is less than $\frac{1}{3}$ because the denominator is greater than 300.

3. 189

$$\frac{x}{630} = .3$$

$$x = 630\,(.3) = 189$$

4. Ⓐ 3 oz $\left(\frac{3}{16} \text{ lb}\right)$ is greater $\left(\frac{1}{8} = \frac{2}{16}\right)$

Ⓑ $\frac{5}{8}$ (0.625) is greater

Ⓒ 30 in. is greater $\left(2\frac{1}{4} \text{ ft} = 24 + 3 \text{ in.} = 27 \text{ in.}\right)$

Ⓓ 45 min is greater $\left(\frac{2}{3} \text{ hr} = 40 \text{ min}\right)$

Ⓔ 15 cups is greater $\left(3\frac{1}{2} \text{ qt} = 12 + 2 = 14 \text{ cups}\right)$

5. $8\frac{1}{8}$ sq ft

$$A = \frac{1}{2}bh$$

$$A = \frac{1}{2}\left(5 \times 3\frac{1}{4}\right)$$

$$A = \frac{1}{2} \times \frac{5}{1} \times \frac{13}{4} = \frac{65}{8} = 8\frac{1}{8} \text{ sq ft}$$

6. $11\frac{2}{3}$ sq ft

$$A = lw$$

$$A = 5 \times 2\frac{1}{3} \left(\frac{4}{12} = \frac{1}{3} \text{ foot}\right)$$

$$A = (5 \times 2) + \left(5 \times \frac{1}{3}\right)$$

$$A = 10 + \frac{5}{3} = 10 + 1\frac{2}{3} = 11\frac{2}{3} \text{ sq ft}$$

7. $\frac{1}{2}$ of $\frac{1}{3} = \frac{1}{6}$

8. In each case, you could first find $1 - \frac{1}{3} = \frac{2}{3}$.

Ⓐ $\frac{\$8.99}{1} \times \frac{2}{3} = \$5.99$

Ⓑ $\frac{\$6.79}{1} \times \frac{2}{3} = \$4.53$

Ⓒ $\frac{\$4.39}{1} \times \frac{2}{3} = \$2.93$

9. 110 stitches

$$10 \div \frac{1}{11} = \frac{10}{1} \times \frac{11}{1} = 110$$

10. Ⓐ $P(\text{a six and a one}) = \frac{1}{6} \times \frac{1}{6} = \frac{1}{36}$

Ⓑ $P(\text{two sixes}) = \frac{1}{6} \times \frac{1}{6} = \frac{1}{36}$

Ⓒ $P(\text{a 6 and a 4, 5, or 6}) = \frac{1}{6} \times \frac{3}{6} = \frac{1}{12}$

Ⓓ $P(\text{a 6 and not a 6}) = \frac{1}{6} \times \frac{5}{6} = \frac{5}{36}$

11. Ⓐ always $(-2)^2 = 4$, $\left(-\frac{1}{2}\right)^2 = \frac{1}{4}$

Ⓑ never $\left(\frac{1}{2}\right)^2 = \frac{1}{4}$, $\left(\frac{1}{4}\right)^2 = \frac{1}{16}$

Ⓒ always $2^2 = 4$, $5^2 = 25$

TEST-TAKING PRACTICE, page 195

1. (4) $\frac{1}{3}$

$$\frac{2}{6} = \frac{1}{3}$$

2. (4) $\frac{1}{8}$

$\frac{1}{2} \times \frac{1}{2} \times \frac{1}{2} = \frac{1}{8}$

3. (4) 40

$15 \div .37 = 40.54$ which must be rounded to 40 in this case.

4. (5) $1\frac{1}{2}$

$4.5 \div 3 = 1.5$, or $\frac{9}{2} \times \frac{1}{3} = \frac{3}{2} = 1\frac{1}{2}$

5. $\frac{3}{16}$

$\frac{3}{4} \times \frac{1}{4} = \frac{3}{16}$

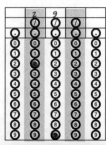

6. (5) 192

$x - \frac{1}{4}x = 144$

$\frac{3}{4}x = 144$

$x = 192$

Lesson 19

Test-Taking Tips, pages 196–201

CHECK YOUR SKILLS

1. (4) 9m

Each yard has 3 ft, so the length is 3m ft
$A = lw$ or $A = 3 \cdot 3m = 9m$ sq ft

2. (1) $4.05

Estimate: $10 - (5 \times \$1.20) =$
$10 - \$6.00 = \$4$
Use calculator: $10 - 5 \times 1.19 = 4.05$

3. 29

Add 10 to both sides: $3p = 87$
Divide both sides by 3: $p = 29$

4. (4) 8.89×10^8

8.89 million is 889,000,000 (8 places)

5. (4) 135°

$180° - 45° = 135°$

6. (2) right

7. (1) 20

$2\frac{1}{2} \div \frac{1}{8} = 20$

Without calculator: $\frac{5}{2} \times \overset{4}{\underset{1}{\cancel{\frac{8}{1}}}} = 20$

8. (5) 42

$(40 - 12) \div \frac{2}{3} = 42$

Without calculator: $\frac{28}{1} \div \frac{2}{3} = \overset{14}{\cancel{\frac{28}{1}}} \times \frac{3}{\underset{1}{\cancel{2}}} = 42$

9. 35

$d = rt = 30$ (1 hr 10 min)

1 hr 10 min $= 1\frac{10}{60}$ hr, so

$d = 30 \times 1\frac{1}{6} = 35$

Without calculator: $(30 \times 1) + \left(30 \times \frac{1}{6}\right) = 30 + 5 = 35$

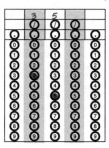

10. (2) 9($8.50)

11. (2) 3 ft 2 in.

$\dfrac{\left(3\frac{1}{2} + 3\frac{1}{3} + 2\frac{2}{3}\right)}{3} = 3\frac{1}{6} = 3$ ft 2 in.

12. (2) $\frac{1}{8}$ in.

Remember: $\frac{1}{8} = \frac{1}{2}$ of $\frac{1}{4}$

$\frac{1}{2} \times 0.25 = 0.12\frac{1}{2}$ or 0.125

13. (5) Not enough information is given.

You need the total seating capacity to find the answer.

14. (4) $6\frac{1}{4}$

$5 \times 1\frac{1}{4} = (5 \times 1) + 5\left(\frac{1}{4}\right) =$

$5 + \frac{5}{4} = 5 + 1\frac{1}{4} = 6\frac{1}{4}$

15. (3) 75°

$\dfrac{180° - 30°}{2} = 75°$

16. **(2)** (6, –3)

17. $\frac{4}{5}$

$$\left(1 - \frac{1}{5}\right) = \frac{4}{5}$$

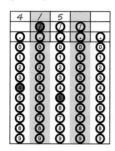

18. **(3)** $\frac{4}{5}$

$$\frac{100}{127} \approx \frac{100 \div 25}{125 \div 25} = \frac{4}{5}$$

19. **(2)** 5.35

$$\frac{1}{10} = 0.1$$

$$5.25 + 0.1 = 5.25 + 0.10 = 5.35$$

20. **(3)** $7\frac{7}{8}\%$

Putting all the rates in decimal form, you are comparing 7.75%, 7.46%, 7.875%, 7.77%, and 7.5%. The highest is 7.875%, or $7\frac{7}{8}\%$

21. **(4)** $5

On the graph: Look above 20 lb. The dollar value of the point on the line is between 4 and 6.

Write the equation: d = 0.25(20) = 5

22. **(1)** 40

On the graph: Look across from 10 dollars. The pound value of the point on the line is between 36 and 48 pounds.

Write the equation: 10 = 0.25n

Divide both sides by 0.25:   40 = n

Lesson 20

Comparisons: Fractions as Ratios,

pages 202–213

M E N T A L M A T H		
1. yes	**4.**	no
2. no	**5.**	no
3. yes	**6.**	yes

1. Ⓐ $\frac{212}{341}$ Ⓓ $\frac{7}{10}$

    Ⓑ $\frac{25}{7}$ Ⓔ $\frac{1}{21}$

    Ⓒ $\frac{23}{180}$ Ⓕ $\frac{1}{9}$

2. Ⓐ $\frac{400 \text{ sq ft}}{1 \text{ gal}}$; 400 sq ft per gallon

    Ⓑ $\frac{4 \text{ glasses}}{1 \text{ qt}}$; 4 glasses per quart

    Ⓒ $\frac{65 \text{ mi}}{1 \text{ hr}}$; 65 miles per hour

    Ⓓ $\frac{\$9.50}{1 \text{ hr}}$; $9.50 per hour

    Ⓔ $\frac{25 \text{ mi}}{3 \text{ hr}}$; 25 miles per 3 hours

    Ⓕ $\frac{\$3}{1 \text{ mo}}$; $3 per month

    Ⓖ $\frac{\$32}{1 \text{ ticket}}$; $32 per ticket

    Ⓗ $\frac{\$.75}{1 \text{ can}}$; $.75 per can

C A L C U L A T O R   E X P L O R A T I O N

Ⓐ $\frac{356}{12} = 29.67$ mpg, $\frac{616}{22} = 28$ mpg; 356 miles on 12 gallons

Ⓑ $\frac{504}{8} = 63$, $\frac{620}{10} = 62$; Shift A with 504 articles in 8 hours

Ⓒ $\frac{\$3400}{1} = \$3,400$; $\frac{\$44,000}{12} = \$3,667$; $44,000 a year

Ⓓ $\frac{\$.75}{12} = \$.625$, $\frac{\$1.08}{18} = \$.06$; 18 eggs for $1.08

Ⓔ $\frac{8.97}{42} = \$.2136$, $\frac{25.97}{120} = \$.2164$; 42 diapers for $8.97

Ⓕ $\frac{9.44}{4} = 2.36$, $\frac{4.94}{2} = 2.47$; $\frac{9.44}{4}$ is less money per tape

Ⓖ $\frac{190}{20} = 9.5$, $\frac{475}{50} = 9.5$; Both gave the same number of pesos per dollar.

USING DATA

Ⓐ

food (1 serving)	calories from fat in 1 serving	grams of fat in one serving	unit rate: calories per gram of fat
muffin	210	23	9.13
peanut butter cookies	80	9	8.89
potato chips	90	10	9
blue corn chips	60	7	8.57
vegetable chips	70	7	10
granola bar	25	3	8.33

ⒷⒸ

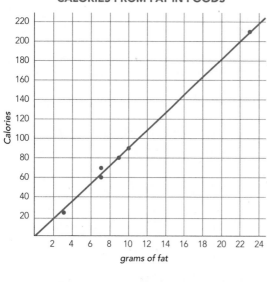

CALORIES FROM FAT IN FOODS

3. Ⓐ The racer was not moving. Distance is the same.
   Ⓑ The fastest rate was during the biking phase. The line segment is steepest there.
   Ⓒ The slowest rate was during the swimming phase. The graph line is most flat there.
   Ⓓ A faster rate will be pictured by a line that is steeper.

4. Ⓐ $\frac{2}{1}$ Ⓒ $\frac{1}{3}$
   Ⓑ $\frac{4}{3}$ Ⓓ $\frac{1}{10}$

5. Ⓐ The order of steepness is as follows: 0.1 for d, 0.33 for c, 1.33 for b, 2.0 for a.
   Ⓑ 9, it rose 9 calories for every gram

6. Ⓐ $\frac{360 \div 3}{3 \div 3} = \frac{120}{1}$ Ⓓ $\frac{100 \div 5}{5 \div 5} = \frac{20}{1}$
   Ⓑ $\frac{250 \div 250}{1,000 \div 250} = \frac{1}{4}$ Ⓔ $\frac{14 \div 7}{7 \div 7} = \frac{2}{1}$
   Ⓒ $\frac{80 \div 8}{8 \div 8} = \frac{10}{1}$ Ⓕ $\frac{12 \div 4}{80 \div 4} = \frac{3}{20}$

7.

$	2	4	6	8	10	12
rolls	3	6	9	12	15	18

8.

length	5	10	15	20	25	30
width	3	6	9	12	15	18

9. Ⓐ 18   Ⓓ 100
   Ⓑ 5   Ⓔ 60
   Ⓒ 500   Ⓕ 60

10. Verifying reasons will vary.
    Ⓐ no, across, 3 × 3 = 9, but 4 × 3 does not equal 16
    Ⓑ yes, across, 4 × 3 = 12 and 5 × 3 = 15
    Ⓒ yes, across, 3 × 5 = 15 and 4 × 5 = 20
    Ⓓ no, across, 3 × 3 = 9, but 5 × 3 does not equal 25
    Ⓔ no, within, 2 × 3 = 6, but 5 × 3 does not equal 9
    Ⓕ yes, within, 5 × 2 = 10 and 22 × 2 = 44
    Ⓖ yes, within, 3 × 7 = 21 and 12 × 7 = 84; across, 3 × 4 = 12 and 21 × 4 = 84
    Ⓗ yes, across, 8 × 9 = 72 and 3 × 9 = 27
    Ⓘ no, across, 3 × 3 = 9 but 4 × 3 does not equal 25
    Ⓙ yes, across, 3 × 25 = 75 and 4 × 25 = 100; within, $\frac{3}{4} = 0.75 = \frac{75}{100}$
    Ⓚ yes, across, 3 × 20 = 60 and 5 × 20 = 100; within, $\frac{3}{5} = 0.60 = \frac{60}{100}$
    Ⓛ no, within or across, 5 × 4 = 20, but 20 × 4 does not equal 100

11. Ⓐ no
    Ⓑ yes, $\frac{40 \text{ miles}}{1 \text{ hr}}$
    Ⓒ yes, $\frac{\text{height}}{\text{base}} = \frac{5}{1}$
    Ⓓ no
    Ⓔ yes, $\frac{3 \text{ red}}{2 \text{ yellow}}$
    Ⓕ no
    Ⓖ no
    Ⓗ yes, $\frac{\text{Thomas}}{\text{Ted}} = \frac{5}{1}$
    Ⓘ yes, $\frac{9}{10}$

J yes, this information can be represented both ways:

(1) 9 more people voted for the measure than against (no ratio).

(2) The ratio $\frac{for}{against} = \frac{19}{10}$.

12. A yes, $\frac{9 \text{ made}}{12 \text{ attempts}} = \frac{x \text{ made}}{50 \text{ attempts}}$

B no, you would add to find this answer

C yes, $\frac{14 \text{ pages}}{1 \text{ hr}} = \frac{49 \text{ pages}}{h \text{ hr}}$

D yes, $\frac{2 \text{ cc}}{25 \text{ lb}} = \frac{x \text{ cc}}{130 \text{ lb}}$

E no, this is a comparison by subtraction

13. A $\frac{4}{5} = \frac{d}{200}$, $\frac{\text{doctors recommend Brand Y}}{\text{total doctors surveyed}}$

C $\frac{5}{4} = \frac{200}{d}$, $\frac{\text{total doctors surveyed}}{\text{doctors recommend Brand Y}}$

E $\frac{4}{d} = \frac{5}{200}$, $\frac{\text{number of reported doctors}}{\text{number of surveyed doctors}}$

CHECK YOUR UNDERSTANDING, page 212

1. A $\frac{8}{1}$ **D** $\frac{5}{8}$

B $\frac{3}{5}$ **E** $\frac{4}{5}$

C $\frac{3}{8}$

2. A $\frac{250 \text{ mi}}{10 \text{ gal}} = \frac{25 \text{ mi}}{1 \text{ gal}}$ (or 25 miles per gallon)

B $\frac{2,400 \text{ ft}}{30 \text{ sec}} = \frac{80 \text{ ft}}{1 \text{ sec}}$ (or 80 feet per second)

C $\frac{\$11.34}{18 \text{ muffins}} = \frac{\$.63}{1 \text{ muffin}}$ (or \$.63 per muffin)

D $\frac{\$2.85}{19 \text{ oz}} = \frac{\$.15}{1 \text{ oz}}$ (or \$.15 per ounce)

E $\frac{384 \text{ calls}}{32 \text{ people}} = \frac{12 \text{ calls}}{1 \text{ person}}$ (or 12 calls per person)

3. $\frac{2}{12} = \frac{1}{6}$

4.

speed (mph)	20	30	40	50	60
car lengths	2	3	4	5	6

5. $\frac{140 \div 70}{210 \div 70} = \frac{2}{3}$

6. $\frac{2}{5}$

7.

c	22	44	66	88
d	7	14	21	28

8. A 100 **D** 110
B 72 **E** 22
C 55 **F** 7

9. A yes **D** yes
B no **E** no
C no

10. $\frac{\$4.29}{4} \approx \$1.07$ per battery, $\frac{\$10.97}{10} \approx \$1.10$ per battery; 4 batteries for \$4.29 is the better buy

TEST-TAKING PRACTICE, page 213

1. (5) 19:20

$\frac{190}{200} = \frac{19}{20}$

2. (1) $\frac{1.5}{1}$

$\frac{60}{40} = \frac{1.5}{1}$

3. (2) The best price per ounce is Box C.
Box A = \$.24
Box B = \$.20
Box C = \$.18

4. 2,500

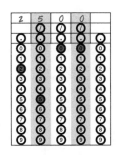

5. (2) year 2
The slope of the graph is steepest during year 2.

Lesson 21

Proportions, pages 214–215

MENTAL MATH	
1. no	**4.** no
2. yes	**5.** no
3. no	**6.** no

1. Ⓐ True: $\dfrac{165 \text{ mi}}{3 \text{ hr}} = \dfrac{55 \text{ mi}}{1 \text{ hr}}$

$165 = 55 \times 3$

Ⓑ False: $\dfrac{2 \text{ oranges}}{35 \text{ cents}} \neq \dfrac{8 \text{ oranges}}{150 \text{ cents}}$

$2 \times 150 \neq 35 \times 8$

Ⓒ False: $\dfrac{1 \text{ table}}{6 \text{ people}} \neq \dfrac{16 \text{ tables}}{64 \text{ people}}$

$1 \times 64 \neq 6 \times 16$

Ⓓ False: $\dfrac{2 \text{ cans}}{5 \text{ cents}} \neq \dfrac{200 \text{ cans}}{1{,}000 \text{ cents}}$ (1,000 cents = $10.00)

$2 \times 1{,}000 \neq 5 \times 200$

Ⓔ False: $\dfrac{1 \text{ oil}}{20 \text{ gas}} \neq \dfrac{2 \text{ oil}}{10 \text{ gas}}$

$1 \times 10 \neq 20 \times 2$

Ⓕ True: $\dfrac{2 \text{ lb}}{6 \text{ people}} = \dfrac{8 \text{ lb}}{24 \text{ people}}$

$2 \times 24 = 6 \times 8$

Ⓖ False: $\dfrac{75 \text{ fat}}{300 \text{ total}} \neq \dfrac{40 \text{ fat}}{175 \text{ total}}$

$75 \times 175 \neq 40 \times 300$

Ⓗ True: $\dfrac{3 \text{ women}}{5 \text{ total}} = \dfrac{12 \text{ women}}{20 \text{ total}}$

$3 \times 20 = 12 \times 5$

Ⓘ True: $\dfrac{2 \text{ men}}{5 \text{ total}} = \dfrac{8 \text{ men}}{20 \text{ total}}$

$2 \times 20 = 8 \times 5$

2. Ⓐ $b = \dfrac{240}{4} = 60$ Ⓓ $d = \dfrac{754}{10} = 75.4$

Ⓑ $t = \dfrac{400}{5} = 80$ Ⓔ $s = \dfrac{454}{25} = 18.16$

Ⓒ $x = \dfrac{357}{7} = 51$ Ⓕ $y = \dfrac{1430}{11} = 130$

3. Ⓐ $c = 4$

$\dfrac{c}{5} = \dfrac{24}{30}$

$30c = 24 \times 5$

$c = \dfrac{24 \times \overset{1}{\cancel{5}}}{\underset{6}{\cancel{30}}} = \dfrac{24}{6} = 4$

Ⓑ $m = 12$

$\dfrac{8}{m} = \dfrac{20}{30}$

$20m = 8 \times 30$

$m = \dfrac{8 \times \overset{3}{\cancel{30}}}{\underset{2}{\cancel{20}}} = \dfrac{24}{2} = 12$

Ⓒ $p = 55$

$\dfrac{5}{8} = \dfrac{p}{88}$

$8p = 5 \times 88$

$p = \dfrac{5 \times \overset{11}{\cancel{88}}}{\underset{1}{\cancel{8}}} = 55$

Ⓓ $b = 75$

$\dfrac{4}{15} = \dfrac{20}{b}$

$4b = 20 \times 15$

$b = \dfrac{\overset{5}{\cancel{20}} \times 15}{\underset{1}{\cancel{4}}} = 75$

Ⓔ $t = 15$

$\dfrac{t}{9} = \dfrac{10}{6}$

$6t = 10 \times 9$

$t = \dfrac{10 \times \overset{3}{\cancel{9}}}{\underset{2}{\cancel{6}}} = \dfrac{30}{2} = 15$

Ⓕ $c = 40$

$\dfrac{10}{c} = \dfrac{25}{100}$

$25c = 100 \times 10$

$c = \dfrac{\overset{4}{\cancel{100}} \times 10}{\underset{1}{\cancel{25}}} = 40$

Ⓖ $w = 25$

$\dfrac{6}{15} = \dfrac{10}{w}$

$6w = 15 \times 10$

$w = \dfrac{\overset{5}{\cancel{15}} \times 10}{\underset{2}{\cancel{6}}} = \dfrac{50}{2} = 25$

Ⓗ $k = 33$

$\dfrac{3}{11} = \dfrac{k}{121}$

$11k = 3 \times 121$

$k = \dfrac{3 \times \overset{11}{\cancel{121}}}{\underset{1}{\cancel{11}}} = 33$

4. Ⓐ $b = 15$ or   Looking across:

$\dfrac{4}{5} = \dfrac{12}{b}$ $4 \times 3 = 12$

$4b = 5 \times 12$ So, $5 \times 3 = 15$.

$b = \dfrac{5 \times \overset{3}{\cancel{12}}}{\underset{1}{\cancel{4}}} = 15$

Ⓑ $k = 9$ or   Simplify first:

$\dfrac{k}{12} = \dfrac{6}{8}$ $\dfrac{6}{8} = \dfrac{3}{4}$

$8k = 12 \times 6$ Looking across:

$k = \dfrac{\overset{3}{\cancel{12}} \times 6}{\underset{2}{\cancel{8}}} = \dfrac{18}{2} = 9$ $\dfrac{k}{12} = \dfrac{3}{4}$

$4 \times 3 = 12$

So, $3 \times 3 = 9$.

Ⓒ $r = 24$ or   Looking across:

$\dfrac{3}{8} = \dfrac{r}{64}$ $8 \times 8 = 64$

$8r = 3 \times 64$ So, $3 \times 8 = 24$.

$r = \dfrac{3 \times \overset{8}{\cancel{64}}}{\underset{1}{\cancel{8}}} = 24$

D $v = 12$ or

$$\frac{3}{v} = \frac{7}{28}$$

$7v = 3 \times 28$

$$v = \frac{3 \times \overset{4}{\cancel{28}}}{\cancel{7}} = 12$$

Looking from top to bottom:

$7 \times 4 = 28$

$3 \times 4 = 12$

E $n = 25$ or

$$\frac{8}{32} = \frac{n}{100}$$

$32n = 8 \times 100$

$$n = \frac{8 \times 100}{\underset{4}{\cancel{32}}} =$$

$$\frac{100}{4} = 25$$

Looking from top to bottom:

$32 \div 4 = 8$

So, $100 \div 4 = 25$.

F $d = 12$ or

$$\frac{3}{7} = \frac{d}{28}$$

$7d = 3 \times 28$

$$d = \frac{3 \times \overset{4}{\cancel{28}}}{\underset{1}{\cancel{7}}} = 12$$

Looking across:

$7 \times 4 = 28$

$3 \times 4 = 12$

G $n = 12$ or

$$\frac{n}{25} = \frac{48}{100}$$

$100n = 48 \times 25$

$$n = \frac{48 \times \overset{1}{\cancel{25}}}{\underset{4}{\cancel{100}}} =$$

$$\frac{48}{4} = 12$$

Looking across:

$100 \div 4 = 25$

$48 \div 4 = 12$

H $r = 4\frac{2}{7}$

$$\frac{3}{7} = \frac{r}{10}$$

$7r = 3 \times 10$

$$r = \frac{3 \times 10}{7} = \frac{30}{7} = 4\frac{2}{7}$$

I $d = 121$ or

$$\frac{44}{4} = \frac{d}{11}$$

$4d = 44 \times 11$

$$d = \frac{\overset{11}{\cancel{44}} \times 11}{\underset{1}{\cancel{4}}} = 121$$

Looking from top to bottom:

$44 = 4 \times 11$

So, $121 = 11 \times 11$.

J $n = 62\frac{1}{2}$

$$\frac{5}{8} = \frac{n}{100}$$

$8n = 5 \times 100$

$$n = \frac{5 \times \overset{25}{\cancel{100}}}{\underset{2}{\cancel{8}}} = \frac{125}{2} = 62\frac{1}{2}$$

K $z = 2$

$$\frac{1.2}{z} = \frac{4.8}{8}$$

$4.8z = 1.2 \times 8$

$$z = \frac{1.2 \times 8}{\underset{4}{\cancel{4.8}}} = \frac{8}{4} = 2$$

L $s = 2$

$$\frac{1.5}{9} = \frac{s}{12}$$

$9s = 1.5 \times 12$

$$s = \frac{1.5 \times \overset{4}{\cancel{12}}}{\underset{3}{\cancel{9}}} = \frac{6.0}{3} = 2$$

M $n = 3$

$$\frac{\frac{1}{4}}{6} = \frac{\frac{1}{8}}{n}$$

$\frac{1}{4}n = 6 \times \frac{1}{8}$

$$n = \left(6 \times \frac{1}{8}\right) \times 4 = \frac{3}{4} \times 4 = 3$$

N $c = \frac{1}{25}$

$$\frac{\frac{1}{5}}{20} = \frac{c}{4}$$

$20c = \frac{1}{5} \times 4$

$$c = \frac{\frac{1}{5} \times 4}{20} = \frac{\frac{4}{5}}{20} = \frac{\overset{1}{\cancel{4}}}{5} \times \frac{1}{\underset{5}{\cancel{20}}} = \frac{1}{25}$$

O $a = 200$ or Looking from top to bottom:

$$\frac{2\frac{1}{2}}{5} = \frac{100}{a}$$

$2\frac{1}{2}a = 5 \times 100$

$\frac{5}{2}a = 5 \times 100$

$$a = (5 \times 100) \times \frac{2}{5} = \frac{\overset{100}{\cancel{500}}}{1} \times \frac{2}{\underset{1}{\cancel{8}}} = 200$$

$2\frac{1}{2}$ is $\frac{1}{2}$ of 5

100 is $\frac{1}{2}$ of 200

$a = 200$

5. A $w = 56$ women

$$\frac{7 \text{ women}}{12 \text{ total}} = \frac{w \text{ women}}{96 \text{ total}}$$

$12w = 7 \times 96$

$$w = \frac{7 \times \overset{8}{\cancel{96}}}{\underset{1}{\cancel{12}}} = 56$$

B $c = \$2.10$

$$\frac{2 \text{ oranges}}{35 \text{ cents}} = \frac{12 \text{ oranges}}{c \text{ cents}}$$

$2c = 35 \times 12$

$$c = \frac{35 \times \overset{6}{\cancel{12}}}{\underset{1}{\cancel{2}}} = 210$$

Ⓒ $s = \frac{5}{4} = 1\frac{1}{4}$ cups

$$\frac{\frac{1}{2}\text{ sugar}}{4\text{ servings}} = \frac{s\text{ sugar}}{10\text{ servings}}$$

$$4s = \frac{1}{2} \times 10$$

$$s = \frac{\frac{1}{2} \times 10}{4} = \frac{5}{4} = 1\frac{1}{4}$$

Ⓓ $f = 7{,}920$ ft

$$\frac{1\text{ mi}}{5{,}280\text{ ft}} = \frac{1.5}{f\text{ ft}}$$

$$f = 5{,}280 \times 1.5$$

$$f = 7{,}920\text{ ft}$$

Ⓔ $d = \$43$

$$\frac{11\text{ pesos}}{1\text{ dollar}} = \frac{473\text{ pesos}}{d\text{ dollars}}$$

$$11d = 473$$

$$d = \frac{473}{11} = 43\text{ dollars}$$

Ⓕ $g = 11.75$ gal

$$\frac{\text{miles}}{\text{gallon}} : \frac{52}{1} = \frac{611}{g}$$

$$52g = 1 \times 611$$

$$g = \frac{611}{52} = 11.75$$

USING DATA

Ⓐ $\frac{25{,}000}{c} = \frac{1187.7}{198.7}$

$1187.7c = 25{,}000 \times 198.7$

$c = \$4182$

Ⓑ $\frac{175{,}000}{h} = \frac{815.0}{434.9}$

$815h = 175{,}000 \times 434.9$

$h = \$93{,}383$

Ⓒ $\frac{150}{m} = \frac{758.1}{80}$

$758.1m = 150 \times 80$

$m = \$15.83$

Ⓓ $\frac{475}{d} = \frac{747.4}{600.8}$

$747.4d = 475 \times 600.8$

$d = \$381.83$

Ⓔ You do not have to add the zeroes because they would be added to both the numbers in the second ratio. You would immediately cancel them when you reduced the ratio.

Ⓕ Answers will vary: calculators, computers, digital cameras are all cheaper than they were years ago.

---

6. Ⓐ $DN = 4m$

$$\frac{5}{x} = \frac{15}{12}$$

$$15x = 5 \times 12$$

$$x = \frac{\overset{1}{5} \times 12}{\underset{3}{15}} = \frac{12}{3} = 4$$

Ⓑ 70°

$180° - (35° + 75°)$

$180° - 110° = 70°$

7. $x = 40$ ft

$$\frac{40}{100} = \frac{16}{x}$$

$$40x = 100 \times 16$$

$$x = \frac{\overset{5}{100} \times 16}{\underset{2}{40}} = \frac{80}{2} = 40$$

8. (1) *A* and *D* are similar triangles.

9. $n = 12$ in.   or   Looking across:

$$\frac{3}{4} = \frac{9}{n} \qquad\qquad 3 \times 3 = 9$$

$$3n = 4 \times 9 \qquad\quad \text{So, } 4 \times 3 = 12.$$

$$n = \frac{4 \times \overset{3}{9}}{\underset{1}{3}} = 12$$

10. $f = 6$ ft

$$\frac{1\text{ in.}}{1.5\text{ ft}} = \frac{4\text{ in.}}{f\text{ ft}}$$

$$f = 1.5 \times 4 = 6$$

11. $n = 350$ ft

$$\frac{1\text{ in.}}{100\text{ ft}} = \frac{3.5\text{ in.}}{n\text{ ft}}$$

$$n = 100 \times 3.5 = 350$$

12. $p \approx 1.5$ in.

$$\frac{1\text{ in.}}{135\text{ mi}} = \frac{p\text{ in.}}{208\text{ mi}}$$

$$135p = 208$$

$$p = \frac{208}{135} \approx 1.5$$

13. Ⓐ $\frac{279}{24} \approx \frac{240}{24} = 10¢$ apiece

$\frac{649}{100} \approx \frac{650}{100} = 6.5¢$ apiece (better buy)

Ⓑ $\frac{159}{22} \approx \frac{160}{20} = 8¢$ per oz

$\frac{249}{32} \approx \frac{240}{30} = 8¢$ per oz

With a calculator, $\frac{159}{22} = 7.227¢$ per oz (better buy), and $\frac{249}{32} = 7.78¢$ per oz.

Ⓒ $\frac{1{,}099}{30} \approx \frac{1{,}200}{30} = 40¢$ per diaper

$\frac{1{,}999}{64} \approx \frac{2{,}000}{60} = 33¢$ per diaper (better buy)

Ⓓ $\frac{63}{8} \approx \frac{64}{8} = $ 8¢ per oz

$\frac{179}{32} \approx \frac{180}{30} = $ 6¢ per oz (better buy)

Ⓔ $6 \times 1\frac{1}{2}$ oz = 9 oz for \$.88

This is cheaper than \$1.09 for a regular-price 9-ounce box.

Ⓕ Often the better buy is found in large packages. However, if the food would spoil before you could eat that much, it is better to buy in smaller quantities.

CHECK YOUR UNDERSTANDING, page 224

1. All of these answers can also be found using the cross-multiplication method.

Ⓐ $x = 24$; Looking across: In denominators $3 \times 6 = 18$; In numerators $4 \times 6 = 24$

Ⓑ $x = 21$; Looking across: In numerators, $5 \times 3 = 15$; In denominators, $7 \times 3 = 21$

Ⓒ $n = 4$; Looking within: $9 \div 3 = 3$ and $12 \div 3 = 4$

Ⓓ $x = 4$; Looking across: in numerators, $\frac{1}{4}$ is half of $\frac{1}{2}$; In denominators, 4 is half of 8.

Ⓔ $n = 5$; Looking within: $54 \div 6 = 9$ and $30 \div 6 = 5$

Ⓕ $x = 9$; Looking within: 0.06 is twice 0.03 and 9 is twice 4.5.

Ⓖ $x = 12$; Looking across: In denominators, $1.5 \times 2 = 3$; In numerators, $6 \times 2 = 12$.

Ⓗ $x = 5$; Looking across: $\frac{1}{5}$ is twice $\frac{1}{10}$ and 10 is twice 5.

2. $d = \$2.50$

$\frac{100}{4} = \frac{d}{10}$

$4d = 100 \times 10$

$d = \frac{\overset{25}{100} \times 10}{\underset{1}{4}} = 250$

3. $y = 56$ oz

$\frac{1}{16} = \frac{3\frac{1}{2}}{y}$

$y = 16 \times 3\frac{1}{2}$

$y = \frac{\overset{8}{16}}{1} \times \frac{7}{\underset{1}{2}} = 56$

4. $t = 150$ shots

$\frac{6}{9} = \frac{100}{t}$

$6t = 9 \times 100$

$t = \frac{\overset{3}{9} \times 100}{\underset{2}{6}} = 150$

5. $d = 86$ ft

$\frac{3}{21\frac{1}{2}} = \frac{12}{d}$

$3d = 12 \times 21\frac{1}{2}$

$d = \frac{\overset{4}{12} \times 21\frac{1}{2}}{\underset{1}{3}}$

$d = (4 \times 21) + \left(4 \times \frac{1}{2}\right)$

$d = 84 + 2 = 86$

6. $x \approx 24$

$\frac{145.6 \text{ mi}}{60 \text{ min}} = \frac{x \text{ mi}}{10 \text{ min}}$

$60x = 145.6 \times 10$

$x = \frac{1{,}456}{60}$

$x \approx 24$

7. $w = \frac{16}{3} = 5\frac{1}{3}$ tsp.

$\frac{2}{3} = \frac{w}{8}$

$3w = 2 \times 8$

$w = \frac{16}{3} = 5\frac{1}{3}$

8. $m = 8$ mph

$\frac{26}{3\frac{1}{4}} = \frac{m}{1}$

$3\frac{1}{4}m = 26 \times 1$

$m = 26 \div 3\frac{1}{4} = \frac{\overset{2}{26} \times 4}{\underset{1}{13}} = \frac{8}{1}$

9. $r = 2\frac{1}{2}$ ft

$\frac{1}{20} = \frac{r}{50}$

$20r = 1 \times 50$

$r = \frac{50}{20} = \frac{5}{2} = 2\frac{1}{2}$

10. $20 - 6 = 14$ passes

11. $n = 750$ parts

$\frac{15}{16} = \frac{n}{800}$

$16n = 15 \times 800$

$n = \frac{15 \times \overset{50}{800}}{\underset{1}{16}} = 15 \times 50 = 750$

12. $\frac{55}{11} = \frac{5}{1}$

13. $\frac{5}{7} \neq \frac{8}{10}$, no

14. The package of 3 rolls for \$2.67 is the better buy.

$\frac{199}{2} \approx \frac{200}{2} = $ 100¢ or \$1.00 per roll

$\frac{267}{3} \approx \frac{270}{3} = $ 90¢ per roll

15. $z = 3\frac{1}{3}$ hr

$\frac{1}{60} = \frac{z}{200}$

$60z = 1 \times 200$

$z = \frac{200}{60} = \frac{20}{6} = 3\frac{1}{3}$

16. $.09 savings per taco

$\frac{99}{2} \approx \frac{100}{2} = 50¢$ each

$.59 - $.50 = $.09

TEST-TAKING PRACTICE, page 225

1. (2) 375

$\frac{2}{75} = \frac{10}{m}$

$2m = 75 \times 10$

$m = \frac{75 \times \overset{5}{\cancel{10}}}{\underset{1}{\cancel{2}}} = 375$

2. (5) 14

$\frac{16 \text{ wide}}{9 \text{ high}} = \frac{25 \text{ wide}}{n \text{ high}}$

$16n = 9 \times 25$

$n = \frac{225}{16} \approx 14$

3. 5

$\frac{10}{12} = \frac{x}{6}$

$x = 5$

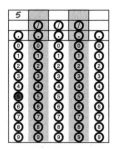

4. (1) Richmond (VA) Expressway

5. (1) 10,200

$\frac{2 \text{ for}}{7 \text{ total}} = \frac{n \text{ for}}{35,700 \text{ total}}$

$7n = 71,400$

$n = 10,200$

6. (1) 10

$90 \div 9 = 10$

Lesson 22

Percent I, pages 226–239

1. $\frac{1}{2}$ **5.** $\frac{3}{5}$

2. $\frac{3}{4}$ **6.** $\frac{2}{5}$

3. $\frac{1}{5}$ **7.** $\frac{1}{3}$

4. $\frac{1}{10}$ **8.** $\frac{1}{8}$

1.

fraction	2-place decimal	percent
$\frac{3}{10}$	0.30	30%
$\frac{1}{4}$	0.25	25%
$\frac{2}{5}$	0.40	40%
$\frac{1}{1}$	1.00	100%
$\frac{1}{3}$	$0.33\frac{1}{3}$	$33\frac{1}{3}\%$
$\frac{7}{100}$	0.07	7%

2. A 9   **D** 14

B 13   **E** 6; 18; 60

C 7

3. A 40; 4; 0.4   **D** 2,000; 200; 20

B 300; 300; 300   **E** 500; 50; 5

C 100; 10; 1   **F** 1,500; 10; 15

4. A $x = 9$ **F** $k = 0.69$

B $g = 9.1$ **G** $x\% = 10\%$

C $p = 8.9$ **H** $n\% = 100\%$

D $n = 0.7$ **I** $p\% = 1\%$

E $h = 0.71$

5. A 20; 10; 5

B 120; 50%; 30

C 80; 80; 80

6. A $x = 4$ **F** $w = 60$

B $b = 8$ **G** $x\% = 50\%$

C $n = 6$ **H** $n\% = 25\%$

D $c = 8$ **I** $p\% = 20\%$

E $t = 40$

7. A 30; 60; 90

B 9; 18; 300%

C 150; 200%; 300%

8. A $c = 16$; $d = 8$; $n = 24$; $t = 64$; $x = 128$

B 10%; 20%; 30%; 50%; 25%; 75%

C $m = 2$; $b = 4$; $p = 22$; $s = 24$

D 100; 200; 900; 1,800

9. **(A)** $\frac{90}{100} = \frac{9}{10}$; true **(E)** $\frac{2}{100} \neq \frac{18}{90}$; false

(B) $\frac{75}{100} \neq \frac{70}{96}$; false **(F)** $\frac{110}{100} \neq \frac{50}{40}$; false

(C) $\frac{15}{100} = \frac{6}{40}$; true **(G)** $\frac{200}{100} \neq \frac{20}{40}$; false

(D) $\frac{40}{100} = \frac{30}{75}$; true **(H)** $\frac{300}{100} = \frac{36}{12}$; true

10. **(A)** $\frac{65}{100} = \frac{n}{120}$

$100n = 65 \times 120$

$n = \frac{65 \times 120}{100}$

$n = 78$

(B) $\frac{x}{100} = \frac{70}{105}$

$105x = 70 \times 100$

$x = \frac{70 \times 100}{105}$

$x\% = 66\frac{2}{3}\%$

(C) $\frac{75}{100} = \frac{45}{p}$

Simplify: or Looking across:

$\frac{3}{4} = \frac{45}{p}$

$3p = 45 \times 4$ $3 \times 15 = 45$

$p = \frac{\overset{15}{\cancel{45}} \times 4}{\cancel{3}_1}$ So, $4 \times 15 = 60$

$p = 60$

(D) $\frac{35}{100} = \frac{s}{80}$

Simplify: or Looking across:

$\frac{7}{20} = \frac{s}{80}$

$20s = 7 \times 80$ $20 \times 4 = 80$

$s = \frac{7 \times \overset{4}{\cancel{80}}}{\cancel{20}_1}$ So, $7 \times 4 = 28$

$s = 28$

(E) $\frac{105}{100} = \frac{42}{b}$

Simplify: or Looking across:

$\frac{21}{20} = \frac{42}{b}$

$21b = 42 \times 20$ $21 \times 2 = 42$

$b = \frac{\overset{2}{\cancel{42}} \times 20}{\cancel{21}_1}$ So, $20 \times 2 = 40$

$b = 40$

(F) $\frac{t}{100} = \frac{9}{72}$

$72t = 9 \times 100$

$t = \frac{\overset{1}{\cancel{9}} \times 100}{\cancel{72}_8}$

$t\% = 12\frac{1}{2}\%$

(G) $\frac{52}{100} = \frac{f}{150}$

$100f = 52 \times 150$

$f = \frac{52 \times \overset{3}{\cancel{150}}}{\cancel{100}_2} = \frac{156}{2}$

$f = 78$

(H) $\frac{250}{100} = \frac{10}{d}$

Simplify: or Looking across:

$\frac{5}{2} = \frac{10}{d}$

$5d = 2 \times 10$ $5 \times 2 = 10$

$d = \frac{2 \times \overset{2}{\cancel{10}}}{\cancel{5}_1}$ So, $2 \times 2 = 4$

$d = 4$

(I) $\frac{36}{100} = \frac{252}{n}$

$36n = 252 \times 100$

$n = \frac{\overset{7}{\cancel{252}} \times 100}{\cancel{36}_1}$

$n = 700$

(J) $\frac{m}{100} = \frac{200}{125}$

Simplify: or Looking across:

$\frac{m}{100} = \frac{8}{5}$

$5m = 8 \times 100$ $5 \times 20 = 100$

$m = \frac{8 \times \overset{20}{\cancel{100}}}{\cancel{5}_1}$ So, $8 \times 20 = 160$

$m\% = 160\%$

11. **(A)** 10% of $46 = m$

(B) $\$1.47 =$ what % of $\$21.00$

(C) 11% of $c = 2,200$

(D) $\$22,500 =$ what % of $\$150,000$

(E) 20% of $\$85 = p$

(F) $12 =$ what % of 30

12. **(A)** $c = 135$

$90\% \times 150 = c$

$0.90 \times 150 = 135$

(B) $x = 60$

$125\% \times 48 = x$

$1\frac{1}{4} \times 48 = (48 \times 1) + \left(48 \times \frac{1}{4}\right) = x$

$x = 48 + 12 = 60$

(C) $x = 62\frac{1}{2}\%$

$55 =$ what % of 88

$55 = x \bullet 88$

$x = \frac{55 \div 11}{88 \div 11} = \frac{5}{8} = 62\frac{1}{2}\%$

D $n = 125\%$

2,000 = what % of 1,600

$2{,}000 = n \times 1{,}600$

$\frac{2{,}000}{1{,}600} = n$

$n = \frac{5}{4} = 125\%$

E $y = 240$

$80 = 33\frac{1}{3}\% \times y$

$\frac{80}{\frac{1}{3}} = 80 \div \frac{1}{3} = y$

$\frac{80}{1} \times \frac{3}{1} = 240$

F $b = 20$

$250\% \times b = 50$

$b = \frac{50}{2\frac{1}{2}} = 50 \div 2\frac{1}{2}$

$b = 50 \div \frac{5}{2}$

$b = \overset{10}{\cancel{50}} \times \frac{2}{\underset{1}{\cancel{5}}} = 20$

CALCULATOR EXPLORATION

A 4.6 ounces

$10\% \times 46 = m$

`1` `0` `×` `4` `6` `SHIFT` `%` ` 4.6 `

B 7%

$1.47 =$ what $\% \times \$21$

$\$1.47 \div \$21 = x$

`1` `.` `4` `7` `÷` `2` `1` `SHIFT` `%` ` 7. `

C 20,000 people

$11\% \times c = 2{,}200$

$c = 2{,}200 \div 11\%$

`2` `2` `0` `0` `÷` `1` `1` `SHIFT` `%` `20000.`

D 15%

$22{,}500 =$ what $\% \times \$150{,}000$

$22{,}500 \div 150{,}000 = n$

`2` `2` `5` `0` `0` `÷` `1` `5` `0` `0` `0` `0`
`SHIFT` `%` ` 15. `

E $17

$20\% \times \$85 = p$

`2` `0` `×` `8` `5` `SHIFT` `%` ` 17. `

F 40%

$12 =$ what $\% \times 30$

$12 \div 30 = p$

`1` `2` `÷` `3` `0` `SHIFT` `%` ` 40. `

USING DATA

A

no. of hours	percent	degrees
5 or less	15%	54°
6 hours	25%	90°
7 hours	30%	108°
8 hours	25%	90°
9 or more	5%	18°

B

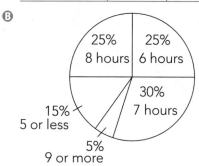

C They are proportional: $\frac{30}{100} = \frac{\text{area of sector}}{\text{area of entire circle}} = \frac{\text{length of arc}}{\text{circumference of entire circle}}$

area of entire circle $= \pi r^2 = \pi \bullet 2.5^2 = 19.6$ cm²

area of sector $= 30\%$ of $19.6 = 5.9$ cm²

circumference of entire circle $= \pi d = \pi \bullet 5 = 15.7$ cm

length of arc $= 30\%$ of $15.7 = 4.7$ cm

---

13. **A** $5500, 25%

10% of $22,000 = $2,200; 15% of $22,000 = $3,300; total = $5,500

$5,500 is 25% of $22,000

B $16,500, $866.25

$22,000 − $5,500 = $16,500

0.0525 × $16,500 = $866.25

C 17; It will take 2 years to get to 75% of its original value. At 5% per year after that , it would take 15 more years. 15 + 2 = 17

D $393.75

7 years would mean 25% + 5 (5%) = 50%

50% of 15,000 = 7,500

0.0525 × 7500 = 393.75

14. **A** $30, $170

15% of $200 is $30; $200 − $30 = $170

B $17, $153

10% of $170 = $17; $170 − $17 = $153

C No, 23.5%

47 is 23.5% of 200

D In this problem, the base of the 10% percent discount was not the original price.

CHECK YOUR UNDERSTANDING, page 238

1. **A** 35   **F** 125
   B 12   **G** 4.5
   C 75   **H** 45
   D 20   **I** 80
   E 0   **J** 12

2. **A** 25% of $110
   B The values are the same.
   C 50% of 90
   D 25% of 1,000
   E $10
   F The values are the same.

3. **A** $\frac{20}{100} = \frac{4}{20}$; true   **E** $\frac{250}{100} = \frac{30}{12}$; true

   B $\frac{30}{100} = \frac{9}{30}$; true   **F** $\frac{1}{100} \neq \frac{3}{3,000}$; false

   C $\frac{80}{100} \neq \frac{35}{45}$; false   **G** $\frac{110}{100} \neq \frac{95}{85}$; false

   D $\frac{10}{100} \neq \frac{2.15}{215}$; false   **H** $\frac{75}{100} \neq \frac{8}{12}$; false

4. 6% of $130,000 = c
   c = $7,800

5. 25% of $78.00 = d
   d = $19.50

6. 20 = 80% of t
   t = 25

7. 5% of s = 200
   s = $4,000

8. 175 = what % of 250
   x = 70%

9. 88 = what % of 400
   p = 22%

10. **A** 40% of 900 = c
    c = $360

    B about 14

    $\frac{\$5,000}{\$360} = 13.89$

11. 36 = 90% of d
    d = 40

TEST-TAKING PRACTICE, page 239

1. 25

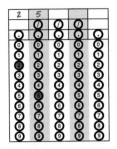

2. (2) 1,120
   $0.35 \times 3,200 = 1,120$
   (est: $\frac{1}{3}$ of 3,200 = 1,100)

3. (5) Not enough information is given.
   The base of the percent is not given.

4. (3) 7.5%
   $\frac{90}{1,200} = \frac{x}{100}$
   1,200x = 9,000
   x = 7.5

5. (4) 43%
   9 is what % of 21
   $n = \frac{9}{21} = 0.429 \approx 43\%$

6. (4) 31.03
   3% of 32 = 0.96
   31.03 is too short

Skill Maintenance

Lessons 20–22, pages 240–241

Part One

1. **A** $\frac{45}{75}$ **D** 24

   B $\frac{45}{120}$ **E** $\frac{24}{120} = \frac{1}{5}$

   C 36   **F** 80

2. **A** 12 oz   **D** $4\frac{1}{2}$ cups

   B $1\frac{1}{2}$ pints   **E** 4 cups

   C $2\frac{1}{2}$ lb   **F** $5\frac{1}{2}$ qt

3. **A** T   **C** F
   B T   **D** T

4. **A** approximately 6
   B 4 hours
   C 80 parts

Part Two

1. (4) 6

2. (2) 5:1

3. (4) 220

4. (2) $\frac{3}{5} = \frac{\$2.88}{x}$

5. (3) $4,400

6. (1) 12%

7. (3) $10,800

Lesson 23

Percent II, pages 242–253

MENTAL MATH	
1. $x = 10$	4. $m = 7.5$
2. $k = 10$	5. $p = 50$
3. $n = 7$	6. $k = 30$

1. Your estimates should be close to these.

   Ⓐ $p \approx 9$
   11% of 90 $\approx$ 10% $\times$ 90 = 9

   Ⓑ $m \approx 30$
   27% of 120 $\approx$ 25% $\times$ 120 = 30

   Ⓒ $b \approx 8$
   20% of 37 $\approx$ 20% $\times$ 40 = 8

   Ⓓ $x \approx 67$
   98% of 67 $\approx$ 100% $\times$ 67 = 67

   Ⓔ $k \approx 1,500$
   296% of 500 $\approx$ 300% $\times$ 500 = 1,500

   Ⓕ $n \approx 110$
   9% of 1,099 $\approx$ 10% $\times$ 1,100 = 110

   Ⓖ $w \approx 32$
   48% of 64 $\approx$ 50% $\times$ 64 = 32

   Ⓗ $v \approx 22$
   32% of 66 $\approx$ 33$\frac{1}{3}$% $\times$ 66 = $\frac{1}{3}$ $\times$ 66 = 22

   Ⓘ $d \approx 4$
   0.8% of 400 $\approx$ 1% $\times$ 400 = 4

   Ⓙ $c \approx 11$
   25% of 45 $\approx$ 25% $\times$ 44 = $\frac{1}{4}$ $\times$ 44 = 11

2. Ⓐ 9.9   Ⓕ 98.91
   Ⓑ 32.4   Ⓖ 30.72
   Ⓒ 7.4   Ⓗ 21.12
   Ⓓ 65.66   Ⓘ 3.2
   Ⓔ 1,480   Ⓙ 11.25

3. Your estimates should be close to these.

   Ⓐ $.75
   $4.88 $\approx$ $5.00
   $.50 + $.25 = $.75

   Ⓑ $1.65
   $11.31 $\approx$ $11.00
   $1.10 + $.55 = $1.65

   Ⓒ $2.70
   $17.65 $\approx$ $18.00
   $1.80 + $.90 = $2.70

   Ⓓ $3.60
   $24.05 $\approx$ $24.00
   $2.40 + $1.20 = $3.60

   Ⓔ $4.80
   $31.72 $\approx$ $32
   $3.20 + $1.60 = $4.80

4. Estimate: $8
   $41 $\approx$ $40
   $40 $\times$ 15% = $6.00
   $41.45 + $6 $\approx$ $48
   $48 $\div$ 6 = $8
   Each person should pay $8.

5. Your estimates may vary from these. Make sure they are reasonable.

   Ⓐ $\frac{102}{400} \approx \frac{100}{400} = \frac{1}{4} = 25\%$

   Ⓑ $\frac{30}{147} \approx \frac{30}{150} = \frac{1}{5} = 20\%$

   Ⓒ $\frac{95}{50} \approx \frac{100}{50} = \frac{2}{1} = 200\%$

   Ⓓ $\frac{8}{83} \approx \frac{8}{80} = \frac{1}{10} = 10\%$

   Ⓔ $\frac{0.9}{100} \approx \frac{1}{100} = 1\%$

   Ⓕ $\frac{398}{500} \approx \frac{400}{500} = \frac{4}{5} = 80\%$

   Ⓖ $\frac{52}{75} \approx \frac{50}{75} = \frac{2}{3} = 66\frac{2}{3}\%$

   Ⓗ $\frac{1.00}{9.95} \approx \frac{1}{10} = 10\%$

   Ⓘ $\frac{1.50}{3.09} \approx \frac{1.50}{3.00} = \frac{1}{2} = 50\%$

   Ⓙ $\frac{19.00}{98.59} \approx \frac{20.00}{100.00} = \frac{1}{5} = 20\%$

6. Use $i = prt$; $t = 1$.

Principal

Rate		$500	$1,000	$1,500	$2,000
	6%	$30	$60	$90	$120
	12%	$60	$120	$180	$240

7. Use $i = prt$; $t = \frac{1}{2}$.

Principal

Rate		$500	$1,000	$1,500	$2,000
	6%	$15	$30	$45	$60
	12%	$30	$60	$90	$120

8. Ⓐ 0.065

$1,000 \times 0.065 = \$65.00$

Ⓑ 0.075

$1,000 \times 0.075 = \$75.00$

Ⓒ 0.1025

$1,000 \times 0.1025 = \$102.50$

Ⓓ 0.0825

$1,000 \times 0.0825 = \$82.50$

Ⓔ 0.066

$1,000 \times 0.066 = \$66.00$

9. Ⓐ actual change: 200

Ⓑ actual change: 200

Ⓒ for part Ⓐ 200 out of $10,000 = \frac{200}{10,000} = 0.02 = 2\%$

for part Ⓑ 200 out of $400 = \frac{200}{400} = \frac{1}{2} = 50\%$

Without knowing the relative change, you would not know how significant the change was in the smaller city. Without knowing the actual change, you would not know how serious the issue of violent crime is in either city.

Ⓓ Jill: $340 + \frac{1}{2}(340) = 510$

Jack: $240 + \frac{1}{2}(240) = 360$

Ⓔ The actual change seems more significant since Jill's new score was a passing score and Jack's was not. While the percent change was impressive for both, it is critical to know, "50% of WHAT?" This question is a particularly important one to ask whenever percents are used in the media.

10.

Marked Price ($)	Discount ($)	Sale Price ($)
50	$0.30 \times 50 = 15$	$50 - 15 = 35$
60	$0.30 \times 60 = 18$	$60 - 18 = 42$
70	$0.30 \times 70 = 21$	$70 - 21 = 49$
80	$0.30 \times 80 = 24$	$80 - 24 = 56$
p	$0.30p$	$p - 0.30p$

11.

Original Value ($)	Depreciation ($)	Value After 1 Year ($)
8,000	$0.20 \times 8,000 = 1,600$	$8,000 - 1,600 = 6,400$
9,000	$0.20 \times 9,000 = 1,800$	$9,000 - 1,800 = 7,200$
10,000	$0.20 \times 10,000 = 2,000$	$10,000 - 2,000 = 8,000$
v	$0.20v$	$v - 0.20v$

12. $100\% - 20\% = 80\%$

80% of $8,000 = \$6,400$

80% of $9,000 = \$7,200$

80% of $10,000 = \$8,000$

80% of $v = 0.80v$

13. 28,200

$100\% - 6\% = 94\%$

94% of $30,000 = 28,200$

or

6% of $30,000 = 1,800$

$30,000 - 1,800 = 28,200$

14.

Price ($)	Sales Tax ($)	Total ($)
40.00	$0.07 \times 40.00 = 2.80$	$40.00 + 2.80 = 42.80$
60.00	$0.07 \times 60.00 = 4.20$	$60.00 + 4.20 = 64.20$
100.00	$0.07 \times 100.00 = 7$	$100.00 + 7.00 = 107.00$
1,000.00	$0.07 \times 1,000.00 = 70$	$1,000.00 + 70.00 = 1,070.00$
p	$0.07p$	$p + 0.07p = 1.07p$

15. $107\% \times \$40 = \$42.80$

$107\% \times \$60 = \$64.20$

$107\% \times \$100 = \$107$

$107\% \times \$1,000 = \$1,070$

$107\% \times p = 1.07p$

16. 104% of $\$350 = \$364$

17. 175% of $40,000 = 70,000$

18. 200% of $\$180 = \$360$

CALCULATOR EXPLORATION

Ⓐ $343.20

Ⓒ 2,124 board ft

Ⓑ $117.76

Ⓓ $592.02

19. Ⓐ 8.4%

42 = what % of 500

$x = 42 \div 500 = 0.084 = 8.4\%$

Ⓑ 25%

7,000 − 5,250 = 1,750

1,750 = what %% of 7,000

$x = 1{,}750 \div 7{,}000 = 0.25 = 25\%$

Ⓒ $18\frac{3}{4}\%$

380 − 320 = 60

60 = what % of 320

$x = 60 \div 320 = 0.1875 = 18\frac{3}{4}\%$

Ⓓ 30%

480 − 336 = 144

144 = what % of 480

$x = \frac{144}{480} = 0.3 = 30\%$

Ⓔ 5 − 4 = 1

1 = what % of 4

$x = \frac{1}{4} = 25\%$

Ⓕ ≈ 10%

Estimate: 76,838 − 69,717 ≈

77,000 − 70,000 = 7,000

7,000 = what % of 70,000

$x = \frac{7{,}000}{70{,}000} = \frac{1}{10} = 10\%$

USING DATA

Ⓐ 26.4 − 25.2 = 1.2; 1.2 ÷ 26.4 = 4.5%

Ⓑ 1,069,899 − 806,038 = 263,861

263,861 ÷ 806,038 = 0.3273 32.7%

Ⓒ 65.5 − 58.6 = 6.9

6.9 ÷ 58.6 = 0.1177 11.8%

Ⓓ 65,000

Ⓔ Area II: 65,000 ÷ 185,000 = 35.1%

Area III: 65,000 ÷ 90,000 = 72.2%

Ⓕ It seems that the relative change is more significant here when you consider the measures that must have been taken to increase the number of test-takers by 72%.

USING DATA

Ⓐ In each grade, the percentage of smokers increases by 3%. You would expect 33% of 12th graders to smoke.

Ⓑ percent decrease = 27%

amount of decrease is 9%

9 = what % of 33

27% = x

CHECK YOUR UNDERSTANDING, page 252

1. Your estimates may vary from these, but they should be reasonable.

   Ⓐ $n = 48\%$ of $32 \approx 50\% \times 32 = 16$

   Ⓑ $p = 25\%$ of $811 \approx 25\% \times 800 = 200$

   Ⓒ 98 = what % of $200 \approx 100 = 50\% \times 200$

   Ⓓ 98 = what % of $498 \approx 100 = 20\% \times 500$

   Ⓔ $m = 19\%$ of $75 \approx 20\% \times 75 = 15$

   Ⓕ $c = 8.9\%$ of $480 \approx 10\% \times 480 = 48$

   Ⓖ $2.99 = what % of $4.99 \approx $3 = 60\% \times 5

   Ⓗ $19.75 = what % of $58.67 \approx $20 = 33\frac{1}{3}\% \times 60

   Ⓘ 38 = what % of $2000 \approx 40 = 2\%$ of 2000

   Ⓙ $t = 6\%$ of $47.50 \approx 6\%$ of $50 = 3

   Ⓚ 35 = what % of $700 \approx 35 = 5\%$ of 700

2. **Ⓐ** 0.03   **Ⓖ** 0.005

   Ⓑ 0.035   **Ⓗ** 0.005

   Ⓒ 0.30   **Ⓘ** 0.0075

   Ⓓ 0.35   **Ⓙ** 0.0075

   Ⓔ 3.50   **Ⓚ** 0.073

   Ⓕ 0.01   **Ⓛ** 8.00

3. 100% − 54% = 46%

4. $6\frac{1}{4}\% + \frac{1}{2}\% = 6\frac{1}{4}\% + \frac{2}{4}\% = 6\frac{3}{4}\%$

5. $12 \times 1\frac{1}{2}\% = 18\%$

6. $\frac{4.00}{19.45} \approx \frac{4}{20} = \frac{1}{5} = 20\%$

7. Estimate: $75\% \times $188.88 \approx 75\% \times 200 = 150

8. $\frac{24}{35} \approx \frac{24}{36} = \frac{2}{3} = 66\frac{2}{3}\%$

9. $800 − $560 = $240

   $240 = what % of $800

   $\frac{240}{800} = x$

   $x = \frac{240 \div 8}{800 \div 8} = \frac{30}{100} = 30\%$

10. 100%

11. 100% − 21% = 79%

    79% of $2,500 = $1,975

12. $360 \div 3{,}000 = \frac{12}{100} = 12\%$

13. $.50 \div $.80 = 62\frac{1}{2}\%$

TEST-TAKING PRACTICE, page 253

1. 85

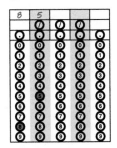

2. (3) 90,000

(10% + 5%) 600,000 = 60,000 + 30,000 = 90,000

3. (4) $21,000 + 0.10($21,000)

4. (2) 25

The base of the percent is the original cost of 2 blankets.

5. (4) 102.60

2(29.99) + 3(19.59) = $118.75 original price
80% of 118.75 = $95 sale price
108% of 95 = $102.60 with tax added

Lesson 24

Relating Rates and Slopes to Graphs,
pages 254–263

CALCULATOR EXPLORATION	
1. $-2 = x$	**6.** $7 = u$
2. $-8 = y$	**7.** $-7 = v$
3. $-3 = r$	**8.** $-4 = m$
4. $-11 = s$	**9.** $-8 = n$
5. $-7 = t$	**10.** $4 = k$

1. $\dfrac{\text{rise}}{\text{run}} = \dfrac{3}{1} = 3$

2. You may have chosen any two points. The slope would be the same.

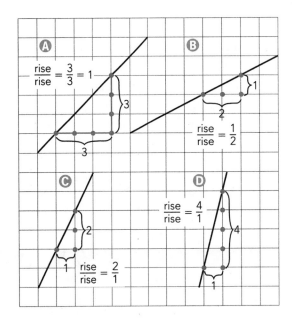

3. You may have chosen any two points. The slope would be the same.

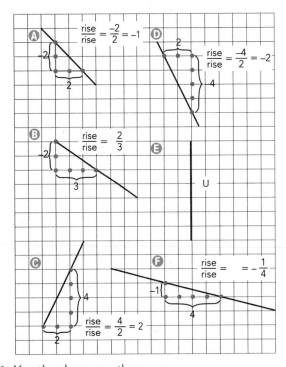

4. Yes, the slopes are the same.

$m = \dfrac{3-1}{5-9} = \dfrac{2}{-4} = \dfrac{1}{-2} = -\dfrac{1}{2}$

5. A (2, 5) D (0, 3)
B (5, 2) E (3, 0)
C (–6, 2) F (2, –5)

6. Ⓐ $m = \dfrac{5-2}{2-5} = -1$

Ⓑ You can see that this line is horizontal, so the slope is 0.

$m = \dfrac{2-2}{-6-5} = \dfrac{0}{-11} = 0$

C $m = \frac{3-0}{0-3} = \frac{3}{-3} = -1$

D You can see that this line is vertical, so the slope is undefined.

$m = \frac{5-5}{2-2} = \frac{10}{0} =$ undefined

E $m = \frac{3-2}{0-5} = \frac{1}{-5}$ or $-\frac{1}{5}$

F $m = \frac{2-5}{-6-2} = \frac{-3}{-8} = \frac{3}{8}$

7. A $(1, -1)$

B $\frac{3-(-1)}{0-1} = \frac{4}{-1} = -\frac{4}{1}$. The new point G is on the line from point D to point F; therefore, the slopes would be the same.

USING DATA

A
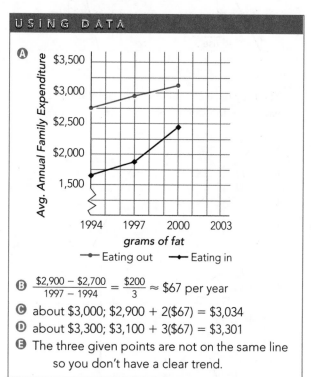
grams of fat
— Eating out   — Eating in

B $\frac{\$2,900 - \$2,700}{1997 - 1994} = \frac{\$200}{3} \approx \$67$ per year

C about \$3,000; \$2,900 + 2(\$67) = \$3,034

D about \$3,300; \$3,100 + 3(\$67) = \$3,301

E The three given points are not on the same line so you don't have a clear trend.

---

8. A

number of bottles	0	100	150	200
cost	200	350	425	500

B $y = 200 + 1.50x$ or $1.50x + 200$

C
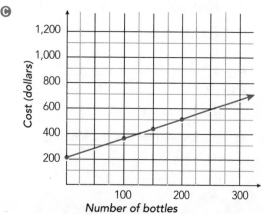
Number of bottles

---

9. A $y = 1.50(50) + 200 = \$275$

B $y = 1.50(250) + 200 = \$575$

C 300 bottles
$650 = 1.50x + 200$; subtracting 200 from both sides,
$450 = 1.5x$; dividing both sides by 1.5
$300 = x$

10. A $\frac{350 - 200}{100 - 0} = \frac{150}{100} = \frac{3}{2} = 1.5$ or 1.50

B $y = \underline{1.50}x + 200$

11. A $y = 4x + 200$

B

number of bottles	0	100	200
cost	200	600	1,000

C
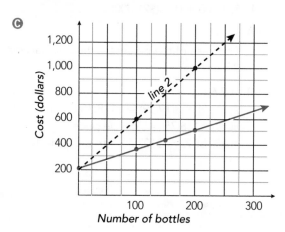
Number of bottles

D The y-intercept (the fixed cost) is the same, the slope (the unit rate) is different.

12. A $y = 4x + 400$

B

number of bottles	0	100	200
cost	400	800	1,200

C
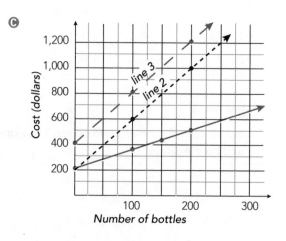
Number of bottles

D The slope (unit rate) is the same, the y-intercept (fixed cost) is different.

13. Ⓐ #1 with a slope of 35
 Ⓑ #2 with a slope of 11
 Ⓒ #2, the y-intercept is 77
 Ⓓ #3, the y-intercept is 10

14. Ⓐ $r = 5.50x$
 Ⓑ

number of cruets sold	0	100	200
revenue	0	550	1,100

 Ⓒ

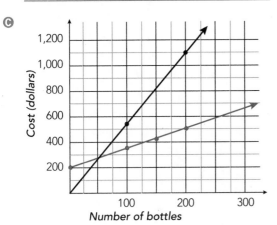

Number of bottles

 Ⓓ $800
 Ⓔ 180

15. Ⓐ 50
 Ⓑ $C = 1.5(50) + 200 = 275$
 $r = 5.50(50) = 275$

16. Ⓐ about $200
 Ⓑ $800
 Profit = Revenue − Cost
 $P = 5.50(250) - (1.50(250) + 200)$
 $P = 1,375 - 575$
 $P = 800$

CHECK YOUR UNDERSTANDING, page 262

1.

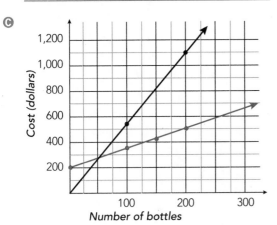

$A = (2, 3)$
$B = (3, 1)$
$C = (-4, 1)$
$D = (-3, -1)$
$E = (0, -3)$

2. For these, you could use either the graph or the formula, $m = \frac{y_2 - y_1}{x_2 - x_1}$
 Ⓐ $m = \frac{3 - 1}{2 - 3} = \frac{2}{-1} = -2$
 Ⓑ $m = \frac{1 - 3}{3 - 2} = \frac{-2}{1} = -2$
 Ⓒ horizontal line: $m = 0$
 Ⓓ $m = \frac{1 - 3}{-4 - 2} = \frac{-2}{-6} = \frac{1}{3}$
 Ⓔ $m = \frac{-1 - 1}{-3 - 3} = \frac{-2}{-6} = \frac{1}{3}$
 Ⓕ $m = \frac{1 - (-3)}{-4 - 0} = \frac{4}{-4} = -1$

3. Ⓐ $15
 Ⓑ $2.50
 Find the slope: $\frac{15 - 0}{0 - 6} = \frac{15}{-6} = -\$2.50$
 Ⓒ 6 days

4. Ⓐ $.25
 Ⓑ $C = 0.05x + 0.25$
 Ⓒ $C = 0.05(16) + 0.25 = \$1.05$

5. Ⓐ The steeper (top) line is Jerry's trip.
 Ⓑ about 10 minutes
 Ⓒ Recognizing that the slope of the line is the same as the rate, the slope of Jerry's line is 70 $\left(\text{or using minutes } \frac{70}{60}\right)$, and his mother's is 55 $\left(\text{or } \frac{55}{60}\right)$.

TEST-TAKING PRACTICE, page 263

1. **(2)** (1, −4)
2. **(2)** −1
 $m = \frac{5 - 0}{0 - 5} = \frac{5}{-5} = -1$
3. **(2)** 1995
4. **(4)** 1994

Lesson 25

Practice Test, pages 264–277

1. **(4)** 252

$$\frac{(334 + 157 + 265)}{3} = 252$$

2. **(5)** 6n

On Friday, the bakery gets 2n dozen.

$2n + 4n = 6n$

If necessary, use an easy number, like 5, in place of n.

3. **(3)** $\frac{3}{8}$

3 divided by 8 = 0.375 or 37.5%

4. 80

$$\frac{16}{21} = \frac{x}{105}$$

$21x = 1680$

$x = 80$

or, looking across, $21 \times 5 = 105$ and $16 \times 5 = 80$

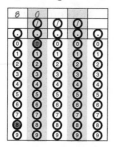

5. 2

$3(-2)^2 + 5(-2)$

$3(4) + (-10) = 2$

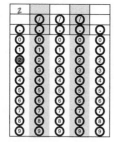

6. **(2)** 14.4

$20 \div 1.39 = 14.3884 \approx 14.4$

7. **(4)** 109.35

Day 1: 0.90(150) = 135

Day 2: 0.90(135) = 121.50

Day 3: 0.90(121.50) = 109.35

8. **(4)** $500 − ($169 + $282)

The negative sign in front of the parentheses applies to both numbers.

9. **(3)** $6

The y-intercept for Plan B is at $6.

10. **(2)** $13.50

Follow the grid line up from 90 to the point (90, 13.50)

11. **(2)** ≤ 33

Look straight down from the intersection of Plan A and Plan B.

12. 70

On the grid line for $20, count the number of units between Plan A and Plan C. There are 7 squares, each worth 10 minutes.

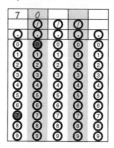

13. 40

The entire circle represents 100%.

$100 − (30 + 25 + 5) = 100 − 60 = 40$

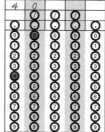

14. **(3)** $142.50

5% of 2850 = $142.50

15. **(4)** 105

$$\frac{3}{7} = \frac{x}{245}$$

$x = 105$

16. **(4)** 20%

amount of change = what % of original number

$4 = x (20)$

$\frac{4}{20} = x$

$0.2 = 20\% = x$

17. (3) (3, −3)

18. (3) 10
$$a^2 + b^2 = c^2$$
$$6^2 + 8^2 = c^2$$
$$36 + 64 = c^2$$
$$100 = c^2$$
$$10 \text{ ft} = c$$

19. (2) $10^2\pi$
$A = \pi r^2$ If $d = 20$, then $r = 10$.
$A = \pi 10^2$ is the same as $A = 10^2\pi$.

20. (2) 8
The arc BD is $\frac{1}{8}$ of the entire circumference because a 45 degree angle is $\frac{1}{8}$ of the entire 360 degrees of the circle.
$$\frac{\pi d}{8} = \frac{20\pi}{8} = \frac{62.8}{8} \approx 8$$

21. 135
$\angle ACB$ and the 45° angle makes a straight angle that totals 180°, so 180° − 45° = 135°.

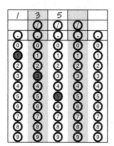

22. 232.8
$$9.7(31 - 7) = 232.8$$

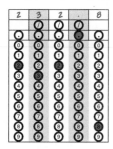

23. (3) Duluth

24. (5) Detroit
The range is the difference between the high and the low. The range in temperatures for Detroit is 30 degrees

25. (1) 18
$$15 - (-3) = 15 + 3 = 18$$

26. (5) $3\frac{1}{2}$ cups
$$2(1 + \frac{3}{4}) = 2 + 1\frac{1}{2} = 3\frac{1}{2}$$

27. (2) 1 hr 25 min
Add: 15 min + 1 hr + 10 min = 1 hr 25 min

28. (2) 9.6%
$$\frac{1}{4}\% = 0.25\%$$
$$9.85\% - 0.25\% = 9.60\% = 9.6\%$$

29. (5) 8n
$P = 2$ lengths + 2 widths
$$P = 2(3n) + 2(n) = 6n + 2n = 8n$$

30. (4) $3\frac{1}{2}$ hours
$$20 (10 + \frac{1}{2}) = 200 + 10 = 210 \text{ min}$$
$$210 \text{ min} \div 60 = 3\frac{1}{2} \text{ hr}$$

31. 150
$$A = \frac{1}{2}bh$$
$$A = \frac{1}{2}(20)(15) = 150 \text{ cm}^2$$

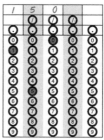

32. (4) 180° − (90° + 35°)

33. (5) 3($12) + 2($24) + $7
This expression represents the cost of the 3 T-shirts plus the cost of the 2 pairs of shorts plus the shipping charge.

34. (1) $C = 20n + 40$
When $n = 0$, the cost is 40. This is the fixed cost. Each of the following costs increase by 20 for each increase of 1 in n. The unit rate is 20.

35. (5) b and c only
25% of $200 is $50. Both prices over $200 will qualify.

36. (3) 162
$$\text{Avg} = \frac{\text{total}}{\text{number of minutes}}$$
$$2.7 = \frac{\text{total}}{60}$$
$$\text{total} = 2.7(60)$$

37. **(4)** (−3, −1)

38. **(4)** 9.2

$$22 − 12.8 = 9.2$$

39. **(2)** 8 mph

$$d = rt$$
$$2 = r(\tfrac{1}{4})$$
$$2 \div \tfrac{1}{4} = r$$
$$8 = r$$

40. **(1)** 112

Look straight up from 33 to the bottom of the target range. The value on the vertical axis at this point is less than halfway between 110 and 120.

41. **(2)** −1

For each year of age, maximum heart rate decreases by 1.

Formula: $\dfrac{190 − 170}{30 − 50} = \dfrac{20}{−20} = −1$

42. **(3)** 57

Follow the line for 130 until it crosses the line for the highest target rate. Look straight down to find that it corresponds to a point that is less than halfway between 55 and 60.

43. $\dfrac{1}{130}$

Total family tickets 10 + 15 + 25 = 50

$$\dfrac{50}{6,500} = \dfrac{1}{130}$$

Estimate $\dfrac{50}{5,000} = \dfrac{1}{100}$

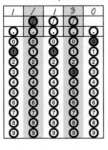

44. **(3)** $13,950

Total income: 6,500 × $5 = $32,500
Net profit: $32,500 − $18,550 = $13,950
Estimate: $32,000 − $18,000 = $14,000

45. **(2)** between 10 and 11 feet

$10^2 = 100$, $11^2 = 121$

46. **(4)** Only C is true.

A. In the earlier survey, the percentage of women, age 20 − 29 is less than the percentage of men who are obese.

B. In the earlier study, the greatest percentage of obesity for women occurred in the age group 60 − 69.

47. **(5)** Not enough information is given

You do not know the number of grams in a glass, the base of the percentage.

48. **(3)** $n = \dfrac{(\$20 − \$13.95)}{x}$

Subtract to find the amount of money remaining after the express letter. Divide the price of one stamp to find how many could be bought.

49. **(1)** $\dfrac{6}{m} = \dfrac{9}{30}$

This proportion compares:

$$\dfrac{\text{height}}{\text{height}} = \dfrac{\text{length}}{\text{length}}$$

50. **(4)** 10

$$A = \pi r^2$$
$$300 \approx 3(r^2)$$
$$100 \approx r^2$$
$$10 \approx r$$